D1350911

Home

BY THE SAME AUTHOR

Fiction

All the Same Shadows
The Guilt Merchants
The Girl in Melanie Klein
Articles of Faith
One. Interior. Day. – Adventures in the Film Trade
The Genoa Ferry
Cesar and Augusta

Biography

Sir Donald Wolfit, CBE: His Life and Work
in the Unfashionable Theatre

Plays

Country Matters
A Family
The Ordeal of Gilbert Pinfold
The Dresser
After the Lions
Tramway Road
The Deliberate Death of a Polish Priest
Interpreters
J. J. Farr
Ivanov
Another Time
Reflected Glory
Poison Pen

Edited by

A Night at the Theatre
The Ages of Gielgud
Dear Alec

HOME

Ronald Harwood

WEIDENFELD & NICOLSON
London

First published in Great Britain in 1993 by
Weidenfeld & Nicolson
The Orion Publishing Group Ltd
Orion House,
5 Upper Saint Martin's Lane,
London, WC2H 9EA.

Copyright © 1993 Sea Point Productions Inc.

All rights reserved. No part of this publication may be
reproduced, stored in a retrieval system, or trans-
mitted in any form or by any means, electronic,
mechanical, photocopying, recording, or otherwise,
without the prior permission of the copyright owner

Ronald Harwood has asserted his moral right to be
identified as the author of this work

A catalogue reference is available from the British
Library

ISBN 0 297 81368 4

Typeset at The Spartan Press Ltd,
Lymington, Hants
Printed in Great Britain by
Butler & Tanner Ltd,
Frome and London

For
Antonia and Harold
who will, I trust, do the decent thing and take full
responsibility for having encouraged me.

Prologue
1983

PROLOGUE

'There it is, look, up there, through the trees, oh God, look!' Natalya held her breath and bit her bottom lip hard. She pointed through the car window, the reflection of her beauty frozen against a moving pattern of snow-tipped leaves.

Varya, the interpreter, who was also their driver for the day, slowed the car a little. Harrison, beside her, ducked and twisted his head.

'Can you see it?' Natalya asked, breathless, urgent.

'Yes, yes, I see it,' Harrison said. The great house, white, serene, stood on the crest of the hill overlooking the small town. The Red Flag fluttered aimlessly from atop the rounded turret.

'It's the same view as in the painting,' Natalya whispered. Wonder and disbelief.

Sobliki.

Varya, whose only pleasure was to dampen the pleasure of others, said in her mournful Slavonic voice, 'It's locked most probably.'

The car crossed over the wooden bridge that spanned the man-made lake. Although it was the second day of May, cloudless and sunny, snow still covered the fields and clung to the trees. The house disappeared from view. The uneven road, pitted with slush and plates of ice, curved in a wide semi-circle so that, for a moment, it seemed as if they were leaving Sobliki behind them. But then, veering left, they entered an avenue of tall pines and directly ahead was the gate-house and the arch. Beyond, stood Sobliki itself, impassive, waiting.

Varya said, 'As I thought. Place deserted.'

'No, it isn't,' Harrison said, pleased to correct her, for no sooner had she spoken than there was movement near the main door of the house. A knot of three people was advancing towards them, two men and a young woman. Another man remained apart, looking and not looking at the approaching car.

Varya parked inside a ring of birch trees and was the first to alight. Natalya took a deep breath to compose herself. Leaning back across the front seat Harrison took her hand. 'Isn't this extraordinary?' he said.

'I can't believe we're here,' Natalya said.

3

Varya returned to the car and poked her head in through the window. 'Please to get out, Natalya. Here is the Chairman of the Sobliki soviet.'

The Chairman, stocky, dark, bald, stood in front of the others, the young woman and the man who had a camera. In his obligatory dark navy suit, white shirt, black tie, the Chairman was a model of soviet officialdom but his eyes were unusually bright, with anticipation, Harrison thought. When Natalya emerged from the car into the crisp Russian sun, there was an audible gasp of surprise from the woman.

Varya made the introductions. The Chairman bowed and kissed Natalya's hand. Harrison had never seen a soviet official perform so old-fashioned a courtesy. The woman was presented as though to a princess: she was the local historian and archivist of the small Sobliki museum. Harrison watched them, his arms behind his back, every inch a royal consort. He caught sight again of the outsider hovering, a man in his early seventies perhaps, white-haired in a light blue suit, plainly nervous, awkward, apart.

The young female historian said something to Natalya in Russian. Varya translated. The photographer danced around them, focusing and clicking his camera. He smiled often at Harrison and appeared to wink or, perhaps, Harrison thought, he had a tic. At one moment he seemed about to say something but was interrupted and resorted to winking again.

'Forgive my shock,' the historian said to Natalya. 'But I could see clearly that you were a Sobelev through and through.'

'My mother,' Natalya said, 'was the last member of the family to be born in this house.'

'Ah!' the historian cried. 'The Countess Iliena Lvovna!'

'Yes,' Natalya said, 'that's my mother, Iliena Lvovna.'

It was the turn of the man apart to react but the sound he made was like a short, sharp cry of pain. The Chairman turned on him and for a moment Harrison thought he was about to utter a reproach but, instead, beckoned with the flat of his hand. The old man shuffled towards Natalya. Harrison noticed he wore no socks.

The Chairman said, 'Allow me to introduce Piotr Kaltikov, our famous artist.'

Kaltikov hesitated and, as though summoning all his considerable dignity, smoothed his hair. He had pale blue eyes which were filling with tears. He could barely speak. He, too, bowed low and kissed Natalya's hand.

Varya translated his words as though she herself were asking the questions. 'Your mother, Iliena Lvovna,' Kaltikov said with a little shudder, 'is she still alive?'

'Yes.'

'And in England?'

'Yes.'

'Thank God,' he said. Then, lowering his voice, he murmured, 'I am a painter, yes, but I only paint one subject. This house. Sobliki.'

Natalya said, 'My mother has a painting of the house. They smuggled it out when they left. By an unknown Italian artist, I think.'

'I have heard of that picture. It was painted, I believe, from the town side of the lake.'

'That's right. It hangs in my mother's drawing-room.'

'Where does she live now?' Kaltikov asked.

'In Godalming. It's a town in Surrey.'

'Oh God, I'm sorry,' he said as if Surrey was the most terrible exile imaginable.

The historian consulted a notebook. 'The Countess Iliena Lvovna married Stepan Kessler, yes?'

'Yes.'

'So you are Natalya Stepanovna.'

'Yes,' Natalya said. 'And this is my husband, Harrison Wilde. We came to Russia to attend the première of his play in Moscow. We are only here because of him.'

While Harrison shook hands with the archivist, he noticed Kaltikov whispering to the Chairman, who nodded reassuringly, and said, 'Yes, yes, yes, of course,' and then turning to Harrison, explained, 'Piotr Kaltikov has something to tell your wife.'

All eyes turned on the artist. He was breathing deeply, fighting tears, and when he was more or less in control of himself, began to speak. What he had to say had obviously been carefully and formally prepared.

'Natalya Stepanovna, this is a great day not only in my life but also in the life of Sobliki,' he began. 'For the town, for all of us who live here, it is a wonderful thing to have a descendant of the Sobelevs return to this hallowed place, especially the daughter of Iliena Lvovna, the last of the family to be born in this mansion. But for me, your visit has a more special and unique significance. Sixty-three years ago, in 1920 to be precise, I was six years old, exactly the same age as your mother, beloved Iliena Lvovna. In that year, your family was expelled from this house. Your grandmother, her three daughters and her son.' At this, the Chairman of the local soviet shrugged helplessly as if to make clear that he was not personally responsible, and cleared his throat.

'What were they to do?' Kaltikov continued. 'Where were they to go? They who had known no other existence but the life they led here in this house. Allow me to tell you then, Natalya Stepanovna, that a certain family of peasants, yes, peasants who had worked for the

Sobelevs on this very estate, offered them shelter, took them into their small house just across the lake, to the south-east, cared for them and made them as comfortable as was humanly possible in the circumstances. Your mother, then aged six, befriended the little boy of that family. Yes, Natalya Stepanovna, this is a great day for me because, yes, it was my family that took them in and I was that boy.' He could no longer contain his emotions. He sobbed silently but uncontrollably.

The Chairman and the historian lowered their eyes. The photographer did his work oblivious to Kaltikov's distress. Natalya suddenly put out her hand and then gently caressed the old man's tear-stained cheek.

The historian spoke to Natalya in Russian. Natalya, who always claimed her command of the language was that of a five-year-old, understood easily. Varya translated for Harrison. 'They will show her house first and park afterwards.'

Again, the photographer winked, nodded, gestured unintelligibly before addressing Varya, who then translated. 'He wants to photograph you single.'

'Perhaps you ought to stick to Natalya,' Harrison suggested. 'She may need help.'

The photographer said, 'Good idea. I speak little English. I'm okay with Mr Wilde,' and he pretended to straighten Harrison's tie and smooth his hair. The moment Varya was out of earshot, he said, 'I am also Jew. My name's Yuri. In this country is not possible Jew marry aristocrat,' and he grinned, revealing several gold teeth. 'I tell you my friend, is glorious—' He stopped, unable to think of the word, and called out a question to Varya.

'Irony,' she replied.

'You say irony?' the photographer repeated. 'Yes, glorious irony, Jew like you make this day possible. I tell you, my friend, today is a kind of justice.'

Varya called, 'Come, Harrison, we are going into the house.'

As Harrison strolled towards Natalya and the others, the photographer's words lingered. A glorious irony, Jew like you make this day possible, a kind of justice. Through Harrison's mind raced a ragged procession, like a tableau vivant, of four families, their families, Natalya's and his, Sobelev, Wildnowitz, Salz and Kessler, whose footprints, individually and collectively, must span half the earth. How did all this come about, he wondered idly? Was it possible to trace their enforced journeys, fuelled by cruelty and cataclysms, abounding with the vagaries and ironies of history, and finally converging to allow Natalya Kessler to meet him, Harrison Wilde, in a small town in England, to fall in love, marry, have children, grandchildren, and to journey here to Sobliki? What anguished decisions had to be made, brutal orders obeyed, sufferings endured, catastrophes experienced to allow her, the descendant of Catherine the Great, and him, the descendant of wandering Jews, to make this journey together?

How has it happened, he asked himself, that I should be the one to complete this circle, the cog to give history such an apparently graceful symmetry? He thought again of Natalya wiping the tears of the artist, Piotr Kaltikov, and he had a strong, irrational conviction that, in some mysterious way, the photographer was right: justice was being done.

He reached Natalya at the foot of the wide steps that led to the open front door. Smiling, she said, 'Hold my hand. We're going into the house now.'

PART ONE

Cogs
(1911)

1

The problem was Isaiah's coffin.

'How will he breathe?' his mother, Leah, asked.

'Through his nose, for God's sake, how else do you breathe?' his Uncle Benjamin, the shoemaker, said. He had an aggressive manner.

'He'll suffocate, he'll suffocate!' Leah said and began to wail, not noisily but like an ailing child who cannot understand pain, soft, long, drawn-out moans of distress and bewilderment.

The male members of the Wildnowitz family were silent: Isaiah, huge brown eyes expressing terror, his father, Solomon, his elder brothers, Baruch and Julius, his uncles Benjamin, the shoemaker, and Laban whom every one called Laban the Idiot because he was a philosopher and composed poems in four languages, all were silent.

Uncle Laban the Idiot said, 'Drill holes.'

'Are you crazy?' Benjamin said as if a criminal act had been suggested. 'They'll see the holes, they'll open the coffin and then what? Laban, you're an idiot, stick to poetry. Drill holes, he says. They'll see the holes.' And, as an afterthought, 'Idiot.'

Laban smiled a mysterious idiotic smile. 'Not if you drill the holes on the bottom of the coffin. Isaiah can lie face down. It's not as if we're going to bury him. Who looks at the bottom of a coffin?'

Now, even Leah was silent and her silence was thunderous.

Solomon, the woodcutter, said, 'It's a good idea.'

And so it was decided. Isaiah, aged twelve, would be smuggled out in a coffin with holes drilled in the bottom before 1 February 1911. Isaiah, who had been listening to his own funeral arrangements, was overcome with disappointment. His Uncle Laban had promised to take him to see a travelling circus which was due on that same day and now he would miss it, but he kept silent.

Silence in the village, too. This was unusual because in recent days – the whole of the second week of January, 1911, to be precise – rumour had been rife and rumour made the noise of a thousand snakes hissing. On the first day of February, the snakes hissed, a spontaneous uprising would result in the slaughter of as many male children as possible but, as is well known, spontaneous uprisings can be haphazard affairs and the gender of the slaughtered impossible to guarantee, so those without young sons were also frightened. The community was paralysed with fear and the only noise to be heard was the snakes hissing. Where and how the hissing began is not known but the terror was confirmed by Dr Stravius, a good man and a true Christian, on his return from seeing an important patient, a retired General, in Vilna. The General had warned the doctor to stay indoors and keep his own family hidden on the night of 1 February 1911 because, the General said, in spontaneous uprisings mistakes can be made not only as regards gender, but also as regards age, race and religion. Confirmation of the rumours abruptly stilled the snakes, which was why the village was silent.

This village was but a speck of dust in the Tsar of Russia's vast empire, an immense domain, one sixth of the land surface of the planet. Nearly a hundred and fifty million people were his subjects, Russians, Georgians, Ukranians, Balts, Jews, Uzbeks, Tartars, Armenians, Germans, Finns, Estonians, Letts. The Tsar himself had more titles than there were inhabitants in this village. Emperor and Autocrat of All the Russias, Tsar of Moscow, of Poland, Lord of Pskov, Grand Duke of Lithuania, and Finland, Prince of Estonia, Sovereign of the Circassian Princes and the Mountain Princes, Lord of Turkestan, Heir of Norway, Duke of Schleswig-Holstein, on and on and on, a laundry list of titles. Yet, no village was too small to feel his might and power. Father of all the Russias.

When alone with his brother, Solomon, Laban the Idiot, who was thirty-three and unmarried, said, 'We must save your boys, Solomon. We must save Baruch and Julius and Isaiah. And if not all, then two. If not two, then one.'

Solomon nodded sadly and sucked in his breath and the sound was like a prelude to weeping. He said, 'But how, Laban? How?'

Laban said, 'Never mind how. The how is always easy. What is difficult is to stand up to fate and say we are not going to bow down. We will change our destiny. That's the difficult thing.'

The consensus of opinion was that the male children should be hidden in the cellars of the tannery. But the brothers Wildnowitz, especially Laban, were cussed, obstinate and nonconformist on principle, any principle, and if no principle was involved, they were cussed just the same. They also possessed more than an instinct for self-preservation and Laban the Idiot, who had planted the seed of resistance, hit upon the idea of the coffin.

Death in general and coffins in particular were an integral part of Laban's life. He was a *nakhtwachter*, literally a night-watcher, a guardian of corpses, for the law states that a corpse must be laid on the floor – all are equal in death – and must never be left alone between the moment of death and burial. So, according to custom, in the house of the dead, two men were employed to wash and dress the corpse, to place it on the floor and to keep vigil through the night. Usually these men were drunks, tramps, black sheep, no-goodniks; night-watching was not a desirable job and it is true that Laban's regular colleague, Fedya Katzenowitz, fitted the mould perfectly. Katzenowitz, ragged, dishevelled, unwashed, thin as a nail, wanted nothing more than a bottle of cognac or vodka to while away the grizzly hours of his watch. He said little, prayed less, slept much. But, for Laban Wildnowitz, the hours from midnight to dawn were the magical hours when he entered a kingdom where poetry, thought, words, imagination and fantasy were the coin of the realm, the kingdom where he, Laban, was king.

Laban was something of a linguist, speaking four languages well and being able to sing snatches of songs in mispronounced English. He composed poetry in Russian, Yiddish, Lithuanian and Hebrew, a different poem for each language, never translating from one to another because, he insisted passionately, each tongue makes its own demands not just of sound but, more importantly, of imagery. A Russian moon, for example, was entirely different from any other moon: the very word *luná*, with the accented second syllable, he explained, suggested sharp, jagged ice, whereas the Yiddish word *levone* called forth milk and ripe pears. This is why, perhaps, he was known as Laban the Idiot.

No one, alas, could judge his poetry because he never wrote down a single line. Nor did he recite his verses in public. In fact, the only man ever to hear a poem by Laban Wildnowitz was his fellow *nakhtwachter*, Katzenowitz, and he was too drunk to remember all the words. One couplet in Hebrew, however, stuck in Katzenowitz's befuddled brain, a couplet he would often repeat drunk or sober, Laban's words, he said, and uttered them as though they explained the meaning of life:

> A pattern of stars on a quilted cradle,
> Dictates the destiny of all mankind.

When Laban was asked the meaning of these words he would reply with his mysterious smile. This was another reason he was known as Laban the Idiot.

He was powerfully built, handsome with a magnificent jet-black mane, an energetic bachelor who, surprisingly, in view of his poetry and poorly paid anti-social work, was an object of envy and suspicion.

13

For, it was said that Laban was an unscrupulous womaniser, a lecher; this reputation was encouraged by his nocturnal profession and, of course, by the hissing of the snakes: Laban, the night-watcher, companion of the dead, they hissed, preyed upon grieving widows, daughters, sisters, indeed any distressed female relative of the deceased. Scandal even suggested that he, on one infamous occasion, had actually had his way with a young widow on the bed while the corpse of her husband lay beside them on the floor. Only Katzenowitz could have been witness to this but he was never heard to speak against his colleague. He was not a malicious man and he respected and loved Laban as he did no other, so perhaps the rumour was pure invention. In certain male quarters, however, Laban was known as Laban Not Such An Idiot.

So it was while keeping company the body of old Reb Tolkowich that the idea of a coffin came to Laban and, as with many a genuine inspiration, the entire plan – Isaiah's accident, the funeral, the journey – was born in that same moment, complete and perfect. Laban wagged his finger at the corpse as though the idea had emanated from the dead man, and smiled.

Katzenowitz said, 'So, what's so funny?'

'Death,' answered Laban. 'Death is very funny.'

'Is that a poem?' asked Katzenowitz, putting the bottle of cognac to his lips and swigging deep.

'No, but it could be.'

After the funeral of the ancient Reb Tolkowich – a learned Talmudic scholar who believed the world was flat – Laban hurried to see his brother, Solomon, hurried through the narrow streets of the place that was larger than a village but smaller than a town.

Put from your mind the rooftops of Chagal. There were no ethereal figures in the sky and no fiddlers on the roofs of Ploemyan. The only music was the cantor's voice on the Sabbath and High Holy Days, the chanting of the Kaddish at funerals, and at weddings the breaking of a glass would be heard, and ritual songs, the stamping of dancing feet to rising, brutal rhythms. The houses had roofs, of course, but they were in need of repair and water found its way through every crack and crevice to soak the crumbling walls. There was never more than one oil lamp alight in any house. Fuel was scarce. People were poor. But, ironically, snow was a blessing; it insulated these hovels and then the need for heat was not so great; and in the second week of January 1911 the snow was heavy and snow was the only blessing to be found that week in Ploemyan or Ploengje, three hundred kilometres south of Vilna.

*

'We *all* accompany the coffin?' Solomon asked.

'Certainly,' Laban said. 'If the militia stop us, if they send us back they'll be giving us a message, won't they?'

'Will they?'

'Of course. They'll be saying, "Oh, no you don't, you're not going to escape so easily." And they won't want to give that message because it'll mean they're in collusion, it'll mean the militia knows in advance of the spontaneous uprising which means it isn't spontaneous and it means the militia already knows what's in store for us. That would be a warning to everybody else. But if they let us through, then they'll think to themselves the others will remain calm and the pogrom can take place as planned.'

Pogrom, incidentally, is a Russian word meaning organised massacre.

Solomon considered Laban's proposal. 'But that means if we accompany the coffin out of Ploemyan, our whole family will escape, not only Isaiah. We'll all escape.'

'I know.' An attractive stillness ensued. Then Laban shrugged. 'It can't be helped,' he said.

Family folklore had it that there were actors in the ancestry of the family Wildnowitz. Well, if not actors exactly then jugglers and story-tellers, magicians and clowns, and there was no doubt that the events of 28 January 1911 seemed to confirm the belief that the family Wildnowitz had actors among their ancestors. The moment before sunset on that day, a terrible cry rose out of the woods, a cry to make the leaves tremble, and presently Solomon emerged carrying Isaiah in his arms like Lear bearing Cordelia. Howl, howl, howl, howl, oi-veh, howl! But it was Leah's performance that most convinced. So terrible was her simulated grief that many attested to her hair turning white in tune with her anguish.

The snakes did the rest. In no time at all everyone had heard the news: Isaiah Wildnowitz had been crushed to death under a falling tree, a tree felled by his own father. Reb Yankel, the spiritual leader of the community, said, 'Tragedy has struck one before tragedy strikes all. God is good.' He, too, was a learned man who believed that God did not rest on the seventh day but instead created Ploemyan.

There is an old adage that money talks. It is a lie. Money does not talk; it shouts, screams, bullies, dictates, commands, decrees, ordains. Money orates. Even Dr Stravius, the good Christian, the very man who confirmed the rumours of the pogrom, was cowed by the stridency of its voice. He took half the family's savings and issued a death certificate.

15

That night, Laban and Katzenowitz sat in the dark back room with Isaiah, who was made to lie on the floor in case anyone happened to look in. The rest of the family were in the small adjoining kitchen, surrounding the stove, and there they rocked and moaned and sobbed and wept in the light of the one oil lamp that yellowed their haggard faces.

Katzenowitz said, 'A pattern of stars on a quilted cradle dictates the destiny of all mankind.' Laban gave him another flask of cognac and then slid to the floor to sit cross-legged beside Isaiah who ate sunflower seeds and stared into the darkness.

Laban said, 'Isaiah, listen to me, because I am going to tell you things that must stay with you for the rest of your days. Listen carefully. God gave Moses ten commandments. I give you only seven, but seven, as you know, is a magical number.

'First, about God. Pray, kiss the *mezuzah* on the gate-posts, lay *tefillin*, keep your head covered at all times, but do me this favour, don't get too involved with God. He's become very forgetful these days. It may be to do with His age. The old are often forgetful. He keeps repeating Himself, because all He does now is test us, over and over again. He keeps on testing us. He can't remember anything else, only to test us and always the same tests. I'll give them a pogrom, I'll expel them from this country, from that country, I'll kill a few hundred, a few thousand, I'll test them, see if they still love me and fear me and honour me. You know what I say, Isaiah? I say, enough already. We've been tested, we love, we honour, we fear, so enough. That's what I mean about God repeating Himself. Testing, that's all He knows. If you want my honest opinion, God is senile, that's His problem at the moment, but please God He'll recover. So honour, love and fear but don't get too involved. Think of Him as a rich elderly relative you visit once, twice a year in the hope you'll inherit.

'Second, about your fellow-men. With them also don't get too involved. The *goyim* say love thy neighbour as thyself. I say, don't be so extravagant. Make it an eighty-twenty split. Because, believe me, love is not the answer. This is a *goyische* invention which, frankly, leaves me stone cold. You love your neighbour as yourself and before you know where you are they're taking advantage. To your fellow-men, Isaiah, you have but one obligation: behave decently. That's all. You may do what you like so long as you don't harm others. But, love? Pfui.

'Third, your parents. Honour thy father and thy mother so thy days may be long on the earth which the Lord thou God hast given thee. Fine, wonderful, terrific. If you want long days on earth be like a child all your life. I say, not. Better a short independent life than three score and ten of bondage. Be decent to your parents, but honour you must keep for other things.

'Fourth, honour. If not your parents who or what will you honour? Honour the world, Isaiah, that cannot be seen. Honour the mysteries and the unknowable secrets. Honour the poets and the makers of music, honour those who write books and those who read them, honour the learned and those who learn, honour the life that all men and women lead inside themselves. Discard the external trappings so you may know what is within. Remember, all men and women live in a secret place in which they are naked and where spirits roam free and magicians haunt the forests.

'Fifth, politicians. Beware the politician who says I am here only to serve you. If you hear these words from the mouth of a politician, run. It means he is here only to serve himself. Conversely, if you should hear a politician say, I like power, I love influence, I want a good time and, along the way, I'll do what I can for you, trust him, for you will have stumbled on an honest man.

'Sixth, remember that we can change our lives. Fate can be fought, as the poet says, and if you ask which poet, I answer, the poet Laban Wildnowitz. Life is not a curse, it is a blessing. So, if life becomes cursed transform it. This can be done. Believe me.

'Seventh, women. This is tricky ground. Women have been given the worst of this world. You know why? They have the pain of bringing men into the world. This is unfair. Not only do they give tyrants life, but they have also to go through terrible agony to do so. That is why they sometimes take their revenge on us. You know how? No? You'll find out. Be decent to women but if you are unlucky enough to fall in love with one, do not blame her, blame only yourself. And remember these words: carnal, erotic, passionate, lustful, titillation, lewdness. Please God, one day you'll find out what they mean.'

These things the night-watcher said to his nephew in darkness. Laban sat cross-legged beside Isaiah, who lay on the floor in imitation of a corpse, eating sunflower seeds and staring into nothingness.

Isaiah was placed in the coffin at dawn on 29 January. He lay face down, his forehead on a silk cushion, arms at his side. He was covered in a patchwork quilt and, to Leah's wailing, the lid was screwed down tight. He breathed through the holes his uncle Benjamin, the shoemaker, had drilled in the bottom.

Laban, Solomon and Reb Yankel, all able men, constituted the delegation to the militia. Reb Yankel, of course, had been by necessity allowed into the conspiracy. A pale winter sun was just visible above the horizon.

The sergeant, fat, unshaven, with mean, close-set eyes like a vole, asked, 'Why do you have to bury him in Vilna?'

Solomon said, 'Because my parents live in Vilna and they are too old to travel here for the funeral.' This, of course, was also a lie since his parents had been slaughtered in another spontaneous uprising at least thirty years previously.

'I thought you people had to bury your dead as soon as possible.'

'Except,' Reb Yankel said, 'in special circumstances.'

'And these,' Laban said, 'are special circumstances.'

'How long will you be away?' asked the sergeant.

'A few days,' Solomon answered.

'How many days exactly?'

'Three, four,' Solomon said.

The sergeant scratched his chin, coughed, spat, sniffed. They could almost hear the wheels in his brain turning. Would they be back by 1 February? Would they return in time for the spontaneous uprising? 'Wait here,' he said and disappeared through a door into a back office.

The delegation was motionless; occasionally their eyes met, questioning, nervous, apprehensive eyes. The three men strained to hear the low rumble of voices from behind the closed door which opened suddenly. An officer looked at them then shut the door again. Laban hoped they were trying to reason as he had reasoned: if we refuse them permission we'll alert the others. If we let them go those who remain will be reassured and calm, and the spontaneous uprising can go ahead as planned.

At last the sergeant returned. 'Permission refused,' he said.

'Refused?' Laban repeated, horrified.

'You heard,' the sergeant said. 'Bury the boy here. No travelling to Vilna.'

Solomon's knees turned to liquid. Reb Yankel grabbed hold of him, tried to keep him from falling.

Laban said, 'But – but my parents will die if they cannot be present at the burial of their youngest grandson.'

'They'll die anyway,' the sergeant said, and added as an after-thought, 'they're old, aren't they?'

Laban opened his mouth to speak but no words came. He stood, open-mouthed, hands outstretched trembling in supplication, help-less and dismayed. A dreadful scene sprang into his mind: Isaiah's funeral, earth pushing its way through the drilled holes in the bottom of the coffin. What would they do? Bury the empty box, smuggle Isaiah out of the village at night? But how? Where would he

18

go? Laban cursed the militia for not reasoning as he had reasoned and for lacking imagination. He cursed their stupidity.

The sergeant said, 'Get out. You smell.'

But at that precise moment, the door to the back office opened. The officer's head was again visible and Laban thought for a moment that perhaps he had no body. 'Wait,' the officer said, and with a jerk of his disembodied head ordered the sergeant to return. Once more the door closed, once more voices rumbled, once more time stood still for the delegation.

The sergeant returned. 'We've changed our minds,' he said, 'that's because we're decent people. Permission granted, get out, you smell.'

Laban silently cursed the militia for not thinking as quickly as he did.

So, at ten minutes before noon, a small procession set forth from Ploemyan on the road to Vilna. The family Wildnowitz huddled on a horse-drawn cart which bore Isaiah's coffin. Isaiah, in cramped darkness, breathed easily but the disgusting smell of horse manure penetrated the coffin and, from time to time, waves of nausea swept over him dispelling his fear. And those who were left in the place attained a sort of calm. The militia would not have allowed the family Wildnowitz to leave with their corpse if there was to be a spontaneous uprising on 1 February, they reasoned. Only Reb Yankel knew the truth and he was victim to nightmares.

The cart trundled on towards Vilna, along the road which scarred the forest. Laban had the impression that they were cogs in an intricate machine beginning to whirr and spin, engage and disengage, but for what purpose was known only to a senile God.

2

In Warsaw, the cogs were turning too, finely honed, almost interlocking, but never quite.

The Russian Military Attaché, Captain Nikolai Nikolaev, looked like an angel in the pay of the devil: tight blond curls, shifty blue eyes, flaccid mouth. Even his cologne smelt of corruption. A few months before Isaiah Wildnowitz's funeral procession would make its way in fading light towards Vilna, Captain Nikolaev and Dr Andrei Bulkarov drank a litre of Polish vodka and ate a jar of pickled cucumbers. Braided tunics unbuttoned, they sprawled in deep armchairs before a log fire in the doctor's surgery. Of the three rooms Bulkarov occupied on the top floor of the Royal Castle, the Governor's residence, the surgery was the most comfortable. The litre of *Zubrowka* was two-thirds gone. The men punctuated their drinking with long silences until Nikolaev suddenly said, 'I'm being blackmailed.'

'By whom?' the doctor asked, a man used to confidences, unshocked, unshockable.

Nikolaev hesitated, shifty eyes more shifty then usual. He gathered the little courage he had. At last he said, 'I am being blackmailed by the Governor-General himself.'

'Are you very drunk?' Bulkarov asked, trying to lean forward to look more closely at his companion but failing.

'No more than you,' Nikolaev said.

'Are you telling me that His Excellency, Giorgy Skalon, the Tsar's representative in Poland, is behaving like a common criminal and blackmailing his military attaché?'

'Yes,' Nikolaev said. 'It's the truth.'

Bulkarov nodded, said, 'Well,' several times, then asked, 'What's he got on you? Little boys?'

'How dare you!' Nikolaev said, wanting to rise then deciding against it.

'What, then?'

'The bastard discovered a little irregularity in my official accounts. Little boys, me? No, sir, just ordinary, everyday, normal embezzlement.'

'What do you do with the money?'

'I bank it in Switzerland. I am building up a fortune in Switzerland. And you should do the same, doctor, believe me. Our days are numbered. The end is in sight. The millenium has arrived. The Tsar's a prick.'

'Spare me from prophets of doom,' Bulkarov said, 'they are always wrong. But, tell me, how do you manage to build up a fortune if you're being blackmailed by His Excellency? Surely his demands are high.'

'No, no, no, he doesn't want money. Skalon's a gentleman. He makes me pay for it in other ways,' Nikolaev said.

'What other ways?'

'He's turned me into a procurer.'

'What do you procure?'

'Whores with big breasts.'

Bulkarov nodded as if to imply he should have guessed.

Nikolaev said, 'His Excellency, Governor-General Skalon, is a pervert.'

'Little boys?'

'No, whores with big breasts.'

'But I like whores with big breasts too,' Bulkarov said. 'That doesn't make me a pervert. As a matter of fact, my late wife had very big breasts.'

Nikolaev explained. His Excellency liked to be tied to his bed fully clothed.

'Fully clothed? That doesn't sound very promising. Where do the whores with the big breasts come in? Do they beat him?'

'Wait, wait. You understand what I'm saying? He likes to be tied to his bed in his uniform.'

'Yes, yes, I've got the point. Does the whore do the tying?' Bulkarov asked.

'No, I do,' replied the Captain.

'You tie the Governor-General to his bed?'

'Yes, and afterwards I cover his face with a silk handkerchief to avoid his being recognised and then I usher in the whore I've procured in town.'

'One with big breasts?'

'Yes, yes, of course.'

'And then?'

'I tell the bitch to remove His Excellency's boots and socks. The great thing about these Polish whores is they don't ask questions, they do as they're told. Once she's done that, I order her to undo her bodice and reveal her large breasts. And then comes the really embarrassing bit for me. I have to tell her that the man tied to the bed wants her to brush her nipples against the soles of his bare feet. She

21

does this. His Excellency squirms with pleasure. After being tickled in this fashion for three or four minutes he cries out, "Enough, my God, enough!" Just those words. Always the same words. "Enough, my God, enough!" Then, I pay the cow and send her back to town.'

'What do you do during all this?' Bulkarov asked.

'I watch.'

'Is that enjoyable?'

'Very.'

They drank. Bulkarov bit into the last pickled cucumber, crisp, tart. He offered the remainder to Nikolaev. Nikolaev refused.

Bulkarov said, 'I don't think that's very perverted.'

'I have to find these whores for him three, four times a week otherwise he threatens to expose me. My life is finished.'

'Nonsense, nonsense—' Bulkarov said.

'And it must never be the same whore.'

'Variety is the spice of life, as the poet says.'

'I can't stand it any more.' Nikolaev wept and, being Russian, real tears ran down his cheeks.

Bulkarov thought of something. 'Wait a moment, wait a moment. You said you cover His Excellency's face with a silk cloth, am I right?'

'Right.'

'Well then, your problems are solved.'

'How?'

'Simple. If His Excellency's face is covered with the silk cloth, the whore can't see him but – and this is the important thing – *he can't see the whore!*'

'So?'

'It means you don't have to produce a new whore each time. You just keep producing the same whore, it'll make your task a lot easier.'

'I've tried it. It didn't work,' Nikolaev said gloomily.

'Why didn't it work?'

'Because His Excellency recognised the whore, that's why.'

'How?' Bulkarov asked, bewildered. 'How did he recognise her?'

'By the feel of her nipples, that's how.'

'His Excellency recognised the whore by the feel of her nipples against the soles of his feet?'

'Precisely.'

'By the feel of her nipples against the soles of his feet?' Bulkarov repeated, his voice rising to a screech.

'Yes!' Nikolaev barked.

Bulkarov shook his head in amazement. 'He must have remarkably sensitive soles, that's all I can say.'

Nikolaev was victim to a renewed bout of crying. 'Curse him, curse him,' he said.

They finished the *Zubrowka*. Bulkarov tossed the remains of the cucumber on the fire. 'For God's sake stop crying,' he said.

'What would my mother say if she found out?' Nikolaev asked, his despair as real as his tears.

'But she won't find out.'

'Yes, but if, if!'

'There's simply no if about it. She's not likely to find out unless you tell her. Or His Excellency tells her. Or one of the whores tells her. Where does she live?'

'Who?'

'Your mother.'

'In Yalta.'

'There you are, your fears are groundless,' Bulkarov said, 'I don't think it likely that any of you are going to go all the way to Yalta just to tell your mother that the Governor-General of Poland likes to have a whore brush his bare feet with her nipples. There's no possible way your mother could find out.'

'Yes, but if, if!'

'There's no if about it. She won't find out.'

'Yes, but if, if!'

The conversation meandered into repetitive, drunken insistence. The clocks of Warsaw struck three. Nikolaev in an effort to stand slipped off the chair on to the floor. He struggled to his knees. '*You* won't tell my mother, will you?' he said, plaintive, pitiful.

'I give you my word.' Bulkarov crossed himself involuntarily.

Nikolaev stood, saluted, made no attempt to button up his tunic and left, a cherub dedicated to sin. Bulkarov recorded the conversation in his dairy and added: I shall go to bed now to dream of nipples and bare feet. Delicious.

Some time between leaving the doctor and six-thirty when his batman came to wake him, Nikolaev shot himself.

Giorgy Skalon, the Governor-General of Poland or, as it was officially designated, the Western Region of the Russian Empire, was appalled. 'What could have induced him to do it?' he asked Bulkarov. 'He was such a decent fellow, and from such a good family.'

Bulkarov had just returned from the Captain's rooms to make his report. Still half-asleep, he had examined the body, observed his drinking companion's brains spattered all over the white wall behind the bed, removed the revolver from what was left of the dead angel's mouth and commanded an orderly to wake the Governor-General's aide-de-camp who in turn made the decision to wake the Governor-General himself.

'Such a useful fellow,' Skalon said. 'He was doing a fine job. Nothing was too much trouble for him.'

Bulkarov saw his own distorted reflection in His Excellency's boots and said nothing.

'I'll telegraph to Moscow for an immediate replacement,' Skalon said. 'I don't want any of this to get out. It can do none of us any good.' He began to pace. His boots squeaked. 'I shall have to write to his mother. I shall say it was an accident. I shall say he was cleaning his pistol, that usually does the trick. Poor Nikolaev.' For a long moment the Tsar's representative was lost in thought. 'I don't know what I'll do without him.' He pursed and unpursed his lips a dozen times.

Three weeks later Nikolaev's successor, Count Lev Borisovich Sobelev, arrived in Warsaw. He was just thirty and his wife, five years his junior, Tatiana Sergeievna, accompanied him. His Excellency said, 'I wish they hadn't sent a married man. I should have specified a bachelor. Bachelors are more diligent.'

They were thought of as an ideal couple. No officer at the court of the Governor-General was more handsome than Lev Sobelev and no gentleman more courteous or more agreeable. His manners were unshowy but always correct. He danced spiritedly, was a lively conversationalist and had a soft, beguiling laugh. If he had a fault in the eyes of others then it was the look of sadness that occasionally cast his face into shadow, a look that suggested a secret sorrow or an unwanted reminder of pain. But the truth was he had never known sorrow or pain and the look that sometimes crossed his face was nothing more than a sign that Lev Sobelev was a Russian through and through and, as everyone knows, all Russians are haunted by spectres of melancholy.

He was of noble lineage. His great-great-great-grandparents were Catherine the Great and an officer of her guard. On their offspring the Empress bestowed the title Count and because the newborn babe was wrapped in the fur of a sable, *soble* in Russian, he was called Sobelev. The family proliferated, and since the law of primogeniture was not applied by the Russian nobility, Count Lev Sobelev, Military Attaché in Warsaw, was just one Count Sobelev among many.

His wife, Tatiana, was also an aristocrat by birth, Princess Souvritzin before her marriage. Tall, erect, imperious, she exuded a manner both haughty and forbidding. In repose her eyes were the grey of an overcast sky but they could turn steel blue to show displeasure. Her figure was spare, angular, and she had practical yet graceful hands. Her three passions were riding, playing the piano and amateur photography.

She was not classically beautiful but striking, her nose a touch too long, her lips a mite thin, her dark hair scraped back too severely. But she had an indefinable style, a subtle economy of dress and adornment, a confidence in her stately walk, so that when she entered a room all eyes, male and female, turned to admire her. That hauteur, that confidence, however, concealed her vulnerability: she was sure of what she was but not of who she was and that made for a social unease which, in turn, made others uneasy.

The Sobelevs had been married six years with two daughters, Xenia and Darya, whom they had left in Sobliki, their country estate; the children were to join them when they were properly settled. In Warsaw they were given a small house near the Castle. Tatiana had brought her maid, Dunyasha Kaltikova, from Russia and between them the two women soon had the furniture rearranged, the paintings of stags removed, new curtains hung, a Bechstein boudoir grand piano in place – the Sobelevs' first purchase, she could not live long without music – all the rooms clean, neat but still lacking a truly distinct personality. The Countess worked as hard as her maid. Russian aristocrats, or at least a great many of them, unlike their English or French counterparts, had no false pride and were not afraid of physical labour. Their pride was genuine which is why many of them survived the tribulations that were to come.

On the piano the Countess arranged a gallery of her photographs. She liked to have around her examples of her hobby which also reminded her of her parents, brother, cousins, aunts, the house in Moscow and the large mansion, almost a palace, Sobliki, near Tula. There was also, in pride of place, a photograph of herself with the Tsar, Nicholas II, both of them on horseback, which Lev had taken on their visit to Tsarskoye Selo.

After the Sobelevs had been in Warsaw barely a month Bulkarov made two entries of interest in his diary in mid-January, 1911:

Warsaw is shortly to have two distinguished guests. Everyone is very excited. First comes The Paganini of Song, La Gloria d'Italia, The King of Baritones, the darling of all Russia, Mattia Battistini. He is to sing Rigoletto and Scarpia. The second visitor is to be Professor Paul Ehrlich, the Jew medical scientist who has discovered the cure for syphilis and was given the Nobel Prize. He's on a triumphant tour of Europe. All the crowned heads and all the uncrowned heads hail him as a saviour – as well they might. Another Jew come to save the Gentiles! Our widowed Governor has asked Countess Sobeleva to be his consort at a gala performance of *Rigoletto*. Many female noses out of joint. The Count and Countess, by the way, give off the odour of monotony. They are forever proper, polite, discreet. In other words BORING. In other words they have a happy marriage.

But a week later:

I detect tension between our Milit. Att. and his wife, the reasons for which are unclear. Could there be SOMEONE ELSE? I doubt it – in both their cases. I hear most things that go on in this town and there's no breath of scandal. Regarding the count, I can see he's handsome but too lethargic to be a rake. Sexual indiscretion, like everything else, requires energy and energy is exactly what the dear Count lacks. As for the Countess, she spends most of her time on horseback. She is a horsewoman *par excellence*. Typical aristocrat. Not a thought in her head. I admit she's handsome on or off her horse, but she's not the sort of woman who makes the pulse beat faster, not the sort you undress with your eyes the moment you meet her, not the sort you want to leap on, not the sort for whom you'd ruin your career. Yet, something has happened to disturb their calm. What? What?

Another week later, at a diplomatic reception given by the Governor-General, Bulkarov overheard a snatch of conversation which provided a clue. Mrs Harrison, wife of the British Minister, said in halting French to Tatiana, 'I expect, Countess, you have heard the great Battistini in your native Russia many times.'

Before Tatiana could reply, her husband intervened. 'Yes. She has,' he said brusquely as if to put an end to the exchange. But Mrs Harrison was insensitive to nuance. She persisted in that particular tone the English reserve for foreigners: loud, blithe and faintly amused. 'I am so excited about the *Rigoletto* next Monday. I wonder, is his voice really so beautiful?' she asked. Tatiana smiled non-committally.

Lev said, 'We are looking forward to Professor Ehrlich's visit.'

Mrs Harrison sailed on. 'And is Battistini really as handsome as everyone says?'

Bulkarov noticed a look pass between husband and wife. Tatiana rose, excused herself and left the reception.

Mrs Harrison announced for all to hear, 'What a charming person the Countess is,' and beamed.

3

The two visitors to Warsaw who interested Dr Bulkarov – Mattia Battistini and Paul Ehrlich – also touched Eva Salz. She loved music and so her pleasure at being given a ticket to hear the mighty baritone sing Rigoletto was easily understandable. But her excitement on hearing of the Nobel prize-winner's impending visit was not so much due to her interest in biochemistry but because her maiden name was Ehrlich and a family legend insisted that the great man was a distant or not so distant cousin.

The provider of both the opera ticket and the news of the putative relation was her Uncle Max, Max Ehrlich, a stationer and newsagent by trade and a bank manager in appearance. He could, like Bulkarov, claim that not much went on in Warsaw without his knowledge. He was a bachelor, asexual, and so had time to indulge passions of a different, gentler kind. He loved giving presents, surprises and good news; he revelled in gossip and intrigue, worshipped the arts, especially literature and the theatre, but, most of all, he adored his niece, Eva Salz, née Ehrlich. Despite these virtues he was thought by many to be 'a difficult man', short-tempered, arrogant and devious, qualities best demonstrated in his relationship to his devoted assistant, Miss Lela Krantnik, whom he had employed for more than twenty-five years and who irritated him almost beyond endurance. Miss Krantnik, on the other hand, slavishly adored Max and sniffed out for him the daily intrigues and excitements of the city so that he could display his intricate knowledge of Warsaw society at all levels.

Their day began at five-thirty each morning but no matter how hard he tried Max always arrived later than his assistant. This was the first source of irritation every day for quarter of a century. To punish her he refused to let her have a key to the shop. In all weathers she was obliged to wait for him outside on the pavement because the bundles of daily newspapers, which were piled under the narrow portico, left no room for her. It was more important to Max that the merchandise was dry and Miss Krantnik approved his priorities. This also irritated him mercilessly. He would have liked her to complain.

On that cold day, the last of January 1911, with snow thick on the ground, he arrived to find Miss Krantnik and the three delivery boys waiting for him. He greeted her as usual with a fierce grunt. 'Morning, Krantnik,' he said. Her response was to sing with a smile, 'Good morning, Mr Ehrlich,' like a cheerful bell-hop. To this he clenched his fists, punched his thighs and opened the door.

Always while sorting the newspapers for delivery Miss Krantnik would offer the first titbit and whenever possible in an underhand, roundabout way. 'Is it true Professor Paul Ehrlich is a relation of yours?' she asked innocently.

'You know he is.'

'Has he told you then he's coming to Warsaw?'

'Who's coming to Warsaw?'

'Your cousin, Paul Ehrlich. I'd have thought he'd have told you. Seeing as he's your cousin.' In truth, Miss Krantnik gave as good as she got.

'Of course I know he's coming to Warsaw,' Max lied. 'But what I don't know,' he conceded, 'is when.'

'I know when.'

'When?'

'Next Thursday. He'll stay two days before travelling to Budapest. There is to be a State banquet in his honour on the Friday.'

Refusing to be placed in an inferior position by his employee, he said airily, 'Yes, Cousin Paul did mention something about a State banquet.'

Miss Krantnik eyed him with a special look – what she called cloyingly 'her Mr Ehrlich look': a mixture of mistrust, amusement, coyness, and love. When Max caught sight of that look, he ground his teeth loudly, gripped his penknife and cut the thick string on a bundle of papers imagining he was severing her jugular vein. Miss Krantnik disappeared into the back room to make coffee – a mocha for him, a *mélange* for herself. While she was gone, Max breathed deeply in an effort to control his annoyance. He should have known Paul Ehrlich was due in Warsaw, he should not have had to learn the fact from Krantnik. Also, he had now to ask her a favour and that upset him even more.

Over coffee he blurted out, 'Krantnik, did you manage to get the two tickets for the opera?'

'I did better than two, Mr Ehrlich,' she said. 'I got three.'

'Three? But I only wanted two. I'm taking my niece. Her husband isn't interested in music. My niece and me. That's two. I only need two. Why d'you want to get three?' Statements and questions barked staccato like a dog about to attack.

'I want to go to the opera, too,' Miss Krantnik said. 'The third ticket is for me.'

28

'You?' Max repeated as though this was the most preposterous thing he had ever heard. 'You? But I thought you were tone deaf.'

'Who says I'm tone deaf?'

'I heard.'

'From whom?'

'I heard.'

'From whom?'

'I heard.'

The repetitions may have continued all morning if the first customers of the day had not interrupted. When he left, Max, ever a surprising man, said, 'All right, Krantnik, give me the tickets. All three of them.'

'I'll give you two, Mr Ehrlich. The third one is for me.'

'I know the third one's for you, Krantnik, but I'd like to pay for it. And I don't want any arguments.' He might have been telling her she was to find other employment.

When Miss Krantnik at last experienced the full pleasure of this unexpected, unprecedented gesture of kindness, she batted her eyelashes, twittered and smiled, caught her breath, produced the tickets from her reticule, dropped them on the floor, retrieved them and held them out to her employer, managing to make them flutter like a fan in the hand of a *femme fatale*. Max took all three, paid her, and ceremoniously returned one which Miss Krantnik slipped into her bodice, a difficult feat since it was buttoned to the neck but it seemed to her an appropriately seductive gesture. In a letter to a cousin in Peoria, Illinois, she wrote: 'Such a happy day. Dear, dear Mr Ehrlich, my beloved employer, is taking me to the opera to hear Battistini. I do nothing to encourage him but his designs are plain for all to see.'

By half-past seven, leaving Miss Krantnik to mind the shop, Max hurried across the city and was to be found pacing up and down outside the entrance to the Faculty of Arts of the University of Warsaw. He knew that Eva arrived each day about this time and contrived as frequently as possible to find excuses to waylay her, take her for a coffee at the café Blikli in the Nowy Swiat and offer her the gossip he had gleaned earlier from Miss Kranknik. Today, however, contrivance was unnecessary, for he had two major items of interest to reveal.

He saw her alight from the tram and head towards him. She bustled rather than walked: head high, chin thrust forward, elbows swinging like pistons, her eyes clear and defiant. The sight of her caused Max's heart to swell with pride and admiration. There was only one word in any language which adequately described what he felt and that was the Yiddish word, *nakhes*, from the Hebrew *nakhat*, meaning contentment, and which implies that particular joy derived from the achievements of a child. His pride in her, it must be said, was justified. Her success was undeniable, rare, probably unique. After glittering academic results as an undergraduate, she had the previous year, in 1910, at the age of twenty-four, obtained the post of junior lecturer in English Literature at the University of Warsaw. She was the first Jewish female to be a member of the Faculty of Arts. Never mind Jewish, just female was enough to mark her out as special. No matter how much the authorities had wanted to appoint someone else, anyone else, her knowledge and quality of mind was so much greater than any other applicant the professors had no choice but to succumb, albeit reluctantly. From these things, and from many other personal qualities of liveliness and energy, her Uncle Max had *nakhes*.

They kissed. 'A coffee, Professor?' he said, beaming.

'So, Uncle Max,' she asked, 'what's new?'

In Blikli, warm and intimate, the ceiling nicotine-stained, the smell of coffee, cigarettes and newly baked rolls producing an aroma of cultured contentment, Max blurted out his two surprises.

Eva kissed him lightly on the cheek to thank him for the tickets but seemed troubled at the mention of the family scientist.

'What's the problem?' Max asked, sensing her mood.

'I'm going to write him a letter,' she said.

'Good. What about?'

'What about? What about? About Zionism, of course.'

'Is he a Zionist?'

'I don't think so. I've never heard that he is. One would have heard.'

'He'd be a great catch,' Max said.

'Yes. He's important. Influential. Dines with kings and queens and presidents and prime ministers, the whole syphilitic crowd. Yes. He'd be a great catch.' Her mind raced and, tormented by an impulsive nature, she came quickly to a decision. 'I'll write to him today. I have a lecture to give but I'll cut it short. This is more important.'

'And what lecture are you giving today?' Max asked with a treacle tone in his voice which was an unattractive by-product of *nakhes* – sentimental and indulgent.

'George Eliot,' she murmured, already beginning to compose the letter in her mind.

'A-ha,' Max said, nodded, smiled a sickly smile. 'George Eliot. My, oh my.'

Eva's lecture – *George Eliot's Daniel Deronda: a real Jew or a Christian fantasy?* – was fortunately sparsely attended so she had no bad conscience about reducing it to a fifteen-minute catalogue of headlines.

She rushed home filled with excitement having made up her mind to write to Paul Ehrlich mentioning their tenuous kinship and to ask if they might meet. She had mixed motives and she had offered to Max the most serious. Eva's total belief in Zionism, in the urgent need for an independent Jewish State in Palestine, consumed her spare time and energy.

Armies of Polish anti-Semites, now led by Roman Dmowski, were on the march. The Socialist Zionist movement, *Po'alei Zion*, had been marshalled to counter the bigots. The Zionists had, in 1909, helped withstand a year-long economic boycott of Jews under the guise of Polish nationalism. Since the last century thousands of Jews had emigrated to Palestine. But Eva's interest was centred on the international implications of the movement. To attract universally renowned Jews to the cause was an activity enthusiastically pursued by Zionists all over the world. She was Secretary of her local branch and had aspirations to shine on the world stage. But therein lay another of her motives for writing the letter. Her instincts told her that to land as big a fish as Paul Ehrlich would greatly assist her political career and, in passing, attract admiration and envy – the two reactions absolutely necessary to those with ambition. Her third motive was the least worthy but may have given her the greatest sense of anticipation. Eva liked celebrities, the more celebrated the more she liked them. To be in the presence of even an infamous adversary gave her secret pleasure. She would too often drop the name in conversation, too obviously glow in reflected glory, so that she had gained a reputation for snobbery and pretentiousness. The prospect of a meeting *à deux* with the most famous scientist in Europe was undeniably thrilling, would do her no harm in the Faculty and would confirm, once and for all, her oft-made claim that Pau' Ehrlich was her cousin.

1. ese impulses – Zionism, personal ambition and self-aggrandisement – may be construed as a sort of single-mindedness for they denoted a sense of purpose and drive. But there was within her a confusion of identity and loyalty that made her seem facile or affected and which lay in her devotion to, and admiration of all things English.

Englishness was the yardstick by which she measured most things from literature to lavatory paper. Style, decorum, decoration, manners, diplomacy, cast of thought, elegance, justice, artefacts manufactured or created, were of quality only if they were English and this conviction was at war with her Jewishness, her Polishness, her aspirations and her Zionism. (Like many an intellectual she viewed the promised land which Zionism offered as a home for Jews less fortunate or less intelligent than she.) No one, least of all Eva herself, could know which of these forces would have the victory and which would, in turn, govern her future.

Was she beautiful or not beautiful? and what was the secret of form or expression which gave the dynamic quality to her glance? Thus George Eliot asked of her heroine, Gwendolen Harleth, Daniel Deronda's love. The same question was to be asked of Eva Salz. No, not really beautiful. Handsome certainly, with a fine straight nose, lustrous hair the colour of ebony, pale skin and a proud carriage. But she was too well-set, almost stocky, and her eyes too steely or defensive, too self-aware or, perhaps, too unconfident. For Eva, like the Countess Tatiana Sobeleva, was certain of only one thing in life, not who she was but what she was. What she knew with crystal clarity was that, of all her contemporaries, male or female, she was intellectually superior. A clever woman, they called her. This was both a curse and a blessing.

Why, then, did this young, brilliant woman fall in love with and marry Adam Salz, apparently a dull, austere dog, a door-to-door haberdashery salesman who specialised in fans, undeniably handsome, outwardly cold and unemotional, rigid in his convictions, and with an unpromising future? She had, after all, countless suitors who ranged from scholars to doctors, from property developers to young bankers. Even the lawyer, Konrad Blokh, said to be richest young man in Poland, had shown interest. But no. Eva had chosen her little Adda. And when he returned home for lunch that cold January day he was astonished to find his wife at her desk, scrumpled pages littered around her feet.

'Something wrong?' he asked.

She explained but he did not really listen. His heart beat faster at the sight of his young wife. She did not write her letter until evening and Adam did not do his afternoon rounds. They found warmth in bed, in each other's arms, in unrestrained, fierce passion.

4

At the time when Isaiah Wildnowitz was struggling to breathe in his coffin and the Count and Countess Sobelev's relationship was under strain, and while Eva and Adam Salz were lost in sensual delights, the members of the Kessler family were experiencing a modest drama which ruffled only the surface of their otherwise disciplined, well-ordered and unremarkable lives.

Despite their name, the Kesslers were as Russian in temperament and mien as any characters created by Leo Tolstoy or Anton Chekhov, and they lived in Moscow. The reason for this was that when, in 1762, Count Sobelev's great-great-great-grandmother, Sophie Friederike Auguste von Anhalt-Zerbst, proclaimed herself Empress of Russia as Catherine II, known now as Catherine the Great, she brought in her thrusting wake a small army of German merchants and professional men who planted their roots in Russian soil. The Kesslers were among these. They set up as textile merchants and by 1850 owned a factory on the outskirts of Moscow. They were the best of the bourgeoisie, the backbone of any decent society, well-educated, responsible, cultured, charitable, proper.

The mild disturbance in their lives took place in the nursery of their Moscow home on a winter's evening in 1911. All the family were present. Stepan Kessler, bald paterfamilias, factory-owner and stoic, and his wife, Anya, her cheeks tear-stained, sat either side of the bed of their elder son, also Stepan, aged five. He was sleeping fitfully and noisily, mouth open. His younger brother, Aleksander, always called Shura, aged three, stared at him, eyes wide with fear but mostly with a lack of comprehension. At the foot of the bed stood Dr Kozlov, the distinguished ear, nose and throat specialist. He removed an apron which was bloodstained and then turned to the maid, Katya, who stood ready with an ewer of warm water which she poured into a basin on the marble-topped washstand. All, except Dr Kozlov, who began to wash his hands and whistle, had that evening a painful not to say terrifying experiece. In the case of the younger Stepan, the most painful and terrifying of his life.

As was the practice then, the removal of young Stepan's tonsils had been performed by Dr Kozlov without anaesthetic. While his father played perfunctorily with Shura in the drawing-room downstairs, Stepan had been laid out, screaming and kicking, on the nursery table, his legs finally secured with leather belts while Anya and Katya held his head over the edge so that, when Dr Koslov forced his mouth open, there was more or less a vertical approach down his throat. 'Don't worry, my boy,' Dr Kozlov said, 'it's like having a tooth out.' This was absolutely no comfort to Stepan. The operation probably took less than a minute but to a boy of five a minute of the kind he had to endure was eternity. The combination of pain, terror and shock was devastating. When it was done he could neither speak nor cry, but lay staring at the white ceiling, trying to catch his breath while Anya cradled him in a warm embrace and Katya whispered words of comfort, telling him how brave he had been.

Now, he was asleep and there let him be with his respectable, high-minded father, his adoring mother and bewildered younger brother. Yes, there let them all be in that dimly lit, warm nursery, the family Kessler in Moscow, certain of their concerns and of their place in the world. Alas, Stepan Stepanovich's tonsillectomy was not the worst thing that would happen to them. Harsher things were in store. Yes, let them be.

5

Isaiah heard strange music. In the darkness of the coffin panic
enveloped him. He twisted his head this way and that, tried to break
free but his shroud was wrapped too tightly. Rigid, terrified, he
seemed able only to harness strength enough to breathe. The music,
tangled, distorted, metallic, came to him as though carried on a
faraway wind, but then he heard the unscrewing of the coffin lid,
shouts and his mother's voice. When at last the shroud was loosened
and he was able to sit up, he choked and spluttered, welcomed the
light which assailed his eyes and saw, as though through a reddish
haze, the head of a beautiful woman encircled in silver spheres above
the trees, below her a tongue of fire and, close by, his uncle Laban the
Idiot dancing with a monkey in the forest.

The going had been hard ever since their departure from Ploemyan
just before noon. Deep, heavy snow covered the ground and they
walked in the ruts made by the wheels of the cart. Laban assumed the
role of leader largely because the entire plan had been his idea and
because he had a natural way with coffins and death. On reaching the
edge of the forest he ordered a brief pause so that Isaiah could urinate
and be fed. 'It may be a little time before you can do that again,' Laban
said to the boy. 'Hold tight. We must keep going until nightfall,' and
returned Isaiah to the darkness of the coffin.

Towards dusk, in the depths of the forest, the sun intermittent and
pale, they saw a thin spiral of smoke a little way ahead. The
procession halted. Laban, like a scout, went to investigate. For those
left with the coffin the wait was cold and agonising. Fifteen minutes
passed, twenty, twenty-five. Then, Laban reappeared, beckoning
them with both hands to come on. A man stood beside him, garishly
dressed in a multi-coloured patchwork coat with a sheepskin collar.
He also beckoned.

The cortège trudged forward. Leah wept loudly again fearing that
Laban had encountered trouble. But he was smiling when they
reached him and so was the man in the multi-coloured coat.

'Who is he?' Solomon hissed.

'You'll see, you'll see,' Laban said.

They heard the music before they reached a clearing where small, gaily decorated caravans surrounded a camp fire. Their eyes were instantly drawn to a young boy with a monkey on his shoulder and a barrel organ. He churned out an unrecognisable tune that kept repeating itself. A woman walked a tightrope, one man juggled silver balls, another spat fire. Laban's companion, swarthy, lively, graceful, said something in a language none of the family Wildnowitz understood but it was obviously a command because, instantly, the others ceased their activities and gathered around the newcomers, gazing at them as though they were freaks. The family Wildnowitz had stumbled on the travelling circus.

They were called the Circus Stoica and the man with Laban was Ion Stoica, fourth-generation acrobat, juggler, tightrope-walker, magician, leader of a small peripatetic troupe which visited towns and villages and hamlets from the Black Sea to the Baltic. While Ion made the introductions Isaiah hid behind his mother's skirts, awed and timorous. There was Raina Stoica, Isaiah's age, dancer and singer; Chivu Stoica, clown and juggler of silver balls; Arpad Stoica, fire-eater; and the most beautiful woman Isaiah had ever seen, Constanta Stoica, a tightrope-walker whose ravishing face he had beheld above the trees. And, like children eager both to show off their talents at any and every opportunity and to welcome the strangers, the Circus Stoica continued to practise their acts, performing impromptu in the forest clearing where the setting sun reddened both the snow and Isaiah's discarded shroud.

The Stoicas delighted in Laban's account of the counterfeit death; they were themselves outcasts, understood persecution and admired ingenuity. Their origin was vague but they boasted of Romanian ancestry with gypsy, Hungarian and Georgian antecedents thrown in. Ion claimed to speak all European languages but Laban, himself a linguist of sorts, had difficulty understanding him in any of them. (Ion's strange pronunciation and syntax Laban said was a wholly original tongue which he henceforth called Ionian.) The Stoicas, however, understood Laban's Russian and at the unfolding of the tale smiled, chuckled, nodded like admiring conspirators.

'But where will you go now?' the beautiful Constanta asked.

Silence answered her, for what other response could be given? To escape Ploemyan had been their priority and as far ahead as anyone had planned. Indeed, when the same question was raised by Solomon Wildnowitz an hour before their departure from the town, Reb Yankel said, 'Don't worry about such things, you'll find a way, God is good,' but no one believed him. Now, the unanswerable hung heavy. They sat around the fire, under the stars, covered in rugs and coats made of animal skins. The Jews ate the food they had brought with them; into the glowing embers the Stoicas dug *shashliks* made of mysterious meats, turning them frequently. The smell made Isaiah's mouth water.

Laban said, 'We want to get to the sea, to a port, but we have no real plan.'

'Sleep on it,' Ion said. 'We'll talk further in the morning.'

A flask of wine was passed around. Laban, alone of the Wildnowitzs, drank. The young girl, Raina Stoica, sang a sweet, sad harmony, to the accompaniment of a balalaika played by Arpad, the fire-eater. Isaiah found himself staring into Raina's eyes which were large and frank; he was overcome with shyness; he knew there was mischief in those eyes and was grateful to the darkness for hiding his blushes. But as he turned away from her he noticed Constanta crawl to Ion and whisper. The leader nodded.

'My daughter, Constanta, has a good idea,' he said. 'If you like, you can use one of our caravans for sleep.'

The half-hearted protests from the Wildnowitzs were easily brushed aside. Circus people, Ion said, were used to hardships and, after all, one night's discomfort was not such a terrible hardship. The preparations were made. The caravan was small and cramped but, somehow, the seven Jews managed either to sit or lie in the confined space. Isaiah was squeezed between his parents on a narrow cot. Laban, climbing to an upper bunk where his brother, Benjamin, was already asleep, said, 'Imagine we're on a ship and this is our cabin. Naturally, we're in steerage, as they call it, where luxury is not readily available. So, dream sweet dreams, my dears. Dream of this ship ploughing through the waves, rocking us gently to sleep. Remember, we have changed our fate and confronted destiny. We have escaped. Dream sweet dreams, my dears, dream.'

Isaiah asked, 'But where are we travelling to, Uncle Laban?'

'To America, of course, where else?'

America had always been Laban's dream, unusual for a Ploemyan Jew. In the past, especially after the pogroms in the 1890s, the majority of those fleeing from the town had sought and found shelter in Germany or England and many, including Wildnowitz cousins, had even made the long ocean voyage to South Africa although no one now knew why. But Laban, being an individualist and cussed, had to be different. 'Yes, my little Isaiah,' he said, 'sleep now and dream of America.'

Isaiah awoke to the sound of angry voices and to find himself alone in the caravan. He peered out of one of the small, frost-encrusted windows but could only make out shapes and icy shadows. Pulling on his coat he tumbled into the biting air. The sun had risen but its rays had not yet reached the clearing.

His family were standing huddled on one side of the rekindled fire. On the other Constanta Stoica was berating her father, watched by the other members of the troupe. Isaiah slipped in beside Leah who, preoccupied with the scene she was witnessing, absentmindedly passed her son a crust of black bread and put her arm around his shoulder, holding him tightly.

Isaiah whispered, 'Why are they fighting?'

Leah shrugged. 'We can't understand,' she said. 'But your Uncle Laban thinks it's about us.' (She always said 'your Uncle Laban': it was a note of disapproval.)

Ion struck Constanta hard across the face. The world froze. Constanta did not flinch but stood her ground, gazing defiantly at her father who, unable to stare her down, marched towards Laban. 'You must go now,' he said, turned sharply and disappeared into his caravan.

The remaining Stoicas gathered round to watch Laban wrap Isaiah in the shroud. Raina cried and Leah, whose own anguish was always assuaged by the sight of someone else's pain, gave comfort by taking her hand. The young girl's tears unaccountably renewed Isaiah's courage and, for the first time since leaving Ploemyan, he had a vague realisation of his own heroism. Once again the lid of the coffin was screwed down and the coffin itself placed on the cart. Isaiah heard words of farewell and wishes for a safe journey as the cart trundled forward. He thought he heard Raina crying still.

Not long after, Isaiah heard another cry.

'Jews!'

A man's voice.

'Jews!'

'Jews,' Ion Stoica said addressing the family Wildnowitz, 'I have been persuaded to allow you to accompany us to Danzig. That's a great metropolis, you know, a seaport, so you may find a ship there to take you to wherever you want to go.'

'America,' Laban said. 'We've decided.'

When Isaiah asked how Ion Stoica's change of heart had come about, his father, Solomon, told him that Constanta Stoica had coerced the others into joining her rebellion against the decision not to give the family refuge. 'This is what they were fighting about early this morning,' Solomon said. 'The good-looking girl, Constanta, had made up her mind to help us, suggested the idea to her father, who gave her a crack across the jaw for her pains. But she's like your Uncle Laban, she's obstinate, and don't ask me how, but she managed to persuade the others to support her. They're like one big family, you see. The father doesn't want trouble so he gave in.'

Later, Laban said confidentially to Isaiah, 'If you want my honest opinion, there is something not quite right about what your father told us. Good-hearted *goyim*, circus people banding together to save seven miserable Jews? No, Isaiah, it doesn't ring true. You know what I think? I think your father paid some money over, probably all he had left, that's what I think.'

Whatever the exact nature of the turn of events, the outcome was undeniable: Isaiah would not have to lie in his coffin again. The family Wildnowitz joined the Circus Stoica and started on the road – but to where? America became an obsessive goal, especially to Laban the Idiot, but America was the future which is by definition unknown and uncertain. To Isaiah what mattered was the present and the present was an idyll, a fantasy, a life beyond the imagination of the twelve-year-old boy who had experienced only poverty, fear, anxiety and a strict code of behaviour by which he was obliged to live. No, this journey upon which he was now embarked represented freedom in a real, finite sense and, for the rest of his life, when searching for a word to describe man's ultimate goal, Isaiah would use the word *frizlitch* which was Ionian and meant freedom.

America, America, America.

These were some of the names that Laban the Idiot repeated along the roads of northern Europe as the family Wildnowitz and the Circus Stoica headed towards the sea: Tsintsinatty, Mishugan, Indernapolish, Tsikargo, Milvorkee, Yelloystoyne, Nyork, Erritzona, Feeladelfya, Yossimight, Missatsippy, Dellas, Oota, Vashinton Dee Tsee, Ellybumma. No one knew where he had learned them but he taught them to Isaiah whose favourite was Ellybumma.

America, America, *frizlitch*, America.

6

Battistini, Battistini, Battistini.

The Countess Tatiana Sobeleva retired to her bed, hiding a letter, written in French, beneath the coverlet.

3 February 1911.

Dear Countess,

I hope with all my heart you remember me. We met in Moscow some years ago when I sang Scarpia and gave several successful concerts. You also attended one of those. We rode horses together. Do you remember? I am sure you agree what lucky fortune we are both here in Warsaw at the same time. May we meet again?

I am your devoted servant and present my sentiments on a grand scale.

Mattia Battistini.

Tatiana read the letter and took immediately to her bed with a savage headache and a mild temperature. She was made ill by a complex sequence of emotional reactions. When she had heard that Battistini was to sing in Warsaw her pulse quickened and her mind flew to the first time she had seen him, almost eight years ago, when she was only seventeen and before she was married.

Battistini on stage, as Scarpia, cruel, cruel Scarpia, always, it seemed to her, bathed in a strong, harsh light which followed him everywhere, his presence overshadowing the other singers, his glorious voice drowning Tosca in the great duet. And, when taking his countless solo bows to the cheers and applause, had he not spotted her in the box? had their eyes not met? had he not given her a special bow all to herself? Tatiana returned home after the performance and wrote an admiring letter careful to mention in which box she had been seated. She wrote in French in which she was more comfortable than Russian. When she woke in the morning, late, she decided not to send the letter but her maid, Dunyasha had, moments before, tiptoed into the room to see if her mistress was awake, noticed the envelope and had it delivered by footman to the theatre.

Battistini replied at once, inviting her to attend his recital at the end of the week and to join him backstage for a glass of champagne. The invitation threw her into a delightful panic. She consulted Dunyasha, a lover of intrigue – should she accept or not? Accept, Dunyasha advised, but do not go alone. Tatiana agreed and invited her brother, the raffish Prince Grigory Souvritzin, four years older than she, to accompany her. Again, she was overwhelmed by Battistini's artistry and the thought of meeting one of the most famous singers in the world excited her more than she cared to admit.

They met in a small ante-room. At first, Tatiana was disheartened because of the number of guests crammed into the room. She knew them all, the Dolgorukis, Bakhrushins, Kutuzovs, Shuvalovs, a chattering, noisy herd of grandees. But on entering to cries of aristocratic delight and more applause, Battistini, wearing a crimson silk dressing-gown with a towel carefully wrapped around his neck, made straight for Tatiana, bowed low and kissed her hand. The women narrowed their eyes and the men, especially Grigory, affected concern. Tatiana was filled with a terrible sense of doom which she was unable to explain.

That weekend they had gone riding together. Riding was the only opportunity members of her class had to engineer trysts. Trotting by her side, Battistini talked mostly of himself, of his great loneliness, of the terrible life he led, a wanderer, a nomad, the recipient of affection, love, adoration from a vast multitude of admirers, but lonely, oh, so desperately lonely. And when he uttered the 'oh' – long drawn-out and sonorous – it was, Tatiana felt, like being Tosca in the presence of Scarpia. They agreed to meet again. A date and time was arranged, but she did not keep the appointment. Her terror, her cowardice, was too great. And that was all. Except for the note in Russian:

Where were you? Why you did not come? I thought we discover something beautiful. I am desolate. M. B.

The note, alas, she kept. Alas, because a week after her marriage, her young husband, Count Lev Sobelev, discovered it while helping her to unpack after their move to the great house, Sobliki, near Tula. His rage was terrifying. 'Who is M. B.?' he demanded. Tatiana struggled for, and achieved calm. She related the facts of what can hardly be called an affair. Lev listened to her story in silence, a silence more terrible than his rage. From that moment, the name Battistini was taboo.

Battistini, Battistini, Battistini.

When the announcement was made of the baritone's visit to Warsaw, Lev Sobelev became morose and embattled. This was the tension detected by Dr Bulkarov and confided to his diaries. This was the reason for the Count's graceless behaviour towards Mrs Harrison, the wife of the British Minister, at the diplomatic reception, which caused Tatiana to depart so suddenly.

Now, in her darkened bedroom lying between crêpe de Chine sheets, she reread Battistini's latest letter. 'I hope with all my heart you remember me . . . I am sure you agree what lucky fortune we are both here in Warsaw at the same time,' and loathing for him surfaced like nausea. She detested his false modesty. How could she not remember him? He whose name was in the newspapers almost daily, whose fame was as great as – as Paul Ehrlich or Sarah Bernhardt. And how dare he presume that she would regard their being in the same city as fortuitous?

Anger, too. How stupid of him to write, how indiscreet and clumsy. Did he not know she was now married? Perhaps not. Even so. Well, what was one to expect from a vulgar, preposterous singer?

Yet, an ache, a longing to see him again, to be in his presence, to hear his voice.

And fear, fear of danger, fear of herself, fear of weakness, fear of catastrophe. Cowardice, plain and complicated. For, at the heart of Tatiana's anguish resided a timid, sensitive temperament and an over-developed conscience. She aspired to the highest standards of behaviour which, she believed, gave the world she lived in order, style and decorum.

Tatiana, as she almost always did when in doubt, consulted Dunyasha. 'Sweetheart,' the maid said, 'be careful. Don't see him in private.'

'I want to see him, Dunyasha,' Tatiana said.

'Go to the opera and see him, my darling, but don't be alone with him. That's all I say.' Tatiana closed her eyes. She knew Dunyasha's advice was sound yet she longed to disregard it. Dunyasha asked, 'Do you think of him often, angel?'

'Often,' Tatiana murmured.

'I would love to hear his voice.'

'His voice is like a priest intoning prayers.'

'Mattia Battistini,' Dunyasha said, playing with the sounds in her mouth.

'Mattia Battistini.'

They heard the front door slam. A flurry in the bedroom. Tatiana slipped Battistini's letter to Dunyasha, who stuffed it into a pocket and then sat by the bedside as though keeping vigil. Lev entered. 'Ssh, she's asleep,' Dunyasha said.

'I'm not asleep. I have to keep my eyes closed. The light hurts.'

Lev flicked a look that told Dunyasha to leave. Alone with his wife, he said, 'Will you be well enough for the Ehrlich reception next week?'

'Of course. I'll be better tomorrow.'

'No,' Lev said quickly, 'don't be better tomorrow. Stay in bed.'

'I'll be all right.'

'Even so.'

'I don't understand.'

'The Governor-General wants us to accompany him to the opera on Saturday. It would be better if I told him you weren't well enough. My advice is to remain in bed until the – the opera company leaves Warsaw.' He thought about kissing her on the forehead but decided against it.

The intrigue of servants is simpler, more discreet, and certainly more effective than the most devious, secret negotiations of governments. All Dunyasha needed was a nudge.

'I want to go to the opera,' Tatiana said through tears, pounding her pillow with clenched fists. A spoiled child.

'But why can't you?' Dunyasha asked.

'Because – because.'

Dunyasha thought for a moment. 'Is Lev Borisovich putting his foot down?' A noise from Tatiana indicated that this indeed was the problem. 'Husbands are meant to be jealous, little darling. That's what husbands are for.'

Tatiana recounted that Lev had more or less ordered her to remain indisposed until Battistini departed the city. 'He said "opera company". He couldn't bring himself to utter the name Battistini but I knew very well what he meant.' She was weeping freely now.

Dunyasha wiped Tatiana's brow with a handkerchief doused in cologne. 'There, there, sweetheart, don't fret. You'll go to the opera, you'll see.'

His Excellency the Governor-General of Poland, Giorgy Skalon was also fretful. He had suffered a dizzy spell while emerging from his weekly bath and had his valet, Arkady, not saved him from falling, might have done himself serious injury. Dr Bulkarov was summoned.

Skalon lay in his bed while the doctor probed and prodded. Arkady, the son of a village priest, a small, bespectacled man who took pleasure in being servile, stood to one side, head bowed, hands clasped at his navel.

Bulkarov said, 'There doesn't seem to be anything organic, Excellency. You have low blood pressure but that's good, you'll live to be a hundred. I think it was just the heat of the bath. Are you working very hard at the moment?'

'Yes, yes, of course I'm working very hard. To serve His Imperial Majesty is not a sinecure, you know. Life just now seems unnecessarily complicated.'

'Why so?' Bulkarov asked and started to pack away his instruments.

'To begin with, I badly need a female chiropodist.'

Bulkarov spluttered.

'Why do you laugh, doctor? It's not funny.'

'No, no reason,' Bulkarov replied airily, 'except that it sounds so – so specific, Excellency. I mean, wouldn't a male chiropodist do?'

'Certainly not, I won't have a man touch my feet. Only women know how to treat a man's feet. Can you find me someone?'

'I'll make enquiries,' Bulkarov said.

'Will you? Will you?'

'But only if you promise to take things easy.'

'How can I take things easy? If it's not one thing it's another. I had word yesterday that the Countess Sobeleva has been taken ill and so now I have the whole business of the opera to reorganise. I'm a lady short and I had the party so carefully balanced. Have you been asked to examine her, doctor?'

'No.'

'So we don't know what's wrong with her. She's probably pregnant.'

'I think I would have been summoned if that were the case, Excellency.'

Arkady said, 'Please forgive me, Excellency, for speaking, but I wonder if you would allow me to be indiscreet?'

'Yes, yes, what is it?'

'I believe, Excellency, that I may be able to lighten your load in one particular respect.'

'Yes, yes, well, get on with it.'

'As is my wont, while Your Excellency dines, I take the air and stroll towards the Square. Last evening I happened to meet the Countess's maid, Dunyasha, in the street. When I say meet, Excellency, it was in fact rather comical because I rounded a corner and collided with her, almost knocking her over. She insisted, Excellency, that I buy her a cognac to restore her spirits. And so, of course, we conversed.'

'Yes, yes, yes, yes, well?'

'Calmly, calmly, Excellency,' Bulkarov murmured.

Arkady continued. 'During the course of our conversation it transpired that the Countess was fully recovered.'

'What?' Skalon barked. 'What time was this?'

'While Your Excellency was at dinner. About nine o'clock last evening.'

'But that is precisely when Count Sobelev told me his wife was too ill to attend the performance.'

'I am only repeating what the serving-woman told me, Excellency.'

'And she said the Countess had recovered?'

'Oh, yes, Excellency, the maid was quite unambiguous on that matter.'

'Then why did the Count tell me she was still unwell?'

'I cannot say, Excellency. And I must add it was all rather droll because this Dunyasha person was at pains to make me promise to inform you, Excellency, that her mistress was recovered but I said, "My dear woman, I do not presume to inform His Excellency of anything. It's not my place." And had the opportunity not arisen a moment ago, I would have remained silent.'

After confiding the exchange between master and servant to his dairy on 4 February 1911, Dr Bulkarov added:

Like me, H. E. misses Nikolaev. There is obviously no one he can trust now and he needs to satisfy his 'podversion'. His man, Arkady, is a simple fellow, son of a priest I believe, and wouldn't understand. And if he did he'd also probably shoot himself. At least the matter with the Countess is sorted out, but there's something fishy there, I smell it. Yes, life is dull without Nikolaev. I've no one to drink with, no one to gossip with. I spend my days reading every word of the Moscow newspapers which all carry the same news – the Tsar receives foreign dignitaries, the police arrest agitators, thirty Jews slaughtered in a spontaneous uprising near Vilna, a chemist in Kiev claims to have discovered a cure for baldness, the Moscow Art Theatre is to revive *The Seagull*. I have nothing to look forward to but the opera and the Jew Ehrlich's visit.

That night, Count Sobelev said to his wife, 'We can't get out of going to the opera. H. E. insists we accompany him.'

'Didn't you tell him I was ill?' Tatiana asked trying to keep the excitement out of her voice.

'Of course I told him but he doesn't believe me. He accused me of lying. I had a terrible scene with him.'

'I'm sorry.'

'Someone's convinced him that you're in perfect health.'

'Who?'

'He refused to say. We should have called in Dr Bulkarov. I could have persuaded him to order you to stay in bed. It's too late now. H. E. commands us to accompany him.'

She kept silent, turning her head away from him in case he detected the pleasure in her eyes.

Lev said, 'I don't want to be embarrassed, Tatiana. You're not to applaud too enthusiastically. Is that understood?'

'Yes.'

'And when that man, that singer, you know whom I mean, when he is being brought up to the box to be presented we should excuse ourselves. I don't think I can bear to set eyes on him.'

'Whatever you say.'

'I shall sleep in my dressing-room tonight.'

Battistini, Battistini, Battistini.

7

Adam Salz was a man described by his wife and by others who knew him well as highly strung, a term used in those days to characterise someone who reacted with exactly the same degree of alarm to events great or small, important or trivial. To his customers and casual acquaintances, however, he was regarded as colourless and some- what rigid, but that was merely a ruse on his part, a demeanour he had developed since adolescence to keep his constant anxiety under control.

His adolescence had been scarred by family misfortune which caused an emotional upheaval that dogged him forever after. His parents, Josef and Esther, had two sons, Karl and Adam who was the younger by seven years. For most of Adam's childhood, certainly until he was twelve, the family was well-off, indeed rich. They lived in a splendid house on Sienna, employed servants and took two holidays a year, in Monte Carlo and in one or another of Europe's more fashionable spas. Monte Carlo was the clue to the catastrophe that ruptured the idyll.

Josef Salz had made his money out of manufacturing paper in Poland and squandered it at roulette and baccarat in Monaco. Gambling was a sickness from which he would never be cured. When his world collapsed, the family moved out of their mansion into a two-bedroomed apartment in Nalewki, one of Warsaw's poorer districts, and Josef found work as a caretaker at a factory he had previously owned. But his optimism, like his gambling, was incur- able. He remained unbearably cheerful, convinced his bad luck would change and that, even on his paltry wage, he would be able to place small stakes judiciously and thus rebuild his fortune.

Karl, the elder son, who had been privately educated in Switzer- land and Germany, was then nineteen and studying medicine in Vienna. Luckily, Josef had set up a trust fund to take care of his education and so he was unaffected by the disaster. Adam, however, was less fortunate. He had nursed, since his earliest years, an ambition to become an artist and had shown a modest gift for drawing and clay modelling. These dreams were, of course, shattered. No private education for him, no sojourns abroad, no expectations, no future. He developed a disgust for his father and a wretched envy of his brother, aggravated by Karl's decision not to return to Warsaw but to set up his medical practice in Austria. Karl wrote occasional brief letters to his mother but even these stopped. After a year or two, Esther heard from him no more and she mourned him as if for a dead child.

The change in family circumstances was hardest for Esther. Never a great beauty but always upholstered in the most fashionable fabrics, she had led a life of ease and leisure. Now, she was reduced to serving behind the counter in a local bakery. Because Josef's gambling and losses continued unabated, the pittance she earned was often all she possessed to pay the rent and to feed herself and Adam.

For Adam, Friday night was the worst night of the week. In happier times, religion had played little part in the family's life. There were occasional visits to the synagogue but neither boy was taught Hebrew nor were they prepared for the rite of bar mitzvah. Yet Josef, for reasons that were never clear, contributed generously to a variety of Jewish causes, and always anonymously. When the fall came, and he was struggling to salvage something from the wreckage, he was dismayed to discover that all the Jews in high places who knew of his charity, shunned him as if he had contracted leprosy. But he explained it away as a vagary of human nature, and kept cheerful.

Esther, on the other hand, found solace in religion and so, on Friday nights, said prayers and lit the Sabbath candles. But this alone was not what made the Sabbath eve so terrible for her younger son. What Adam found unbearable was to see her sitting in her squeaking rocking-chair, waiting for her husband's return from work with his weekly wage packet. She would wait and wait, rocking to and fro, the squeaking of the chair grating on Adam's nerves as though someone were running fingernails down a blackboard. That was how he remembered his mother: a broken woman, her eyes swollen from crying, waiting until dark, her face lit by flickering Sabbath candles, before she said, 'Don't worry, Adam, I have something put by. We won't wait, we'll eat. Thank God I've got a job. God is good.' Long after Adam was in bed, he'd hear his father return and his mother's inevitable angry reproaches. In the morning, she'd say, 'Same as usual. His pay packet was empty. How can he do it to us?'

These emotional disturbances laid the uncertain foundations for the persona that Adam was to develop. His reactions bordered on the extreme. He determined to be as unlike his father as possible. He never gambled; he was financially prudent to a fault; he believed in being responsible, conscientious and diligent. Above all, he sought stability in the world outside as though to insulate the rampant insecurity within. At fifteen he went out to work and on every Friday night thereafter presented Esther with his pay packet and she gave thanks to God with a fervour that sickened her son. Yet, he paid for her to have a Jewish burial and was never heard to complain. He refused to do the same for his father but a charity devoted to impoverished Jews footed the bill.

In his adult life, apart from the almost continuous habit of playing rapid five-finger exercises on his thighs, nothing of Adam's inner confusion could be easily detected. He seemed much older than twenty-eight, was fastidious in appearance, rather handsome in a vapid sort of way, moustache neatly clipped, suit immaculate, fingernails pristine, his conversation careful, diction precise. Someone meeting him for the first time would mark him down as, well, yes, dull and the more discerning might have regarded him as eccentric. He had a habit of making sudden announcements out of the blue which those, unaware of his background, found puzzling to say the least. 'I'm a Freethinker, thank God,' he'd say, or 'The worst thing in life is an empty pay packet,' or 'It's nothing that a drop of oil won't cure,' or 'I don't want to be disturbed.' None but Eva had encountered his deeper layer, his abandoned passion, and that was because, of course, it was revealed only in love-making.

On the Monday of Battistini's *Rigoletto*, Adam's interior disturbances were particularly active. Waking, he remembered Eva was to accompany her Uncle Max to the performance and he was immediately put out. The five-finger exercises at breakfast would have done credit to Paderewski. Adam, unlike Count Sobelev, was not a jealous man; he was too confident of his sexuality to be jealous, but he was possessive and wanted Eva to spend an evening, any evening, either in his presence or alone. So his wife's impending visit to the opera caused his day to start badly. Then, there was the matter of the lost key to his sample case. The case itself, a large rectangular wooden box, contained threads, cottons, laces, ribbons, the samples of tortoiseshell, mother-of-pearl and ivory which ladies could have made into combs, needles and pins, bobbins and reels, diamanté, swatches of silks and, in pride of place, miniature ostrich feather plumes so fashionable in fans and capes and head adornments. 'I have lost my key,' Adam said, 'and I cannot make a living without my key.'

Eva found it for him in the lower right-hand pocket of his waistcoat, its usual place. 'Odd,' he said. 'I looked there. Well, it's nothing that a drop of oil won't cure.' He kissed her. His hands found her breasts and thighs. He would have delayed his departure for work, was indeed about to lead her back to the bedroom when a paroxysm of coughing overpowered him and dispelled his lust. She laughed gently and lovingly. He said, 'There's always tonight,' but remembered the opera. Irritation and anxiety returned. He set off on his rounds across the city of Warsaw.

Most of Adam's customers were Poles and Adam hated the Poles, hated their anti-Semitism and arrogance. He preferred to think of himself and to be thought of as German. At least, Adam reasoned, in Germany Jews were assimilated, accepted and welcomed in business, industry, finance, the arts, politics, journalism, in every walk of life. It felt to Adam that the culture of Germany was enriched by Jews. Not so in Poland. Here he had to put up with the sneers and disdain that were his daily expectations. His anxiety trebled when customers would say, 'What have you got for me today, Jew?' or 'You Jews drive hard bargains,' or 'Isn't your wife the clever Jewess who teaches our young?' Adam especially loathed the word Jewess; it made him shudder but, being Adam, the shudder was concealed. He did make it known, especially to other Jews, that he was a non-believer who scorned all Jewish observances. He worked on the Day of Atonement, ignored the dietary rules and attended the synagogue only for weddings. All religions enslave mankind, was another of his sayings, and he would have no part of it. He allied himself to the Assimilationists, did not approve of Eva's Zionism although was careful not to allow it to become too great an issue between them. But these small acts of defiance could not effect a complete retreat from his collective identity. The inheritance was too powerful; the numberless ancestors who accounted for his existence and moulded his very being had fed into him a code of behaviour, a pattern of thought, genetic, ancient, arcane and compulsive, from which it was impossible ever to escape. Which is why he reacted so badly to the news Uncle Max gave him in the late afternoon.

Adam had never warmed to Max Ehrlich but tolerated him for Eva's sake and took to visiting him, once a week perhaps, in the newspaper shop. On that cold Monday in February, it had crossed Adam's mind that there might be the slim chance of a spare ticket to the opera and, although he was unmusical and positively disliked opera, he had a fancy to be with Eva that night, to watch her pleasure and enjoy the event vicariously.

'Is Mr Ehrlich in?' Adam asked of Miss Krantnik.

'In the back,' she said and, as she lifted the counter flap to let Adam pass, added in an excited whisper, 'He's taking me to the opera tonight. With your wife. We're closing early to give us time to dress. I'm so excited I can hardly breathe—'

'Who are you whispering to, Krantnik? What's going on?' Max called.

'It's Mr Salz,' she replied.

Adam joined Max in the back room. Miss Krantnik made them

glasses of lemon tea and then returned to man the counter and to continue a long letter she was writing to her cousin in Peoria, Illinois, and in which she intended to include a description of her night at the opera. Adam and Max discussed the possibility of a fourth ticket to *Rigoletto* but Max said it was pointless even to think about it.

'And what news from abroad?' Adam asked. 'Anything of interest?' He held the glass of tea in both hands to warm them.

'The Russians are at it again,' Max said.

'What's that supposed to mean? At what again?'

'What do you think?' Max said and reached out for a copy of *Hatzefirah*, the Hebrew organ of Warsaw Zionists, from the shelf behind him. Licking his middle finger he flicked through the journal and explained that he had come upon an especially interesting item of news but that the *goyische* Warsaw press had ignored the matter entirely. 'I kept this for Eva in case she didn't see it. We Zionists have to know about these things. I'll read it to you,' Max said. 'The headline is: "Thirty slaughtered in pogrom", and it goes on to say that on 1 February a so-called spontaneous uprising against the Jewish population took place in a village to the south of Vilna. There have been others, too. A man's on trial for poisoning wells, another for eating Christian babies. It's the old, old story. The Tsar's under pressure at home and whenever he needs to divert attention from his own troubles he turns on us. They want him to become a democrat. Some chance. He'll resist until all the Jews in his empire lie buried and then who will he blame? Mark my words, Adam, it won't be long before they organise a few spontaneous uprisings in Poland. The Poles have never needed encouragement when it comes to slaughtering Jews.'

A gloomy silence ensued. Adam said, 'I don't want to be disturbed,' and left.

When locking up the shop, Max said, 'What does a clever woman like my niece see in that man, for God's sake?' and shook his head.

'There's no accounting for love,' Miss Krantnik replied coyly.

The opera, the lost key, a coughing fit, disagreeable customers, a pogrom, all were equally upsetting. Adam returned home irritable and anxious. While he watched Eva dress he uttered for the first time the words, 'We should emigrate.'

Eva was putting her hair up but allowed it to fall again to her shoulders. She peered more closely into the looking-glass as if to bring his reflection nearer and a nervous smile played at her lips. 'What did you say, we should what?'

'Emigrate.'

She started on her hair again as though keeping her hands busy made light of his words. 'Don't be silly, Adda, where would we go?'

'I don't know. But I really hate it here.'

'You've always hated it here but it's your home so don't be silly.'

'I've never felt at home.'

'But, Adda, you're the one who's always saying you want peace and calm and security. You're the one who doesn't want to be disturbed. Now, you're inviting upheaval. Why?'

'I don't know. I can't help what I feel. We should emigrate,' and he went on to recount the news of the pogrom Max had given him that afternoon.

'But where would we go? Palestine?'

'No, thank you. I don't want to die of sunstroke.'

'It's our homeland, Adam. We have to fight for it. All of us,' but even as she uttered the words she wasn't sure she meant them.

'Not me,' he said. 'My heritage is Europe not the desert. I will not end my days with my eyes and mouth filled with sand.'

'Where would we go, then?'

'Germany. That's where we belong. We could have a decent life in Germany. My father was a German. Your grandfather was a German, Salz is a German name, Ehrlich is a German name, Germany is where we should go.'

'But neither of us speak the language. How would we manage? What would we do?'

'I could write to my brother, Karl, in Austria, and ask his advice.'

'You haven't seen or heard from your brother for twenty years, don't be ridiculous. And you loathe him, don't you? And Austria's more anti-Semitic than Poland.'

Her argument went unanswered. Adam's fingers worked overtime. He stared at his wife, impulsively lent forward and kissed her long slender neck. 'Stop that at once,' she said. 'I simply can't be late.'

'I don't like the comb in your hair,' he said. The ornament in question was tortoiseshell.

'You gave it to me,' she said, 'and it's the only one I have.'

He unlocked his sample case and produced the most expensive comb he carried, mother-of-pearl, fashioned into an undulating wave. 'I can't afford to give you this,' he said, 'but you can borrow it for tonight. Only don't lose it.'

She dug the comb into her hair.

'You look like a queen,' he said.

It was her turn to kiss him. She held his face in her hands. 'Adda, don't talk of emigrating again. Please. We'll be all right. Our life is here. We'll be all right.'

But he said, 'I don't want our children born here, Eva. I don't want our children born in Poland.' He pulled away and sat on the bed. She gazed at him, uncomprehending. He muttered, 'The worst thing in life is an empty pay packet.'

8

On that Monday night, for just over three hours, Eva Salz and Countess Tatiana Sobeleva were, unawares, of course, in each other's presence, occupying the same space, the auditorium of the Warsaw opera house.

Uncle Max and Miss Krantnik arrived first and made their way past a Russian guard of honour into the spacious, pillared foyer with its twin marble staircases. There they waited for Eva and for the arrival of the Governor-General. Max's appearance, because of his white tie and tails, was transformed. No one would have thought of him now as a bank manager. He seemed to have grown in height and he gazed on the assembly with none of the mean arrogance bank managers exude, but rather with tender pride, superior, indulgent, his eyes twinkling with enjoyment and confidence as though he were somehow host to this distinguished gathering. In evening wear his arrogance might have led others to think he was a philanthropist or an opera critic. Miss Krantnik's appearance, on the other hand, was not quite so successful if the description of her dress she gave to her cousin in Peoria is anything to go by. 'I wore velvet,' she wrote, 'of the brightest blue embossed with red roses that wound up silver stems. My neckline, not too *décolleté*, was trimmed with gold braid, the sleeves with an off-white lace and I wore the amethyst ear-rings and necklace which had belonged to our grandmother. I swept my hair to one side, secured it with a diamanté wedge-shaped comb – Aunt Frieda's – and my mother's cameo pinned just below my left shoulder. Even though I say it myself, I looked quite something, I can tell you.' Max later whispered to Eva, as they were settling in their seats, 'Krantnik has let us down. Have you ever seen anyone so *ongepotchket*?' Which means overdecorated, unaesthetic, tasteless. Yiddish is nothing if not economic.

Max glowed, however, when he first caught sight of Eva. Although Miss Krantnik regarded her black gown as much too plain and severe, Max's admiration knew no bounds for what he called her dazzling simplicity and he said so pointedly, complimenting her also on the mother-of-pearl comb. The three of them stood at the foot of the staircases celebrity-spotting, craning their necks this way and that, standing on tiptoe to catch a glimpse of the rich, the powerful and the famous. This, they all three instinctively felt, was undoubtedly going to be a great evening in their lives. Just before eight o'clock uniformed trumpeters entered and the buzz of excitement was reduced to a murmur as the eight bandsmen, helmets, breastplates and trumpets gleaming, marched slowly through the foyer, four up each staircase, and into the auditorium. This was the cue for the audience to follow and a slow, stately procession began, an elegant shuffling of slippered feet on marbled floors.

'I congratulate you, Krantnik,' Max said, 'these may be the best seats in the house.' Miss Krantnik reddened with pleasure, for indeed they were finely positioned in the fifth row of the stalls with Max taking the seat on the central aisle. Eva gazed in wonder at the glittering scene. To her right, on the level of the first tier, the spacious Royal Box; to each side smaller boxes and loggias; above, reaching to the heavens, it seemed, the upper balcony and gallery, all filling with chattering people as excited as she. The orchestra began tuning to make its curiously thrilling harmonic dissonance. The trumpeters marched on to the stage in front of the curtain and faced the auditorium. Minutes later, a bewigged major-domo came through the doors of the Royal Box and gave a signal with his gold staff. A mighty fanfare sounded. His Excellency the Governor-General and his party made a grand entrance and took their places. Eva gazed directly at Tatiana who stood on the Governor-General's right. Miss Krantnik wrote that His Excellency's consort, a certain Countess Sobeleva, was plainly dressed, extremely haughty and epitomised Russian brutality. When the fanfare finished the audience applauded and cheered.

Max said, 'Listen to them. They hate the Russians almost as much as they hate the Jews, but just listen to their cheers.'

'Power, Uncle Max, subdues prejudice,' Eva said, smiling.

The Governor-General and his party sat and the audience followed suit. The conductor, Maestro Vittorio de Concini, rotund and sweaty, entered the orchestra pit. More applause. He raised his baton and the orchestra played the Russian Imperial anthem. All stood. The anthem finished. All sat. The lights dimmed. Miss Krantnik turned to Max and smiled. Max turned to Eva and smiled and the smile did not leave his face the entire evening. Conversation dropped to a mumble. Maestro de Concini raised his baton once more. The mumble faded to silence. A cough. Another. More coughs. Silence again. The first notes of the overture sounded.

A moment after the music began, Adam's words, 'I don't want our children born in Poland', echoed in Eva's head. Even when the curtain rose and Battistini made his first entrance to a tumultuous reception, Adam's voice persisted and she knew that the evening was

55

somehow poisoned. She rehearsed their conversation over and over again – emigrate? where? we don't speak the language, Palestine? eyes and mouths filled with sand, I don't want our children born in Poland, emigrate? where? we'll be all right, we belong here, emigrate? don't be silly, Adam, where? Occasionally, she would be jolted back into the reality of the opera house, recognise some snatch of Verdi's glorious music, applaud an aria, marvel momentarily at Battistini's artistry, but try as she might she could not completely control the disturbance her husband had provoked.

One incident during the tenor's second act aria provided relief. He had sung a few phrases when Max whispered to her, 'Too slow,' and then, as if he'd overheard, the conductor, Maestro de Concini, took out his pocket watch, held it up by the chain for the tenor to see and swung it urgently like a demented pendulum. 'What did I tell you?' Max said. The tenor snarled. The conductor looked to his orchestra for approval and the strings tittered sycophantically. In Italy the conductor's gesture of impatience would have been greeted with cheers and catcalls but in Poland the audience was scandalised and the affronted whisper that filled the house was like a brief cloudburst. Eva turned to look at the Royal Box and saw the Governor-General confide his opinion to the lady on his right and then shake his head disapprovingly. But again: emigrate? Where? Why? Where?

Eva continued distracted during the intervals and Max felt obliged to ask if she was feeling quite well. It was while the great quartet – *Bella figlia del amore* – was in full blast and while Battistini was singing shamelessly to the Royal Box, that Eva was possessed of a sudden insight. For the first time, she understood Adam's alienation through her own awareness of what it meant to be foreign. Here she was, Eva Salz, a Pole, junior lecturer at the University, with Polish friends and colleagues, undeniably privileged, here she was, sitting amidst the cream of Warsaw society, in the presence of Russian and Polish nobility, but knowing with absolute certainty that she did not remotely belong in this company. She felt as though an invisible wall surrounded her, a wall that isolated her completely even from her uncle and Miss Krantnik. When Battistini stepped forward from the other singers of the quartet to bow this way and that, as though he alone had produced all the four voices, he seemed bathed in so bright a light that he was separated from the others, who were now reduced to nothing more than bobbing shadows, Eva, too, felt separate from the great shadowy assembly around her, bathed in a harsh light of her own and Adam's making. Emigrate. Where?

Miss Krantnik was the first to stand and shout 'Bravo!' as the final curtain fell. 'Exhibitionist,' Max whispered to Eva. Presently, most of the audience also rose. The cheers echoed and re-echoed. Battistini did not at first take a call but allowed his colleagues to soak up the initial enthusiasm and it was only when the gallery started to call 'Battistini! Battistini!' that he came through a parting in the curtain, arms outstretched as if to embrace all present. Miss Kranktnik described what followed with girlish, breathless excitement:

Flowers rained down on him. He stooped to retrieve a rose. We cheered until it seemed we'd lose our voices. The great Battistini pressed the rose with one hand to his heart and then held it out, appearing to offer the flower to the Governor-General. Although I thought it a silly gesture for one man to make to another, I was nevertheless so caught up in the moment that I nearly fainted. But this gesture caused some commotion in the Royal Box. It was impossible to see clearly, first, because there wasn't much light and, secondly, because people standing obscured my view. But we gathered that somebody in the box was taken ill. Before one was really aware of what was happening, the Russian party seemed to vanish. The Royal Box was suddenly empty. And when we turned back to look at the stage, Battistini was still in front of the curtain, motionless, the hunchback Rigoletto, the jester, forlorn and alone. He backed away, bowing, taking his leave of us as though we were all royalty, out of sight for ever.

Afterwards, when we were in the street, a most exciting incident occurred. We were following Mr Ehrlich who was trying to find a taxi when a woman's voice, obviously in distress, called out, 'Does anyone here speak English?' Well, of course, Mrs Salz answered at once that she did and a pretty rather dowdy blonde woman with a clear, perfect complexion pushed her way through to us. It turned out she was a Mrs Harrison, wife of some British diplomat from whom she had been separated. Gallantly, Mr Ehrlich insisted that we escort her to her home. In the taxi, she explained what had happened. She and her husband had been seated in the loggia beside the Royal Box. Apparently, at Battistini's curtain call, the Countess Sobeleva, the haughty woman I had observed earlier, had slipped off her chair in a dead faint. That was what had caused the great commotion. Mr Harrison immediately offered his assistance although, Mrs Harrison said, there were several men in the box who were perfectly capable.

Somehow or another Mr Harrison was caught up in the fuss, called across to his wife, 'We have to get her to a doctor, make your own way home, have you money for a cab?' and that was the last she saw of him. Imagine, cousin dear, me, Lela Krantnik, sharing a taxi with the wife of a British diplomat! All in all, it was the most wonderful, unforgettable evening of my life!

For Tatiana, too, the evening was unforgettable. She had dressed with extreme care in a gown of ice-blue satin, striking in its simplicity. She wore for the first time in her life the tiara – known in the family as the Small Tiara – given to her by her mother-in-law, an elderly and stylish woman who had lived in St Petersburg, and the matching sapphire ear-rings. Tatiana attended to her appearance slowly, carefully placing the tiara in her hair herself but allowing Dunyasha to pin on her breast the exquisite cabochon surrounded by rubies, a present from the Tsar's sister, Grand Duchess Olga. She looked magnificent.

Lev, too, looked magnificent in his white dress uniform. They set off for the Castle but exchanged hardly a word. Each admired the other's appearance and said so. Apart from that, silence. Once at the Castle, they were caught up in the preparations for the departure to the opera house. The *chef du protocole* fussed and fluttered, waving a list which gave the order of precedence: Lev and Tatiana, presumably because of their aristocratic status, were to ride with the Governor-General; on arrival, Lev would drop back and join the aide-de-camp and his wife, while Tatiana took the arm of His Excellency.

It was Tatiana's first experience of a State function and she detested it. Her natural reticence contrived to make her feel more awkward than ever. She did not take to being the centre of attraction; she did not enjoy the stares and whispers; she did not like being on show. Yet, her nervousness gave her an icy dignity, a stillness, a shield for her emotions. The hauteur remarked on by Miss Krantnik was nothing more than a mask. For, while Tatiana processed to the Royal Box, her lips drawn in what might have been mistaken for the faintest of smiles, her heart pounded and her mind raced with thoughts of Battistini and what effect being in his presence again might have on her.

As it happened, on his first appearance, when the audience welcomed him so noisily, she was disappointed. True, his make-up was convincing, the hump on his back pronounced, and he hobbled about the stage like a crippled orang-utang. Was this the man, she asked herself, who had caused her so much anguish? Was not the entire history of the affair – the letters, the ride in Moscow, the revewal of contact here in Warsaw – and the notion that there could possibly be any true feeling between them, was it not all simply an idle fancy, like a schoolgirl crush or rather like the opera she was witnessing, a contrivance born of ennui? She was a married woman, a mother, with standards of behaviour to maintain, too timid for scandal, the whole thing was ridiculous. But oh, his voice, his voice, so rich and compelling it seemed to pervade her entire being and transported her from her surroundings, easing her anxiety. Her thoughts floated free and she was once again in Sobliki, imagining herself in cool, empty rooms or strolling in the arcadian park Balutan had designed and which surrounded the great house. Oh, his voice, his voice. Battistini.

Her reverie was disturbed by the conductor, de Concini, waggling his watch at the tenor. The Governor-General whispered to her, 'Bad form. Very bad form. Italians have no manners.' And, later, when the great quartet began, she could feel Battistini's eyes on her and knew he was singing for her and for her alone. The anxiety returned, the heat was unbearable, the Small Tiara felt like an enormous weight crushing her. She wanted to vomit. She closed her eyes and dug her nails into the palms of her hands. She could not, would not, suddenly rise and leave the box. She must hold on.

All she remembered thereafter was the nausea and the panic. When the final curtain fell and the singers took their bows, Tatiana was fighting for control. She kept her eyes closed to stop the world from spinning. She did not see Battistini holding out the rose to her. Lev mentioned it later but then circumstances had changed and he had overcome his anger. She fainted because she could no longer suppress the nausea. She slipped off the chair, was vaguely aware of voices, of being lifted. And then, nothing.

Dr Bulkarov, who had not attended the performance because of a mild bout of influenza, was woken from sleep. He dressed hurriedly, sweated profusely, examined the Countess and reported to his diary:

Feeling as though I had swallowed broken glass, I made my way into my surgery where the Countess Sobeleva was laid out on my examination couch. Her husband was hovering over her, the way husbands do, wringing his hands. He said, 'Oh, the scandal, the scandal,' but I was feeling too shaky to ask what he meant. The rest of the vice-regal party had repaired to the banqueting room for refreshments, H. E. included. I asked the Count to wait outside while I examined his wife. Reluctantly, he obliged. She was semi-conscious. I administered sal volatile and she came to with a start. 'I'm going to be sick,' she said. I grabbed an enamel basin, held her head, but all she did was wretch violently. I proceeded with my examination. One did not have to be a medical genius to diagnose the cause of her distress. I summoned her husband back into the room and told him my conclusions. 'Nothing to worry about,' I said. 'She's pregnant.'

Another incident in young Stepan Kessler's life.

Katya, the nanny, needed the attention of a dentist. Young Stepan, now about seven years old, accompanied her. Since Katya was the patient, the dental practice was in a working-class district of the city. Katya was the last patient of the day. Winter, early evening and already dark. The receptionist occupied a desk in the bare waiting-room and kept glancing this way and that, flicking anxious glances at Katya and Stepan and at the two doors that led from the room, one to the surgery, the other to the dentist's private quarters. 'Why's she so nervous today?' Katya asked Stepan. A patient emerged from the surgery, paid the receptionist and left. Katya stood and was about to cross to the surgery door when the receptionist hissed, 'No, no, sit, not yet, there's an emergency.' But nothing happened for a few minutes. Katya held Stepan's hand. The door to the surgery opened. The dentist looked out. He, too, was unusually anxious. He nodded to the receptionist and then retreated. The receptionist quickly went to the second door, the one that led to the private quarters, opened it and said, 'Now.' A man, his head thrust down in the collar of his coat and wearing a fur cap, crossed the waiting-room at speed and disappeared into the surgery. The receptionist seemed to be made more nervous than ever and her tension was infectious, increasing the natural anxiety Katya felt at the prospect of dental treatment. Perhaps a quarter of an hour passed before the mysterious patient reappeared. He no longer wore his fur cap but held a bloodstained handkerchief to his mouth. He had dark wavy hair and wore pince-nez. Just as the man was leaving, he turned to the dentist who was hovering in the surgery door, and said, 'Thank you, comrade,' and was gone.

Stepan thought what a funny thing it was for a patient to call a dentist comrade.

'The American quota is full.'

'Full?' Laban the Idiot repeated.

'Yes. Full.'

'Full for Jews?'

'Of course for Jews. Who else?'

Isaiah's idyll had long since come to an end yet the dream of America had remained a constant, the only possibility, the only hope. But that, too, was shattered now. He had travelled almost five hundred miles, seen the end of a cruel winter, encountered the glory of spring and summer, and now, in a heavy autumn rain, stood on a quayside in Hamburg, holding his Uncle Laban's hand, feeling the grip tighten at those terrible words, 'The American quota is full.' America, America, *frizlitch*, America.

From the forest beyond Ploemyan, the Circus Stoica with its newest members had set off in a westerly direction following the highways and paths that led towards the sea, first to Königsberg and then, after some argument, along the coastal road to Danzig.

'We've never performed in Danzig,' Ion Stoica said.

'There's always a first time,' the beautiful Constanta, his daughter, countered. She had taken it upon herself to champion the family Wildnowitz's cause as though for some reason she, too, needed to reach Danzig.

'I don't know about Danzig,' Ion said. 'Danzig. Danzig. Doesn't sound like a place that likes the circus.'

'Does Ploemyan?' Laban asked.

'Does Ploemyan what?'

'Sound like a place that likes a circus?'

Ion, full of doubt, pulled at his drooping moustache.

Laban said, 'If you want my honest opinion few places sound as if they'd like a circus. I don't think you can judge your potential audience by the sound of the town in which they live. I mean, what about Riga? Or Smolensk? Or Minsk? How do they sound to you? You think you'd get an audience in these places? Now, as a poet, I grant you there's only once place you might get an audience just from the sound of it, and that's Vladivostok. To my ear, the people of

Vladivostok would be circus-minded. But, and this is just a personal opinion, I don't think you'd get much of an audience in Minsk. Not from the sound ot if. Now, Danzig, on the other hand—'

Constanta cut him short. 'We'll make for Danzig,' she said.

The adult males of the Wildnowitz family entered joyfully into the life of the Circus Stoica. Laban the Idiot rejoiced in wearing a leotard and in learning to be the base of a human pyramid. He smiled his inane smile while trying, unsuccessfully, to master the art of juggling three Indian clubs. Isaiah's father, Solomon, the woodcutter, took on the role of general factotum, seeing that the caravans and horses were in good order, laying the communal bonfire in the evenings and going ahead of the troupe to announce the advent of the Circus Stoica to the villages and towns. Uncle Benjamin, the shoemaker, turned wardrobe master: he was dextrous and quick-witted, learning fast how to darn tights, repair the soft-leather pumps, and even began designing and making new costumes. About this line of work he complained bitterly, yet both men were secretly proud they were earning their keep and that Ion Stoica began to rely on them.

But the Wildnowitz boys, Isaiah, Baruch and Julius felt out of it. All three tried their hands at various jobs. Early on they had their faces painted by Chivu Stoica, the clown, who dressed them in outsize costumes and threw buckets of water over them in front of a small audience in a village near Koyno. Afterwards, Chivu said, 'Sorry, boys, but you're not clowns. Clowns have to be agile. You are not agile. Clowns have to be half-and-half funny, half-and-half sad. You are not even a quarter funny and you are seven-eighths sad. You are *drebshen*,' which was Ionian for lifeless. The boys were relieved.

The flirtatious Raina Stoica, the young dancer and singer, tried to teach Isaiah a simple *pas de deux* and duet, but soon was forced to say, 'I'm sorry, Isaiah, but you have no rhythm and you sing in three keys.' She kissed him on the cheek and he fled into the woods to hide for the rest of the day. Thereafter, he avoided her eyes which seemed always to mock his timidity.

His mother, Leah, wept a good deal but she never explained the reason. She cooked for the family, tried to keep kosher, lit the candles on Friday night, and wept. Her main preoccupation, however, was to keep her brood clean. 'It's a struggle,' she said, and wept.

For the first few weeks the family were bewitched by the novelty of their existence; the frequent change of scene, the constant rehearsals and the occasional performances both delighted and tired them. But towards the end of February, when they reached

Königsberg in a blizzard, they heard the news of the Ploemyan pogrom.

'You see? We were right to leave,' Laban the Idiot said.

'Shame on you,' Leah said. 'How can you take pleasure in our safety when so many of our neighbours lie dead?'

Laban smiled his idiotic smile. 'I don't rejoice in their death,' he said. 'I rejoice only in the knowledge that fate is a miserable creature who can be cowed and frightened like any other bully.'

Benjamin said, 'We must find a *schul* and say Kaddish,' which is the prayer for the dead.

Isaiah, because he had neither lost a close relative nor celebrated his bar mitzvah, was not eligible to intone the solemn prayer and so remained in the caravan with Leah. Solomon, Benjamin, Laban, Baruch and Julius set off in search of a synagogue to pray for the victims of the massacre. Laban the Idiot was particularly joyful at the prospect. 'It'll be nice to say Kaddish again,' he said. 'I've missed the dead.'

It was in the days following that Isaiah noticed his father's change of mood. Solomon became taciturn, hardly speaking and, although he performed his various tasks diligently, he worked to an accompaniment of woeful sighs of his own making. At first no one dared to ask him the reason for his obvious distress but eventually Leah, who must have known all along what was troubling him, blurted it out. 'He's worried that Isaiah won't be able to have a bar mitzvah. He's been worried ever since he came back from the *schul* in Königsberg.' Once the problem had been so succinctly stated Solomon's cares seemed to lift. 'A problem aired is a problem shared,' he said. From then on, family councils were frequent.

It was a genuine dilemma. Every Jewish male, at the age of thirteen, celebrates his bar mitzvah, which comes from the Hebrew and means 'son of the commandment'. The bar mitzvah ceremony is not a law, not a sacrament but a tradition and not a very ancient tradition at that, having only come into existence in the fourteenth century. It marks the boy's entry into manhood and is obviously related in some way to pubescent initiation rites which often occur at the age of thirteen in other cultures. In modern times the bar mitzvah is thought of as a confirmation of faith, but in earlier times Orthodox Jews, even mildly Orthodox Jews like the Wildnowitz family, believed that the Jewish faith needed no confirmation. To be a Jew is to be a Jew. It does not need to be confirmed, it needs to be celebrated. And that's what a bar mitzvah is: a celebration. However, certain observances have to take place in a synagogue. The boy is obliged to read, or rather sing in that particularly mournful, difficult cadence decreed by tradition a portion from the Torah, the scroll of the law, the Pentateuch, which is written in Hebrew but without vowels and takes some study. (It is as if, for example, the opening of Psalm 90 was written: *Lrd, th hst bn r dwllng-plc n ll gnrtns.*) He would also have to sing a corresponding portion from the latter part of the Bible called the *Haftarah*. He might even be called on to give a scholarly address on some aspect of the interminable Talmud, the commentary on, and often bizarre analysis of, Mosaic law. And although the ceremony is an indescribable source of pleasure to parents and grandparents and from which *nakhes* is derived in bucketfuls, for the boy himself it is often an agony because it usually occurs just as his voice is breaking with the result that the singing can turn into an uncontrollable demonstration of falsetto and basso profundo, sometimes mid-note. Nevertheless, the preparation requires tuition and study and this was at the heart of Solomon's concern. Where would they find a teacher, a rabbi, a scholar? After all, they were circus folk now, itinerants. 'What should be done?' asked Solomon.

Laban said, 'I have the answer.' They all turned to him, expecting an ingenious solution, at least as inventive as a coffin with holes drilled in the bottom.

'What? What?' Benjamin barked. 'What's to be done?' He cupped his hands like a would-be strangler.

Laban nodded, smiled, fuelled Benjamin's vexation, then said, 'Nothing is to be done.'

'What?' from all present.

'We don't do anything about Isaiah's bar mitzvah. In short, he doesn't have one.'

There was not much discussion after that. There was a lot of shouting but not much discussion. While Isaiah tried to settle for sleep he could hear the arguments continuing.

How can you suggest such a thing?

Call yourself the boy's uncle?

But no one can deny it isn't a solution!

Wash your mouth out, Laban!

He heard also Ion Stoica's voice calling from another caravan for silence and silence descending. Isaiah fell asleep hoping that Laban would win the day.

Isaiah had, of course, begun his studies for the ordeal months before, but the flight from Ploemyan had proved so great an interruption that when Solomon tested him he could hardly remember a thing. This failure increased the family's concern. Night after night, possibilities were explored and madcap schemes suggested.

'We could leave him behind somewhere, find a nice family to look after him, he can learn what he has to learn.' This from Benjamin.

'Leave him behind? And then what?' from Laban.

'Leave him behind? Oh my God!' from Leah.

Benjamin again: 'We can keep in touch with the family that takes care of him. We can let them know where we are.'

'Keep in touch? How? By carrier pigeon?' from Laban.

'Have you never heard of something called the telegraph?' from Benjamin with an arrogant sneer.

'The telegraph, he says. We can't afford a bagel and he's talking about telegraphs.'

In the end, Leah solved the problem. 'Laban,' she said in a tone that would not be defied, 'you must teach him.' It was probably the first time she had ever exerted her strength and her intervention caused immediate consternation.

'Laban?' from Solomon and Benjamin as one. 'Laban?'

'Yes. Laban. He's good at languages. He'll teach him. And when we get to Danzig, we'll consult a rabbi and ask his advice.'

The portion of the Torah which Isaiah had to learn was appropriately the opening of the eleventh chapter of the Book of Exodus: *And the Lord said unto Moses, Yet will I bring one plague more upon Pharaoh, and upon Egypt: afterwards he will let you go hence.* 'Please God,' Laban said. 'For Pharaoh read Tsar.'

Each afternoon, after the midday meal, when the others were resting or performing their ordinary, everyday chores, Laban and Isaiah found a place well away from the camp to conduct the lesson. Even in that miserable winter Laban was at pains to search out a hut or some sheltered spot.

'Can't we just find somewhere near the camp?' Isaiah whined. 'Why do we have to walk so far?'

Laban the Idiot smiled his idiotic smile.

Isaiah was an average pupil; he did not have his uncle's linguistic flair but Laban was a patient, kindly teacher, easily diverted into poetic or philosophical discourse.

'Remember,' Laban said, 'this one outstanding quality of the Jews. They are obliged, because of the bar mitzvah, to learn to read. Literacy marks us out. Even my fellow *nakhtwachter*, Fedya Katzenowitz – may he still be drawing breath – yes, even Katzenowitz, that decent *alcoholnik*, even he could read. Furthermore, consider this for ingenuity. So that we could all understand each other wherever we travelled, we invented Yiddish, what is called a lingua franca, and, and it's a big and, with a wonderfully simple embrace. Yiddish is written with Hebrew characters. So, from day one, a Jew can read two languages. This is an artful invention of the highest degree and unknown, to my knowledge, in any other culture. It also makes us very unpopular.'

After about a week of lessons, Laban introduced a variation in the arrangements that soon became routine. On one particular day, when an hour or so had passed, Laban became restless, scratched his beard, smiled idiotically and banged his knees together in an irregular rhythm. He said, 'Isaiah, I want you to do me a favour. I am going to ask you to lie on my behalf. Now, if you feel morally unable to do so, you have only to say as much and I will devise some other plan. It's not a very big lie I'm asking you to tell, and, who knows, you may not even be called upon to tell it.'

'What's the lie, Uncle Laban?' Isaiah asked.

Laban sniffed deeply before launching forth. 'It's this. I am going to leave you now. I shall be gone for half an hour, maybe an hour. I want you to wait here until I return. But, if anybody asks, I want you to say I was with you all the time. So, do you feel morally disposed to help me in this fashion? I am unable to reward you, as you know, because I have nothing to reward you with. But you will have my eternal gratitude and that, after all, I give to few men.'

'Where will you be going, Uncle Laban?'

'Ah.' A short, sharp sound. 'Where will I be going?' He thought about the answer for some time and then his eyes twinkled. 'I will be going, as they say in Ionian, to *shligalick*,' he said, and scurried away.

Isaiah puzzled over the meaning of this Ionian word. Was it a town, a restaurant, what? He asked his brothers but they didn't know; he wanted to ask Raina Stoica but hadn't the courage. He hoped that one day he would have an explanation.

The thaw made the going hard as ice turned to sludge and sludge turned to mud. The horses slipped and the wheels skidded. Progress was slow. The men walked behind the caravans giving occasional shoves to keep the little procession moving. And Laban sang,

> Oi, Tsutsanna! Oi, don't you cry for me,
> I come from Ellybumma mit mine banjer on mine knee.

and

> I'm down dere mit mine hat bust in,
>> Doodah! Doodah!
> I'm go beck hoim mit a pucket full tin,
>> Oi! doodah day!
> Gunna run all night!
> Gunna run all day,
> I bet mine geld on de boptail neg,
> Tsomebody bet on de bay.

The going was even slower as the days grew hot and long. The Stoicas stopped frequently, not to perform but to bathe in the sea and

66

to sleep the afternoons away. Sometimes, when the heat had been stifling they travelled at night. In late September, with autumn having taken hold, they reached an inland village some twenty miles from Danzig where they were to give two evening performances in a barn belonging to the local mayor. On the afternoon of the second performance, Isaiah and Laban lay by the bank of a lazy stream, books spread before them. The day was unusually warm and pleasing to the senses but Laban was restless. Something worried him. He was unable to concentrate until his eyes lit up with a sudden insight. 'You know why I can't settle today?' he asked.

'No, Uncle Laban, why?'

'I'll tell you why. Because I hate the countryside, that's why. But, why? Why do I hate the countryside?'

'I don't know, Uncle Laban, why?'

'Give me a chance and I'll tell you.' Laban, who was constantly fascinated by facets of the Jewish psyche with all its protean contradictions, launched forth on yet another aspect that had just taken hold of his fertile brain. 'I hate the countryside because I am a Jew. Jews in general hate the countryside. Again, why? Again, I'll tell you. Why does a Jew consider rural silence an affront to his ear-drums yet loves the noise of the city? Why does he wake if a cock crows at dawn yet can sleep through a brawl outside his bedroom window? Why is it he cannot abide a picnic in an open field but loves a crowded café with everyone shouting so you can't hear yourself think? Why does he object to the sweet fragrances of nature as though his nose had been insulted yet notices not the stench of sewage in city streets? Why does he despise insects and worms and all things that creep and crawl but regards fleas and flies as fellow urban-dwellers who are only trying to make a living? Why is he indifferent to the sight of trees, flowers and haystacks yet his heart lifts at the sight of tightly packed houses, restaurants and factories? Why, Isaiah, why?'

'I don't know, Uncle Laban. Why?'

'It's a matter of tempo. In the countryside the turnover is too slow. The Jew likes speed, results, quick answers. He's not a man to wait a year to see a flower bloom. He plants a seed today, he wants the flower tomorrow. And something else. There are just not enough people in the countryside.' He looked around as if he hoped to prove himself wrong. 'It's too empty. The Jew likes people, crowds, bustle, toing and froing. In the countryside everything is predictable. In the city, the unexpected is the expected. This makes for excitement, which is, after all, one of life's condiments.' He smiled, pleased with the dissertation, then stood. 'Enough. I'm off to *shligalick*,' he said. 'Isaiah, sit further downstream, by those trees, no one will see you there. I won't be too long.' The boy had begun to collect up the books when Laban dropped to his haunches and took his face in his hands. 'You're a good friend, Isaiah,' he said. 'A little bit *drebshen*, but a good friend.'

Isaiah found a shady hollow where he settled down to watch the water trickle over stones and pebbles, meander through reeds and tall grass, skip from light into shadow to make continuous and unreliable patterns. A bird skimmed low along the water following the path of the stream. Unidentifiable insects hummed monotonously. Isaiah experienced an unaccustomed feeling of detachment, as though he had no place there. He acknowledged the beauty of his surroundings but his uncle's words had somehow sapped his ability to submit even a little to nature's spell.

Gunshots shook him from his reverie. Male and female voices, angry, screaming, crying. His mother calling, 'Isaiah! Isaiah!' Panic and confusion took hold. He did not want to be caught alone either here by the stream or returning to the farmyard and let his uncle down. But then he heard Laban's voice shouting, 'Don't shoot! Don't shoot!' and another shot. Isaiah, clutching his books, ran for dear life.

When he reached the farmyard an amazing scene, a nightmare, greeted him. Ion Stoica, shotgun in one hand, a pair of men's trousers in the other, was firing wildly at the barn doors which were peppered with holes. Constanta Stoica was beside him trying to pull the gun from his hand but she was stark naked and his first sight of a nude woman both embarrassed and electrified Isaiah. Beyond them, behind the animal drinking trough which was also punctured with gunshot and leaking like a colander, cowered the rest of the Stoicas and the family Wildnowitz. Leah put her head up to call Isaiah but Ion swung round and fired in her direction. She screamed and fainted. Isaiah stood trapped like a petrified rabbit in no man's land.

Ion screamed, 'Come out, you dirty *shligalicker*!'

'Father! Father!' Constanta pleaded. All Isaiah could think of was that her breasts were wondrous things, undulating with her passionate attempts to pull the gun from Ion's hands. And her thighs, too, were wondrous things, he thought, and the triangle of black hair between them was also wondrous.

His father, Solomon, shouted, 'Close your eyes, Isaiah, don't look!' but for once Isaiah disobeyed.

Uncle Benjamin risked an inch of his forehead above the trough, 'Laban, it's no use! He'll kill us all, give yourself up!' and ducked out of sight.

Ion turned viciously on Constanta. 'How long has he been *shligalicking* you?' he demanded. 'How long?'

'Isaiah, shut your ears, too!' Solomon called.

Arpad Stoica, the fire-eater, saved the day and Laban's life. Unseen, he had crawled off to his caravan, collected what was necessary, returned, and then with devastating accuracy spewed a tongue of flame at Ion's feet. Ion reeled with surprise, dropping the gun, which Constanta instantly grabbed.

'Laban, come out. I've got the gun,' she called.

This was a general cue for everyone to regroup. Uncle Benjamin hared across to Isaiah and clamped his hands over the boy's eyes and started to lead him towards the caravans. Baruch and Julius, too, were heading in that direction when the barn door opened a crack, then a little wider and, at last, Laban appeared. He, too, was naked.

> I'm down dere mit mine hat bust in,
> Doodah! Doodah!
> I'm go beck hoim mit a pucket full tin,
> Oi! doodah day!

The horse and cart that had once borne Isaiah's coffin now carried the family Wildnowitz towards Danzig. Laban sang, Benjamin stared angrily at the horizon and it was Solomon's turn to weep. Leah comforted her husband silently and her sons were silent, too. Isaiah looked back and saw the members of the Circus Stoica grouped in a tight knot, watching their departure, receding. Only Raina Stoica had the courage to wave, but Isaiah thought he saw Ion slap her.

Isaiah was not privy to the post-mortem. Baruch and Julius, older than he, were able to shed some light on what had happened. Laban's affair with Constanta had begun almost from the start; indeed, she had hoped to leave the circus in Danzig and travel with Laban to America. When Ion Stoica accidentally discovered them in the barn, both naked, entwined, he lost all control, fetched his shotgun and determined to murder Laban.

'What does "going to *shligalick*" mean?' Isaiah asked.

His brothers, who now understood the word, sniggered and tried to explain the tricky details.

Julius said, 'You have to aim for the navel.'

'And, remember,' Baruch added, 'it's not *shligalicking* unless the woman locks her legs round you and holds you tight.'

'Constanta, being an acrobat, was good at that,' Julius said. More sniggering.

At once Isaiah knew he had been let in on the mystery of existence. His dreams were haunted by either Constanta or Raina, sometimes both, holding him between their legs in a vice-like grip and he woke with his first ecstatic orgasm and the inevitable embarrassment that followed. But Laban said, 'You see? It's not just for *pishing* out of.'

Isaiah himself came in for terrible censure from both Benjamin and Leah. Solomon had more or less collapsed emotionally, unequal to the crisis, bewildered and despairing. 'Never,' Benjamin said, 'lie. Never give a criminal an alibi. Never betray the whole family for the sake of one member!'

Leah sat and rocked as though in mourning. 'It's all your Uncle Laban's fault. But you should have told us,' she moaned, 'you should have said he told you to lie.'

Laban, however, was unperturbed and unrepentant. He continued to smile his idiotic smile, offered no apologies, and sang as the cart headed slowly towards Danzig.

> Gunna run all night!
> Gunna run all day,
> I bet mine geld on de boptail neg,
> Tsomebody bet on de bay.

When they reached the main road to the port they became aware of a line of other wagons and carts, about twenty of them, heading in the same direction. Benjamin, who was at the reins that day, urged the horse onward and soon drew level with the rear of the column. He saw at once the passengers were Jews and that the carts were loaded with their belongings. Brief greetings were exchanged and explanations given. Yes, all the conveyances were carrying Jews. Russian Jews.

'We're fleeing the Tsar,' the driver of the nearest wagon said. He was a bearded man in a black frock coat and a Homburg, named Abraham.

'Why? What's happened?' Benjamin called across to him.

'Stolypin's been assassinated in Kiev,' Abraham called back.

'Who's Stolypin?'

'The Tsar's prime minister,'

'So?' Benjamin said. 'One Russian less in the world is a cause for rejoicing not for flight.'

'The assassin was a Jew,' Abraham said.

The story was quickly told. Two or three weeks previously, Piotr Stolypin had accompanied the Tsar to Kiev to unveil a statue of Alexander III. By way of celebration they had attended a performance of *Tsar Sultan* by Rimsky-Korsakov at the Kiev Opera House. The Tsar was in a box with his two eldest daughters, Olga and Tatiana, Stolypin in the stalls. During the second interval, a young man approached him, drew a Browning revolver and shot him twice in the chest in full view of the Tsar and his daughters. Stolypin lived for five days, then died. The assassin's name was Mordka Bogrov, a revolutionary.

70

These Jews on the road to Danzig and who came from a village near Pasym, had feared reprisals and fled.

'Join the party,' Abraham said, 'one more family won't sink the ship.'

In Danzig they were given shelter by Reb Grossman and his flock. They were told at once that this was not the best place to find passage to America. Few ships sailed the Atlantic from Danzig and those that did were mostly cargo vessels. Hamburg was a better bet, an international port servicing many great ocean liners. Each day, however, a delegation set off for the harbour only to be told the same story. After a week, the Pasym Jews and the family Wildnowitz took to the road again and headed for Hamburg where Laban and Isaiah, standing in the rain, heard the dread words: 'The American quota is full.'

Solomon took no part in the deliberations that followed. Broken, he sat, nodding his head slowly as if to agree with anything that was said.

'There must be a way out,' Laban affirmed, 'there must be,' his spirit indomitable.

'We can emigrate somewhere else,' Benjamin said. He, too, showed signs of strain. 'Lots of our people went to England and, don't forget, the Horowitzs ended up in South Africa, in Kep Tovn, we could find a ship for South Africa. Or we could stay here.'

'South Africa? Stay here?' Laban repeated as though a blasphemy had been uttered. 'Benjamin, stick to your last. Leave the travel arrangements to me. We'll get to America if it's the last thing we do.'

11

The State banquet in honour of the Jew boy Ehrlich was a most enjoyable affair with one splendid moment provided by the ancient Princess Radziwil who is quite a card. But first, let me set the scene before it all fades from memory.

Dr Bulkarov began his account in the early hours of the morning following the banquet, after the guests had departed and he had made his way up to his rooms, heavy-footed, tired, chewing the butt of a lifeless cigar, a little drunk.

To begin with, the doctor dealt with Tatiana's condition. Although during her first two pregnancies she had experienced no problems at all, she was now not at all well, vomiting in the mornings and suffering from dizzy spells and fatigue. She was also emotionally weak which the doctor put down to her condition. He ordered her to stay in bed and noted her husband's deep and sincere concern – 'Lev Borisovich fusses around her a good deal' – and wondered if the Count did not hold himself in some way responsible for her emotional state.

Bulkarov reported Tatiana's pregnancy to Skalon, the Governor-General.

'But I thought you said she wasn't expecting,' Skalon barked.

'That was before I examined her.'

Skalon paced, hands clasped behind his back, his boots squeaking with every step. 'This is most inconsiderate,' he said. 'She seems to be a very selfish person.'

'Why so, Excellency?'

'First, she faints at the opera and denies that singer fellow Battistini the chance of meeting me, and now she gets a bun in her oven, as our soldiers say on manoeuvres, and I'm robbed of a lady to sit beside that Jew boy Ehrlich at the banquet.'

'I'm not sure it's entirely her fault, Excellency.'

But His Excellency was not convinced. 'A very haughty woman. Never liked the family. She's a Souvritzin, you know. They think everyone else is beneath them. I'm told there was a lot of objection when she said she'd marry Sobelev. They didn't think he was good enough for her. No, she's not my glass of vodka, by any means.'

'If I can be of any assistance with the arrangements,' Bulkarov said with a vague gesture.

'Good of you, Bulkarov, good of you. But I've already made my decision. I shall put that old Polish cow Radziwil next to the Jew. I'll have her granddaughter beside me. Sobelev can sit on his own at the far end.'

'But you know that Princess Radziwil is as deaf as a post.'

'Can't be helped.'

'You will remember not to get too excited, won't you, Excellency?'

'Yes, yes,' Skalon said, terminating the interview. But as Bulkarov reached the door, he asked, 'Any luck with a chiropodist?'

Bulkarov smiled crookedly, shook his head and slipped out of the room.

The tables in the magnificently ornate State banqueting hall were arranged in a T and Bulkarov was placed at the top table, not on the same side as the grandees but opposite them, more or less diagonally across from the guest of honour and his ravaged dinner companion. Orders were worn and Ehrlich, as befitted the discoverer of the first cure for syphilis, sported the sash and medal of *Wirklicher Geheimer Rat* or Privy Councillor bestowed upon him by Prussia. This entitled him to be addressed as *Exzellens*. He had been honoured all over the world but he was especially proud of doctorates from Oxford and Chicago; he was also an honorary citizen of Frankfurt am Main where he founded an institute which bore his name. He was fifty-seven but looked much older. A serious face, receding temples, neat white beard and moustache. Oval-shaped glasses. Delicate hands with long, elegant fingers. Bulkarov reported that it was said of Ehrlich that he had no interest in money or earthly rewards – 'unusual for a Jew' – but that his sole interests were research and to toil in his laboratory.

The achievement that won him the Nobel Prize in 1908 was for his pioneering work on immunity and serum therapy, begun in the 1890s, not the cure for syphilis which was to come later. Success with serum therapy led to him being given, in 1899, what amounted to an unlimited budget at the Royal Institute for Experimental Therapy in Frankfurt and told that no restrictions applied to the direction of his research. It was here that his great discovery, the preparation known as 606 or Salvarsan and still later Neosalvarsan and popularly as 'the magic bullet', had been made.

'But my God, what a bore he turned out to be!' Bulkarov wrote.

Before dinner I was presented to him by H. E. himself. No small talk. Stared at me through those intellectual glasses. Desperate, I said in French, 'Tell me, *Exzellens*, how did you come upon

73

Salvarsan?' He replied at once and at speed in a heavy German accent, as though delivering a prepared speech. I hope I've got it right. 'It was like this,' he said showing life for the first time. 'I had recognised the limitations of serum therapy. Many infectious disorders, in particular those caused by protozoa rather than bacteria, failed to respond to serum therapy. This led me to what I call chemotherapy, the treatment of disease by chemical means.' Here, H. E. approached with Sobelev but Ehrlich held up his hand and kept the couple waiting while he continued to explain to me how he had started trying to find synthetic substances to kill parasites without destroying the organism. Success eluded him until he turned his attention at last to *Spirochaeta pallida*, the organism which causes syphilis. At this point, H. E., who was bouncing on his toes, could contain his impatience no longer. He pushed me aside and presented Sobelev to the Jew.

Bulkarov enjoyed official dinners, liked the formalities, the interminable courses, the good wines and the fine champagne for the toasts. He particularly savoured that moment when the servants padded from one male guest to the other offering choice Havana cigars. When it came to his turn, Bulkarov studied the boxes on the silver tray, tried to decide what length would satisfy his taste that evening and settled on an Anguila de Ora Corona Imperial. He noticed that Ehrlich chose similarly. The two men exchanged a nod and raised their cigars as if they were toasting each other. Ehrlich tried to make conversation with the aged Princess Radziwil but she, unaware that he was speaking to her, surveyed the assembly and smiled serenely. Then, the speeches began.

After proposing the health of the Tsar and his family, the Governor-General rose to laud the guest of honour. He began. '*Exzellens*, you have opened new doors into the unknown. The whole world is in your debt.' Bulkarov thought he should have stopped there but the Governor-General did not oblige. Ten minutes later, having added little to his opening sentences, he sat to polite applause. The guests rose, drank to Privy Councillor Paul Ehrlich and awaited his reply.

Ehrlich made his speech in French which was reported by the press in full the next morning. There was one passage of particular interest:

I want to make it clear that the work I have done and for which I have been generously rewarded would not have been possible without the help of a great many people, especially my esteemed colleague, Emil von Behring. [Applause.] I mention this because scientists, like artists, cannot, do not, exist in a vacuum. As Your Excellency expressed so eloquently, it does not matter in what

74

country we were born, to what race we belong. Our work, be it humble or important, is for all mankind. [Sustained applause.] As a matter of fact, it may interest you to know that this very morning, on my arrival in Warsaw, I opened several letters that were awaiting me and more than half of my correspondents asked me to lend my name to one political faction or another. I consigned these letters to the waste-paper basket. [Laughter and applause.] I am a scientist whose greatest wish is to serve humanity. [Applause.] If I am anything else, I am a citizen of the world and that is a very daunting burden. [Applause.] Thank you for your generous welcome. [Applause. All those present stood.]

The applause and chatter subsided. Then, the Princess Radziwil turned to Ehrlich and her voice rang out, silencing all present.

'And what is it you discovered? No one seems able to tell me,' she bellowed. Ehrlich muttered in her ear. 'What? Speak up!' Ehrlich, embarrassed, sensing all attention was on them, muttered again. 'The cure for what?' she asked, cupping her ear. Ehrlich took a pen from his inside pocket and scribbled on her menu. An auspicious silence ensued while the Princess searched for her lorgnette, found it, brought the menu card into focus and read what Ehrlich had written. 'Syphilis?' she cried. The guests held their collective breaths. 'What a shame,' the Princess said, 'you didn't do that earlier. My poor, dear husband might still be alive.'

A POSTSCRIPT.

After Lev Sobelev had departed for the banquet, Dunyasha tiptoed in to see Tatiana and found her awake.

'All well, sweetheart?' she asked.

'I'm fine,' Tatiana said.

From her bodice Dunyasha produced a postcard-sized photograph of Battistini. 'I found this in Lev Borisovich's study, when I was cleaning up. He'd torn it in half but I pasted it together for you.'

Tatiana gazed at the handsome face and read the inscription: À ma chère comtesse, avec mes sentiments énormes – Mattia Battistini, Varsava, 1911.

Later, just before midnight, she heard the front door open and close, which signalled Lev's return. He was cold sober, having endured the sort of evening he abhorred, and came into Tatiana's room to see how she was. She pretended to be asleep. Dunyasha, seated in a rocking-chair, was keeping vigil at the bedside and put a finger to her lips. Lev kissed his wife on her forehead and retired.

In some mysterious way, Tatiana reflected as she settled for sleep, the torn photograph and her husband's goodnight kiss symbolised the end of *l'affaire Battistini*. The tension she had experienced for the past weeks began to evaporate. I want to have my baby in Sobliki, she decided. And I will go to church on Sunday and thank God I have not harmed anyone.

12

JEWS GIVE CHRISTIANS SYPHILIS!
'Is that an order or a statement of fact?' a wag shouted.

The banner was raised above the heads of the crowd awaiting Paul Ehrlich's arrival at the State banquet. The Warsaw police on duty nodded and smiled. Three young Jews hastily scrawled a slogan of their own:

CHRISTIANS NEED JEWS TO CURE THEM!
and were immediately beaten up by the patrolling officers, hauled off to the nearest police station, charged with disturbing the peace and their improvised banner ripped to pieces.

Eva and Uncle Max stood near the ornamental gates of the Castle watching the grandees arrive. She had received no reply to the letter she had written to cousin Paul. She had, in fact, written two letters: one to the institute in Frankfurt, and a copy to await his arrival at his hotel, the Bristol, in Warsaw. She had no idea whether or not the famous scientist had even received them. She took to delaying her early morning departure for the university to await the arrival of the postman which meant that disappointment was her daily bread. Ever since the night at the opera, the night Adam first mentioned emigration, the night she first felt her isolation, her mood had been downcast. The one bright spot was the pleasure she received in recounting the story of how she, Miss Krantnik and Max had rescued Mrs Harrison. She made much of it, talked of it often and produced the card Mrs Harrison had given her by way of proof. There was little else to lighten her days. She told Adam that she felt in a state of suspended animation.

Ehrlich's carriage passed through the gates to a mixture of cheers and hissing. Eva glimpsed the imposing figure, saw the glint of his medal and his eye-glasses and that was about all. The crowd dispersed. Eva and Max wandered down side streets, heading for the café Blikli in the Nowy Swiat and a nightcap.

'He probably didn't receive the letter,' Max said, sensing his niece's mood.

'He received it. I bet he did.' She felt defeated and depressed.

'So, it's not such a terrible thing,' Max said. 'Look at it logically.

Cousin Paul is a busy man. Fêted wherever he goes. Invitations to answer, lectures to give, God knows what else. He receives a letter from you, he says to himself, I'll deal with it tomorrow, something else comes up, and he forgets. He's human, that's all there is to it. Don't be disappointed, Eva, don't take it to heart. So the great man didn't reply. Great men are like that.'

But Eva's depression had more tangled roots than Max could guess at. She had set store by her letter to Paul Ehrlich, had imagined meeting him, impressing him, interesting him in the cause of Zionism. Being clever, she also knew what benefits to her personally the results of such a meeting could bring. Prestige, advancement, influence, benefits that would change her life. For, she realised, at the heart of her present inertia lay a longing for a magical transformation which might present her with new horizons, interests, activity and so dispel the unbearable isolation she had felt ever since the night at the opera. Paul Ehrlich had come to embody a symbol of escape. And even then, when she had tracked the causes of her mood and arrived at a rationale, she accounted herself stupid and immature and pathetic, which merely deepened her depression.

The next morning Max awaited her arrival at the University. He held in his hands copies of several morning newspapers all of which carried Paul Ehrlich's speech. Once again, seated in Blikli, they pored over the reports, reading and rereading the passage:

As a matter of fact, it may interest you to know that this very morning, on my arrival in Warsaw, I opened several letters that were awaiting me and more than half of my correspondents asked me to lend my name to one political faction or another. I consigned these letters to the waste-paper basket. I am a scientist whose greatest wish is to serve humanity. If I am anything else, I am a citizen of the world and that is a very daunting burden.

'He's an assimilationist,' Max said. 'Like your husband.'

'He's a pompous, self-opinionated fool,' Eva said. Max wanted to add 'also like your husband' but bit his tongue. 'Political? What does he mean political? I wanted to talk to him about survival and nationhood and pride in who we are! Citizen of the world, I consign *you* to the waste-paper basket.'

Throughout that summer and the onset of autumn Eva's unhappiness persisted. Adam continued to press for emigration to Germany. Max, to keep her close, argued for her remaining in Warsaw and continuing her work for the Zionist cause. Ehrlich's speech preoccupied her for weeks, made her question all the opinions she held and the stand she had taken. Was it best to assimilate, as Adam argued? Could she ever imagine herself a Pole? Wasn't a Jewish homeland the only answer? But Eva's motives for asking these questions, like those of all activists, political or social, arose out of her personal needs and the inherent flaws in her personality; these motives were then subtly and subconsciously rationalised and articulated as causes or philosophical abstractions. All her self-searching could be reduced to one question which was simple and primitive: where do I belong in the scheme of things?

In September and at the beginning of October three events conspired to transform her life but not in the way she had either expected or hoped. First, she discovered she was pregnant which filled her with both joy and concern for the child's future. I don't want the baby born in Poland, Adam had said and, now, nor did she. Two weeks later the news came of Stolypin's assassination. The Jewish community was thrown into turmoil. Rumours besieged the city of Warsaw. The assassin, Mordka Bogrov, it was said, was a double agent, a revolutionary and a police informer, but for which side he was working when he shot the Tsar's prime minister was not clear. Nor did it matter much to Eva and her circle. What mattered to them was the undeniable fact that Bogrov was a Jew and that talk of revenge was in the air. Then, shortly after the new academic year began, Dr Chaim Shapiro, a member of the Faculty and a renowned expert on Charles Dickens, was suspended from his duties. No explanation was given. The next day Eva was summoned to the office of the Dean.

She dreaded these interviews. The Dean was a hunchback with a high, domed forehead who crouched at his desk, his chin almost touching the polished surface. He appeared to Eva like a prehistoric predator about to pounce.

'Please forgive me, Mrs Salz,' he said, 'but I have to ask you some personal questions. I believe you are expecting a happy event next year.'

'I am pregnant, yes.'

'Yes. Well. Now. Then. The Faculty have come to the decision that it would be unwise for you to continue in your present position and so must ask for your resignation.'

'Why?'

'For two reasons, my dear Mrs Salz. First, for your own sake, for your health and the health of the unborn child.'

'I'll worry about my health and the health of my unborn child, thank you.'

'Yes, yes, I'm sure, but we cannot help but take some responsibility in the matter. Secondly, we do not feel it would be seemly for an expectant mother to stand before a class of young persons.'

'Why?'

'Please don't be difficult, Mrs Salz, you know very well why. I am talking about decorum and certain standards of decent behaviour which we are obliged to maintain.'

'I'm a married woman. I'm pregnant. What's indecent about that?' The Dean winced. Eva's eyes narrowed and she thrust her chin forward defiantly. 'Explain this to me, then. Why was Mrs Motyka allowed to go on teaching French literature almost until she gave birth?'

The Dean shifted uncomfortably. 'We felt that was a mistake and have revised the rules.'

'Why don't you tell me the truth, Dean?' Eva asked as though she pitied him.

'I have told you the truth, Mrs Salz.'

'No, you haven't. Isn't the real reason I'm being asked to resign connected with the murder of Stolypin? Isn't this the beginning of a purge of "undesirable" elements from the Faculty?'

'Certainly not!' The Dean raised his head momentarily and appeared outraged.

'Why was Dr Shapiro suspended?' Eva demanded.

'I am not permitted to discuss that matter.'

'No, I'm sure you're not. Why haven't you the courage to admit that you are getting rid of the Jews from the Faculty?'

'Because it isn't true.'

She stood and gazed at him with unconcealed contempt. 'You know what I loathe most about you, Dean? It's not that you're fraudulent and unprincipled and immoral. You're all those things. No, what I hate most about you is that you're a coward. You haven't even the courage of your corrupt convictions. I resign, Dean. Good morning.'

Before she told Adam the news, Eva wrote a letter:

3 October 1911

Dear Mrs Harrison,

I do hope you remember me. My uncle and I were fortunate enough to be of some service to you following the performance of *Rigoletto* with Mattia Battistini. Presuming on that slight acquaintanceship, I wonder if it would be possible for you to grant me a short interview. I look forward to hearing from you at your earliest convenience.

13

'A no-goodnik poet,' Laban the Idiot said, 'would compare the cranes in the harbour of Hamburg to wading birds or birds of prey. But to me they are like fingers wagging a warning to a blind God. You understand my meaning?'

But Isaiah could not see admonishing fingers. He could not see wading birds or birds of prey. Standing on the quayside, holding his uncle's hand, he looked out at the harbour through a mist of tears and rain and saw little but blurred, strange, unidentifiable shapes against the grey sky. The American quota is full. Was the antonym of *frizlitch* despair?

They rejoined the other members of the family and the Pasym Jews, about twenty all told, in a large, cold shed, empty but for an insistent echo that mocked everything they said. The shed was ordinarily used to receive noisy, disembarking passengers who would find their luggage piled, as in all dockside arrival halls, under initial letters painted on card and suspended from the high beams. Now, the vast space of the hall was occupied by a small island of travellers who knew neither their destination nor their point of departure. By chance, they sat under the letter J which, later, Laban said, was apt. One man stood apart, Solomon Wildnowitz, who could not bear to hear any longer the repetitions of disappointment and doubt from the others. He moved away, came to rest under the letter Z, arms folded across his chest but tucked his hands into his coat so that it looked as though he was hugging himself for warmth and comfort which was not far from the truth.

All were waiting for the return of a small delegation which included Abraham, the bearded man in a frock-coat and Homburg, and two or three other leaders of the Pasym contingent who had set off, an hour before sunset, in search of help. It had been decided they must find a local Jewish community who could, perhaps, offer shelter for a few days until some sort of plan for the future was decided. Since none had visited Hamburg before, the whereabouts of the nearest Jewish quarter was uncertain. 'We may be some time,' Abraham had said. 'Be patient. God is good.' The light slowly faded and a chill invaded the shed.

When Laban and Isaiah returned all faces lit up with expectation but, at the sight of them, hope was immediately extinguished. They shuffled across to Leah and Benjamin.

'*Nu?*' Benjamin, the shoemaker, said.

'*Nu,*' Laban the Idiot repeated.

The word *nu* which is pronounced to rhyme with Jew is, philologists claim, the most versatile word in the Yiddish language, if not in any language. It can, with the appropriate inflection, gesture or facial expression, convey anything from interest to boredom, indignation to finality, helplessness to defiance, doubt to certainty. In the case of Benjamin's *nu* which was accompanied by a cautious frown, it conveyed, 'Have you found out anything of interest that won't upset me too much?' In reply, Laban's *nu*, coloured by the slightest shrug of resignation, said, 'It's the same story everywhere. The American quota is full, that seems to be the long and the short of it.'

The sun set, a pink glow lingered, then it was dark and the Jews turned into huddling shadows. Laban repeated his thoughts on the poetic metaphors which might be applied to cranes and produced an angry rebuke from Benjamin. 'For God's sake, Laban, don't be an idiot all your life. They are cranes in the harbour of Hamburg, that's all they are, nothing more, nothing less. Enough poetry. We're in trouble, can't you understand? See things as they are. Idiot.'

'Where will we spend the night?' Leah asked but the only reply she received was an attenuated cry from one of the Pasym women, an '*oy-yoy-yoy*' of such anguish that it seemed to insinuate itself into every corner of the shed only to be doubled and redoubled by the echo. Fearful of again upsetting the woman, Leah whispered to Benjamin, 'Have we enough money for rooms?'

'If I knew how much rooms cost in Hamburg, I could answer your question,' he replied unhelpfully.

Leah noticed Solomon, a bulky, lonely silhouette. She called to him, 'Come, sit with us, Solchik, we have to talk.' But he did not move. He remained where he was, isolated, aloof and cold under the letter Z.

Isaiah snuggled up to Leah, who held him close and stroked his hair. His brothers, Julius and Baruch, had made friends with a couple of Pasym boys their own age, and sat with them, talking in murmurs, occasionally laughing, but their laughter drew hisses of reproach from the elders as if, in the circumstances, laughter was sinful. Loaves of black bread were passed from one to the other, hunks torn off, blessings murmured. 'Praised be Thou, O Lord our God, King of the Universe, who causes the earth to yield food for all.' A child began to cry which first elicited sympathy and then, very quickly, annoyance.

The child was silenced by the noise of one of the small side doors rattling. A terrified stillness. A match flared followed by noisy relief.

Abraham and the others had returned, and even in the light of a single match it was possible to see his smile and sense his cheerfulness. Now, more matches flared and candles were lit so that those who had waited saw that strangers were also present, a man in his early thirties, like Abraham in apparent high spirits, and his wife who, by contrast, exuded timidity and caution as though experience had taught her that life was full of unpleasant surprises.

Abraham said, 'All is well. Allow me to introduce Herr Alfred Bronstein and Frau Bronstein.'

'Katarina, Katarina,' Frau Bronstein said with her eyes downcast and a smile like a nervous tic.

Abraham explained the Bronsteins' presence. He and the others had found a synagogue not far from the harbour. The *shammas*, the caretaker, directed them to the rabbi's house. The rabbi, Reb Leitermann, who was in the middle of his evening meal, irritably directed them to the mansion of a banker, Herr Sigmund Frankfurter, who was also the president of a committee which administered a Jewish charitable trust. He, too, was in the middle of a meal and so ordered a servant to lead the Jews to Herr Bronstein's house. The Bronsteins generously put aside their meal and returned to the shed with the delegation. Abraham did not know that Herr Bronstein was the newest member of Herr Frankfurter's committee and was, therefore, keen to impress Herr Frankfurter. Most of Abraham's audience found his story difficult to follow but were reassured when Alfred Bronstein addressed them in German.

'Ladies and gentlemen,' he said, 'I bid you welcome to Hamburg.' He had a high-pitched, nasal voice, precise diction, a pompous manner, and he pursed his lips after each sentence as if about to blow a kiss. 'I represent an organisation whose chief purpose is to help our less fortunate brethren.'

At this point, Katarina revealed a deeply irritating habit: she talked at the same time as her husband. Lowering her voice, she leaned close to Leah, who happened to be nearest to her, and asked, 'Have you eaten, are you very tired, do you have small children, I don't have any children, where are you from, where are you going?' and so on. Her husband, obviously accustomed to his wife's ways, took no notice but continued to speak. Leah, however, wanted to yell, 'Shut up, for God's sake, I'm trying to listen,' but hadn't the courage.

'You will be pleased to hear,' Bronstein said, 'that we have hostels which will accommodate you.' An 'Ah!' of relief and pleasure, sighed in unison, greeted this welcome information. 'But I am bound to tell you that the conditions of the Trust insist men and women live separately. There are two houses, therefore. One for men, one for women.'

83

'*Oi!*'

'However, on the Sabbath, on *shabas*, families, of course, are permitted to come together in whichever house is most convenient.'

('Two hostels, yes, well, never mind, they're very clean, and there are less than a half a dozen people in each at the moment, the beds, I believe, are comfortable, and the houses are not too far from each other, your children can spend the days with you but, as my husband says, the men are definitely not allowed in the women's hostel and the women are not allowed in the men's hostel—')

'The Trust will also provide a little money for each family to buy food and clothes, should this be necessary. Tomorrow, volunteers will come and ask you questions to ascertain your individual circumstances—'

('Yes, you can light candles, say the blessings, have a nice Sabbath meal, but unfortunately your husband won't be permitted to stay the night, or fortunately, as the case may be, what do you say to that?')

' – so, if you would kindly collect up your things and follow me, I will see that you are settled and fed.'

It could have been worse, Laban decided, and all members of the family agreed. At least they were warm and had been given a breathing space. But Isaiah cried himself to sleep for the first few nights because he so missed his mother and he remembered a nightmare in which Leah died and Solomon said, 'Look on the bright side.'

In reality, Solomon was not so optimistic. Ever since the parting from the Circus Stoica, the gravity of his family's situation gradually bore down on him, as if each day weights were being added to a scale, so that as he realised more and more clearly the prospect of a hopeless and frightening future, his growing awareness tipped the balance of his spirits into melancholy. For reasons he was unable to fathom let alone articulate, he took upon himself the responsibility for all the disasters which had befallen them and began to believe that he and he alone had brought the family to the very brink of catastrophe. If only he had never agreed to Laban's plan in the first place, if only they had never left Ploemyan, if only he had known or guessed about Laban and Constanta Stoica, if only he had accepted what fate had in store for them as his forefathers had always done. If only, if only, if only until he wanted to scream. Now, his days were dark and his heart heavy. His sons were without a future. Laban's eternal hopefulness and Benjamin's bad temper fuelled Solomon's self-reproach. He saw no avenue of escape and was, therefore, unable to appreciate the one dispensation in an otherwise bleak world: his decline fed Leah's ascendancy.

At first, unaware of the depth of her husband's depression, Leah instinctively did what was required of her, practical, ordinary things expected of a wife and mother. But she also discovered that words of encouragement were needed daily in order to harness the family's collective will and, in so doing, gave each one a sense of purpose, a belief in a roseate future that could not, must not, dare not be questioned. Like a general trying to inspire a demoralised army, Leah led by example. She meant her courage and certainty to be infectious and, to some extent, they were. She was no more than thirty-five at this time but already had the figure of a matriarch and was possessed of unusual physical strength. The one thing of which she never complained was tiredness. In a thousand unspecified ways the Wildnowitz men came to rely on her.

A day or two after they were settled, a family conference was held in a dockside café. The men agreed they must all look for work. Leah listened to their chatter, heard them describe what sort of jobs they were after, speaking as if they were qualified professionals looking to buy into some fancy partnership, and knew at once that she must take immediate action. By chance, when she returned to the women's hostel she found Katarina Bronstein inspecting the kitchen. 'I need work that'll pay, Frau Bronstein,' Leah said. 'I need to work tonight so that I can have money tomorrow.' She spoke in Yiddish, of course, which Katarina had difficulty following.

Katarina Bronstein, unlike her husband, was genuinely interested in the plight of these uprooted people. Bronstein, however, lost interest the moment the refugees were settled and processed. He was a branch manager of one of Herr Frankfurter's banks and therefore lacked human sympathy, which is why he had such excellent prospects as a banker. He engaged in charitable work merely to advance his career but then, perhaps, the motives for charity are unimportant so long as the charity itself is advanced. Katarina, on the other hand, despite her diffidence, took the work seriously, visited the hostels at least twice a week, saw to it that the occupants kept themselves and the houses clean and enquired after each individual's well-being. To Leah's demand for immediate work, Katarina's eyes danced nervously as though she'd been asked for a loan, but she said, 'Do you mind what work you do?'

'Certainly not,' Leah said. 'I'll scrub out lavatories, I'll clean floors, I'll carry bricks on my back, whatever's required.'

Katarina closed her restless eyes and thought for a moment. When she was apart from her husband, Leah noticed, Katarina's manner, while still betraying insecurity, was more subdued, almost calm. 'Will you wash and iron?' Katarina asked.

'Give me the tub, give me the soap, give me the clothes, the sheets, the blankets, give me the iron, I can't wait to begin.'

Leah's forcefulness caused Katarina to retreat a step or two; she put a hand to her forehead as though the light was too bright. 'One of the women who left recently for Australia – or was it Austria? – had some clients, bachelors, widowers and the like. Of course she had to abandon them once she had found a passage. I mean, it would have been impossible for her to go on doing their laundry from the ship.' She twitched a smile, Leah looked blank, the smile disappeared.

Leah said, 'But they must have found another washerwoman by now.'

'Not necessarily. I'll talk to Ludwig Kahn. He's a bachelor and was one of her clients.' With that, she seemed to curtsy to Leah and then fled. But, true to her word, the next day she was back at the hostel with two bars of yellow soap and a list of names and addresses. By evening, Leah was employed, her strength was increased and she held her head high.

Of course, she was right about the men or, at least, about Laban and Benjamin. Something in the air of this thriving port gave them a mild but thankfully brief dose of *folie des grandeurs*. Alfred Bronstein's persona also made a contribution, for he was unlike any other Jew they had met, neither speaking nor understanding Yiddish, running the branch of a bank, obviously well-educated, confident, respectable, respected. 'That's how I'd like to be,' Benjamin said in the dockside café. 'I'd like to wear a collar and tie to work. And a suit.'

'It is clear,' Laban said, 'that in Germany anything is possible. Jews can alter their destiny in this country. Perhaps I could get a job with books. That's what I'd like, I'd like to work with words. And when I get to America I shall write a long saga entitled, *The Circus of Life*.'

'Me,' Benjamin said in one of his rare moments of expansiveness, 'I'd like to sell shoes instead of making them.' (It was at this point that Leah decided she had to find work at once.) 'One of the men who asked us all those questions yesterday gave me a couple of names. What about you, Sol?'

Solomon shrugged. 'Me? Whatever's going.'

A plan was hatched. It was decided that in the mornings they would search for employment; in the afternoons they would return to the dockside offices and make enquiries in the hope that one of the shipping lines would risk breaking the American embargo and carry them all across the ocean. For, America remained the goal. Even Benjamin, who had, under stress, suggested they emigrate elsewhere, now fixed his sights once more on America.

When the conference broke up, Julius and Baruch decided to accompany Benjamin. They were hoping to find work, too. Isaiah said, 'Can I come with you, Uncle Laban?'

86

Leah was about to object, fearful of where Laban might lead her son, but Laban said, 'It'll be my pleasure,' and it was settled.

What the men had not anticipated was the snobbery of German Jews who, over hundreds of years, had wriggled out of their ghettos, wormed their way through cracks in the walls into towns and cities until they were almost indistinguishable from their German neighbours. The Rothschilds, for example, began in a Frankfurt ghetto and weren't they now all great lords whose influence spread from one end of the continent to the other? Adam Salz had been right when he claimed that German Jews were the most assimilated in Europe. Most had endured persecution, some overcame poverty and achieved acceptance. To many, especially the bourgeoisie, German patriotism and nationalism were passions which grew naturally and were used as badges, shields, camouflage. The Kaiser had few more loyal subjects. That is not to say there wasn't a goodly amount of prejudice and hatred about but it was toothless and either ignored or somehow overcome. A Lithuanian Jew, therefore, in his shabby clothes, speaking his unpleasant liquid Yiddish, which was after all the ghetto vernacular, was a reminder of an unhappy past which was best forgotten. When Benjamin and his two nephews entered a shoe-shop owned by Jakob Dobermann and asked if a salesman was needed, the look of horror and embarrassment on Herr Dobermann's face could not have been more pronounced if the three of them had entered the store naked. Dobermann bundled them into a side room, gave them fifty pfennigs, and ushered them out through the back door into an alley. 'Don't come back, please don't come back,' he called.

Laban was met with laughter. Holding Isaiah's hand, he sailed into Adler's, a large bookshop, and demanded to see Herr Adler himself. He was asked the purpose of his call. 'I am Laban Wildnowitz,' he said airily. 'A poet. What work can you offer me?' The assistant could not control his laughter; Laban pretended not to understand and proudly smiled his idiotic smile; Isaiah blushed with shame.

Outside in the street, Laban said, 'The biggest anti-Semites are the Jews themselves.'

Solomon fared better although that is a matter of opinion. His melancholia did not allow for pretensions so he kept away from the more fashionable parts of the city into which his brothers had ventured. He attended morning service in the synagogue near the harbour and, afterwards, asked the *shammes*, Yitzchak, for advice. Yitzchak was a small, mischievous man who gave off a smell of stale onions and naphthalene.

'You want to be a *nakhtwachter*?' Yitzchak asked, eyes twinkling.

'Thanks, no, not my style. My brother, Laban, used to be a *nakhtwachter*.'

'Tell him to see me, I'll have work for him. Death's always a good business. You have a trade?'

'Woodcutter.'

'Not much wood in Hamburg.'

'No.'

'Can you cook?'

'No.'

'Are you an all-weather man?'

'What do you mean?'

'Do you mind working out of doors no matter what the weather?'

'No, I don't mind,' Solomon said. '*Nu?*'

'*Nu*, go to this address. They have work most days for all-weather men.' Yitzchak began to scribble the address.

'Write in Yiddish. I can't read German,' Solomon said.

He found a small doorway through which he passed into a courtyard. A line of a dozen or so men, tramps, drunks, derelicts, shuffled towards a trestle-table which was set up at the furthest end. Solomon joined the line and noticed that each man, on reaching the table, was given two boards roped together which were placed over his head before leaving. On the boards were written slogans, exhortations, advertisments which Solomon could not understand and he was puzzled as to what was expected of him.

When his turn came, the sandwich-boards were placed over his head. 'What am I supposed to do?' he asked.

'Walk the streets, take only twenty minutes for lunch, don't drink, and return at five o'clock. We'll pay you then. Don't try and sneak into the warmth anywhere. We have inspectors all over the city.'

Ideal, Solomon thought, just walk, think, keep going, walk, ideal. Once or twice passers-by slipped him a few pfennigs. Mid-morning, he was stopped by a tall, erect, white-haired man, all in black, plainly distinguished, but with an oily, unctuous manner.

'Excuse me for asking this,' the man said, 'but are you a Jew?' He talked slowly enough for Solomon to understand.

'Why do you want to know?' Solomon asked, immediately suspicious and fearful.

'Simply that I work among Jews and you seemed to me to look like one of that noble race.'

'Aren't you a Jew yourself?'

'Alas, not,' the man said with a sad but unconvincing smile which Solomon mistrusted. 'I am a Lutheran minister. I am Pastor Naupert. Tell me about yourself.'

Solomon gave his name and explained his present circumstances.

The pastor nodded. 'I shall pay the hostel a visit. I think what you are doing is very fine and you will be rewarded in heaven.' He tipped his hat and rewarded Solomon on earth with a few coins.

What am I doing, Solomon wondered, that will earn me a seat among Lutheran angels? Momentarily, he was cheered by the thought. It was only later that day, when returning to the courtyard, that he understood. He encountered Laban and Isaiah on their way back to the hostel. Laban took one look at him and burst out laughing.

'What's so funny?' Solomon asked.

'What's so funny? You know what's written on those baords?'

'What?'

'"Jesus Saves."'

'*Oi gewalt!*' Solomon wailed.

'And I hope,' Laban said, 'on what they're paying you, you'll be able to save, too.'

The next day Solomon, the sandwich-board man, was to be seen in the streets of Hamburg advertising Finkelstein's Kosher Restaurant.

Leah collected her first load of dirty laundry from Ludwig Kahn, the bachelor, who lived alone in two rooms above the office where he worked. He was a shipping clerk, a handsome, kindly man in his forties, with an encyclopaedic knowledge of the shipping timetables. 'Only one thing, Leah,' he said, 'don't starch the collars. I get boils on my neck.'

From Kahn she went to the synagogue and introduced herself to Yitzchak, the *shammes*. This was not a professional call because Yitzchak did not know the meaning of the word wash let alone laundry. No, Leah wanted advice about Isaiah's bar mitzvah lessons. Yitzchak told her to bring the boy the following afternoon to meet Rabbi Levi which she did and Isaiah resumed his studies. For a while Leah was happy.

So, within a matter of days, having travelled over five hundred miles across northern Europe, the family Wildnowitz from a small town in Lithuania, was sniffing out the life of one of the most populous centres in Germany, the Free and Hanseatic City of Hamburg. Propelled by an atavistic instinct for survival, they scurried across the bridges and along the *fleete*, the web of canals which connect the rivers Alster and Elbe, lost themselves in the maze of alleyways and streets in the *Alstadt*, only to find their bearings again speedily and safely. Seven impoverished Jews, shabbily dressed, rendered unable by circumstance to exploit their true talents, yearning for a life in a land they called America but which was, in reality, only a word, as in a code, a cipher identifying a dream of freedom, promise and security. They were not unique. There were twenty-five thousand other Jews, or thereabouts, in Hamburg. Stop any one of them on the street and they would have a similar family history to tell, a story of upheaval and resettlement, if not today then yesterday, if not yesterday then the day before.

The ability to settle quickly, to adapt to circumstances, to make a new life of a sort, may be a genetic inheritance which has been bred into the system by two thousand years of necessity. The pattern repeats itself time and time again and confounds Darwin's theory that only the fittest survive. Or, perhaps, proves it.

Benjamin, shoemaker but would-be salesman, soon realised he was not going to find a job that required a collar and tie and settled for humping and sorting skins in a leather warehouse on the left bank of the Elbe where new docks and wharves had recently been constructed. His temper was not improved. Solomon advertised Samuel Finkelstein's Kosher Restaurant, walked in circles, and with each step his despair deepened. A week after he first donned the sandwich-board, he was given a voucher for a free meal at the restaurant he advertised and took along his sons, Julius and Baruch, to share it with him. Because neither of the boys could speak German they had difficulty finding employment, but after lunch that day, Julius happened to ask Herr Finkelstein if he knew of any jobs in the offing. Finkelstein was enormously fat and poured sweat even in the coldest weather. His eyes bulged alarmingly and his voice was always hoarse which made his question, 'Can you wash a plate?' sound as if it was the most brutal enquiry he had ever made. 'Certainly,' Julius replied. Ten minutes later he and Baruch were in Finkelstein's basement kitchen, wearing soiled white aprons, scraping, washing, drying, earning.

Laban, although he still nursed a fancy for the literary life, had no choice but to take up his former trade. Solomon had mentioned that Yitzchak, the *shammes*, promised to be helpful and so he was. Most nights, Laban found himself in the houses of the dead, rich and poor, keeping vigil beside a corpse on the floor, either contemplating fate or allowing his fertile imagination to run free through forests magical and mysterious. He also thought often of Constanta Stoica, of her breasts and her limbs, of her mouth, her tongue, her passion, and felt a familiar craving that needed to be satisfied.

Reporting for work one evening, he found Yitzchak in a particularly cheery mood. 'Have I got something for you tonight!' Yitzchak said with obvious enjoyment.

'What? Who? Where?'

'A murder victim.'

'A Jew's been murdered?' Laban said with alarm, instantly fearing another spontaneous uprising.

'Yes, a woman.'

'*Nu?*'

'Her name is Karin.'

'That's all? Karin?'

Yitzchak chuckled and chose to remain mysterious. He drew a map, gave Laban a bottle of schnapps, said, 'You'll be needing this,' and sent him on his way.

Laban hurried along ancient passages, down winding back streets and, after many wrong turnings, found the house which was small and squat. Two policemen guarded the door. 'It's closed,' said one of them. 'Go fuck somewhere else.'

Laban was taken aback by their language. 'But I am the *nakhtwachter*,' he said trying to sound dignified. 'I have to sit with the body. I've been sent by the synagogue.'

They let him pass and he entered into a narrow hallway lit by a single gas mantle which popped and spluttered. He paused to listen for the sounds of mourning but heard nothing. He was conscious, however, of a not unattractive pungent smell. Then, he heard a woman's laughter and another voice ordering quiet. He coughed loudly but without effect. There were doors leading off the passage but they were closed. 'Hell-o-o,' he called, and again, more loudly. Upstairs, he heard a door open. 'Who's there?' asked a woman, and a light came on which illuminated the staircase. Laban said, 'It's the *nakhtwachter*.' Hurried steps and then the woman appeared on the first landing. Laban was astonished. A beauty stood before him in a shiny black dress, the neckline cut so low it almost revealed her nipples. Impossible to guess her age, no longer a girl, yet sensual, desirable, and instantly he knew simply from the way she stood that she was available. On seeing Laban, the woman narrowed her eyes, as if assessing him and seemed satisfied with what she saw.

'Where is Karin, please?' Laban asked gently.

'Upstairs. What's your name, handsome?'

'Laban Wildnowitz,' he said.

'I am Madame Europa Altona.'

'Pleased to meet you,' he said. 'Are you a relative of Karin?'

'Certainly not, she was a stupid bitch, I told her to be careful, but would she listen? No, she always knew better, I said don't get involved in ropes and whips, it's not worth it, and was I right? I was right. The poor bastard, a respectable man, is in prison and she's lying dead in her room.' She beckoned him up the stairs and he followed cautiously. She was the source, he now realised, of the pungent smell, a sweet yet peppery scent which excited him. 'Mind you, she was a religious girl, never worked from sunset Friday to sunset Saturday. Yet, our Jewish clients never wanted her. Funny, don't you think? She always lit candles. She used to say to me, "Madame, when I die, don't leave my body unattended." That's why you're here. I ordered the police to bring her back from the morgue. They weren't too keen but I have friends in the police.'

Laban, unsophisticated though he was and inexperienced in city life, understood instantly he was about to keep vigil over a *kurveh*, a *nafka*, Yiddish words for prostitute, in a house of shame. He was shown into the room where Karin's body lay on the bed, a sheet for a shroud. At his insistence, Madame Altona helped him lower Karin to the floor and in the process Madame Altona's bodice loosened a little and revealed her breasts. Left alone with the corpse, Laban realised his mouth was dry and he licked his lips.

Across the city, in the women's hostel, by the light of a solitary candle, Leah slaved over a sink, washing and rinsing other people's clothes. Down the street, in the men's house, Benjamin slept the sleep of a labourer and Isaiah slept, too. But Julius and Baruch kept themselves awake, waiting for the house to settle down for the night, so that they could eat in secret the food they had stolen from Herr Finkelstein. Solomon twisted and turned in his lonely bed, was twice woken by the mournful blast of a ship's hooter and wiped away the tears that streamed down his cheeks. And Laban the Idiot kept a dead whore company, wondered what delights fate had in store for him, and murmured his famous line of verse, 'A pattern of stars on a quilted cradle/Dictates the destiny of all mankind.'

PART TWO

Turning Points
(1912–1919)

1

Sobliki is a large house and a large village. The Sobelevs owned both. From the village, through the trees, a huge man-made lake can be seen. The far bank rises steeply and becomes a hill, rich with beech and sycamore, and it is on the very crest of this hill that the house nestles.

The house is white, its central section rounded like a graceful turret; the abutting wings rectangular but in no way severe. It is in reality a mansion but somehow, whether by design or accident, of a modest scale, domestic and welcoming. To the rear is the park Balutan designed or, rather, seems not to have designed, for he so managed to make nature an ally that the paths through the woods, the sloping lawns, the ponds embraced by reeds, the avenues of birch trees, all give the impression of having been there since time began. Only the unexpected folly or monument testifies to man's intervention.

While Lev and Tatiana were in Warsaw, the only adult Sobelev in the house was Lev's father, Count Boris, a widower. He missed his son and daughter-in-law and longed for their return. He kept ennui at bay by indulging his chief interest which was genealogy, and spent much of his time studying the latest *Almanach de St Petersbourg* or finding fault with a book his cousin had produced on the Sobelev family. A solitary man by nature, he preferred the company of his family, alive or dead, to friends or strangers. In truth he had in all his life considered only one man a close friend and that had been his celebrated neighbour, Lev Nikolayevich Tolstoy, whose country estate, Yasnaya Polyana, was a day's ride away.

Apart from being landowners and aristocrats, the two men had apparently little in common; at their first meeting, before the turn of the century, Count Boris had tried to provoke Lev Nikolayevich by criticising the epilogues of *War and Peace*. 'Individuals matter more, Lev Nikolayevich, than this historical movement of which you write. Individuals affect history. Individuals change history. And what's more, insignificant accidents are often the pivot for great events and disasters. I know this very well from studying the history of my own family.' He then launched into a catalogue of incidents, of how this Sobelev gambled and that Sobelev did not, of how another had revolutionary tendencies and yet another was close to the Tsar, on and on, all of which were meant to reinforce his argument.

Lev Nikolayevich was not disposed to engage Count Boris. His powerful intellect, he knew, was no match for his neighbour and, moreover, he was not used to being criticised in any way whatsoever, certainly not so crudely and openly. While Count Boris raged, he listened patiently with a nod, a smile, a shrug, but was determined not to bring his great authority into play. Count Boris, however, persisted. He wanted a fight. He was not intimidated either by Lev Nikolayevich's fame or by the awe in which others, especially the Tolstoy family, held the great writer. 'And what's more I don't believe in the perfectability of man,' he continued, 'or in some harmonious system after which you seem to hanker. There is, in my opinion, no vast, single vision to be had of mankind. We are base creatures, we do the best or worst we can, and individuals, yes, Lev Nikolayevich, individuals drag us out of the mud or push us further into it. I do not deny you are a great story-teller, perhaps the greatest who has ever lived, but please, leave philosophy to philosophers.'

At this Lev Nikolayevich's beard trembled; he did his best to control his temper. He rose from his chair, went to his bookshelves and removed two books. One was *Soirées de St Petersbourg* by Count Joseph de Maistre; the other was *La Chartreuse de Parme* by Stendhal. 'Be so kind, Boris Lvovich, to read *War and Peace* again, and then these two volumes. Let us argue no further until you have digested their contents. Then we may discuss these matters in greater detail.' And as he sat again, he added, 'And please return those books. They are very precious to me.'

Thereafter, the two men met about twice a year. Count Boris returned the books but without comment. Historical movements, the importance of individuals, whether or not accidents and quirks of history and significance, were never again discussed. The truth was that Count Boris had not finished either of the works Lev Nikolayevich had lent him. After reading a mere ten pages of the Maistre he knew he was out of his depth. His only word on the subject was, 'You see, Lev Nikolayevich, I feel things instinctively and I speak only from personal experience.' To which the writer replied with enormous enthusiasm, 'Exactly!' for the conflicts and confusions within him were as intense, perhaps more intense, than in any other human being. Conflict, not certainty, was the motor of his greatness. His belief that the personal life alone was real warred with his theory that individual behaviour did not explain the history of societies. 'Exactly!' he said again and seemed about to embrace Count Boris but then thought better of it.

Count Boris tried to bait his neighbour on one other occasion. This time he mocked the opening lines of *Anna Karenina*. 'Happy families do *not* resemble one another,' he asserted. 'They are quite as unique and individual as unhappy families. My late wife and I—' but he got no further. The mere thought or mention of his dead spouse caused Count Boris to weep, for which Lev Nikolayevich was extremely grateful.

But the two men did discover a bond which was their love of the land and the peasantry. In the author this belief arose out of a mystical conviction. In Count Boris the reasons were more selfishly motivated. He was awkward in high society or in the presence of politicians and intellectuals. He much preferred the company of his steward, his house servants or the labourers on his estate. Like Konstantin Levin in *Anna Karenina* Count Boris had worked side by side with his farm workers gathering hay. He counted those glorious, long-lost summer days among the happiest in his life.

When the news came of Tolstoy's death at the Astapovo railway station in 1910, Count Boris wept for two days and nights. It was kind and wise, therefore, of the Tolstoys to keep secret part of a letter Lev Nikolayevich had written to a relative:

> Boris Lvovich Sobelev here. The man is obsessed with family trees. Of all the bores in the world he is undoubtedly the greatest. But he is so stupid that I have a sneaking affection and regard for him.

To Count Boris's delight Tatiana and Lev returned from Warsaw three months before she was due to give birth. Their son, Vladimir, came into the world in October 1911. Tatiana had wanted him born in Sobliki and, besides, was more confident of the local midwife than she was of Dr Bulkarov. The couple had also missed their two daughters, Xenia and Darya who, now aged eight and five, were in need of a governess. Miss Agnes McMurray from Edinburgh joined the household at the beginning of the year. Firm but affectionate, she was a no-nonsense, red-haired young woman whom the children called Mac but which their Russian accents turned into Muck. They adored her.

Tatiana was happiest in Sobliki. The great world vanished. Intrigue, protocol and restlessness were unknown. Any memory of Battistini was consigned to the shadows. She rode in the mornings, practised the piano for an hour each afternoon and managed effortlessly the affairs of both The Annex and the main house. Count Boris was devoted to her and depended on her for his comforts and peace of mind, leaving the running of the estate to Lev.

To the Sobelevs the world was settled, secure and permanent. The measure of country life, as Laban the Idiot once observed, is stately and predictable; little changes but the seasons. The greatest excitement was the biannual visits to Moscow and St Petersburg where they stayed in family houses either with Tatiana's parents, the Souvritzins, or in the Sobelev town house on the Moscow River. Once back in Sobliki, tranquillity returned and they continued on the unquestioned, unquestionable advance towards old age and death. Or so they believed, for country life, just as much as life in any city, encourages illusions and false perceptions and nothing could have encouraged illusion on a grander scale than the events in which Tatiana was to play a minor role.

A week before the Christmas of 1912, a military despatch rider from the garrison in Tula spurred his horse through the village and made for the road which borders the lake and leads past the side of the house. Up the hill he galloped, through the heavy snow, catching occasional glimpses of the impressive white building. Then, he wheeled his horse in a wide arc and took the drive towards the gatehouse. Once through the arch he saw, to his right, the family church and the mausoleum. To his left, The Annex, a small country house in itself, and beyond it, the stables.

His approach has been observed by the elderly steward, Pavlik, whose family had served the Sobelevs for more than a hundred years. When the horseman came to a halt and began to dismount, Pavlik opened the main door and slowly shuffled down the steps to greet him. From The Annex came the laughter of children.

'A message,' the despatch rider said, 'from Her Imperial Majesty for the Countess Tatiana Sergeievna Sobeleva.' He took from a leather case embossed with the Tsarina's coat-of-arms a large envelope which bore Tatiana's name written in the elaborate script employed by Imperial clerks and bureaucrats.

'Tatiana Sergeievna lives in The Annex,' Pavlik said wearily as though he were exhausted by the need to repeat this information. 'Take it there, please, and save my legs. And, afterwards, if you go to the back, they will give you refreshment.'

Dunyasha delivered the envelope to Tatiana, who was pasting photographs into an album.

'Well, what's it say, sweetheart?' Dunyasha asked impatiently.

'Where is Lev Borisovich?' Tatiana asked. She could not conceal her excitement but the words were hardly out of her mouth when Lev and his father, Count Boris, burst into the room. 'What's this Pavlik tells us about a despatch from the Empress?' Count Boris asked, half-way through the door.

'I am commanded,' Tatiana said a little breathlessly, 'to attend the Empress as lady-in-waiting when the Imperial family celebrates the tercentenary of the Romanov dynasty.'

Count Boris, as was his habit on hearing news good, bad or indifferent, burst into tears. Lev embraced his wife and Dunyasha said, 'You'll have to go to Moscow and buy some pretty clothes.'

The festivities began in St Petersburg, in the Cathedral of Our Lady of Kazan, with a glorious choral *Te Deum*. On that day, in February 1913, Tatiana rode in a carriage down the Nevsky Prospect, following a long way behind the carriages occupied by the Tsar and the Empress, but the cheering of the vast crowd that lined the street was so constant and deafening that Tatiana and her companion were forced to shout at each other to try to make themselves heard above the clamour. Tatiana's companion, whom she had only just met that morning, was another of the young noblewomen the Empress had invited to wait on her during the tercentenary celebrations, a Countess Maria Obrunina, a retiring, sensitive woman, younger than Tatiana and unmarried. Their first conversation, however, was not promising.

'What a to-do!' Tatiana cried.

'What?'

'What a to-do!'

'I paint!' yelled Maria.

'What?'

'I paint! I'm an artist!'

'What?'

'I thought you asked, "What did you do?"'

'No, I said, "What a to-do!"'

'Oh! I am sorry. I misunderstood.'

'What do you paint?'

'No, I'm feeling perfectly well, thank you.'

After that, they resorted to smiling at each other and to marvelling at the cheers, wave upon wave, that greeted the Imperial procession.

Both women were to find the ensuing weeks exhausting. Their days were crowded with ceremonies at which, from all over the empire, delegations wearing colourful national dress were allowed to pay allegiance and respect to their Sovereign Lord. In St Petersburg, Tatiana and Maria were present at a ball which was attended by a thousand guests and, later, they witnessed the adoring reception accorded the Imperial couple's appearance at the opera house to see a performance of Glinka's *A Life for the Tsar*.

Tatiana wrote to Lev, 'Oh, the standing for hours on end, the longing to close one's eyes, to rest them from the dazzling colours of the uniforms, the medals, the gowns and the jewels. We were sated

99

with splendour. If the strain on us was great, think of the poor Empress who is not a strong woman at the best of times. It has been unbearable for her. In fact, she confessed the other day, to Maria Obrunina and me, that she was near to fainting on more than one occasion.'

In May, they boarded a steamer on the Upper Volga and set sail for the ancient Romanov seat of Kostroma where, three hundred years before, Mikhail Romanov was informed of his election to the throne. Peasants in their hundreds of thousands lined the banks and some even waded into the water to get a closer look at the Father of all the Russias. The displays of loyalty bordered on hysteria. But the climax came in June, in Moscow, when the Emperor rode into the city alone, sixty feet in advance of his Cossack escort. In Red Square – its ancient name – he dismounted and followed chanting priests through a gate into the Kremlin. What touched Tatiana most, however, was an image of the nine-year-old Tsarevich, Alexis. With his mother, he had followed in an open car but was also meant to walk across the square. He was too ill and was carried in the arms of a Cossack. Tatiana was overcome with sadness at the sight of this helpless child, afflicted it was rumoured with an incurable disease, who was heir to the throne and might of the Romanovs. She shuddered as though visited by a dismal, tragic vision of the future, of impermanence and human frailty. But what renewed her confidence was the knowledge that she had seen with her own eyes people from every corner of the Tsar's vast domain fall down and kiss his shadow as he passed. She was certain there could be no end to such worship, such devotion and loyalty.

On her return to Sobliki, after she recounted these events, Count Boris said, 'It's as I've always said. The Duma is a barrier between the Tsar and his people. He has the unbounded love and loyalty of his subjects. I pray to God he does not give into these miserable politicians who want him to become a democrat and behave like his dreadful cousins in England. No. The Tsar can do anything he likes because he is loved and revered and worshipped. I used to argue these things with my old friend, Lev Nikolayevich Tolstoy. He disagreed but I have been proved right. The Romanovs will rule for ever! And there are those, closer than I to the Imperial couple, who hold similar beliefs and voice them just as vigorously.' He raised his vodka glass and began a long series of toasts which started with him clearly enunciating Nicholas and Alexandra, but his words became slurred through the host of Grand Dukes and Duchesses, and he was totally unintelligible in the descent to minor princelings. Tatiana retired long before he and Lev downed the last drop with which they drank the health of all the Sobelevs.

Tatiana wrote to her new friend, Maria Obrunina:

Thank you so much for your beautiful self-portrait. I shall treasure it always. Such excitement. Kurugin, the station-master, came galloping up to the house to tell us he'd received a telephone call from one Denisov in Moscow to say there was a parcel for me on the next train. He returned to the station, waited for the train, then came back to the house bearing your portrait. What a to-do! My strength is not yet returned. But I devour the indescribable beauty of Sobliki, the stillness and peace make me strong. The days when I could not find the energy to rise from my bed are fewer and fewer. I take such pride and pleasure in remembering our experiences, the kindness of the Empress, the beautiful brooches she gave us and, most importantly, the honour and delight I feel at having been part of something so glorious and worthwhile. And, dear Maria, what a privilege it was to meet you. My father-in-law has climbed your family tree and discovered that we have at least six great-aunts and many more cousins in common, not to mention H. S. H. Prince Alexander Wasillyevich Souvoroff-Rymniksky who led the army into ninety battles and never lost one! Another to-do! I hope we meet again soon.

The haunting self-portrait of Maria, Tatiana hung in her dressing-room beside the painting of Sobliki completed thirty years before by an unknown Italian artist.

A footnote. Dr Bulkarov recorded on the 30 January 1913 that he, too, was leaving Warsaw. 'I have failed His Excellency, the Governor-General,' he wrote, 'having been unable to find an expert to minister to his feet. Time to go home.'

2

It is necessary to return to 1911, the year Mrs Harrison replied to Eva's letter. 'Of course I remember you, and with gratitude. (I remember especially your beautiful mother-of-pearl hair adornment.) If it is convenient, please take tea with me next Thursday at four o'clock.' At that meeting, Eva wasted no time. 'We want to emigrate to England,' she said. 'We want our child born in London. Can you or your husband help us?' She explained the reason for her urgency, for attempting to bypass official channels. 'In 1905,' she said, 'your Parliament passed a law, the Aliens Immigration Act, to stop the tide of Jews flooding into England from eastern Europe. It makes things extremely difficult.'

Mrs Harrison, although a little taken aback by Eva's request, agreed to try and help.

She broached the subject with her husband that same evening over dinner, repeating Eva's words. 'She's pregnant and they want their child born in London.'

'Well, let them apply in the usual way.'

'But there's a law, isn't there, that makes things difficult.'

'Not my department, old girl. Consular. Lot of foreigners wanting to emigrate to dear old England. Jews especially. Don't want too many of them, you know. Hence the law.'

'But she's the very best type of Jewess,' Mrs Harrison said. 'Frightfully well-educated. My dear, she seems to know the whole of Shakespeare, Dickens and George Eliot by heart.'

'Got to be careful with educated Jews, old girl. Could be anarchists.'

'Oh, I don't think so. She doesn't strike me as in the least bit revolutionary. Surely you can help. You could have a word with Tubby Ravenshaw. He keeps telling me what a fine chap you are and that you were the best fag he ever had at Eton. And what's the point of being Minister if you can't pull a few strings? And Mrs Salz and her uncle were awfully kind. I mean you didn't have to go to the aid of that Russian iceberg, Sobeleva, and if I hadn't found Mrs Salz and her uncle, I'd probably have been kidnapped and sold off in the Polish white slave traffic or something.'

Mr Harrison laughed. 'Don't be such an ass, old girl.'

'And she does speak the most perfect English. And she does think England the best country in the world. And I did promise I'd help her.' She fought back tears.

'All right, old girl, don't take on so. I'll have a word with Tubby in the morning.'

Two weeeks later, Eva received a letter from the British Embassy which cleared the path of red tape and official forms. They could leave for England whenever they wished.

Eva kept her plans secret from Adam. She wanted to present him with a *fait accompli*. When the letter from the Embassy arrived, he recognised the crest on the envelope and naturally wanted an explanation. Before she had time to discover its contents, Eva was pressed into translating the favourable reply. At first, Adam was too bewildered to react. He exercised his fingers on his thigh for almost a minute and then burst into an angry reproach, castigating Eva for not letting him in on her machinations. When he left to do his rounds of the city he barely kissed her goodbye, but on his return that evening was less embattled. All he wanted, he said, was to discuss what would, after all, be the biggest decision either of them had ever made.

His objections were chiefly linguistic. He had half a dozen words of English and so demanded to know how he was expected to make a living without being able to communicate his simplest needs. Eva had prepared her arguments carefully and began by suggesting she could teach him the rudiments of the language. Once in the country she was certain he'd improve rapidly. Furthermore, she said, the haberdashery company who employed him as their Warsaw representative imported a good many items from England and surely he could obtain a letter of recommendation to one of their London associates. Last but not least, ostrich feathers, the most lucrative commodity in his sample case, were mainly channelled through London to all the capitals of Europe. Was there not a commercial opportunity in that department?'

Although he did not want to relent too quickly, Adam was almost instantly won over by the ostrich feather argument. It took his fancy to think of himself as a supplier rather than a tradesman, and he had visions of independence, of striking out on his own and, of course, making a fortune. But the impending upheaval only served to increase his internal alarm which was ordinarily activated by less momentous concerns. He agreed to his wife's schemes but spent his days before their departure in a see-saw state of excitation, feverish misgivings and of muttering, 'I do not want to be disturbed,' and 'There is nothing so terrible as an empty pay packet.'

For Eva, the most painful wrench was from Uncle Max. 'Why do you want to leave?' he said helplessly. 'Why? Why?' Eva avoided the truth. She did not tell him her real reasons which were entirely subjective. Had she confessed her profound sense of isolation, her conviction that she felt she no longer belonged in this society, she knew she would hurt him irreparably, for he was bound to misinterpret, bound to take the explanation as a personal insult. Would he not have argued, 'But I'm here, we're family, you belong?' She did not know if she had the strength to be implacable in the face of emotional blackmail.

She put the blame on Adam and on his fear of renewed Polish anti-Semitism. 'And he has every right to be afraid,' she said. 'They dismissed me from the University, for God's sake, and that's only the beginning.'

'Go to Palestine, then,' Max countered. 'Why England? Why?'

Again she used her husband as the obstacle. Adam flatly refused, she said, to settle in Palestine but, of course, the real reason was her own ambivalence. She had over the weeks refined her rationale. Her Zionism, the notion of a Jewish State, while passionately felt and believed in, was somehow an ideal to be achieved for others, for those who genuinely needed to escape persecution. Like many crusaders, Eva loved the cause more than the individuals it was intended to serve. As a matter of fact, individuals hardly came into it which is why she was able to be unsentimental and combative. She viewed Zionism as the means to rescue not people she knew, not people like herself or Adam, but rather an abstract mass of suffering humanity. This absolved her from what she regarded as martyrdom. Besides, she told herself, she did not have a pioneering spirit but, perhaps, at some future date she would reconsider. This was nothing more nor less than the cant of self-deception. Her cultural ties to Europe were too strong to contemplate a severance which would be immutable and final. Eva, for all her cleverness, was driven by the universal human motive of wanting it every which way.

Miss Krantnik summed up the parting in one of her last letters to her cousin in Peoria:

Eva and Adam Salz left for London yesterday. Mr Ehrlich went to the railway station to see them off. He wore black as though he were in mourning. When he returned he looked completely drained and retired to the back room where I heard him sobbing. Poor, poor man. Mrs Salz is a strange woman and not easy to know. Her manner intimidates me. She is always so self-confident and a little condescending. She has emigrated because she fears a new wave of anti-Semitism. It is true she was sacked from her university post like other Jewish professors but surely that in itself is not an augury of persecution? I am not sure that I shall miss her.

Mr Ehrlich may be desolate for the moment but I know he will soon be over it and I hope to be of some help to him in healing his pain.

If Tatiana Sobeleva was at her most content in the stillness of Sobliki, then Eva was happiest in movement. The train journey across Europe was a constant pleasure. On the second night, while Adam slept, she first felt her baby kick. She lay in the dark of the couchette, rocked gently by the speeding train, and accounted the awareness of life within her a splendid omen. Each time the train stopped, she peeped out of the curtained window, saw the names of unknown towns and villages and then lay back, filled with excitement. Warsaw was fast becoming like a dream she could no longer remember.

'How d'you say this, then? S-a-l-z?'

'Salz,' Adam said as distinctly as possible.

'What's it mean?'

Eva explained in her precise English. 'It means, literally, salt. It is German although we are Polish.'

'Right. Well, from now on, forget the ruddy z, we don't have names in English ending with z, you're Salt, plain and simple and not S-a-l-z. Next!'

Thus was the family renamed by an unknown English immigration officer in a shed in the port of Harwich. Adam was outraged and objected loudly but Eva calmed him down, for she secretly welcomed the change. It felt as though she had been made the gift of something she long craved: a new identity, an almost English identity.

The newly named Salts arrived in England at dawn on 22 March 1912. By late afternoon they were crossing London in a taxi which set them down at Mrs Figg's boarding house in Stepney, an address Eva had been given by Dr Chaim Shapiro, her fellow-academic who suffered suspension from the English faculty. He had stayed with Mrs Figg while researching his biography of Charles Dickens. Two days later, the couple were in rented furnished rooms.

London was a noisy, chaotic, civilised glory. It made Warsaw seem like a village. Eva did not notice the squalour of the tightly packed houses, the lack of running water, the incessant noise, the unbearable humidity, the stench in the streets. Friends had warned her that London was the most dangerous city in the world but she never once felt threatened. On the contrary, the kindness and humour of neighbours, not all Jews, made her feel at home. She liked being called 'ducks' or 'ducky' and she quickly made friends and found her feet. Mr and Mrs Antisorski, who lived above them, took a particular interest. Mrs Antisorski, mother of five, recommended Dr Kantor to look after Eva when her time came. 'A first-class man, perhaps the finest doctor in all London town,' she said. 'With this man I trust my life.'

At Mr Antisorski's suggestion, Eva put cards up in the display cases outside newsagents offering to teach Poles English. Mr Antisorski was her first pupil. Within a week she had half a dozen more. Her belly grew apace, her complexion took on a healthy glow and, for the first time in years, Eva knew contentment.

Adam also took to London or, as he liked to say, London took to him. He had brought with him two letters of introduction, both to importers of ostrich feathers. The first had gone out of business. The second was James MacCleod of D. D. Graham & Sons, but when Adam presented the letter he was told Mr MacCleod had recently died. However, Alistair Graham, the present head of the firm, asked if he was able to translate letters from German and Polish into English. Adam, whose English could not have inspired much confidence, said that he was more than able and Mr Graham, perhaps out of kindness, employed him on a part-time basis at threepence a letter.

Each day, Adam reported at the offices of D. D. Graham & Sons. If there were letters from abroad, the Chief Clerk would hand them over, and Adam would then hurry to the Warsaw restaurant at 32 Osborn Street in Whitechapel, a kosher eating-place. There, he would consume countless glasses of lemon tea, buy lunch for less than a shilling and find someone who knew the appropriate tongue to help him with the translation. (It was, incidentally, an infamous establishment, for in 1911, the owner, Leon Beron had been murdered by one of his customers, Steinie Morrison, who was still serving a life sentence in Dartmoor.) Once the text had been rendered into rough English, Adam trotted home to Eva so that she could check the grammar and spelling before delivering the final version to the Chief Clerk. It was a satisfactory arrangement for both parties and, after a month or so, the Chief Clerk employed Adam on a regular basis as a filing clerk.

The Salts were happy. In late June, Dr Kantor delivered their baby, a boy, whom they named George, for George Eliot, Maximilian, for Uncle Max, and Harrison, for their benefactors. George Maximilian Harrison Salt weighed eight pounds four ounces, refused to sleep when requested and his parents doted on him. Eva prayed that one day he would go to Eton.

3

'Ich habe, du hast, er hat, wir haben, ihr habt, sie haben.'

Stepan Kessler performed his obligatory Saturday morning chore. Spring, 1913, Moscow. Stepan, now aged seven, was at the dining-room table with his father, Stepan Senior. The boy chanted, declining a German irregular verb. For the past six months his father had insisted on him having a weekly German lesson and Stepan was not doing too badly. 'You cannot start learning a language early enough,' Kessler was fond of saying. 'After all, you begin to learn your first language the moment you are born.' He was pleased with his son's progress, for Stepan displayed a gift for languages which was due mainly to his self-confidence and the fact that he did not mind making a fool of himself. He was bright, outgoing, vigorous and energetic.

Although Kessler had always intended to teach his son German, the need for tuition became more immediate because of a letter from a cousin, Karl Lohmeyer of Chemnitz in Germany. Lohmeyer, like Kessler, was also in the textile trade, and planned a visit to Moscow with his wife, Liselotte, and their son, nine-year-old Willi. The trip was to combine work and pleasure, for Lohmeyer and Kessler had close business connections.

In July the Lohmeyers arrived. Karl Lohmeyer was correct, formal and spotlessly clean. Stepan once watched him scrub his hands and nails with such gusto that he wondered why the man didn't bleed. He changed his collars twice a day and doused his top pocket-handker-chief in *kölnischwasser*. Liselotte was also somewhat stiff but more animated than her husband. She enjoyed gossip provided it dealt with moral indiscretion, for she liked best of all to disapprove. The centre of her life was her son, Willi, upon whom she doted. Both Lohmeyers were deeply religious and, each evening, at Willi's bedtime they knelt with him by his bed and said their prayers.

Willi, although two years older than Stepan, had a babyish quality which made the age difference irrelevant. He was always neatly, not to say daintily, dressed. He was, after all, an only child. Stepan's mother, Anya, was of the opinion that Willi was effeminate but she kept the thought to herself.

In the late afternoon of the Lohmeyers' arrival, the two boys were playing in the upstairs nursery with young Shura Kessler, taking the first awkward steps towards friendship, when they were all summoned to the drawing-room. Willi said, 'I know what's going to happen now.'

'What?' Stepan asked.

'You'll see.'

What happened was that Willi was put on show. He was, his parents claimed, a musical genius and would now display his talents to his hosts. Five instruments were produced, a violin, a drum, a penny-whistle, cymbals and a trumpet. These were arranged on a table. '*Ein, zwei, drei!*' from Liselotte and Willi set off like a frenzied hare playing on the five instruments the German national anthem, '*Heil dir im Siegerkranz*', which has the same tune as 'God Save the King'. He produced the first phrase on the violin, then banged the drum, moved on to the penny-whistle, clashed the cymbals and finished with a flourish on the trumpet. The sounds were excruciating. The Kesslers, especially the boys, watched with wide-eyed astonishment. The Lohmeyers radiated pride. Anya, foolishly she later realised, applauded and cried, 'Bravo!' which Willi took as his cue for an encore. He went through the whole agonising performance once again. This was too much for little Shura who began to giggle. His giggle was infectious and set Stepan off. Steely parental glares could not still them. Stepan rose from the floor and began to stagger about the room, near to hysteria. He ignored a sharply hissed reproach from his father. Willi played on unperturbed. Then, out of control, Stepan grabbed the violin, tucked it under his chin, picked up the bow and played almost faultlessly the Tsarist national anthem. It was the first time he had been near a violin in his life. The silence which followed was more deafening than the music.

'Do that again,' Willi said, staring at his cousin in wonder. Stepan obliged and once more played the anthem even more expertly than the first time and with a sweetness of tone that was beguiling to all but the Lohmeyers.

Dinner that evening was a desultory affair. With the children in bed the four adults sat round the table struggling to find topics of mutual interest, for they were all preoccupied in various ways with the thought that Stepan Kessler showed a musical gift which eclipsed the much-vaunted talents of Willi Lohmeyer.

That night, in their bedroom, Anya said, 'It was all very unfortunate. We should have stopped him.'

'Yes,' her husband replied. 'Stepan is a very exuberant boy. He will need controlling.'

'Nonsense. He is full of life and that's all that matters.'

'I have a feeling Karl and Liselotte and Willi will not stay as long as they intended.'

He was right. On a pretext, they cut short their visit and returned to Chemnitz. After they were gone, Stepan pleaded for a violin of his own and his entreaties were answered. Lessons were arranged and, after six months, the teacher informed Anya that the boy needed a more expert tutor. Enquiries were made and Anya discovered that, in the neighbourhood, lived Valentin Manishowitz, the distinguished virtuoso, now retired but who gave occasional lessons. After listening to Stepan, Manishowitz declared, 'Yes, this boy is good. Just how good I'm not sure, but we'll find out. Music could be his career.' Twice a week, Stepan presented himself to Manishowitz, proved a conscientious and inspired pupil, and was inflamed with the idea of becoming a world-famous musician.

4

Laban the Idiot was in love. It was the first time he had known such overwhelming passion which he both blessed and cursed. He blessed the variety and incongruity of his emotions. In his loved one's presence, his self-esteem and virility were invigorated, and he experienced delicious sensations of drowning and delirium; separated from her, he encountered unfamiliar anguish, anxiety, longing, desperation; all of these he blessed. What he cursed was his realisation that he was no longer in control of his life, that here was a fate, like death, impossible to change.

Madame Europa Altona returned Laban's love. It was not, of course, the first time she had been pierced by what she liked to call 'Cupid's male member', but she was certain that this was the first time her feelings were genuine. During the night of Laban's vigil beside Karin's body, she had entered the room often, bringing him sweetmeats to accompany his schnapps. At dawn, when the undertaker came to remove the dead girl, she asked how much she must pay Laban for his night's work. He hesitated and in that careless moment his future was settled. She caught the sparkle in his eye, a look both searching and suppliant. She answered by opening her mouth a little, as though catching her breath, then smiled, narrowing her eyes, sensual, seductive, welcoming eyes. They made love all that morning and missed Karin's funeral.

He taught her the Yiddish word for fornicator which is *yentzer* and the Ionian synonym, *shligalicker*. He made himself useful around the house, fulfilling the duties of caretaker and strong-arm man. He was popular with the girls but careful not to look at them too longingly, for Europa had a jealous nature and a vicious temper. When one of the whores said Laban was a pimp, Europa cracked her hard aross the face and called her a lying bitch. Strictly speaking Europa was right: although Laban was not a pimp it was undeniable that, because of Europa's possessiveness, he did live off her immoral earnings. She was generous with money, clothes, books and cigarettes. She insisted he give up being a *nakhtwachter* and demanded that he move into her apartment at the top of the house. He obliged but did not tell his brothers or, indeed, anyone else, for there was no need. His nightly absence from his hostel bed needed no alibi. But Benjamin glimpsed him once in the street wearing a pearl-grey suit, a matching bowler, a cerise polka-dot cravat and demanded an explanation. 'A widow,' Laban said, 'wanted me to have the last suit of clothes her poor husband bought but never wore. *Nu.*'

No one suspected his secret life, but on two occasions he took Isaiah to meet his paramour because he longed to show her off to someone, to share his pride in her. He swore the boy to secrecy. Isaiah thought Constanta Stoica more alluring – but then, of course, he had seen her naked – yet he could not deny that Europa had style and warmth; no one had ever fussed over him so much, or plied him with so many pastries and chocolates.

Within a month after entering into this liaison with a brothel-keeper, Laban's dream of America receded like a ship sailing into a heavy mist. 'I used to think we could make fate our servant,' he said to Isaiah. 'But beware. I was wrong.'

A fog enveloped Isaiah's father, Solomon, a fog of despair and hopelessness. He trudged the streets of the city weighed down not only by the sandwich-board around his neck but also by the depression that was now his constant, unwanted companion. From morning until night his entire being wept.

Each evening, after his work was done, he and Leah met in Finkelstein's restaurant where their elder boys were now permanently employed as kitchen porters. There, husband and wife drank hot lemon tea, each holding the glasses in both hands for warmth. Somewhere in Herr Finkelstein's bloated body, beneath his desperate and often brutal manner, there must have lurked a human heart, for he never charged them. Every day Leah offered to pay, and every day Finkelstein opened his arms as though prepared for crucifixion and said, 'A robber of the poor I am not!' It was his way of concealing his generosity.

There was no particular moment when Leah realised just how ill her husband was. The effect was cumulative, a growing recognition which probably occurred at the same pace as Solomon's despair deepened. These daily meetings, which were meant to be family progress reports and serious discussions of their future plans, degenerated into Solomon shedding tears and moaning, 'We'll never get to America, never, never, never, I feel it in my bones, I don't want to carry sandwich-boards all my life, I need air, I hate it here,' and Leah would pat his hand gently and repeatedly, saying, Solchik, Solchik, Solchik.

It came to Leah that she must obey Laban's dictum decreeing fate can be confronted and changed. This was ironic in view of the fact that

Laban now took precisely the opposite point of view. He'd resigned himself to being a passive victim who had been bewitched. Not Leah. She could no longer bear Solomon's misery. She made up her mind to ask one of her bachelor clients, the shipping clerk, Ludwig Kahn, for help.

Usually, she called on him around eight o'clock in the morning, just as he was about to descend to his office beneath his rooms. But on this day, a Thursday, she changed her routine and decided to deliver and collect in the late afternoon when he would have finished work; this, she reasoned, would offer the opportunity to ask his advice and allow him the time to give it.

It was already dark when she crossed the city in a persistent drizzle. People were scurrying home, swathed in cloaks, hats pulled low, huddled under umbrellas. Carrying in a wicker basket Kahn's crisply ironed laundry, she was half-way up the stairs to his rooms when she heard angry voices, a door slam, and the sound of a woman crying.

Then, Kahn's voice, 'Come back, don't be silly, I didn't mean it—'

Leah paused and just then, into view round the bend of the staircase, came Katarina Bronstein, obviously and deeply distressed, buttoning up her bodice. Seeing Leah, she stopped dead, cried out, 'Oh my God!' and hurried past. Leah turned to continue up the stairs but saw Kahn himself on the landing, in his dressing-gown, his face lopsided in a crooked, apologetic smile. 'This isn't your usual time, Leah,' he said severely. 'Don't do it again. It doesn't suit me. Just give me my laundry and go.'

'But I want to talk to you,' Leah said.

A moment that changes lives. It rushed into Kahn's mind that his washerwoman meant to blackmail him. He said, 'How much do you want? I'm not a rich man.'

'What are you talking about?' Leah demanded. 'I want what you owe me for your washing, that's all. What else should I want? I don't care what you get up to, but don't you worry, I've noticed the stains on the sheets, I'm not blind, and they're hard to get out, believe me.'

He recoiled as though physically assaulted. He said, 'Why do you want to talk to me?'

'I need advice,' Leah replied.

Even then, Kahn's suspicions were not allayed. Something in her manner, her determination, made him mistrust her. 'You mean money, say it, say it, you mean money not advice, you mean money!' and he banged the banister with his fist.

'Herr Kahn, calm down,' Leah said plaintively. 'I need advice. I give you my word. Only advice. Please.'

He was rigid for a moment, still trying to decide her true motives. Finally, with a furtive gesture he beckoned her to follow him into his cramped, dimly lit hallway.

'What is it? Be quick, I'm going out shortly,' he said uneasily, fidgeting with the cord of his dressing-gown.

She began by describing Solomon's state of mind and the difficulty with the American quota, but she could see Kahn wasn't really listening although he nodded impatiently from time to time. 'I think we should give America a miss,' she said. 'Maybe it's not meant for us to go to America. Tell me, Herr Kahn, please, you know the ships. Where else can we go? There must be other places where we can make a life. Isn't there a ship going somewhere, anywhere in the whole wide world that will carry us out of our misery? Help us, Herr Kahn, I beg you.'

'Why not stay here in Hamburg?' he said brusquely, but the moment he'd made the suggestion he realised how unintelligent it was. Leah, from now on, would always be an embarrassing, not to say dangerous, presence. Better to be rid of her, easier than sacking her, think of somewhere she could go. 'Or Berlin,' he said.

'No, Herr Kahn, cities don't like my Solchik and my Solchik don't like cities. There are no opportunities for a woodcutter. He misses the outdoors. He needs to make a new life, that's what he's set his heart on. He needs to start again. Are there other places?'

'Of course there are other places,' he said impatiently.

'Tell me, I beg you.'

'There's Australia or South Africa,' he said. 'Lots of Jews are going to South Africa.'

Leah nodded. 'Yes,' she said. 'Families from Ploemyan, that's where we're from, they went to South Africa. They've got open spaces there?'

'Certainly. It's all one big open space,' Kahn said.

'Where is it exactly?' Leah asked.

'Six thousand miles away,' he answered, and the enormous distance comforted him.

'Australia I heard of, too. The woman who did your washing before me—'

'Dora—'

'Yes, Dora, she went to Australia. But South Africa has people from Ploemyan there,' Leah muttered, weighing the choices.

'South Africa, yes, it's a wonderful country, a new, young country, the streets are paved with gold, the sun shines every day, it's a land flowing in milk and honey.' His enthusiasm was too forced, his manner too urgent.

'They've got forests there?'

'Forests? They've got more trees than you can count. You'd have a wonderful life there, Leah. You'd have servants in South Africa, you'd have other people to do the washing for you—'

'How can I afford servants? I can't afford to stay in the same house as my Solchik.'

'I'm telling you, Leah, even poor Jews can afford servants in South Africa, they have black people there, *schwarzes* there who do nothing else but work as servants. And they want white people just now. Yes, I think you should go to South Africa. I'll give you an address of a friend of mine, Herr Adolf Wassermann, I've got his card somewhere—' and he was already on the move, darting into one of the rooms, but calling to her, 'He's a shipping man like myself, he knows all about South Africa—' and he returned with his dirty washing wrapped in a sheet and Adolf Wassermann's visiting card.

'Six thousand miles,' she said sadly. 'It sounds you'd have to pay a lot to travel six thousand miles.'

Kahn stiffened. 'I knew you wanted money,' he said.

Leah's eyes half-closed with pain. 'Don't insult me, please, Herr Kahn. Life is hard enough as it is.'

The next day, Friday, in the afternoon, after his morning Hebrew lesson, Isaiah was in the men's hostel, in the room with rickety wooden tables and chairs where they ate and passed the time of day. Some of the Pasym men were just finishing a game of cards and set off for the synagogue, the *schul*. Left alone, Isaiah sat in a corner, his back to the door, struggling with his bar mitzvah portion without the vowels, '*nd th Lrd sd nt Mss, Yt wll brng n plg mr pn Phrh, nd pn gpt: ftrwrds h wll lt y g hnc.*' He heard a cough. He turned. A white-haired man, clothed in black, had entered, hat in hand, and stood gazing at him with a sad, sickly smile. 'I'm looking for Solomon Wildnowitz,' he said. 'The sandwich-board man.'

'He's my father. He's at work,' Isaiah said. He was made uneasy by the visitor's gentleness.

'What time will he return?'

'Not till later. It's Friday night. He'll go to *schul* first, I'll meet him there, and my uncles, and then we'll all come back here for the *shabbas* meal. My mother should be here soon to light the candles and do the cooking. I'm just about to go—'

The man slapped his forehead. 'Friday night, of course! How stupid of me!' he said and sounded as if he meant to leave. But he remained in the doorway for a moment, then slid into the chair opposite Isaiah. 'I am Pastor Naupert,' he said. 'I know your father. I promised to visit him. I'm from the Society for the Conversion of the Jews.'

114

Isaiah said nothing, just stared at Naupert, waiting for him to continue.

The pastor thrust his head forward and said softly, almost a whisper, 'Do you know who Jesus is?'

'No,' Isaiah replied although he had heard the name but no more than that.

'Jesus was a Jew. Like you. But He was the Son of God.'

Isaiah made no comment. A voice told him he shouldn't be listening to this man.

'And do you know what happened to Jesus?' Isaiah shook his head. 'Other Jews killed him. Wasn't that wicked of them? Yes, Jews killed the Son of God. Now, you wouldn't do such a thing, would you?'

Isaiah, by dint of his continuing silence, appeared non-committal.

'Of course, you wouldn't. But that's what the Jews did. They gave Jesus Christ, the Son of God, our Saviour, to the Romans and the Romans crucified him. Do you know what crucifixion is?'

'No.'

'They nailed Jesus to a cross. Drove nails into His hands and feet. The blood poured from Him and His agony was great. That's what the Jews made the Romans do. And do you know why? They hoped to kill Jesus Christ. But, He was, as I have said, the Son of God and so He didn't die. Do you know what He did? Three days after He was crucified, He rose from the dead. And you, young man, will, when your time comes, also rise from the dead if you believe in our Lord Jesus Christ and make amends for all those Jews who murdered Him. I want you to kneel down with me and pray to Jesus Christ and ask His forgiveness. Will you do that?' Naupert slipped noiselessly to his knees. 'Come along,' he said. 'Join me. Put your hands together like this. Do as I tell you, boy.'

Isaiah knelt.

'Put your hands like this,' Naupert commanded, pressing his own hands together in prayer, 'and say after me, "O Lord Jesus Christ—"'

'What are you doing? Get up, get up at once!'

Leah had entered the room carrying a grease-stained brown paper bag containing food for the Sabbath meal. Isaiah, relieved at seeing her, ran to her and held her hand tightly.

'Is this your mother—?'

'Never mind who I am,' Leah said, advancing on Naupert. 'I want to know who you are—'

'Pastor Naupert of the Society for the Conversion of the Jews.' He remained on his knees and smiled his unctuous smile.

'For what? For what of the Jews? For what? For what? For what of the Jews?' Although she did not know the meaning of the word conversion, Leah's instincts rose up and screamed. She pushed Isaiah aside. Consternation burst out of her. 'How dare you make my son kneel? Jews don't kneel! How dare you! You *gonif!*' which means, among other things, thief, crook, no-goodnik. Out of control, she swung the brown paper bag aiming for Naupert's head. To avoid the blow, he scurried away on his knees like a clown playing for a cheap laugh. Leah pursued him. 'Get out from this house,' she yelled, once more swinging the bag, and this time grazing the back of his neck.

Stung, Naupert managed to get to his feet, found his hat, turned on her and was about to remonstrate when Leah advanced on him growling like a savage animal. Naupert fled.

Leah went to the window to look out and make certain of his departure. Isaiah, terrified, watched her. After a while, she turned to him and said, 'The *goyim* hate us, oh my, do they hate us. But, why? Why?' Then, she added, 'Don't mention this to your father. It'll only make him cry. And don't tell anyone else either. I want everybody peaceful and calm this evening. Now, go to *schul*. You'll be late.'

When the men returned from the synagogue, Leah and a couple of Pasym women had lit candles, said the blessings, making mysterious passes over the flames and then covering their eyes with their hands. Three individual tables had been laid, the largest with seven places for the Wildnowitz family. Only a handful of Pasym Jews remained in the hostel, presumably because many of the others had enough money to afford better accommodation.

To preserve the fiction that he was still a *nakhtwachter*, Laban attended the services in the synagogue on Friday nights and Saturday mornings, and Friday night was the one night he slept in the hostel. He donned his oldest clothes and his most battered hat to pray beside his brothers and nephews. For all his mistrust of Jehovah, he rather liked the rituals and the traditions, was warmed and comforted by them and, although he would never admit it publicly, knew they helped him live from one day to the next. In this he was no different from a multitude of Jews around the globe.

There is a school of thought which teaches that the miracles reported in the Pentateuch have a scientific or logical explanation which is why, as science and logic have become the dominant faiths, miracles are no longer reported. That school of thought would have been exploded had its adherents been present in the men's hostel on that Friday night in late November. If not by a miracle how else did Leah manage to serve *gefilte* fish, chicken soup with dumplings called *knaydlak*, the horseradish, and *tsimmes*, which is a dish of mashed and sweetened carrots? How else can the chopped liver, celery, radish and olives be explained? And if not by a miracle how could she afford apples to purée for dessert? But all these traditional delicacies Leah provided and her menfolk ate. And the two Pasym women worked similar miracles.

After the meal, over the glasses of lemon tea, Leah watched and waited. Laban was telling the story of a widower who tore his hair out over the corpse of his wife, threw himself into her grave, had to be dragged screaming from the cemetery and yet, within a week, remarried. The men smiled and nodded wisely. The boys sniggered. An amused, contented silence ensued. Leah pounced.

'I think we should forget America,' she said. All eyes turned on her. 'One, there's the quota. Two, how long can we live like this? Three, Solchik needs a change of air.'

Benjamin said, 'Not go to America? Where else should we go?'

'South Africa,' she said and repeated much of what Ludwig Kahn had said to her. She told them of sunshine and servants and streets paved with gold. But she had new and important information to add. That very afternoon she had been to see Adolf Wassermann, an expert, a specialist in South Africa, and his man had informed her there were berths on a ship sailing in two weeks' time. This was not all. The South African government gave financial assistance to those wishing to emigrate, Jews and gentiles alike, so long as they were white-skinned. 'We're white-skinned,' Leah said. 'We should go.'

Benjamin said, 'Financial assistance, yes, but that means we have to have some money, they're not going to pay the whole trip—'

'We'll find the money!' Leah said. 'We'll beg, borrow, steal, work twice as hard—'

'Find the money in two weeks? It's not possible, Leah,' Laban said, trying to sound reasonable. 'You know what you are, Leah? A *meshuggeneh*!' which means one who is crazy, mad, absurd.

The argument erupted, as she knew it would, with angry recriminations and accusations.

'You've lost your mind' from Benjamin.

'Not go to America?' from Laban.

'Where is this place South Africa, just tell me where it is?' from Solomon who began to cry almost immediately and through his tears added, 'Isn't that where the Horowitzs went and were never heard from again?'

'Not only the Horowitzs,' Benjamin said and began to list the names of Jewish families from Ploemyan who had sailed into the southern hemisphere.

The Pasym Jews fell silent and listened, for the Wildnowitz clan did not know the meaning of discretion or of civilised discourse. They raised their voices to fever pitch, ignored arguments that contradicted their own points of view, and shouted and shouted and shouted. In the end, Leah banged the table with her fist so that the candlesticks trembled and the flames danced. 'I'm telling you now once and for all: Solkchik, the boys and I are going to South Africa. We've made our decision,' she said.

'You're breaking up the family, Leah,' Benjamin warned, wagging a finger.

'It's better than breaking Solchik's heart,' she countered.

'I'm staying here,' Laban said, 'until the boat sails for New York. That's my dream, that's my fate.' But he was lying and knew it.

'Please yourselves. It's your lives. You do what you like. But I'm not going to allow Solchik to die of misery in a hostel in Hamburg. Finished. Final. Good *shabbas*. Goodnight.'

Isaiah did not sleep easily and was prey to nightmares. In the most terrifying, from which he woke screaming, Pastor Naupert drove nails through his hands and feet and made him drink his own blood. Europa said, 'He's a good man, do what he says,' and Isaiah was again in his coffin, rising through the lid, hovering over the earth at a great height until, like a punctured balloon, he swooped and plunged headlong towards the ground.

'Ssh! Wake up! Don't make such a noise, what's the matter?' Laban asked. He sat on Isaiah's bed mopping the sweat from the boy's brow.

'I had a terrible dream, Uncle Laban.'

'Don't tell me, please,' Laban whispered. 'Only one thing scares me in this life and that's a bad dream. You know why? I'm frightened to death it could come true.'

'I dreamed—'

'Don't tell me, I beg you, Isaiah. You want to get rid of a bad dream, write it down. It's an old tradition. My father, your grandfather taught me. All poets do it. That's how we write poetry. We simply write down our bad dreams.'

'But it's Friday night, Uncle Laban, you're not supposed to write on the *shabbas*.'

'For a bad dream, break the rules.'

Isaiah took his uncle's advice and scribbled down the fast-fading memory of the dream. But it did not help him sleep. He hid his head under the blanket, fearful that Pastor Naupert would tiptoe into the room with a hammer and nails.

Katarina Bronstein was waiting for Leah at the women's hostel. Leah returned with the two Pasym women and saw her the moment they turned up the gaslight just inside the front door.

'I'd like to see Leah alone,' Katarina said. The Pasym women hurried away to the kitchen at the back of the house.

Katarina at first avoided Leah's eyes. She played with her handbag, opening and shutting the clasp. At last, she looked up. Her gaze was unusually steady. She said, 'I'm sorry about what happened yesterday—'

'Please, don't, Mrs Bronstein, please, not another word. It's your life. It's none of my business.'

'I feel so ashamed.'

'*Nu*, what can I say?'

'Mr Bronstein isn't an easy man to live with.'

'I understand, no man is easy to live with—'

'But Mr Kahn is kind and—'

'Yes, yes, I know. A very kind man, Mr Kahn, very kind indeed.'

Without warning, Katarina once more opened her handbag, took out an envelope, thrust it into Leah's hands and ran out into the night. It happened too quickly for Leah to protest. When the sound of Katarina's footsteps receded, Leah opened the envelope. It was stuffed with paper money, more money than she had ever seen. There was a handwritten sentence on blue writing-paper but she could not understand it. She hid the money in her bodice and joined the Pasym women in the kitchen. 'Can you read this?' she asked.

One of them took the piece of paper and read: 'South Africa is a beautiful country.' And that was all.

Two weeks later, on 8 December 1912, Leah and Solomon Wild-nowitz, their three sons Julius, Baruch and Isaiah, set sail aboard the *Southern Cross* for Cape Town which they pronounced Kep Tovn. Benjamin and Laban stood on the quayside and waved them farewell. The parting had been an agony for all concerned.

Benjamin's decision not to make the journey arose out of his perversity, his innate contrariness, and a closed mind. Once he had set his heart on America, nothing, except natural disaster, could alter the course he had planned. The very fact that others were more flexible served only to make him more obstinate. No amount of pleading or cajoling could shift him. After days and nights of turbulent debate, Leah said, 'It's your decision. We're going. You're staying. That's how it is.'

'I'm not staying,' Benjamin said. 'I'm waiting. I'm waiting for passage to America.'

Laban used the same argument but, as only Isaiah knew or guessed, for very different motives. Because he had been the one who first invented the family's American dream, his insistence on remaining in Hamburg was more readily accepted. He took Isaiah aside, hugged him fiercely, and said, 'Remember all I told you and your life will be a bed of roses. Remember especially that where a man lives inside himself is the most important address in the world.'

5

Tatiana's fourth child was born in the early hours of a freezing January morning in 1914. A servant was despatched to the railway station where the clerk on duty tapped out a telegram to Dr Volkov in Tula requesting that he come to Sobliki as quickly as possible. As a precaution, the servant was also instructed to wake Old Matriona, the midwife, and bring her as quickly as possible to the house. It was just as well. Old Matriona reached Tatiana's bedside with only minutes to spare. The baby, a girl, came hurtling into the world as though unable to bear the suspense of waiting any longer. The doctor arrived in time for lunch. By then, father and grandfather had inspected the newest Sobelev and expressed their joy. Count Boris, of course, wept. Xenia, Darya and Vladimir, who was now inevitably known as Valodya, were allowed in to see her. It was decided that the child should be named Iliena.

Her birth caused Count Boris particular excitement because it meant he could add her name to the family tree, a scroll kept in a silver tube fashioned by the Moscow jeweller, Serge Cabrol, a former employee of the great Peter Carl Fabergé. The night after the birth Count Boris cleared his desk and spread the parchment, anchoring the four corners with icons. He cleaned his eraser, sharpened his pencils and laid them out neatly to one side. He rubbed his hands with anticipation. While Pavlik, the steward, prepared the samovar, Count Boris said, 'I have decided to redraw the last few generations. I shall begin with my great-grandfather and work down until I have added little Iliena Lvovna.'

'Whatever you say, Boris Borisovich.'

'I do not want to be disturbed.'

'You must eat, Boris Borisovich.'

'Well, of course, I must eat. I'm not going to work at meal times. I shall work at night.'

'And what about sleep, Boris Borisovich? A man of your age needs sleep.'

'A man of my age needs very little sleep.'

'We're more or less the same age, Boris Borisovich, and I need a lot of sleep.'

'My dear friend, will you please stop fussing over me like a nanny? You may need sleep, I do not need sleep, that is how the world is. Now, please, leave me in peace. I have an important task to perform.'

Pavlik shrugged, shook his head, and withdrew. In the morning, he knocked gently on the study door but received no reply. He entered and drew the curtains. Count Boris's forehead rested on the desk.

'Well, well, well,' Pavlik sang with icy satisfaction. 'I thought you said you didn't need sleep, Boris Borisovich. No, no, don't explain. I know, you've only closed your eyes and you're thinking. Yes, yes, I know. Come along, now, it's seven o'clock.'

But Count Boris didn't respond. The pencils at his right hand had not been touched. Iliena Lvovna's name had not been added to the tree whose roots began with Catherine II's illegitimate offspring.

Count Boris was interred in the family mausoleum at Sobliki. He was laid in an open coffin, his family, friends, retainers and many inhabitants of the town filed past to gaze on his untroubled face. The coffin was sealed. The priest, Father Astasi, who had a splendid bass voice, sang the glorious Orthodox liturgy. The heavy stone flags in the mausoleum were lifted and Count Boris was lowered into the crypt.

The birth of Iliena and the death of Count Boris were the two most important events in the Sobelev household for many a year. The Tsar's foolhardy and disastrous adventure against the Japanese, his defeat at Port Arthur, the political agitations from one end of the empire to the other, barely ruffled the peace of Sobliki.

Maria Obrunina wrote a long letter to Tatiana to congratulate and condole: 'A birth and a death in so short a space of time seems to epitomise the very essence of what it means to be Russian. I sometimes think that God treats us with unnecessary cruelty.' And on the last page: 'My cousin, Fedor, who works in the Foreign Ministry, is in a state of constant depression. He says that mighty and destructive forces are being marshalled, indeed, are poised to strike. My father disagrees vehemently, but I can't help siding with Fedor. God help us all.'

Tatiana replied: 'I suppose we could be accused of indifference. We are insulated from the world here at Sobliki. And what in the order of things can rival the birth of a child and the death of an old man?'

The Sobelevs mourned Count Boris and rejoiced in their children. Tatiana and Lev decided not to move out of The Annex into the big house which would in future be used for guests and entertaining. Lev developed a persistent backache which Dr Volkov was unable to diagnose or cure, but because of Lev's condition, Volkov visited the house often in the spring of 1914. He was a likeable, hard-working man who drank a little too much but who was genuinely concerned for the well-being of his patients, rich and poor. Tatiana enjoyed his company. He once happened to remark that what the young women of Sobliki badly needed was instruction during pregnancy and assistance after their babies were born. Tatiana decided, with the doctor's encouragement and help, to open a clinic in one of the disused barns near the stables. Once a week, women from the village trooped up the hill to listen to lectures and partake in practical demonstrations. The clinic was accounted a success.

There was little affectation in the Sobelev household; their style was never ostentatious. Among themselves the family conversed in French but talked in Russian to the servants. Miss McMurray, Muck to the children, sang Scottish lullabies to Iliena, taught the other children English and arithmetic, and secretly kept the servants in order. Lev read the latest pamphlets and books on agronomy, was unusually efficient in running the estate, and saw to it that his workers were well cared for. Occasionally, he visited Yasnaya Polyana to compare notes with Sergei Lvovich Tolstoy. Tatiana learned Beethoven's 'Waldstein' Sonata, photographed her family and the women who attended the clinic, and rode for an hour in the afternoons.

These were insulated, gentle, decent, proper lives.

6

Adam Salt, arms outstretched like a sleepwalker, felt his way along White Horse Lane and hoped he would know when he reached the Mile End Road. His eyes smarted and his chest ached. The fog, dense and lifeless, humbled the city. Human shapes loomed and receded. Near by, a horse whinnied and he heard a motorist trying to crank an engine into life. The diffused lights from shops or houses mysteriously emerged out of the gloom like ectoplasms which hovered, held steady, faded. The laughter of children from high above his head mocked him. In the fog he was unable to keep his constant, inner anxiety at bay; all his unspecified fears ran amok. He was overcome by a fit of coughing.

'You all right, mate?'

Adam, bent double, struggled for breath, felt a comforting hand on his elbow offering support. He recognised first the silver badge, then the shape of the helmet. 'Am I near the Mile End Road, please?' Adam asked.

'You should be indoors, you know.'

'I am going to see doctor. For results of X-rays.'

'Good idea. 'Spect he'll be busy today, doctors always are in a pea-souper.'

'I am near, you say?'

'Another twenty yards. Hold on to me and I'll take you to the door.'

'Thank you, officer, you are most kindly.'

The policeman delivered Adam to Dr Kantor's basement surgery. 'Mind how you go, sir,' he said, climbed the stone steps and instantly vanished.

The fog invaded the waiting room. Adam joined the other patients who sat on wooden benches, coughing, spluttering, blowing their noses. Every now and then, the door to the consulting room opened, a huddled form hurried out, and Dr Kantor's voice called, 'Next!'

The man seated beside Adam said, 'In Odessa I never once was offered a fog. Here, you can buy them wholesale.' His laugh turned into a wheeze, and the wheeze into a noisy, awful rasping. He tapped his chest. 'Chronic bronchitis, me,' he said. 'My brother had identical. He was dead before he got to fifty, God rest his soul. Me, if I live out this week, I'll give up snoring.'

I, too, will die before I'm fifty, Adam thought, and thrust his hands into his overcoat pockets in an effort to keep them still.

By any standards the Salts had settled well. Adam was in regular employment at the warehouse, and Eva taught English to as many Poles as she could reasonably manage. Their first London winter and the inevitable fog had been, to Eva at least, a source of excitement, bringing instantly to life the London of Dickens and Conan Doyle. Although little George developed perpetual colds and was forever snivelling, Eva delighted in the enforced darkness, the yellowish haze in which everything was suffused, even tolerated the unpleasant taste, and the smuts and acrid smell which invaded her nostrils. She stood for hours gazing out of the upstairs window, losing all sense of day or night, while George played at her feet.

Adam suffered in the fog and, even when it cleared, the damp, cold days and nights made breathing difficult. More than once he was too weak to work. The Chief Clerk at D. D. Graham & Sons accepted his absence, and those of many other workers, as the penalty of winter but stopped their wages just the same. Adam was ill and knew it, yet he put off seeing the doctor, telling himself he would be better when spring came and, indeed, the warmth of May gave some relief and reassured him. But at the height of midsummer, the humidity and airlessness again brought him low and dashed his spirits.

He frequented the Warsaw restaurant less and less because the walk tired him unduly. His lunch-break he spent at his desk, eating the sandwiches Eva prepared for him. Sometimes he wandered into the storeroom to look at the ostrich feathers. He enjoyed reading the labels which told him where they had originated – Australia, the southern states of America and from the Grahams' own ostrich farm in a place called Oudtshoorn, in the Cape Colony – and he thought of this merchandise dispersed the length and breadth of the British Isles and further afield across Europe. Each time he saw a picture of a queen or a princess in her plumage, he liked to imagine that her finery had once been stored in this place. Eva bought him a pamphlet about the ostrich and he was pleased to learn that its feather had been the emblem of the Egyptian god Shu, the god of light and air, and that ostrich plumes had once adorned the helmets of medieval knights. The knowledge gave him confidence that the commodity would always be in demand.

He concealed the seriousness of his condition from Eva, did not even tell her that Dr Kantor had sent him to the hospital for X-rays. When she asked why he spent so long in the outside lavatory, he'd say he was constipated. The truth was that he hid there to cough until he thought his lungs would burst. He'd drag himself to work, buy a cheap new handkerchief each day and carefully dispose of it on the way home.

Eva, by contrast, was full of energy, both physical and intellectual. She gave her lessons in the mornings. After a few months she was earning almost as much as Adam. They were by no means well-off, of course, but they managed, and were even able to save a little. Her real pleasures were sightseeing and visiting the public library, activities made possible by Mrs Antisorsksi, her neighbour, who was only too pleased to look after George for three ha'pence an hour. Once a week Eva borrowed the latest novels, biographies, histories. She was a fast reader and her son's noise did not disturb her. Other young mothers, whom she met at Dr Kantor's, confessed to being too fatigued to read. Eva's energy seemed inexhaustible. When she was not at the library or immersed in a book, she set off on what she called 'a jaunt'. After an early lunch, she sallied forth on her own, either walking or by tram, or, most exciting of all, on a Circle Line train, discovering the city she had known only from travellers' tales and books. These journeys were like visits to another foreign country.

Her erstwhile Warsaw colleague, Dr Shapiro, had steered her towards Chelsea. When in London to research his biography of Dickens, he'd spent his Sundays there, walking the narrow streets, marvelling at the variety of houses and cottages, large, small, straight and crooked. For lunch, he took to sipping warm beer and eating cold sausages in the public houses that seemed to stand on every corner. He discovered, too, the homes where some of the great literati of the past had lived and this list he handed on to Eva.

Chelsea was a raffish enclave, the haunt of poets, artists and Bohemians, bordered to the south by the River Thames and to the north by smart, smug Kensington. Eva was entranced by it. Dr Shapiro's list in hand, she visited Thomas Carlyle's house and, from the Embankment, stood and gazed at 4 Cheyne Walk where her heroine, George Eliot, died. On another outing, she walked to World's End, to Hobury Street, and saw George Meredith's home. These trips excited her imagination and she spent her spare money buying books at second-hand bookshops in the King's Road, and then devouring them on the journey back to Stepney.

'When we have a little more money, Adda, we're going to move to Chelsea.'

All Eva's activities were animated in part by her surplus energy. She had never discovered a completely satisfactory outlet for her vitality and gifts and, even with a small child, her restlessness tormented her. But there were other reasons for what amounted to her almost frenzied need to keep occupied.

The word neurosis was not yet in common use but no other word adequately describes the state to which Eva succumbed. A year after George was born she suffered a painful miscarriage followed by severe anxiety and depression; by an act of will she fought off the condition, or thought she had, but there remained scars which never quite healed. She tried to renew her passion for Zionism but discovered that, among the Jews of the East End, the movement was driven in the main by Socialists, like the *Bund* in Poland, and she had little sympathy for them. Her instincts rejected the communal and paternalistic approach to the future Jewish State. She was too much an individual, too independent, to subscribe to any notion of egalitarianism and so felt isolated and at odds with the fashionable current of thought. Yet, this rejection of Socialism was to trigger an uncomfortable inconsistency of attitude because, in contrast, to the north and west of London, she collided with the English disease of snobbery. Ludicrous though it seemed to her, the Jewish families long established in England and those who had fought their way out of East End poverty treated immigrants with noticeable disdain. Of course the better-off contributed generously to charities and good causes which served their poorer brethren but that did not mean they wanted to sit with them on committees or invite them into their homes. The smart end of the Zionist movement was also, therefore, denied her. For the rest of her life, Eva regarded English Jews as the worst snobs in the world and warned all and sundry to be wary of them.

Her struggle to rid herself of depression following the miscarriage and her useless attempts to serve Zionism coincided with an apparently mundane incident to which she reacted irrationally. Dr Kantor paid her a routine visit and, as he was leaving, said, 'Mrs Salt, you won't forget to bring George to the surgery for his vaccination, will you?'

Panic seized her. A neighbour's daughter, Mary O'Malley, had been inoculated and reacted badly. Her little arm swelled, she ran an alarmingly high temperature and seemed to cling precariously to life. There were countless stories in the newspapers about children dying from vaccination and she was filled with dread. Into her mind, a personification of the terror she felt, came the face of Paul Ehrlich, but why he was suddenly transformed into an ogre she was unable then, or later, to explain.

'I'll think about it,' she said to Dr Kantor.

'Mrs Salt, please, it's no good thinking about it. It has to be done. It's the law. We don't want a repetition of the 1902 epidemic.'

'I'll bring him in a day or two.'

She confided her fears to no one so that now both she and Adam had secrets they kept from each other. This did not in any way undermine their relationship, for they continued to find solace in love-making. Her pregnancies had been agony to Adam who found the wait to satisfy his fierce sexual hunger almost unbearable. Not that Eva kept him at a distance for longer than was necessary. Her libido, too, demanded to be fed. When she discovered she was pregnant for the third time Adam had to reconcile himself yet again to more months of celibacy.

Eva's preoccupation with Paul Ehrlich did not leave her. The more she tried to rid herself of his distorted image, the more deeply the image embedded itself. The more deeply it embedded itself the more she tried to be rid of it. The vicious circle is the wormcast of a neurotic impulse. She tried to banish her fears by writing them down:

I fear for my child's life. I fear Georgie will die if he is vaccinated. This I believe to be quite rational and intelligible because there is much evidence of children reacting so badly to vaccination that the dose proves fatal. I am not reassured by Dr Kantor or by the memory of how poor little Mary O'Malley suffered.

But this is only a part of what I feel. I have a terrible – and this, I know, is irrational – a terrible fear of a plague sweeping Europe. I cannot explain this. When I try to sleep, my mind is suddenly filled with visions of the dying as though I were looking at a tableau-vivant by Brueghel. Central in this chimera is Paul Ehrlich. I hear him say quite clearly, 'Salvarsan doesn't work, you see. It doesn't cure, it kills.' I am relieved if Georgie wakes; but even at other times, not only at night, I hear Ehrlich's voice, 'It doesn't cure, it kills.' I can be doing quite ordinary things, teaching, washing, cleaning, shopping, walking, and into my mind, unasked for, comes the nightmarish image and Paul Ehrlich, as though choreographing the death of millions, crying, 'It doesn't cure, it kills.' He seems gleeful. I know him to be a good man, a benefactor of mankind, yet his voice persists, 'It doesn't cure, it kills.'

I realise I am suffering from some form of mental aberration. I know also that I am not insane. I don't think anyone believes I act strangely or dementedly. Certainly Adam shows no signs of being concerned for my health.

I want to protect us all from the plague that I know is coming, but I do not know how.

I want to be free of it.

*

'Next!'

Adam left the gloom of the waiting-room for the gloom of the surgery where Dr Kantor was drying his hands. He looked over his shoulder and greeted Adam with a thin smile. Adam knew at once the news must be bad. Dr Kantor, although only in his early thirties, had the look and posture of an old man upon whose shoulders all the cares of the world had been laid. His dark brown eyes were reservoirs of apology and compassion. He said, 'Mr Salt, I'm pleased to tell you, it's not as serious as I thought.'

'Not?'

'No. Frankly, I thought it might be TB, but the tests and X-rays are negative.'

'What, then, please?'

'Chronic bronchitis. I'm sorry.'

'Oh, God,' Adam murmured. His mind raced. He remembered the man from Odessa in the waiting-room. I'll be dead before I'm fifty, he thought. 'Is there a cure?'

'Not really. I'm sorry, but—'

'Yes?'

'A different climate would help. I'll tell you honestly, Mr Salt. If you go on living in this country, it'll get worse and worse. I'm sorry.'

'No cure, you say?'

'I can give you medicine to help the cough but I'm not going to lie to you. It's a chronic complaint. Next winter, you'll be ill again.'

'Different climate, you say?'

'Yes. Somewhere warm. Or dry. Or both. But this may be impossible, I know. If you were rich—'

'You mean, like Palestine?'

'Yes, Palestine. Yes, why not? Palestine, yes.'

'Other examples, please, where?'

'Switzerland. Many people with chest complaints go to Switzerland.'

'Switzerland?'

'Or the Austrian Alps, perhaps.'

'Or the Obersalzburg?'

'Yes. Or South Africa.'

'South Africa?'

'Yes. If you promise not to mention this to anyone,' Kantor said, 'I myself am thinking of emigrating to South Africa.'

'Are you ill, too, doctor?'

'Asthma.'

'Where in South Arica?'

'Cape Town. I have a cousin there. He's a solicitor or attorney, as

128

they call it. They want doctors. European doctors. They want Europeans. They'd help you with the fares.'

'South Africa.'

'Wonderful climate. Wonderful opportunities. Do you the world of good. Frankly, Mr Salt, London is not your friend. Yes, you need a warm, dry climate. Think about it. In the meantime I'll give you the medicine.'

'Please don't mention to Eva,' Adam said. 'I myself will tell.'

'I understand,' and as Adam was leaving to brave the fog, he added, 'Oh, and remind her to bring George in for vaccination. He's long overdue. I'm sorry.' He smiled sadly.

Ordinarily, the journey by foot from Dr Kantor's surgery to the warehouse near Narrow Street would have taken Adam at most forty-five minutes. In the fog, which showed no signs of lifting, he crawled along for more than three hours. Exhausted, breathless, he reported for work just after lunch. Alistair Graham was conferring with his Chief Clerk when Adam sloped past into the general office where the junior clerks laboured over dockets and receipts and bills of lading. Graham, like many a Scot, presented to the world a stern manner, but in reality gave the lie to the stereotype, for he was a generous man; he was also perceptive.

'What's the matter with Salt?' he asked. 'He looks like death warmed up.'

'Fog,' the Chief Clerk said, smiling grimly. 'That's what's the matter with him, sir. Fog. That's what's the matter with all the foreigners, sir, can't take the fog.'

Graham nodded but he had sympathy for the men who had to work in all weathers, in sickness and in health, or lose a day's pay.

'He's a good worker is Salt,' Graham said. 'Intelligent man, knows the market.'

'Yes, sir, all the Yids are good workers.'

When he had finished his business with the Chief Clerk, Graham wandered into the general office, greeted those he knew, then crossed to Adam's desk.

'You don't look well, Salt,' he said. 'Should you be working?'

I'm going to die before I'm fifty, Adam thought, and burst into tears.

'Here, man, what's the trouble?'

Adam stammered, trying to find words; he screwed up his eyes as though in terrible pain.

'Come now,' Graham said, 'come into my office, have a wee dram of whisky, that'll set you to rights. These pea-soupers are good to neither man nor beast.'

He led the way up a flight of rickety wooden stairs into his office and

129

poured Adam a Scotch. 'You want to tell me what's troubling you?' Graham asked.

Adam gulped his drink, took deep breaths and then, in a rush, reported Dr Kantor's diagnosis.

'It could be worse,' Graham said. 'What's this doctor of yours advise?'

'He give me medicine. He say also perhaps to live in better climate. He gives to me four choices,' Adam said. 'Palestine, Switzerland, Austria or South Africa.' He coughed painfully.

Graham watched him. 'We have the farm in South Africa,' he said.

'Yes, sir.'

'Would you like me to write to my brother, Donald, see if there's an opening? There's the warehouse in Cape Town, he might need someone with experience of the London end.'

'You think this is possible?'

'I don't mind writing to him. I can't promise anything.'

'I would like it, yes, please, for you to write. I am grateful to you, sir.'

'Don't be grateful. I haven't done anything yet.'

These events belong to November, 1913. Adam decided not to confide in Eva until after Graham had received a reply from his brother which arrived at the end of January:

3/1/'14

Dear Alistair,

Thank you for yours of 19/11/'13.

Could always do with an experienced man. Quality of personnel here pretty poor. Your Kaffir is lazy, your Boer is stupid, your Englishman is English.

If this man Salt is all you crack him up to be let him come out, but at his own expense. I will, however, guarantee him a suitable post. Let me know soonest what he decides.

Hope this finds you as it leaves me and I send my best wishes to you and Margaret for a happy and prosperous 1914.

Your brother,
Donald.

When Adam broke the news to Eva, showing her the letter Donald Graham had written, her relief was tangible. 'You are pleased,' he said, astonished. 'Why are you so pleased? I thought you would be heartbroken to leave London.'

She thought for a moment. 'I am and I'm not,' she replied. Of course she would miss London, but an avenue of escape from her macabre obsessions seemed to open out before her, sun-blessed and full of hope. Still, she did not share that secret with him, but said, 'If I seem so pleased it's because I want you to get well, Adda,' which was also true.

'There's always Palestine,' Adam said carefully.

'No. I don't think Palestine would suit us. I don't want to be a pioneer, Adda. You'd find the life too hard there. It wouldn't do you good. No. Let's make enquiries about South Africa.'

There was one more obstacle yet to be overcome. The Union Castle Line refused to carry women in their last weeks of pregnancy. The problem was solved by the birth on 26 March 1914, of Isobel. A month later, the Salts boarded the *Warwick Castle* at Southampton and set sail for the southern hemisphere. On only the second day at sea, Eva was astonished to wake with a lightness of spirit she had not known for almost a year. Paul Ehrlich no longer blighted her consciousness and she was convinced that she and her family had managed to escape the plague. And as the ship sailed into warmer weather, Adam coughed less and less.

At the time the Salts were at sea, in the European spring of 1914, the Wildnowitz clan had been settled in Cape Town for over a year. Their journey had been marred by Leah's perpetual seasickness and she vowed never to travel by ship again. The highlight of the voyage was Isaiah's bar mitzvah, held on deck, on 16 December 1912, which happened to be both his thirteenth birthday and a Saturday. Rabbi Zuckerman, who had carried across Europe the Torah from his synagogue in Vilna, conducted the service. Isaiah sang well and, as was only to be expected, gave his parents *nakhes*. Their fellow passengers in steerage rummaged through belongings and produced gifts for the bar mitzvah boy – cufflinks, studs, cravats and even a Homburg which was too big for him. An Irishman, Liam O'Mally, said, 'God, that were a beautiful thing to hear the boy converse so sweetly with the Almighty,' and gave Isaiah the pocket-watch which had once belonged to his father.

They arrived in blazing January heat. The first sight of their new home filled the passengers, crowded at the ship's rail, with wonder and optimism, for there is little anywhere in the world to match the beauty of the graceful mountains, Devil's Peak, Table Mountain and Lion's Head, which cradle the town. The newcomers were met on the quayside by a small delegation led by Zalman Mauerberger, who represented an organisation for the settlement of Jewish immigrants. Mauerberger was short and aggressive. (Julius said he made Uncle Benjamin seem docile.) To Leah's question, 'Are you going to put us in separate hostels?' he said, 'What are you talking about? What are you talking about separate hostels? Who said anything about separate hostels? What are you talking about? We give you a flat for six months, not big, not small, but a flat. After that you've got to afford a place of your own. What are you talking about hostels?'

Another member of the delegation, Mrs Klingman, officious and orderly, asked, 'Town of origin?'

'Ploemyan,' Solomon said.

'Ploemyan?' she repeated. 'You hear that Mr Mauerberger? The family Wildnowitz come from Ploemyan.' Mauerberger grunted angrily while supervising the loading of luggage into the back of a van. 'We already have people here from Ploemyan,' Mrs Klingman explained.

'Who? Who?' Solomon asked.

'There's a Mr Katzenowitz—'

'Fedya Katzenowitz, the *nakhtwachter*?'

'Yes—'

'And the family Horowitz?'

'Yes, yes, Horowitz, oh, and a whole host of others.'

On his first night in Cape Town, Isaiah was unable to sleep. The excitement of the arrival, the heat, the new surroundings all contributed to his restlessness. But he was also troubled by an ache, a yearning. He missed Laban. He tossed and turned, and when sleep finally came there lingered in Isaiah's mind a disembodied image of his uncle smiling idiotically while Europa Altona popped into his mouth rich, dark chocolate.

On the second night Isaiah prayed before sleep, 'Please, O Lord Our God, King of the Universe, allow me to see my Uncle Laban again.'

In Hamburg, Laban discovered the legend of Oedipus and his life was transformed. He had struck up an acquaintanceship with one of Europa Altona's regular clients, Andreas Kleiber, a young theatre and literary critic, who visited the house once a week on Saturday evenings. After Kleiber had, in Europa's words, 'done the business', he took to sipping a cognac with Laban in a back room. Kleiber's interest was engaged by what he regarded as Laban's original and lively mind and he brought Laban books, pamphlets, exhibition catalogues, and talked of the latest opera and theatre productions. Laban, Kleiber learned, had never seen a play and so gave him a ticket for *Oedipus*.

Laban was not carried away by his first visit to a playhouse. He did not know what to make of a group of people who moved and talked in unison, ('How a fellow knows what his fellow-fellows are going to say, and say it at the same time, beats me!'), wondered why all the juicy bits in the story happened off-stage and was puzzled by the actor playing Oedipus because he looked old enough to be Jocasta's father. But what really bothered him was a lack of confidence in his grasp of German. He was not certain he understood every nuance in the translation of Sophocles, and was unsure as to whether or not he had followed the story accurately. He waited impatiently for Saturday and Kleiber's weekly visit.

'Herr Kleiber,' Laban said, pouring the cognac, 'I am not one hundred per cent certain I've got this right. Tell me if I'm wrong. Oedipus is born. They make a prophecy. He will murder his father and marry his mother. So far correct?'

'Correct.'

'For his parents this a terrible thing to hear. Talk about a curse, this is a curse. So, they give the baby to a shepherd and tell the man to make sure the baby is put to death. Correct?'

'Correct.'

'But, watch out, here comes human feelings. The shepherd can't carry out his orders. This man, he looks after lambs, how can he kill a baby? So, *nu*, he ties the baby's legs together and leaves him by the road. Still correct?'

'More or less.'

'By good luck, people find the baby, take care of him, he grows up into a fine young fellow and before you can say the Ten Commandments, he kills his father and marries his mother. Correct?'

'Correct.'

'I got it right, then. This man Sophocles has taught me something.'

'How so?'

'I used to think a man can alter his fate. But recently I've changed my mind. In fact, I came to believe it's quite the reverse. But Sophocles tells me something else again. Because this story of Oedipus has a simple moral, and the moral is this: the more we do to change our fate, the more certain that fate becomes.'

'Precisely.'

'Good. Then let's have another cognac and drink to Sophocles. He's put my mind at rest.' They drank.

'What was worrying you?' Kleiber asked.

'Well, it's like this. I believed all my life you could take fate, give it a shake, a kick in the *tochas*, a slap round the face, and you don't have to accept what it offers. Some time ago, I got into my mind an ambition to go to America. This is all I could think about. America, America, America. A voice in my head told me this was my fate. America. *Nu*, all seemed to be pointing in the right direction, I travelled many miles, reached Hamburg, and then, *feh*, fate takes me by surprise. Instead of me doing the shaking, the kicking and the slapping, fate brings a knee up into my crutch and says, "Laban, you're a *shmuck*." You know what means this word *shmuck*? Not like in German a piece of jewellery, oh, no. In Yiddish it means, pardon the language, your penis, but it also means a fool or, like they've always said about me, an idiot. So, fate says to me, "*Shmuck*, you're not going to America. You're going to stay here in Hamburg, because I'm going to make you a slave to a woman—"'

'Europa Altona?'

'That's her. A slave, me, Laban the Idiot. And America? *Pfui!* So, you say to yourself, all right, tell me something I didn't know, fate has the last word. But now, thanks to this man Sophocles, I understand I was wrong. You see,' Laban said, dropping his voice to a whisper, 'I now know for certain my fate is to end up in America.'

'Really?'

'Absolutely. So, please, not a word to Europa Altona, she can get very upset. But the fact is, it doesn't matter what I do, by hook or by crook, by fate or by schmate, I know I'll end up in America singing, "I come from Ellybumma mit mine banjer on mine knee!"'

Kleiber, perhaps more of a journalist than a critic, wrote an article for the Hamburg daily newspaper *Altonaer Tageblatt* in April 1914, entitled 'Sophocles and the Wise Jew'. It began, 'The other night I had a conversation with Laban, a wise Jew, who is an acquaintance of mine.' Kleiber, of course, did not describe the precise circumstances of the conversation but he summarised the discussion and transformed it into a jingoistic diatribe about Germany's future. It was neither intelligent nor well-written; he did not once question how Laban could be so certain of what fate had in store for him. He implied that the destiny of individuals or nations, was, finally, a matter of belief. He ended:

> No matter who our enemies are, whether they reside within our borders or beyond, whether they seek to undermine us politically or take up arms against us in battle, nothing will alter Germany's destiny which is to be the dominant force in Europe. German culture, German civilisation, no matter what, will triumph.

Benjamin Wildnowitz could not believe the words he read. Never mind Laban the wise Jew, this Laban he read about, he knew for certain, was none other than his brother, Laban the Idiot.

They had lost touch since the departure of Solomon and Leah. The brothers waved goodbye from the quayside, both too numb to cry, and returned to the men's hostel. Laban began to pack the few old clothes he kept in a battered suitcase under his bed. 'Benjamin,' he said, 'I won't be sleeping here again. I've got somewhere else to sleep.'

'Where?' Benjamin demanded but Laban remained silent, and Benjamin knew from his manner there was no point in questioning him further.

To begin with, they met in the synagogue on Friday evenings but, after a month or two Laban was no longer to be seen. Perhaps, Benjamin reasoned, he goes to another synagogue; later he decided that perhaps Laban didn't go to a synagogue at all. This neither surprised nor saddened Benjamin. Laban had always been a misfit, an idiot, a *meshuggeneh*; his behaviour was only to be expected.

In the weeks that followed, Benjamin earned enough to rent a room of his own. He was lonely and miserable. He continued to pester the shipping lines but without success. He did not bother to learn German, for he had no intention of remaining in the country. He bought a Yiddish newspaper once a week and it was in its pages, in April 1914, that he read Kleiber's article about Sophocles and the wise Jew, reprinted from the *Altonaer Tageblatt*.

In the same week, Benjamin discovered that a ship was willing to take Jewish immigrants to America. He also discovered, or believed he discovered, a conspiracy that he was certain had been hatched by the shipping lines against Jews trying to sail across the ocean. The reason was not clear, but Yitzchak, the *shammes*, muttered, '*Geld*, what else?' and to the disadvantaged, whether true or not, money is always an acceptable explanation for why they remain disadvantaged. Benjamin could never get to the bottom of the quota mystery, but the upshot was that he needed to find Laban urgently. He visited the offices of the Yiddish newspaper and was shown into the shabby, shelfless but book-filled office of the editor, Josef Herbstein, a man in his forties, with shifty eyes, a suspicious nature, and who jerked his head from right to left, left to right, as if he expected sudden arrest. A cigarette dangled from his lips and the lapels of his jacket were patterned with ash. He poked his head above the columns of paper that rose from his desk. A whisper: '*Nu?*'

Benjamin explained the problem. 'So, how can I find this wise Jew who is my brother, Laban?' Benjamin asked.

With his little finger, Herbstein delicately flicked ash from his cigarette on to his tie. 'He owes you money?'

'No one owes me money, I haven't got any money, how can anyone owe me money?' Benjamin retorted.

Herbstein nodded, then came the sudden, furtive jerk of the head from side to side. 'Come back in two days' time,' he said confidentially.

'But it's urgent, I have to find him quickly.'

'All right, don't come back in two days' time,' Herbstein said, and disappeared behind the piles of paper, a trickle of smoke the only evidence of his existence.

Two days later, after work, Benjamin returned. Herbstein said, 'Let's go for a meander.'

'Have you found my brother?'

'Is he a bit of a *yentzer*?' Herbstein asked, closing one eye.

'You've found him!'

'Could be.'

On the way to Europa Altona's, Benjamin asked, 'How did you find him? From this *goy*, Kleiber, who wrote the article?'

Herbstein stopped, looked over his shoulder as if to make sure they weren't being followed. 'I have my ways,' he said.

'What ways?'

Herbstein stopped again, gripped Benjamin's arm tightly, and said, 'You're right. I found out from Kleiber.'

'So, what's the big secret? That's all I wanted to know.'

Herbstein said, 'In this life, you can never be too careful.'

Laban was astonished to see Benjamin on the doorstep. Herbstein was introduced. Laban smiled sheepishly and led them into the back room where clients sometimes waited for the girl of their choice, or returned to be refreshed after doing the business. The brothers said little to begin with; the atmosphere was awkward, attempts at conversation halting. Herbstein lit one cigarette from another and watched the two men through curling smoke.

Europa Altona poked her head round the door. Herbstein pulled his hat over his face. Laban said, 'My brother and a friend.'

'Don't be too long, sweetheart, I'm running a business not a charity,' she said, blew him a kiss and withdrew.

Laban said, '*Nu?*'

'*Nu,*' Benjamin replied.

Herbstein said, 'You get here complimentary tickets?'

The brothers looked at him blankly.

'Any chance of a free passage, you get my meaning?'

Laban said, 'Like she said, she runs a business not a charity. No free passage, no.'

'Talking of free passage,' Benjamin said, and launched into an account of why he had come to see Laban. He explained the sudden disappearance of the quota, the possibility of sailing to New York in a week's time. 'What's more,' Benjamin said, 'the people who put us in the hostels, that fellow Bronstein, they'll help with the fare. Assisted passage, they call it. *Nu?* Do I book two berths, Laban?'

Laban the Idiot, poet, philosopher and *shligalicker*, smiled his inane smile, and said, 'No. Don't book for two. You go, Benjamin. I'll join you later. But don't worry, I'll join you in America.'

Benjamin rose immediately, raised his forefinger at Laban and shook it relentlessly while he tried to find words. 'You, you,' he growled, 'you were always an idiot. You think I can't see what's going on? You think you're living here a life that's all roses and *gefilte* fish? I know you, Laban. You're *yentzing* that *kurveh*, that's what's keeping you here, I got eyes in my head, Laban, I saw her blow you a lovey-dovey kiss, you think I'm blind? I'm not blind. How long you think that's going to last? I'll tell you how long. As long it takes to blow a kiss, that's how long. You know what you are, Laban? I'll tell you what you are. You're a – you're a – you're an idiot, that's what you are!'

Herbstein said, 'You sure you can't even get me a little tickle on tick?' and looked hopeful.

'An idiot! Yes, that's what you are!' and he stormed out, convinced he would never see his brother again.

Laban harboured no such misgivings. He was confident of his own future. 'Give me your poor,' America said. 'I am your poor,' Laban answered. 'I'll be with you in a moment.' He could imagine the scene: an automobile and chauffeur in the background, Benjamin, in a suit and tie, waiting to greet him on the New York quayside, a millionaire, arms outstretched in welcome.

Laban's pressing difficulty, however, was Europa Altona. Whenever possible, he would worm America into the conversation but the fish would not bite. 'I belong here,' she said. 'That's why I chose the name Europa.'

'You chose the name Europa?' Laban said, astonished. He watched her undress for bed in the early hours of a Sunday morning. The last customer had departed. The exhausted girls were already asleep.

She was silent for a moment. 'Europa Altona,' she said, 'is not my real name.'

'Not? You never told me that.'

'You never asked.'

'To me it sounds like your real name.'

'No. My real name is Theodora von Tresckow.'

'That's some name,' Laban said.

'It's some family.'

'So, *nu*, tell me, *bubee*, how did you come from Theodora von Tresckow to Europa Altona?'

'I made it up when I went into the business. Altona because that's where I was born, and Europa after the goddess Europe who was a whore.'

'Europe was a whore?' Laban repeated, scandalised.

'Don't you know the story of Europe?' she asked.

'Can't say as how I do.'

'You're supposed to be an expert on the Greeks.'

'Me? Never. Only on Oedipus I'm an expert.'

'She was a Greek whore.'

'Europe was a Greek whore?'

'A goddess but a whore.'

'A goddess. Ah.'

'She was raped by an eagle.'

'By an eagle? My!'

'Or it may have been a bull.'

'An eagle or a bull, there's some difference, make up your mind.'

'People tell different stories. Anyway, whichever, eagle or bull, the rapist was actually Zeus in disguise. He became her pimp.'

'That Zeus, what a fellow—'

'Because after he raped her she put flowers in his mouth and hung garlands from his horns. It's obvious. He was her pimp and that's the kind of whore she was.'

Laban was silent.

'Europe,' she said. 'Everyone's after her. She's a slut. And Zeus is disguising himself all the time. You know what disguise he's in now?' Naked, she slipped in beside him and he cradled her in the crook of his arm.

'No idea,' Laban said.

'The Kaiser,' she said.

'The Kaiser is Zeus in disguise?'

'Of course. He's ready for rape, I can smell it a mile away. And she'll let him, the whore!'

'What's all this got to do with why you took it as a name?'

'Because it's the story of my life. The pimps I've known. No more, thank God, not now I've got you.'

'But isn't this a good reason we should pack our bags, board an ocean steamer and set sail for America? You don't want another rape on your hands.'

Her answer surprised him. 'I'll think about it,' she said. It was the first time he detected a softening, however tenuous, in her attitude.

'Yes, think about it, *bubee*. No more rapes, no more eagles or bulls. You and me in America.'

'And will we be married or will I just be Europa in the New World?'

He squirmed a little. 'It's my turn to say I'll think about it.'

She laughed softly and started to caress him, her mouth and tongue finding a path to his thighs. Laban lay back and lazily reached out to stroke her buttocks. He murmured, 'You'll be Mrs Laban Wildnowitz. Or Theodora Wildnowitz. Me, I prefer Europa Altona,' and laughed. 'Now,' he said, 'let me be an eagle or a bull!'

Benjamin watched the spires of Hamburg disappear as the ship nosed its way out of the harbour, into the North Sea on its voyage to America. But from the moment the aggressive, thrusting skyscrapers of New York materialised out of mist and sea, Benjamin Wildnowitz was filled with loathing for every square inch of the United States of America, seen and unseen. The rage, which anyway accompanied all he did and felt, ran riot, producing in him a scowling, belligerent, indiscriminate aggression towards anything and everything, humans, animals, inanimate objects. He cursed the heat, the humidity, his sweat, the multitude, Ellis Island, immigration officials, medical officers, skyscrapers, the Statue of Liberty, the metallic twang of the language, the noise, incessant movement, the blacks, the Italians, and he cursed most of all his own poverty and the crushing, damning weight of his new world.

He resolutely refused to make friends or to learn English. He found work as a cobbler on the Lower East Side, near the lodging house in which he shared a cell with two brothers, butchers from Odessa. He worked a twelve-hour day, from seven to seven; each evening, he ate a hot meal in a kosher diner on Rivington Street, then repaired to his room where he sat on his bed, staring into darkness, his eyes red with fury. On Friday afternoons he received his wages from his boss, Emanuel Kaufmann, and made for the synagogue, swayed angrily to chant his prayers, and then it was back to the room to glower and brood. When the butchers from Odessa were present, he turned his back on them. Apart from a 'Good *shabbas*' on the Sabbath, and on High Holy Days, a 'Good *Yom Tov*' he exchanged not a word with them. I am doomed, he said to himself over and over again. Doomed.

In moments of deepest despair he thought of Solomon, Leah and their boys and longed to be with them again but he could not bring their faces clearly to mind. Neither could he imagine South Africa or Kep Tovn. He thought of Laban, too, but cursed him for his degeneracy. That a brother of his should end up *yentzing* a *kurveh* for the rest of his life. Idiot! Idiot!

The Idiot, however, had never been more content. Europa Altona continued to love him as she had loved no other, and he continued enslaved. He was certain of the future, convinced that no matter what he or anyone else did, fate or destiny, call it what you will, would so dispose events as to make his journey to America inevitable. Alone or in company he sang often of Susanna, Alabama, of banjos and a bobtail nag, doodah, doodah, day.

8

Three bodies dangle from lampposts. Three policemen in uniform twist this way and that in a light fall of snow, winding, unwinding, and the ropes creak. Stepan clutches his violin case, unable to move, and stares at the hanged men, their necks elongated, tongues swollen and protruding, their uniforms stained and smelling of excrement. The sight scorches his consciousness and forever after his image of the Communist *coup d'état* will be three distended corpses sprinkled with snow spinning slowly on an October afternoon.

'Run, boy! Stop staring or they'll come back and hang *you*!' Stepan sees an old man's head peering around the corner of a wall. 'They'll be back!' the man sobs. 'That's my son up there, the middle one. Run for your life or the Pharaohs will come back and hang you like they hanged my son. Run!' Pharaohs is the name for the police, the oppressors of the people.

There are no trams. Stepan's instinct tells him not to take shortcuts but to keep to the main streets which are filled with people, soldiers and sailors mostly, eight, nine abreast, rank upon rank, milling aimlessly. He keeps his eyes lowered, for to catch another's glance can be, he knows, fatal. Distant shots and screams, the breaking of glass. When he reaches home, his mother, Anya, bursts into tears and hugs him with relief. A brooch she's wearing scratches his face.

The impressions of a twelve-year-old boy. Moscow, 1917.

The Kessler house and factory are appropriated by the new state which, according to the creed, is to wither and die so humankind may be free. Katya, the maid, faithful, devoted Katya, drunk, lifting her skirts, yelling, 'Lick my bare ass, you fuckers! Lick the shit! I'm taking the best room for myself, rotten fucking bastards! You'll be in the attic or the cellar, and you can fucking wash and iron *my* fucking clothes. Pigs! Pigs! Fucking pigs!'

Anya, dignified, erect, gathers her two sons and, followed by her husband, mounts the stairs to the bedroom. They lock the door, and push a heavy wardrobe hard against it. But only Katya haunts the house, drinking their vodka and their wine, and screaming obscenities. The next morning, she weeps at the locked bedroom door, begging forgiveness. But the Kesslers ignore her and she is neither seen nor heard of again.

Another day, a week later, perhaps. Stepan watches from the bedroom window and sees twenty or so men and women trooping into the house. These are the new occupants. No abuse from them, only unspoken satisfaction at being warm and dry, and at humbling the former owners. The glint in their eyes is the triumph of envy satisfied.

Presently, a terrifying breed of man appears, the district commissar. He has power over their lives and uses it ruthlessly. Furniture, paintings, lamps, knick-knacks, plates, silver, cutlery, the artefacts of comfort and home-making, are either smashed or removed. The reign of terror is mild in the Kessler household but it has begun; each day they wake not with the unknown excitement of what life may have in store, but with the certainty that they will be frightened. Fear rules their lives. From one end to the other of Comrade Nicholas Romanov's former domains, fear has taken his place.

Stepan's refuge is his violin. Once a week, in all weathers, he trudges to the studio of Valentin Manishowitz, his teacher, nearly eighty now, long white unruly hair, hedgehogs for eyebrows, small blue, watery eyes that can suddenly turn to ice. The studio used to be an adjunct to his apartment but the apartment has been appropriated, so now he lives in the studio. A grand piano takes up too much space, so all movement in the room is like an elaborate dance around the instrument, sidling and shuffling. The walls are hung with the mementoes of a career – programmes made of silk, posters in a dozen languages, signed photographs, and a framed personal letter from Johannes Brahms.

The lessons are an hour-long flight from fear. Manishowitz is fond of saying, 'Art, Stepan, is the only universal language. Man will be saved by art or he will not be saved at all,' and 'The harp is the instrument of the angels but the devil plays the violin.' His laugh is silent, his enjoyment immense.

Months later. Talk of foreign armies landing in the north to destroy the Communist regime. Talk of Whites and Reds. Talk of the government moving from Petrograd to Moscow to put distance between itself and the onslaught. Talk of Lenin and Trotsky occupying the Kremlin. Always Lenin and Trotsky as if they were one person. Talk of the massacre of the Romanovs in Ekaterinburg. Everything said in Moscow is said in a whisper. The snakes hiss.

*

'Jews,' Stepan's father says. 'It's the Jews. Trotsky's real name's Bronstein. Kaganovich is a Jew. Marx and Engels were Jews. It's a Jewish plot, a Jewish revolution.' Kessler paces what was once his bedroom but is now his entire home; out on the landing, the floor covered in the best imported Wilton, four women cook their family's food over small makeshift stoves burning wood. Anya is one of them and she is used to it by now though she will never accept it. The carpet is pockmarked by flying sparks, the ceiling blackened by smoke. 'Jews! They killed Christ! Now they kill the Tsar!' Kessler hisses again. He hasn't shaved for days because water is scarce and fuel to heat it scarcer. 'The Jews will kill us all.'

Stepan says, 'Valentin Manishowitz is a Jew. He won't kill us. He's an artist, a musician.'

'I forbid you to see that man again. I forbid you to see that Jew. You are not to take any more lessons.'

But Stepan decides to disobey. He has a deep-seated, inexplicable need to stand before the old man in the studio, violin tucked under his chin, and to play so that the sounds drown reality.

The city struggles back to some sort of life but there seem always to be crowds, knots of people gathered around street-corner orators, or at newspaper displays, or queuing for food, clothes, vodka, cigarettes, or just wandering aimlessly. To reach the studio Stepan is obliged to cross Red Square. Here, a mass of people are gathered, silent and still. A man's voice, sonorous, insistent, holds them spellbound. Stepan pushes his way through towards the Kremlin wall and catches sight of the speaker, a man with dark wavy hair and pince-nez. Stepan holds his breath, for he has seen him before, in a dentist's waiting-room, and heard him call the dentist comrade.

'Who is he?' Stepan asks.

'Trotsky. Ssh.'

'Maestro, my father says I musn't see you again.'

'Oh? Why is that?'

'He says – he says—'

'Tell me.'

'Because – because—'

'Because he can't afford the fees any more?'

'No—'

'Why, then?'

'Because you are a Jew.'

'I see. But I've always been a Jew. Why does it suddenly make a difference now?'

'Because he says you killed the Tsar.'

'A-ha! I didn't know I killed the Tsar.'

'That's what my father says. He says you'll kill us, too.'

'Me, personally? Or just the Jews in general?'

'He didn't say.'

'And what do you think, Stepan? You think it's possible I might kill you?'

'No. I told my father you were an artist, a musician, and you wouldn't kill us.'

'Good. And please assure your father I had nothing to do with the execution of the Tsar and his poor family, though I don't suppose it will make any difference.'

'May we start my lesson now, please, maestro?'

'We certainly may. Oh, just one thing. If it becomes difficult for you to come here again, or to find the money to pay me, come just the same. You have a gift, you have feeling. I enjoy teaching you.'

'_'

'Ah, don't cry, Stepan Stepanovich. Don't cry, little Stepan.'

'_'

'If I give you a present will you stop crying?'

'_'

'Here. This is not my best violin but it's a good one, just the same. It was made for me by Hills of London in 1891, when I played before Queen Victoria. Oh, yes, it's a good violin, all right. Not Stradivarius, but good. Take it, please. I've got six violins, I can only play one at a time.'

'_'

'Play for me on your new violin, little Stepan, and let us lose ourselves in music, which is, after all, the only way of discovering the real world. At least, for you and me. Don't cry.'

His mother's tears, or rather the stains of her tears on her cheeks. The family, in their one room, are anguished and tormented. Kessler paces and his shoes squeak. Little Shura sits on the floor, hugging his knees and rocking to and fro. Stepan stares straight ahead not daring to catch his parents' eyes. His future has been decided.

At last, he speaks. 'When will I leave?'

'Tonight,' his father replied. 'We dare not delay.'

His mother rips open the seam of his overcoat, and stitches into the lining a mat of used rouble notes. He puts on the coat and walks up and down. The notes do not rustle. In icy darkness, the family leaves the house.

The Finland Station is a cauldron of confused humanity. People sit or stand, huddled, freezing, questioning, bewildered, numb. For most of the time, there is little sound save for a constant, subdued murmur, but when a train snakes into the station there is a great hopeful rush to the platform, a noisy stampede. Everyone knows they will not find a train going precisely to their desired destination but the general direction will do: Poland, Finland, Germany.

Stepan and Shura sit either side of their mother, her arms encircling them. Stepan clutches his violin case which contains the Hills violin. Anya cannot stop stroking his face and the back of his neck. Shura sleeps. Kessler makes forays into the cauldron for information, disappears for minutes on end, reappears disappointed. Hours pass. A drunk sings the Tsar's anthem and is abruptly silenced. A train arrives. Another stampede ensues.

'Germany, it's going to Germany.'

Stepan is bundled into the corridor of a carriage already full. An old woman, seeing Anya's agony, says, 'Don't worry, mother, I'll look after him.' Anya nods gratefully, biting her lips and screwing up her eyes in an effort to fight her misery.

Kessler says, 'Chemnitz. That's all you have to remember. You are going to Chemnitz. And when you get there, you ask for the family Lohmeyer.' A whisper. 'If they say you have to pay for this or that, don't hesitate, pay. You have the money. Do you understand, Stepan?'

'Yes, Father.'

A guard's whistle, answering calls, and the wailing of women. Anya hugs Stepan for the last time, smothers him in kisses, lifts Shura, whom his parents consider too young for this journey. He says, 'Auf Wiedersehen.'

Kessler's turn to hug his elder son.

Stepan's eyes fill with tears.

'Chemnitz, remember, Chemnitz, the family Lohmeyer.'

Tears and steam shroud his parents and his brother. He holds his violin case more tightly than ever and wishes he could have said farewell to Valentin Manishowitz.

9

Loose ends.

A faded picture postcard from Max Ehrlich to his niece, dated 31 May 1913. The picture is a photograph of Battistini.

> Warsaw is dead without you. Otherwise all is well! How I'd love to see your children. Are they clever? Krantnik is more inquisitive than ever so I tell her nothing! Am thinking of visiting London next year. Write again soon. I love your letters. Pleased you are so happy and well. Your loving uncle, Max.

And from Miss Krantnik's last letter written to her cousin in Peoria, Illinois, dated 9 January 1919:

> When the year began, I was so full of hope. The misery was over and I believed a new age awaited us. Perhaps it does, but I cannot help allowing everything to be coloured by my own distress. Mr Ehrlich is to marry a rich widow, Anita Posniak, whose late husband, a newspaper reporter, was killed in the war. I learned about the wedding in a most brutal way. I simply received an invitation to the reception. You can imagine my disappointment, for I had always believed Mr Ehrlich entertained a certain regard for me. I see now I was dreadfully mistaken.
>
> Although I cannot fully justify what I'm about to say, I shall nevertheless say it. I blame his niece, Eva Salz or Salt as I believe she now calls herself. Not once, not once, has she written to her beloved uncle. As far as I know, he did not have an address for her in London and none was ever sent. Can you believe it? He was devoted to her and I think that his disappointment somehow poisoned all his former affections.
>
> You say you are moving to Chicago. Please be sure to send me your new address.

A history of the Frankfurter Bank in Hamburg, published by the bank itself in 1919, records that Herr Alfred Bronstein received the Iron Cross, second class, for extraordinary bravery in the face of the enemy.

And, after a long gap, the final entry for that decade in Dr Bulkarov's diary, dated October of the same year, 1919:

I have thrown caution to the wind and joined the Whites. We will smash the Red scum, I know it.

I write this in a tent by the light of a kerosene lamp. I am serving under General Nikolai Nikolayevich Iudenich, who has a grotesque squint, is short and fat, bald with a drooping moustache and inspires no confidence at all. He's a savage aristo and I have absolute faith in him.

We are not far from Petrograd which will be ours in no time at all, and then the Red bastards will crumble into dust.

Oh, the things I have seen. The Reds have no mercy. They destroy whole villages, bury people alive, babies, pregnant women, the old and the infirm. (Mind you, we are not much better. One of our officers lost all control and hanged twelve children in front of their parents and this, I am told, is not an isolated incident.)

Near Pskov I saw the corpse of His Excellency the former Governor-General of Poland, Georgy Skalon. The Reds had chopped him to bits. Literally. And I could not help noticing that his feet were nowhere to be seen. God is a better novelist than Tolstoy.

10

Countess Maria Obrunina made a sketch in charcoal which she called *A Nest Of Aristocrats*, and signed it, M. A. Obrunina, Sobliki, May 1919. There are ten figures, each identified by name. Tatiana and Lev are in the centre, surrounded by their four children, Xenia, Darya, Valodya and Iliena. Tatiana's elderly parents, Prince Sergei and Princess Ekaterina Souvritzin stand in the left foreground, apparently observing them. In the right-hand corner, seated, are the artist's mother and father, Countess Sophia and Count Alexei Obrunin. They are gazing at each other. Counting the artist herself, there were eleven awaiting their fate in Sobliki in the spring of 1919.

In many regions of the former Tsar's empire there was arson, rape, summary executions and destruction, but the revolution was tardy in reaching the environs of Tula. There is no reasonable explanation except, perhaps, for the vast space of Russia, the difficulties of organisation and communication over enormous distances, and to acknowledge that more important centres of influence or danger were given priority in the seizure of power.

All but the Sobelevs had been caught in Moscow by the Bolshevik *coup d'état*. To begin with, both the Obrunins and the Souvritzins had no choice but to stay put, trapped by anarchy, confusion and the continuous hissing of snakes. At the beginning of the new year, 1918, the Moscow soviet ordered them to vacate their homes. The Obrunins immediately made hurried preparations to leave for their country estate but news reached them that their house had been burned to the ground and Count Alexei's brother, his wife and children, murdered. The Souvritizins fared somewhat better: their house, too, had been razed but their son, Prince Grigory, had only been arrested and taken to an unknown destination. The elderly couple decided their one hope was to flee to their daughter, Tatiana, in Sobliki. They telegraphed a message and waited for a reply. None came. They waited and waited, seated among trunks and suitcases, distraught and helpless.

'Let us simply go,' the Princess said.

'No, Ekaterina,' Prince Sergei replied. 'The world may be falling about our heads but that is no reason to behave indecorously. One cannot visit without either an invitation or permission.' He had been *chef du protocole* to Tsar Alexander III.

'But she's our daughter, Sergei.'

'Nevertheless.'

They sat and waited.

The idea of fleeing to Sobliki occurred also to Maria Obrunina. At first, the Obrunins discussed various possibilities of refuge – relatives, neighbours, friends. For one reason or another all were rejected until Maria hit upon Sobliki. With remarkable courage and composure, and against her parents' wishes, she ventured out alone in mid-afternoon and headed for the telegraph office. A queue stretched half-way down the street. A moment's panic immobilised her. Then, she had an idea, or an inspiration. Out of the depths of her subconscious, the memory of a letter Tatiana had written to her years before suddenly burst upon her, ice splintered by an axe. Controlling her excitement, and unperturbed, she strolled down Tverskaya Street as if all were as it should be, buffeted by wave upon wave of drunks, mutinous soldiers, and curiosity-seekers. Once only was she afraid. A couple of soldiers tried to block her path, but her demeanour intimidated them and they stood yelling insults at her back as she continued on her way. She made for I. M. Denisov, supplier of artists' materials from whom, for many years, she had bought her oils, crayons, watercolours, paper and canvas. The shop was locked and barred. She rang the bell. A curtain flicked on the first floor. Seconds later she heard footsteps and Denisov's voice from behind the door, 'Countess, please, it's not safe, go away.'

'I must talk to you, Ivan Mikhailovich,' Maria replied. 'Let me in.'

Denisov obeyed and she hurried into the darkened shop. He looked more like a professor of fine art than a tradesman, with a wonderfully chiselled face dominated by a long thin nose and crowned with impeccably waved iron-grey hair. He made no effort to conceal his alarm, constantly wringing his hands or pressing them together as if in prayer. Each time there was an unexpected noise, gunshots or breaking glass, he winced and squeezed his eyes tightly. 'Countess, you shouldn't be out. We're all going to be murdered,' he said.

'No, we're not,' Maria replied calmly. 'I need a favour from you, and I need it urgently.'

'A favour? From me? But what can I do? What can any of us do?

'Do you remember, some years ago, you sent one of my paintings by railway train to the Countess Tatiana Sergeievna Sobeleva in Sobliki, near Tula?'

'Countess, how can I possibly remember every painting I've sent—?'

'Do you keep records?' she asked, interrupting him sharply.

'Of course I keep records, but—'

'Find them. It's a matter of life and death.'

He hesitated but then went quickly through a curtained arch into an office. 'What year was it?' he asked.

'Nineteen-thirteen. August or September.'

He opened cupboards and drawers and after much shifting of books and blowing of dust found the appropriate ledger. He licked his fingers to turn the pages and at last came to the entry. 'Yes, here it is,' he said.

'Did you not telephone the station-master at Sobliki to tell him the painting was being sent?'

'Yes,' he said, baffled as though by a clairvoyant.

'And did you record the telephone number of Sobliki station?'

'Yes, of course I did. I have it here. Tula eleven.'

'Where is your telephone? I wish to use it,' Maria said.

'But – but the lines – the operators – I'm not sure you'll – it's – I—'

'Where is your telephone, Ivan Mikhailovich?'

After three hours of waiting, a frantic operator at last connected Maria to Kurugin, the Sobliki station-master. She told him her name. 'Will you please get a message to Countess Tatiana Sergeievna? Tell her my parents and I are coming to Sobliki. If it is inconvenient we will only stay a short time. Please tell her we have no choice. Do you understand?'

'Yes, yes,' Kurugin shouted. 'And, Countess, could you possibly do a favour for me?'

'If I can.'

'The Countess's parents, Prince and Princess Souvritzin telegraphed a similar message. I have been unable to reply because my telegraph key is broken. Could you be so kind as to tell them that Tatiana Sergeievna insists they come as soon as possible?'

The next morning, the Obrunins and the Souvritzins travelled the icy roads south to Sobliki.

For more than a year the families lived together. Maria occupied a guest-room in The Annex. The elders were made comfortable in the main house. These were not the death agonies of the old order, but its rigor mortis. As though frozen in an immense avalanche, the aristocrats were rendered impotent and inert. They lived out those days and nights in perpetual terror, starting at the least noise, haunting the windows to watch the drive for unexpected visitors.

There were bizarre anomalies in their existence. Because of the sudden increase in the household, more servants were required. When word reached the town, volunteers, not recruits, arrived offering their services to the embattled grandees. The additional staff could not be paid since bank accounts had been seized, but Lev saw to it that they were compensated in kind with food from the estate. There is no record of complaint or rebellion. Sobliki survived in suspended animation.

During the harvest of 1918, Tatiana and her elder daughters, Xenia and Darya, worked with the peasants from dawn to dusk. So, too, did Maria Obrunina and Agnes McMurray, the children's Scots governess who refused to leave her employers. Yet, after each day's labour, the family were waited on by their servants without question or rancour. Their baths were drawn, clothes laundered, meals cooked and served, formalities observed, respect shown. Only in Russia, Maria said, could such complex relationships be accommodated with such unaffected simplicity.

During that year of waiting, Tatiana came to understand, in a mysterious, intuitive way, that she was being prepared for what was to come. The terror of the unknown gave her the strength to face the terror of the known.

Preparations less inward were also undertaken. Contingency plans were made and remade so obsessively and so often that the planners could not remember what they had finally decided. This was particularly true of the jewellery. First one hiding-place was decided on, then another, and another, and another, until Tatiana, for one, was made so anxious by the constant changes that she endured days of agony unable to remember where her valuables were stashed. Maria supervised the preservation of the best paintings which she removed from their frames, and then carefully rolled the canvases and stored them in handmade hessian sleeves. China and silver were crated and hidden in the bell-tower of the church.

Tatiana had other more serious causes for anxiety. Lev's health deteriorated. He developed jaundice and was confined to bed. This meant that Dr Volkov continued to visit the house regularly. He was the main source of intelligence from the outside world although Father Astasy also provided information. Both men had access to all sections of the community and through their personalities the news was filtered. Dr Volkov was forever optimistic; Father Astasy talked mostly of death and salvation through suffering; thus, the mood of Sobliki oscillated between hope and despair depending on the latest visitor to the nest.

In August, Pavlik, the steward, informed Lev that an itinerant Jewish orchestra had arrived in the town. The leader had requested permission to play for the aristocrats. Lev asked his guests if a musical performance would be welcome.

Count Alexei Obrunin was outraged. In his early sixties, short and overweight, he had an air of self-importance. 'Jews, Lev Borisovich? Jews? Don't you realise that the Jews are behind this whole ghastly business? Marx, Engels, Trotsky, all Jews. I shouldn't be surprised if Lenin himself isn't an Israelite. What was one of his first acts after seizing power? He repealed all the laws that keep the Jews in their place. Only the other day Father Astasy told me the Bolsheviks believe that Jews should have the same rights as other citizens.'

'And so they should,' Prince Sergei Souvritzin said quietly. The hauteur which others found so forbidding in Tatiana was inherited from her father in whom dignity and pride were exaggerated. There was a strong physical resemblance, too, and in the male the long Souvritzin nose and thin lips conveyed even greater severity, almost grimness. The former *chef du protocole* of Tsar Alexander III, not surprisingly a stickler for form, was, however, difficult to read. His opinions often surprised his family and friends. His attitudes and beliefs were not in any way conventional and he took particular pleasure in confronting Count Obrunin whom he considered a well-bred oaf.

The oaf said, 'I beg your pardon, Prince? You believe the Jews should be treated the same as everyone else?'

'I believe all men should be treated equally.'

'You sound like a Bolshevik, Prince.' This, from Sophia Obrunina, who always took the same view as her husband.

'I am a liberal. As was my father before me.'

'So you keep telling us,' the Count said.

'And I became more of a liberal while serving the Tsar when I gained some insight into the filth and inefficiency of the administration.'

'What has all this to do with the Jews?' the Countess asked.

'My family,' the Prince said, 'the Souvritzins, have a long tradition of judging men not by their rank or wealth or position, but by their behaviour towards others. We were always kind to our Jews.'

Maria, to put an end to the discussion, said, 'I should love to hear an orchestra, Jewish or otherwise.'

It was decided that the performance should be given in the park towards evening. One of the follies, no more than a small cupola with four supporting columns, made an ideal platform. Chairs were arranged in a semi-circle for the adults, while the children and Miss McMurray sat on the ground on rugs. There were five male musicians, all somewhat dishevelled in appearance, two violins, two cellos, and a viola. The leader, Mordecai, had slicked-back hair, a trim moustache and a flat nose that looked as though he had once been a pugilist. His manner added new meaning to the word servility. To begin the concert, he gave the peasant's traditional bow: hands crossed on the forehead and then a great sweeping gesture, his arms flowing sideways like a swan's wings, as he bent double.

'Highnesses,' he said, 'in these troubled times, I hope you will find solace in our music. We have prepared a programme of some of the most beloved works by the great masters and also, of course, traditional Russian folk-songs. With Your Highnesses' kind approval, we shall begin with the slow movement to the quintet by Franz Schubert in C major, for strings, opus one hundred and sixty-three.' He made another elongated obeisance before taking his seat beside his colleagues. He gave a nod and the concert began.

And at least one listener did seem to find solace or what passed for solace. The sun dipped behind the avenue of birch and a comforting breeze ruffled the leaves. Imperceptibly, the day began to fade and all were momentarily enveloped in a numinous light, as though they were being sanctified and given a glimpse of eternity. But the light quickly vanished and they became shadows.

The quintet played without music, every note and phrase deeply felt, the sounds speaking directly to those wishing to hear, for Schubert's Adagio is the most profound musical expression of the inner life, a confirmation of the belief that the world of the spirit is more potent than reality. It evokes pain, suffering, and a sense of loss but, much more importantly, it testifies to a glorious, aspiring human quality, mysterious and triumphant, which transcends all and in which, Tatiana thought, only the greatest artists seem to believe, or are able to detect and transmit. So, in that brief twilight, listening to Schubert, she was overcome with joy. The music coaxed from her an affirmation of life and survival. She gazed at her children and thanked God for their existence, and for Miss McMurray, strong, modest, loyal. She turned her eyes on her husband. The last pink rays of the sun touched and enlivened his sallow complexion. He had the appearance of a marble statue. And her father, almost eighty, straight back, proud chin, a prince. Her mother, who had been considered one of the most beautiful women in Russia, was wrinkled now and her head trembled slightly, but Tatiana felt as though the music was an emissary reaching out to embrace them all. For the older Obrunins she felt nothing. The Count, determined to resist the power of the music, waggled a foot in time to his own displeasure. His wife slept, oblivious to the beauty around her, unaware of the five Jews under the cupola who, Tatiana realised, were not only intimates of human tragedy but also witnesses to the glory. Tatiana caught Maria's eye just as darkness overtook them. They exchanged a smile and Tatiana believed that Maria was able to read her thoughts. She had the notion that they both prayed at that moment the same prayer. God, give us the strength to endure.

Inexplicably, Tatiana was aware that she was happy. She tried to remember other moments of similar contentment and then realised that pain was easier to recall. She understood that happiness is rare and leaves behind only the most illusive fragrance.

'I have faith in the Russian people,' Count Alexei Obrunin said. Each evening, after dinner, in the music room on the ground floor, he partnered his wife against the Souvritzins at bridge. Lev, the children and Miss McMurray retired to The Annex early; Maria sketched and Tatiana played the piano. If arguments erupted, as they often did, Tatiana hammered the opening chords of Tchaikovsky's Fifth Piano Concerto to drown or silence them. Tensions were never far beneath the surface.

'In what particular aspect of the Russian people do you have faith?' Prince Sergei asked. 'In their cruelty? Their stupidity? Their cowardice?'

'In their goodness. I have faith in the soul of Russia.'

'Ah! In Russia's soul. I see.'

'You may sneer, Prince, but let us face reality. No people on earth have had to suffer as Russians have suffered.'

'And who's to blame?' the Prince asked, throwing down his cards. 'Answer me that, who's to blame for Russia's suffering?' His wife, Ekaterina, gently patted his hand to calm him but he brushed her off irritably.

'Who's to blame?' the Count said. 'No one's to blame. Our suffering is in God's hands.'

'In God's hands, oh, very good, yes, that's right, blame God. He can't defend Himself.'

Countess Sophia said, 'I agree with my husband,' and then enquired sweetly, 'But you, Prince, have, I suspect, some other theory?'

'Oh, let's play bridge, let's not argue,' Ekaterina said.

'No, no,' Count Alexei persisted. 'I want to hear who the Prince blames for our suffering.'

The Prince exploded. 'Our suffering? Our suffering? You, my dear Count, have never suffered in your whole life. You have been pampered and spoiled from the moment you first drew breath. When the doctor first slapped you to make you cry, he probably wore a velvet glove. You want to know whom I blame for Russia's suffering? I'll tell you. We are to blame. You, me, the Tsar, the Russian people, all of us.'

'All of us?' repeated Countess Sophia, shocked at this revelation.

'All of us?' her husband echoed. 'How dare you, Prince? I have done nothing to make Russia suffer.'

'Forgive me, you have done nothing, Count, and that has been enough to make Russia suffer.'

'This is objectionable,' the Count said. 'You talk like a Bolshevik not like a former servant of the Tsar.'

'The Tsar did not deserve to have servants. He was a bully with a closed mind. And his son, God rest his soul, was a weakling and a half-wit.'

'I cannot listen to this any longer,' the Countess said, rising from the card-table.

Tatiana banged out Tchaikovsky.

Prince Sergei raised his voice and bellowed over the music. 'I have sympathy with the people although they don't deserve it. They should have risen up years ago but they haven't the sense or the courage. I believe we have had a good run for our money, and enough is enough. Our time is over. We are irrelevant. We are the scum of the earth. We are dead only we won't admit it. I wish they'd come to bury us tomorrow.'

The tomorrow he wished for arrived in the spring of 1919. The thaw, like the revolution, was late in reaching Sobliki. In May, the park was still a patchwork of snow and ice. When darkness fell, the cold was intense and there was talk of a bad harvest.

The first warning was the sound of marching feet breaking the ice. Tatiana and Maria hurried to the window. The card-players froze. The glint of something catching the moonlight caused Maria to catch her breath. It was a sword held by a sailor at the head of a dozen or so men marching up the drive. One or two at the rear carried flaming torches. Tatiana remained motionless.

'They're here,' Maria said.

And from Tatiana, 'At last.'

The impatient banging on the door echoed through the house. Pavlik and Dunyasha shuffled down the passage to admit the visitors. The sailor, muscular, close-set eyes, a shining bullet for a head, introduced himself as Comrade Platov. He held the sword in a careless salute but the courtesy was too casual and, therefore, threatening.

Pavlik said, 'How can I help you?'

'I wish to see Comrade Sobelev.'

'The Count has retired for the night.'

'Wake him.'

'He's not well.'

'Wake him.' Platov pushed past into the hall. His followers remained outside on the steps, silent, but he looked back at them and with a curt flick of the head beckoned them to follow. They shuffled

155

uncomfortably into the hallway. All were men from the town; none had been in the house before and they stood uneasily, stealing glances at the finery. Platov paced while Pavlik, with an exaggerated limp, slowly hobbled into the night to summon the residents of The Annex. 'A couple of you go with him,' Platov ordered.

Dunyasha suddenly cried, 'Ivan, what are you doing here?' She had spotted among the men her cousin's son, a ploughman, an ungainly youth with a button nose and massive shoulders. 'Does your mother know you're out?' His comrades laughed, Platov loudest of all but there was no humour in the sound he made.

Tatiana emerged from the music room. 'I am Tatiana Sergeievna,' she said. 'What it is you want?'

Several of the men now removed their caps; one or two bowed. Not Platov. He said, 'We have come to search for arms. And to – to question the men.'

His hesitation signalled a warning. Tatiana said, 'We have no weapons in the house.'

'You expect me to take your word for that, comrade?' Platov asked.

'On whose authority are you here?'

He smiled and Tatiana was surprised at how handsome he suddenly looked. He said, 'On whose authority? On the authority of the Russian people, comrade, and the Tula soviet.' Still smiling, he sheathed his sword. Somewhere in the house a clock struck nine. He turned to his men. 'I'm not waiting any longer. We'll start at the top and work down.'

Platov put a man on guard in the music room. The rest he divided into two groups. One he dispatched to The Annex, the others followed him up the stairs to the top of the house. The search lasted for more than five hours and ended at dawn. Every drawer and cupboard was emptied, every possible hiding-place uncovered. Lev, the children and Miss McMurray joined the others in the music room and Miss McMurray read stories to them in English until they slept. Princess Ekaterina held little Iliena on her lap. Dunyasha came and went with refreshments. The guard, Yakimov, was a baker's assistant and his face was speckled with flour. Lev invited him to sit but he refused. He stood by the door, arms folded, ill at ease.

Platov and his men, banging and shouting, worked their way through the house. There were sounds of breaking glass and wood splintering. When midnight struck, Tatiana went to the piano and played the third movement, the Rondo, of the 'Waldstein' Sonata. Later, she played Mozart's *Eine kleine Nachtmusik*, and later still, Chopin's Prelude Number 15, called the 'Raindrop Prelude'.

Little was said in the music room. As time passed Lev looked more and more haggard. Dunyasha mixed his medicine for him but it

156

seemed to do him no good. Valodya woke with a nightmare and Miss McMurray sang a Scots lullaby to soothe him. Count Alexei Obrunin paced, sat, paced, sat. His wife played patience. Prince Sergei sat perfectly still, preserving his dignity. Maria draw in charcoal *A Nest of Aristocrats*.

Finally, at sunrise, Platov entered, holding in his hand an antique duelling pistol that had once belonged to Lev's grandfather and which had not been used for forty years. 'No weapons, eh?' Platov said trying to sound triumphant. He ordered Yakimov and others to search the music room. 'The rest of you, follow me.'

He led them into the hall. Iliena began to cry and no one was able to quieten her. They stood carelessly grouped at the foot of the staircase, Tatiana with Lev and the children. Platov, his hands clasped behind his back, surveyed each face in turn, nodding every now and then as though in recognition. His men gathered behind him. They had helped themselves to vodka and were flushed now, more confident, less circumspect. Platov whispered an order, and two of them hurriedly left the house.

Platov said, 'So, here we are, comrades, and a nice little bunch you are. This is no longer your property, is that understood? It belongs to the State now, to the people.' He turned suddenly on Count Obrunin and asked his name.

'Obrunin. Alexei Alexeievich.'

Platov took hold of the Count's lapel between his thumb and forefinger as if frightened of catching a disease, gingerly pulled him forward and discarded him in the direction of the men. The Countess demanded, 'What are you going to do to him?'

Platov did not reply, but turned his attention to Lev. 'You're Sobelev, yes?'

'Yes.'

Platov flicked his thumb indicating that Lev should join Obrunin. Lev kissed Tatiana and the children and, while he did so, Platov approached Prince Sergei. 'Name?'

'Sergei Lvovich Souvritzin.'

'A-ha! Souvritzin!' Platov crowed, then turned to his men. 'We've got a Prince here, comrades. All right, you, too.'

The Prince kissed his wife on both cheeks and then Tatiana and the children. He kissed the hands of Countess Obrunina, Maria and Miss McMurray. 'Quite the gentleman,' Platov said, smiling again. 'Right, take them outside.'

Princess Ekaterina screamed, 'What are you going to do?' and began to sob.

Platov ignored her and marched out of the house to join his men and the prisoners. The women hurried after him. The sun was higher now but it gave no warmth, and an icy wind stung their faces. The two men Platov dispatched had brought a horse and cart to the foot of the terrace steps and Platov gave orders for Lev, Prince Sergei and Count Obrunin to be put on the back. The Princess screamed, 'Don't, don't, please!'

'Where are you taking them?' Maria asked. 'What is going to happen to them?'

Platov enjoyed this moment. He turned to Maria, smiled, and said, 'We're not going to shoot them, don't worry. Although if I had my way, I'd hang them from the nearest tree. No, no, it's all legal and proper. They're enemies of the State, you see, sweetheart, and we're taking them to prison. To Moscow.'

Princess Ekaterina ran forward. 'No, no,' she cried, 'you can't, you mustn't, he's an old man, and he believes in what you stand for, he's your friend, he's not your enemy—'

Tatiana marched up to her mother, put an arm around her shoulder and whispered to her, 'Please, mama, stop that. It's not dignified,' and led her back to the steps. The Princess fought for control.

'You women may collect up your personal things and then we want you out of here, understood?' He hopped up on to the back of the cart with the three prisoners, his legs dangling over the tailboard. He clenched his fist in the new salute and the cart set off with his men following on foot. Lev waved. The women and children watched until the procession disappeared.

Dunyasha said, 'I hope Lev Borisovich will be all right. He's never been in a cart before.'

PART THREE

Tracks
(1920–1928)

1

Stepan screamed but his scream was drowned by the noise of the train screeching to a halt in a tunnel. Only when the train was still in the intense blackness were his cries heard. 'What's the matter, little one, what's the matter?' the old woman asked. 'Are you sick?'

'My violin!' he cried. 'Somebody's stolen my violin! I was holding it, somebody stole it while I slept—' He flailed his arms wildly, searching, groping, desperate to find the missing instrument.

The woman tried to comfort him. In the dark he could feel her bony hands flapping around his face but he shied away. 'Who took it?' he demanded, and then yelling, 'Who stole my violin?' He was answered by shouts to keep quiet. He stood. 'I must find my violin! I want the thief who took my violin!' He stepped forward, tripped over something, stumbled, half-fell. 'Where's my violin?' he whimpered.

A hand gripped him. Stepan froze. His eyes were more accustomed to the darkness now and he discerned the silhouette of a long, thin, bearded face amidst the huddled shapes of the other refugees. 'Be quiet, boy, and sit down. Conserve your strength. Losing your violin is a trivial matter. Losing your life is more serious.' The voice was cultivated, Russian spoken with a French accent, an aristocrat.

'But – but you don't understand—' Stepan began.

'No buts. Sit down and be quiet. Accept your fate. In hell do as the damned.'

'Here, little boy—' the old woman said, reaching out her hand again, this time to guide Stepan back to his seat.

He sat, crushed between the carriage window and the old woman, grateful that no one could see the tears coursing down his cheeks. More than leaving his parents, or parting from his brother, the theft of his violin, Manishowitz's Hills of London violin, consumed Stepan with despair, a sense of loss the like of which he had never known, deep and gaping.

He grieved. How could anyone be so disgusting and cruel? he asked. It's my own fault. I should have kept awake, I should have guarded it more closely. But I was clutching it all the time, what more could I do? How could anybody have slipped it out of my arms without waking me? It's my own fault, I—

A boy cried out, 'I shall never see my mother again!' and his wailing enveloped the carriage. But he was soon comforted by reassuring voices.

I will never be comforted, Stepan decided. If I don't find my violin, I will never play again. I swear, I will never play again.

For more than two hours the train remained stationary, the darkness occasionally splintered by a match flaring, and the silence by sporadic murmurs, 'Where are we? What's happening? Where are we?'

From the outset, the journey had turned into an alarming succession of stops and searches and incomprehensible diversions. They crossed the border into Poland but then, mysteriously, snaked back into Russia and then once again into Poland. To Stepan, Moscow was a million miles away. He lost all sense of time and had no idea of how long he had been travelling. But the press of people, crammed tightly one against the other, ensured warmth, and he did not go hungry. It was somehow taken for granted that the food each traveller had brought would be shared among all. The privations were of another kind: bewilderment, fear, confusion. Now, in the tunnel, he was unable to tell night from day. He had slept frequently, empty, untroubled sleeps but he regretted them and wished he had kept awake, guarding more vigilantly the most precious object he owned.

He had also lost count of the times they had been made to detrain. The engine shuddering to a stop at yet another station or siding heralded the cries of 'Off! Off!' from young Red Guards, rifles in hand, prodding, shoving, herding. The constant, endless examination of documents, the questions, the insults: 'Running away, bourgeois scum? You should all be lined up and shot!' And the repetitive message, variously phrased, but always the same: 'The personal life is over. Long live Vladimir Ilyich Lenin! Long live the Revolution!'

His worst memory was of one stop where an overweight, middle-aged woman who might in other times have passed for a schoolteacher or a post-mistress, commanded two dozen men. Her black hair, streaked with grey like barbed wire, was scraped back into an unruly bun and she wore the cap of a Tsarist officer. A faint moustache clouded her upper lip. She scanned the refugees as though looking for someone in particular. Her eyes lighted on Stepan. She ordered him to be brought into the station-master's office which she had commandeered.

Alone with Stepan, she asked, 'Name?' Her breath smelt.

He clutched his violin case tightly. 'Stepan Stepanovich Kessler,' he replied.

'You must say comrade,' she said. 'I am your comrade, you understand, and you are mine.' Her smile was joyless, unconvincing. 'You understand, comrade?'

'Yes, comrade.'

Carefully she studied his documents. 'These are not in order,' she said. 'I'm sending you back to Moscow.'

'I have to get to Chemnitz,' he protested.

'To hell with Chemnitz,' she said, 'I'm sending you back. We are all suffering so that young people like you can have a decent future and you are running away.'

'I am not running away, comrade, my cousins are expecting me. Herr Lohmeyer of Chemnitz.'

'Don't give me shit, comrade. They probably don't even know you're coming. Back you go.'

'Is it money?' he asked urgently. 'I can pay more. I've got money. Do I need another ticket? Can I buy new documents?'

She slapped him hard across the face. He caught his breath. 'Open that case,' she commanded.

'It's only my violin—'

'Open it.'

He obeyed. She took up the violin roughly, shook it, tried to peer through the frets, felt the lining of the case. 'Where's your money?' she asked, thrusting the violin into his hands.

Out on the platform, commands were being shouted, 'Back on board, back on board! The train is leaving immediately.' The engine's whistle sounded.

The woman said, 'You are a piece of shit.' She took hold of his ear and, pinching it tightly, dragged him out of the office back on to the platform where people, seven or eight abreast, were pushing and shoving to reboard the train through the narrow doors.

'I want this boy searched,' she shouted. 'He's confessed. He's a currency smuggler.'

She let go of his ear for a moment to beckon one of her men. The train started to move. There were still knots of refugees struggling at the doors. Stepan darted off like a whippet, diving into the midst of the nearest group who were now running to keep pace with the gathering speed of the train. Hands reached out and pulled him and the others on board. They tumbled one on top of the other. He heard the enraged shouts of protests from the woman but she was impotent. The train was on its way again and not to be stopped, at least not by her.

Now, in the dark of the tunnel, Stepan put his hand to his ear-lobe. He could still feel the pressure of the woman's thumb and finger. How long ago was all that, he wondered?

'We'll die here in this tunnel,' somebody said.

'No, no, we'll move soon.'

'We'll die for want of air.'

'We've been travelling for seven days and seven nights.'

'Eight.'

'No, seven.'

'Eight!'

The train jerked forward. Gasps of relief, bursts of excited chatter. 'We're moving, we're moving.'

And from the aristocrat: 'Damned fools, of course we're moving.'

Minutes later, light so sudden and intense it caused Stepan pain. He turned sharply away from the window, closed his eyes, and then slowly opened them again. Windows were forced to let in welcome blasts of cold, fresh air.

The brakes screamed. A great mournful cry of disappointment. Then, *'Raus! Raus!'*

The aristocrat grabbed Stepan's hand. 'Stay with me,' he said.

'I think we're in Germany again,' Stepan said, uncertain but hopeful.

'I think so, too. By the way, boy, my name is Vladimir Ivanovich Belaev,' he said with a curt nod of the head. He was tall and gangling, like a scarecrow in need of straw. His beard reached well down to his chest. 'Actually, I am Count Belaev, originally from Rostov. And you, what's your name?'

Stepan told him.

'Kessler, Kessler, yes, German origin, I fancy,' Belaev murmured as though vaguely disapproving.

Belaev and Stepan were made to line up with the others in neat ranks, ten in each rank, three columns the length of the platform. Stepan was amazed by the appearance of the station, the flowers in tubs, the absence of refuse, the neat uniforms of the railway officials. Those in charge, the ones forever consulting lists, seemed firm but not unkindly.

'Do you speak German?' the aristocrat asked.

'A little,' Stepan said.

'Good boy. I speak only French and a smattering of Italian. Do you know enough German to ask where we are?'

'I think so.'

As if he still were master of a thousand serfs, the aristocrat snapped his fingers and beckoned one of the railway porters, a short, fat man, with a small, square moustache. To Stepan's surprise, he came scuttling over and bowed to the Count.

'Ask him where we are,' Count Belaev ordered Stepan, who obliged.

'You have crossed the border. You are in Görlitz,' the porter said.
'Ask him how far it is to Dresden.'
'About seventy-five kilometres.'
And Stepan asked on his own behalf, 'How far to Chemnitz?'
'About the same again.'
The porter bowed and waddled away.

The atmosphere abruptly changed with the arrival of the police. Two black vans, which Stepan at first thought were hearses, drew up near the platform and out poured twenty or so uniformed men. Immediately, their leader began shouting orders and a noisy argument erupted between him and the railway officials.

'What are they saying?' Belaev asked.

'I think the police are in charge now,' Stepan answered. 'They've had refugees here before.'

'Oh God. Time for prayer.'

The Görlitz policemen took up positions at strategic points so that the refugees were more or less surrounded and their commanding officer seemed to win the day. He mounted a bench and shouted, 'Russians, listen to me,' and he beckoned them towards him. The refugees broke ranks and swarmed round the man. Belaev and Stepan pushed to the front and Stepan translated for those near enough to hear and they, in turn, passed the word back.

'Russians, we have no facilities to house you here. Unless you have German money to buy tickets to your destination we will have no choice but to send you back to Russia. If you do not have the money you will spend the night in police cells and be transported back tomorrow morning at dawn. We deeply regret this action but we have no alternative. You will now be questioned by my men. There will be no appeal. Understood?' But he didn't wait for a reply. He stepped down off the bench and disappeared.

'Do you have money?' Belaev asked.

'Yes. Do you?'

'I have gold. That's better than money,' and he pulled nervously at his long beard.

Three trestle-tables were set up in a locomotive shed; at each, three policemen asked questions and filled in forms. The remainder of the force either stood blocking the wide door that let in sunshine or lounged behind their colleagues who were doing the paperwork. The refugees were seen singly.

'Good luck, Stepan Stepanovich.'

'Thank you. And good luck to you, Count,' Stepan said. He was confident all would be well. He surreptitiously felt the money in the lining of his coat and it gave him confidence.

'Next.'

Stepan's interrogator had several chins which were damp with sweat. He wore no cap and was almost bald except for three thin strands of hair combed sideways across the dome. Stepan's first reaction was to chuckle inwardly. He looked ridiculous, like an actor made up to amuse. But Stepan's laughter shrivelled when he looked into the man's eyes, small, black dots which never caught the light.

'So, Russian. My name is Alfred Schmidt. What is yours, please?'

'Stepan Stepanovich Kessler.'

Alfred seemed impressed. Documents, please, Stepan.'

So far so good. Stepan produced his papers. The policeman studied them perfunctorily. 'Kessler,' he said. 'You are German?'

'No, I am Russian but my ancestors were German.'

'Ancestors? You are very little boy to have ancestors. How old are you?'

'Twelve.'

'I have a son your age,' Alfred said with sentimental indulgence and then, because it only just dawned on him, he exclaimed, 'But you speak our language!'

'A little. My father taught me.'

'And where is your father? And your mother?'

'In Moscow.'

'You are alone?' Alfred's little eyes widened a crack.

'Yes.'

'You have come on this train all alone?'

'Yes.'

'And you are how old?' he asked again.

'Twelve.'

Alfred shook his head. His chins remained stationary. He said, 'I do not think I could let my son travel on his own. Your parents must be very brave. And you are bound for?'

'Chemnitz. Family Lohmeyer.'

'Money. You have money. Or gold.'

'No, I don't have gold—'

A scream from a woman interrupted him. Two policemen hauled her and a child away. Alfred smiled and nodded as one who liked to watch the world go by. He returned his attention to Stepan. 'Yes? Your money?'

Stepan carefully pulled at the stitches with which Anya had sewn the notes into the lining of his coat but they wouldn't give. Alfred watched for a moment, then produced a pocket-knife. 'Here,' he said, and cut the seam not bothering with the stitches. The bundles of notes fell to the ground. Stepan hastily retrieved them and handed them over to Alfred who flicked through them like a bank clerk and then burst out laughing.

166

'But these are Tsarist roubles.'

'Yes. There's enough there for the fare to Chemnitz.'

'They're useless.'

'Useless?'

'Your Comrade Lenin has declared Tsarist roubles no longer legal tender.'

'When, when did he do that?' Stepan demanded, fear rising to form a hard lump in his throat.

'Last week, maybe the week before. Tsarist roubles are no longer legal tender.'

Another scuffle at one of the tables and two men were marched away.

'Probably they also have Tsarist roubles. You have no gold, no jewellery?'

'No—'

'Next!' Alfred ordered and as he did so signalled his colleagues to bustle Stepan away. Stepan looked back and saw Belaev about to be questioned. Belaev waved, and Stepan thought he heard him call, '*Au revoir*, comrade.'

He was too numb even to weep. In the small cell, with eight others, women and children, Stepan sat on the floor, hugging his knees instead of his violin. No one talked. Night and cold enveloped them. They were served a bowl of watery soup which was at least hot, and a hunk of rye bread. At ten o'clock the solitary electric light was extinguished. A bucket in the corner served as a lavatory and all who had need used it. The stench was unbearable. Silence and misery. One of the young girls cried. Her mother sang:

> The sun has set and is sleeping,
> Stop the tears now, stop the weeping,
> Close your eyes, little baby, hush,
> The night is at hand, hush-a, hush.

The woman had a mournful alto voice which soothed and gave comfort. The little girl stopped crying. Stepan's eyes grew heavy. Moscow, he thought. I am going back to Moscow and to dead men dangling from lampposts. That's how it is. Nothing to be done. He was calm. But into his mind came the face of Manishowitz and with it genuine terror which banished briefly any possibility of sleep. How, Stepan agonised, would he explain to the old man the loss of the violin? He was puzzled as to why he should be so frightened of Manishowitz, yet felt no joy at the prospect of seeing his parents again. And then, just before sleep finally came, the words of Count

Belaev unaccountably crept into his thoughts. In hell do as the damned.

Footsteps in the corridor. Stepan's eyes snapped open. Was it morning already? Were they about to begin the return journey? No. Black in the cell and for a moment he thought he was again in the dark, airless tunnel. A rattle of keys, and the cell door opening.

'Kessler?'

'Yes?'

A torch was switched on and the beam swung from one face to another until it found Stepan. 'Come with me, please.'

Stepan recognised the voice of Alfred Schmidt and his round shape behind the beam of torchlight. 'What – what is it?' Stepan asked.

'Come with me, please.'

Stepan gathered his things and manoeuvred towards the door.

A woman asked in German, 'What time is it?' but Alfred did not reply.

Out in the corridor, Alfred barked, 'Follow me, Russian,' but pushed Stepan ahead, prodding him with the torch to keep him moving.

From the adjoining cell a male voice called out, 'What's going on?'

'Please to shut up and go to sleep,' Alfred answered and gave Stepan a sharp prod in the small of his back. They mounted a short flight of stone steps that led to a wooden door, painted dark green. 'Wait,' Alfred said, juggled with a bunch of keys, unlocked the door, shoved Stepan through and turned on the light.

The room was small, the walls painted from floor to the one windowsill a dull brown, and cream up to the ceiling. A table took up most of the floor space; on one side of it a chair, on the other a bench. Stepan was told to sit on the bench. With his back to Stepan, Alfred removed his cape and cap and carefully hung them on a hook behind the door. He turned to face Stepan. He held a plain buff-coloured file under his arm.

Stepan knew at once the man had been crying. His eyes were almost totally closed by puffy red sacs. The three strands of hair across his pate were damp which gave him an even more forlorn look. Stepan gazed at him, apprehensive, waiting. Alfred's bottom lip trembled and he bit it in an attempt to control his emotions.

At last he said softly, 'I could not sleep.' He waited as if expecting Stepan to comment, but the boy just sat and stared. 'No, I could not sleep. You know why?' Stepan remained motionless. 'Because I could not forget you, that's why. Usually, I am sleeping like a dead man, but not this night. I tossed and turned, seeing your face, and those big eyes of yours, staring at me, saying, "Alfred Schmidt, you are a cruel person, a very cruel person." Then, I must have slept and had bad dreams, for my wife, Katarina, was obliged to wake me. She said, "Why are you crying, Alfred, beloved?" And so I told her of you, the little Russian boy, the same age as our Hermann, all alone, sent from Moscow by his parents to escape those goddam Communists, and his Tsarist roubles worthless. She was unhappy with me. She said, "Alfred, bring him here to our home immediately." I said, "This is not possible, Katarina. There are forms, papers, documents." A long time we argued. You know then what she did? I am telling you the truth, Russian. She rose from our bed, did not even put on her dressing-gown or slippers, but went straight into Hermann's room, woke him, and brought him by the hand to face me. He was rubbing sleep from his eyes. He asked me what was the matter? I could not answer him because my unhappiness was too great. I tried to hide my face so he could not see my tears, but he's a clever boy and grossly observant. He said, "Why are you crying, papa?" Still I could not tell him, so Katarina said, "Look at your son, Alfred. Imagine he is in a prison in Russia, alone, escaping goddam Communists, and his German marks worthless. Think." Then, Hermann said, "But I don't want to go to Russia, mama." I looked into my boy's eyes and, I confess, I wept, oh, such tears. And Katarina said, "Fetch the little Russian."'

They slipped out of the back door of the police station and hurried down narrow streets, Alfred holding Stepan's hand and shining his torch on the cobbled paving stones although the night sky was already lightening. The policeman said, 'I am risking much. That's why I must pretend to be stern with you when I removed you from the cell. No one must suspect. I have here your file which I will destroy. They will not notice one Russian more or less.'

The Schmidt apartment was on the third floor of a squat block of workers' flats. As they mounted the stairs, a delicious aroma invaded Stepan's nostrils and when they entered the front door he was made almost dizzy by the smell. Hermann had been sent back to bed but Katarina, as round as her husband, was in the kitchen to greet them. She was at the stove when they entered.

Stepan removed his cap and bowed his head in greeting. 'Good evening, Frau Schmidt,' he said. It was the first time he had uttered since being awakened and his voice was cracked, his throat dry.

'Ah,' Katarina said, 'such a good-mannered little boy. I have here sausages and many potatoes for you.'

'You must be quick,' Alfred said. 'I will tell you why while you eat.'

'Do not be quick, little Russian,' Katarina said. 'Eat nice and slowly, each mouthful to be chewed thirty times, and pay no attention to Alfred.'

Stepan ate, trying to obey Katarina's dictum but failing. She watched him with an indulgent smile, identical to Alfred's, sickly and sentimental. It made Stepan uncomfortable. Alfred, meanwhile, removed a cover on the stove, jammed the buff-coloured file and its contents down into the embers and made sure the papers burned. He said, 'My brother-in-law, Josef Wessel, is this day delivering pigs to Dresden. He has a fine truck for this purpose and leaves always at first light. On my way to release you, I stopped by his place. This was Katarina's idea. He is married to her sister, Frederika. Thank God he was already awake. He has agreed to take you in his truck with the pigs. In Dresden, his cousin, Wilhelm Jaeger, a goddam Communist but it can't be helped, is an official of the railways, and will see you on a train to Chemnitz.' Alfred watched the last of Stepan's papers burn, replaced the cover, and went to the sink to wash his hands. 'So, Russian. All is in order. On Sunday I will go to church and give thanks to God.'

'That is also my idea,' Katarina said.

Alfred excused himself. 'I will now go and watch from the window for the arrival of my brother-in-law.'

After eating the last mouthful of sausage, Stepan sat back, dazed but contented. Katarina washed up his plate and the frying pan, chatting, as if to herself rather than to Stepan, about the importance of Christian behaviour in a wicked world. Stepan did not really listen. His attention wandered. His eyes lit on a photograph on a wooden dresser, in pride of place among blue and white cups: an elderly man in full military uniform with flowing white moustaches. Katarina turned and noticed. 'You know who that is?'

'No.'

'That is General Ludendorff, a great man, alive now. Erich Ludendorff, yes? He is the hero of Alfred, me and Hermann.' And she smiled at the general with exactly the same indulgence she had shown Stepan.

'He's here!' Alfred called and came scuttling back into the kitchen. 'Put on your cap and hurry.'

In turn the Schmidts shook Stepan's hand, wished him well and bade him goodbye. It was only when he was half-way down the stairs that Stepan realised he had forgotten to say thank you.

2

Herbert Clark Hoover, who was in charge of American food aid to Europe, said, 'Emmett, it's young men like you who give me confidence in the future. I speak on behalf of President Wilson when I say thank you for volunteering.' He shook Emmett's hand and was impressed by the firmness of the grip. 'May God bless you.'

Emmett Brumby was twenty-four years old in 1920 and, although his blond hair was already thinning, gave the impression of a fresh-faced teenager. He had the tall, stringy figure of an athlete and had, indeed, in his second year at Princeton broken the record for the mile. His freckled face shone with inexperience.

The Brumbys were bankers from Philadelphia, had been for three generations, but Emmett's father smashed the mould preferring to try his luck and his large private income at being a painter. In 1891 he emigrated to Paris, then moved to Florence where he met Miss Amelia Jordan, daughter of another ex-patriot American family, and the couple finally settled in Rome where Emmett was born. Sent back to be educated in the United States, Emmett took a degree in law, passed *cum laude*, and was destined for the family bank. But Emmett knew only one thing for certain which was that he had no intention of becoming either a lawyer or a banker. In the summer of 1918 he enlisted in the Army but the Armistice was declared before his services were needed. He returned to Europe and spent an aimless year or two not knowing what to do with himself. He had inherited a strong if somewhat simple romantic streak from his father, and read *The Three Musketeers* and Tennyson's *The Idylls of the King* over and over again. He determined to perform at least one heroic act in his life and light upon a cause, preferably a noble cause, which would not only serve humanity but also help him to find what he called 'self-fulfilment'.

The cause was at hand. Famine crippled Russia. Herbert Clark Hoover initiated a relief programme and asked for volunteers to administer the aid. Emmett responded immediately and believed that his self was about to be fulfilled.

Blizzards paralysed the country. Men, women and children starved and froze to death in numbers too immense to have meaning. Their bodies littered the roads and fields as though they were a crop that had been crudely harvested. No one could remember a winter so savage. Herbert Hoover's young men were given their orders: the cities were starving; go out into the countryside, assess the situation and organise the distribution of surplus food. Speed was of the essence if lives were to be saved.

Maps, like everything else, were in short supply. On his way to Russia, Dean Jackson, a career diplomat with a fey manner, had filched a pre-war German atlas from the American Embassy in Berlin. He had the task of assigning the volunteers their operational areas. Jackson summoned Emmett to his side, the atlas opened to the appropriate page. 'Tula, three hundred kilometres south of Moscow,' he said, pointing. 'Co-operate with the local soviet although they'll deny they have a spare potato. If they prove obstructive, and they will, just tell them you got your orders in Moscow. By the way, soviet means council. But I guess you know that because you speak Russian, don't you?'

'No, sir, I don't,' Emmett said, puzzled.

'Oh. It says here you're a linguist. I took that to mean you spoke Russian.'

'Italian. I speak Italian.'

'Oh. Well, heigh-nonny-no. Do the best you can, and promise nothing. Apparently, they make samovars in Tula, so at least you'll get a cup of hot tea. Don't touch anything stronger. These Reds will drink you under the table. *Arrivederci*.'

Trains were still erratic but Emmett was reliably informed by an official in the transport commissariat that a train would be leaving for Tula at precisely six a.m. the following morning. Dutifully, Emmett was at the railway station a half hour before the appointed time of departure. He waited three hours for a train to appear and another two before it started the journey south. He wore a shaggy teddy-bear coat, much favoured then by young American males and vaudeville comedians, and was at least warm. Nevertheless, huddled into a compartment with eight others, his coat embarrassed him acutely, for he could sense all eyes on it, envious eyes, as though each of his travelling companions was working out how best to steal it from him. He was also hungry, but kept telling himself that self-fulfilment was close at hand. To his surprise, a short time after they had pulled out of Moscow, a fierce woman wrapped in scarves and shawls appeared selling hot tea and stale bread. He bought both and felt better.

Emmett tried not to catch the eye of the man directly opposite him who was studying him closely. He was in his late thirties, Emmett guessed, dressed in black but wearing at a rakish angle a once white fedora with an undulating brim. When he removed the hat he revealed thick black hair that straggled over his fur collar. His drooping moustache was also lustrous black, not a streak of grey anywhere. A crooked cigarette dangled from his lips. Emmett had the impression that the man might be dangerous, a wild Georgian perhaps, or a Tartar. He seemed to be in a constant state of readiness, as though he was about to bare his teeth, growl and draw a sabre. However, when the man leaned forward and tapped Emmett on his knee, as Emmett knew he would, his voice was surprisingly gentle and he spoke excellent if idiosyncratic English.

'You are American, I think?'

'That's right, how d'you do, my name's Emmett Brumby.'

He leaned closer, lowered his voice and said, 'I am Grigory Souvritzin,' then flicked his fingers nervously across his mouth as if to imply the words had never been uttered, and glanced at the other travellers. None took any notice. He nodded conspiratorially to Emmett, then addressed the compartment. 'Do any of you speak English?' he asked cheerfully.

All answered with baleful looks.

He smiled without showing his teeth. *'Parlez-vous Français?'* he enquired.

A young woman with bulging eyes said, ' *Un peu.'*

Grigory returned his attention to Emmett. 'I think we're safe. They are not educated people. We talk in English.'

'I have Italian,' Emmett said.

'Alas, me not, although I believe it is somewhat beautiful language. You have not Russian?'

'No.'

'No. Good. English will be our lingua franca.' Now, he put a single finger to his lips, again to imply a shared secret, and produced from his hip pocket an exquisite silver flask. 'Cognac,' he said. 'The real MacKay.' The appearance of the flask caused the others to stir and cast even more envious glances but Grigory offered it only to Emmett who took a polite swig. Grigory himself drank deeply, savoured the liquid in his mouth before swallowing with a sound of satisfaction. 'Beautiful, no?'

'Very welcome, thank you, sir.'

Grigory stroked his moustache. 'And you are going to?'

'Tula.'

'A-ha. I am beyond. So. We have much time together and may exchange informations.'

'I'd really like that, sir,' Emmett said.

Grigory became suddenly alert and again confidential. 'Please, not to call me sir. The days of sir are over.' More secret looks, a wink, a surreptitious nod towards the others, then the lips drawn in a smile, blithe and expectant. He said, 'If I am to say you Mr Hoover, I am hitting the dollar, yes?'

'Yes, indeed. I am one of the volunteers to administer the President's famine relief.'

'I guessed. But why you go to Tula?' He was genuinely puzzled.

'Oh, just to assess the situation, then see how best to get food to the cities.'

'Big mistake,' Grigory said. 'They will tell you they also have famine in Tula.'

'Well, sir, they can tell me what they like but I'll be there to see for myself.'

'They will wink hood you, my friend, believe me. All in Tula are, how you say, obese. All are eating like pigs. But they will tell you they have no food to spare. Especially— ' He broke off and made mysterious passes with his hands. Emmett pretended to understand and nodded. '*Au contraire*, where I am going, there is great need.' He took out a cigarette with a hollow tube which he pinched and twisted as if it were something he loathed.

'And where is that?'

'Where is what?' he asked, lighting the cigarette and puffing deeply. He exhaled the smoke through his nose in two thin streams.

'Where are you going that is in such great need?' Emmett asked.

'Sobliki. Small village. Much hunger. Tula people suck them dry.'

'Is that right?' Emmett took out a notebook and jotted down the name. Sobliki. 'Is that your home town?'

'No, no, no. I am Muscovite. No, my sister is in Sobliki and her four children, so I know about which I am talking.'

'I take it you're going to visit them.'

'You take it absolutely correct. Otherwise, believe me, there is no reason ever to visit Sobliki. I have spent many times there. Bloody boring. One-horse town you say in America?'

'That's right, that's what we say,' Emmett said, warming to his new friend.

'Only trouble with Sobliki, it is one-horse town but no horse.' Grigory chuckled with enormous pleasure. His eyes twinkling, he said, 'I am family of jail-birds, you know.'

'Really?'

'Oh yes, one year for me. Six months for poor father. God knows how long for brother-in-law.'

'What was your offence?'

Grigory exploded with laughter. 'Offence? Offence? You Americans, you are so innocent. You know my offence? This will

174

amuse you, I hope.' He leaned forward again to whisper, 'My offence is my name.'

'Grigory?' Emmett asked, bewildered.

'No, Souvritzin,' he cried, but the moment he had inadvertently spoken the word so loudly he became nervous and looked at the others for their reaction. The young woman with bulging eyes stared at him, impossible to know what she was thinking. An elderly man in the far corner bowed his head.

After that, Grigory was less communicative, only uttering from time to time cryptic *non sequiturs*. Emmett was not encouraged to comment.

'I am bringing good news to Sobliki, that is why I am happy.'

'I am also sad because the news I bring is not that good.'

'I say to myself always, there must be a way.'

'I waited four days and nights for this train.'

'Hope springs internal.'

'I spent a summer holiday once in Scarborough.'

'Scarboro, Maine?' Emmett asked.

'No. Scarborough, Yorkshire, England. Is more beautiful than Cannes.'

'My sister, Tatiana, and I made sand-castles on the beach. In Scarborough, England.'

'My brother-in-law's uncle has villa in Cannes. God knows what now.'

Emmett dozed but was woken twice. First, to be offered food by the others. He declined.

'Eat,' Grigory said. 'Is insult to say no.' But Emmett would not be persuaded. He did not think it right that a famine relief worker should take food from those he had come to relieve. Grigory made a sound of disgust. 'You Americans, you are crazy,' and bit into a pickled cucumber.

The second time Grigory shook him vigorously and urgently. Emmett opened his eyes to find his companion's face barely an inch away. 'Please to wake, young friend. I have plan,' Grigory said. Emmett became aware that the compartment had emptied. Only the old man who had bowed his head to Grigory remained. Emmett realised he must have slept through a stop. 'You are awake?' Grigory asked.

'Kind of.'

'We are near Tula. You will soon be gone. Here is plan. You come to Sobliki. You ask for me. I write my name in case you are forgetful. And Russian names very difficult for foreigners. Come to Sobliki. I shall be your interpreter. Then you shall see what shall be seen. Please to give me paper and pencil.'

Emmett again pulled out his notebook and handed it over. Grigory wrote his name and returned the book as if he were passing dangerous secrets. He glanced at the old man who nodded again and seemed to smile.

It was already dark when the train pulled into Tula. Emmett heaved his suitcase down from the rack. Grigory stood and gripped his arm. 'You promise. Sobliki. Ask for me. The name is written. Promise.'

'I don't think I can promise until I know more — '

'Promise,' Grigory insisted. 'It is a matter of lives and deaths.'

The snow fell ceaselessly and swirled in great spirals, reducing visibility to a few feet. Emmett stood on the platform and waited. He could barely see the lights of the train he had just left. A man, or rather a huddled shape, approached and said, 'Brumby?'

'Yes.'

The man said something in Russian. Emmett shrugged helplessly. 'Soviet,' the man barked. 'Tula soviet.'

An old woman who was introduced as Comrade Likhanova waited with four men in the foyer of an hotel. She was to be Emmett's interpreter. She looked like a dignified mouse, watchful but timid. The men were members of the local soviet. The chairman, Popov, did the talking for all of them. He was impatient and decisive and continually clenched and unclenched his fists. He made Emmett nervous.

Emmett was led into a private dining-room. On a long table, covered in a white linen cloth, stood a plate of pickled cucumbers and a large bowl of potato salad.

'You see?' Popov said through Comrade Likhanova. 'There is not much food in Tula. We have so little for ourselves we cannot send to Moscow.' Then, to confuse Emmett, Comrade Likhanova added on her own behalf, 'Don't believe him.'

Emmett said, 'Ask the Chairman if I can see for myself?'

'Certainly,' Popov said. 'You may do a tour of inspection of our beautiful city tomorrow morning.' Likhanova again added her own postscript. 'They will only show you what they want you to see.'

'But,' Emmett said, 'perhaps I could go out into the countryside.'

'No need.' ('He is lying.')

'I have my orders,' Emmett said, trying not to react to the interpreter's comments. He reached into his pockets for documents signed by Communist officials in Moscow.

Popov banged the table with his fists. 'You may go where you like. This is a free country. But first you will inspect the town.'

'I suspect people out in the country may have even greater need than you have here in Tula.'

'Nonsense. We all suffer. There is famine everywhere.' ('Yes, there is famine but not in Tula.')

'I've been told you have food here but that there is great suffering in – in — ' He referred to his notebook, ' – in – in Sobliki.'

A look of panic crossed Popov's face 'Who told you that?'

'Officials in Moscow,' Emmett lied.

Popov at once turned to his colleagues and spoke rapidly. He was clearly agitated. Likhanova, while staring at some distant point and never once even glancing at Emmett, said without apparently moving her lips, 'My husband was owner of metal works. I was ballerina. Don't react.'

Emmett folded his arms across his chest and fixed his gaze firmly on the table.

Popov continued to explain or lecture to his comrades. Likhanova said, 'They are worried because you tell them officials in Moscow know about conditions here. Don't look at me.'

Popov said something and his friends laughed, then Popov turned back to Emmett, smiled and raised his vodka glass. 'Let us drink to Vladimir Ilyich Lenin.'

'Lenin.'

All, except Likhanova, drank and ate *zakuski*.

Popov's deputy rose and said, 'President Wilson.'

'President Wilson.'

'Your turn,' Popov said to Emmett.

Emmett stood unsteadily. The vodka was stronger than he thought. 'The Russian people,' he said.

The third member of the soviet said, 'Lev Davidovich Trotsky.'

'Trotsky.'

Other toasts were proposed but Likhanova didn't bother to translate. Popov, still smiling, watched Emmett who, as the toasts continued, leaned a little sideways so that he looked as if he might rest his head on Likhanova's shoulder. His lips were numb but his mind was remarkably clear. He lost all sense of time.

'Tell them,' Emmett said, 'that I want to visit Sob – Sob – Sobliki – tonight, no, I mean tomorrow.'

Popov waited for the translation and his smile vanished, never to be seen again. He stood, gave Emmett a sharp nod, and marched out of the room followed by his comrades. Likhanova gathered her things. 'Good boy,' she said. 'But always remember, you don't have to drink the whole glass. Half at a time will do. It's a trick ballerinas learn.'

Popov returned briefly and ordered Likhanova to leave. She kissed Emmett on his forehead, and said, 'And remember also, food is not the only thing we are short of. There is also famine of truth.' And she was gone.

*

177

Emmett first saw the Sobelev women grubbing for cabbage stalks in a field a mile or so from their former mansion. An icy wind billowed their long skirts. Grigory said, 'There they are, my sister, Tatiana, my nephew, Valodya, and my nieces, the three sisters, Xenia, Darya and Iliena. Iliena is little one.' He flicked the reins of the covered cart and headed across the field towards them.

After two days in Tula, Popov had finally agreed to let Emmett make his tour of inspection. He was put on a train which stopped at every siding. When at last he alighted on the platform at Sobliki, the station-master, Kurugin, came rushing out of the station-house and consulting a piece of paper asked nervously and with care, 'Yermit Brumbi. Hirbit Hoova. Amerikanski. *Da?*'

'Emmett Brumby, that's right.'

Again Kurugin read from his notes. 'Plyess to white in awfice. Maia awfice.'

Emmett followed him into a small office, overheated and airless but unnaturally clean. Kurugin made many gestures that Emmett took to mean he must be patient. Kurugin then lifted the ear-piece from the small telephone exchange, pulled and plugged wires, dialled a number, cranked a handle and, when he was answered, said no more than three or four words before disconnecting himself. He turned to Emmett and again gestured for patience. From the top of a small samovar he took a teapot and poured Emmett a glass of delicious and welcome tea.

Twenty minutes passed. On four occasions Kurugin left Emmett alone for a few moments only to return with a helpless shrug. The fifth time he returned with Grigory Souvritzin.

'You kept promise. Emmett Brumby, you are good fellow.' He hugged Emmett tightly but had trouble getting his arms all the way round the teddy-bear coat.

'I was supposed to be met by the Chairman of the Sobliki soviet.'

Grigory's hands fluttered as though he were trying to imitate a bird in flight. 'Don't worry, you will meet. First, let *me* show you,' and he jabbed his chest with his thumb for emphasis.

He was dressed exactly as before, the off-white fedora pulled low over his right eye, a cigarette with its hollow tube twisted in his mouth. He was about to lift Emmett's suitcase but Kurugin intervened and carried it outside, loaded it on the cart and then bowed low to Grigory, who exploded with fury and spoke severely to the man. Kurugin was not offended. He smiled and again shrugged helplessly.

As they were setting off towards the town, Emmett asked, 'Why did that man bow to you?'

'Because he is old bloody fool.'

'Are you sure you're not the Chairman of the Sobliki soviet?'

'Me? Soviet? Me? Ha!' He flicked the reins hard but the horse did not increase its pace. A little later, he motioned towards the hill that dominated the town. 'See the white house on top of hill?'

'Yes.'

'That's why he bow to me.'

'Was that your house?'

'No, my sister and brother-in-law, poor Lev Borisovich. But I, too, had splendid house. Three splendid houses to be truthful. What I tell you now you must forget. I am Prince. Prince Souvritzin. My father also, naturally. My sister is Countess Sobeleva. Was. Now all comrades.'

'*Prince* Souvritzin?' Emmett repeated with that special note of awe Americans reserve for titles.

'I say to forget. Please always to call me Grigory. Tell me how it was in Tula.'

Emmett described the meeting with Popov, how reluctant the man was to let Emmett out of his sight and how, over the days following, he had done everything to divert Emmett. 'In the end,' Emmett said, 'I had to insist on sending a telegram to Moscow explaining the situation. He said that wasn't necessary and let me go.'

'Who was interpreter for you?'

'A lady named Likhanova.'

'Svetlana Likhanova? My God! She is still breathing? My God! My grandfather wanted to marry her, she was beautiful woman, beautiful ballerina, better than Pavlova. Svetlana Likhanova, my God!' He shook his head in disbelief. 'She married merchant. Jew, I think. So, tell me, you see much suffering in Tula?'

'No. I found stores with food. A church was being used to store grain. I can't say I ate well but I ate. It became obvious that Popov and his boys were hiding something.'

'Sure,' Grigory said. 'What they hide is food. And truth. Communists can do no wrong. They are new Church, new religion. Lenin is Jesus Christ. No, he is Jesus Christ, God, Holy Ghost. Impossible for Communist to admit error. Like Pope.'

'But it's not their fault the harvest failed.'

'It's their fault. Don't be kind. They are bastards.' He steered the cart down a wide street. 'So, you see nothing in Tula. Keep eyes wide open now, Emmett Brumby from Mr Hoover. See?' he said. 'Street empty. But wait. Look now.'

They rounded a corner and came to an intersection which formed a square. A crowd of people stood silently, about two hundred of them, Emmett guessed. Old women bowed as the cart passed. Grigory spotted someone he knew and pulled on the reins. A woman scuttled over. Grigory said, 'This is Dunyasha Kaltikova, saviour of my sister

179

and family.' They talked. Grigory said, 'All are waiting for bread. Seven hours they have been waiting. That's today. Yesterday also. And day before. No bread. Nothing. Tula soviet take all their grain.' He shuddered as if fighting tears and again talked to Dunyasha. She disappeared for a moment, returning with a young mother carrying a child tightly wrapped in a shawl. Grigory talked to her softly and indicated Emmett. The mother unwrapped the shawl from around the baby's head and turned her child's face for Emmett to see. The child was dying, Emmett knew that at once, its two enlarged eyes stared at him out of a grey, emaciated face. Grigory nodded and stroked the mother's cheek. 'You want to see morgue or cemetery?' he asked Emmett. 'You will have to cover nose with 'kerchief. Many bodies, many burials.'

'I think I ought to see the Sobliki soviet first.'

'As you wish,' Grigory said. 'But you will need luncheon. This I will arrange.' He asked Dunyasha a question and Dunyasha pointed. Grigory steered the cart towards the field where Tatiana, her daughters and her son, Valodya, grubbed for cabbage stalks.

The Sobelevs shared the boiled cabbage stalks with Emmett and Grigory. They ate at the long wooden kitchen table in the house of Dunyasha's sister-in-law, Sonya Kaltikova, situated on the outskirts of the town. They had been living there for almost a year. Although Sonya had wanted to prepare the food, Tatiana insisted on doing it herself. Now, they ate. Not much was said. Sonya sat by the stove and sewed a patchwork quilt. Her son, Piotr, and Iliena played at her feet with building blocks rescued from the children's nursery. Emmett was struck by the beauty of the two older girls, especially Xenia, who was petite and vicacious. He caught her eye and she seemed amused by him. Embarrassed, he looked away and noticed a pile of photograph albums stacked in a corner with rolls of hessian in varying sizes. Some time later, Dunyasha returned and reported that there was again no bread. She joined her sister by the stove and stared into space.

After the meal, when the girls were clearing the plates from the table, Grigory offered his flask of cognac. Only he and Emmett drank. Grigory said, 'If not for these good people, the Kaltikovs, God knows what happens to Tatiana.'

Xenia said, 'I'll remember Dunyasha on that night for the rest of my life. We stood outside the house, watching father, grandfather and Count Obrunin being taken off, and we didn't know what to do. Should we go back in, or did we have to stay outside? Darling Dunyasha gathered our things and said, "Come." And that's really all that happened. We slept here in the kitchen. There were eight of us.

God knows how we managed. But we were all women so that made things easier.'

'You weren't all women,' Valodya said. 'What about me?'

She laughed and Darya smiled fondly.

'What happened to the others?' Emmett asked.

Darya said, 'Oh, Maria Obrunina and her mother insisted on trying to get to Moscow. Our governess, Miss McMurray, accompanied them. We have no idea what happened to them, we don't know whether they got there or not. Pavlik, our old steward, escorted my grandmother a few days later and settled her with friends.'

'We should have gone then, too,' Valodya said. 'Now, we need documents and passports and money and – what's going to happen to us, mama?'

The question went unanswered.

Darya said, 'Poor old Pavlik. He was away a month, and two days after he returned he simply died.'

'My God,' Grigory said, eyes filled with tears. 'Russia, Russia, bloody Russia,' and he shook his head slowly.

Tatiana had remained silent. She sat erect as though an iron rod supported her back, her hands folded on her lap. She said, 'Now we know that Lev is at least alive, we must go to Moscow, too.'

'That was the news I am bringing to Sobliki,' Grigory explained. 'For almost a year my sister has no news of her husband. But when I myself am out of jail I make enquiries. I know people. I find out. He is in Lubyanka. Not best hotel in Moscow.' He flicked a glance at Emmett. 'You understand now, Emmett Brumby, yes?'

'Understand what?'

'When I say to you on train I have a plan, this is my plan. You will help to get my sister and her children to Moscow. Yes?' He smiled bewitchingly.

'I'd rather,' Xenia cried passionately, 'he'd help get us out of Russia. Oh, can you help us, Mr Brumby, can you?'

Tatiana stiffened. There was no mistaking the look of disapproval she fired at her eldest daughter. Her eyes turned steely blue and Xenia lowered her head, understanding the reprimand. Her plea to Emmettt had been undignified and she knew it.

That night, in the only hotel in Sobliki, Emmett wrote in his notebook: 'The Sobelevs are fine people and what has happened to them is tragic. I'd like to help but don't know how.' The next morning he recorded: '6.07 a.m. Didn't sleep very well. Woke from a nightmare in which Xenia Sobeleva held up to me a dying child and said, "Please arrange the funeral." I couldn't get back to sleep. I can't get warm and I can't get Xenia's face out of my mind. I'd never imagined that after what they've been through people could remain so – I can't think how to describe them.' Later, he added one word at the foot of the page as though it were to remind him of something: decent.

3

Thousands of miles away, at the bottom of the world, the day was hot and dry. Two men sat on the verandah, the stoep, of a farmhouse looking at a herd of ostrich grazing peacefully on a gentle slope that ran down to a dried-up riverbed. Oudtshoorn in the Cape Province, three hundred odd miles east of Cape Town.

'In all my years, I've never seen an ostrich bury its head in the sand, have you, Salt?' Donald Graham said.

'No, never.'

'And we mustn't bury our heads in the sand either.'

'No, Mr Graham, that must we never do.'

Both were unsuitably dressed for the heat. They wore suits, stiff collars, ties and bowler hats, and looked as awkward as the strutting ostriches. Graham took out a cigar, bit the end and spat it out. 'Well, we've had a good run for our money, that's for certain.'

'Yes, there's nothing that a drop of oil won't cure,' Adam said absent-mindedly. He was waiting to hear more.

Graham said, 'How many shares do you have now in the business?' and lit the cigar.

'Fifty shares, thanks to you.'

'You earned them. And you were right to take them. Better than a cash bonus. Have you been able to save as well?'

'A little. Yes, thank you,' Adam said. Four hundred pounds which he regarded as a small fortune, but he wasn't about to divulge the figure to his employer. He said, 'The worst thing in life is an empty pay packet.'

Graham was used to Adam's unintelligible *non sequiturs* and ignored them. He said, 'There's no good bluffing ourselves. Ostriches are dead ducks.' He smiled wryly. 'No one wants the feathers and what other use has a bird who cannot fly? No, no, we'll sell up, get the best price we can for the farm and the house. We'll sell the warehouse in Cape Town, too. We'll lose, of course, but we'll lose a lot more if we wait any longer.'

'Have you heard from Mr Alistair in London?'

'Oh, aye. He's written. My brother leaves the decision to me. I'm the man on the spot.'

'So, how will we proceed?'

'I'll play fair with you, Salt. You've worked hard and you've been loyal. I don't think you've ever asked for an increase in salary. You can choose. You can sell your shares to me for eight hundred pounds, or you can take your chances on the price we get for the properties on the open market. It could be more, it could be less. You'll want to think about it, no doubt.'

'No. I do not need to think about it,' Adam said, hoping Graham would not detect undue excitement in his voice. 'I'll sell to you, Mr Graham. You have always been fair to me. No one could have had better employer.' Eight hundred pounds was much more than he'd expected.

'Good. Let's shake hands on it then and call it a day. And to hell with ostrich feathers.'

A month later, on a Friday evening, the Salts were about to sit down to dinner in the dining-room of their rented house in Mill Street. The windows were open wide and a friendly breeze tickled the net curtains. Sunset was no more than ten minutes away. The Jews of Cape Town were about to welcome the Sabbath; the men walking to their synagogues to pray, the women staying at home to light the candles, murmur blessings, and to serve the Sabbath meal. But not in the Salt household. Adam stubbornly refused to conform; he did not believe in God and in all the mumbo-jumbo. 'I will not be told what I can eat, when I can work, or whether or not my head should be covered. I will not be a hypocrite. I am a Freethinker, thank God.' Their two children were made to go to school on Jewish holidays which especially unsettled little Isobel although she was, of course, unable to articulate her embarrassment.

The sun plunged behind the horizon. Dusk was fleeting. One moment it was light, the next dark. Night surprised them, as it always did. The city of Cape Town began to sparkle with a random pattern of electric lights. Isobel, now aged six, kissed her father goodnight and went dutifully to bed. Eva accompanied her while the maid, Selina, began to put the food on the table.

Meals were strict affairs. Adam insisted on good table manners and was hard on George, who had a tendency to slouch. Conversation was desultory. Questions about the boy's progress at school were answered grudgingly. George, aged eight, was again top in arithmetic, and had been told by Mr Wilkinson, the cricket master, that he showed promise as a wicket-keeper. Eva reported that Isobel showed a talent for recitation. The moment the last mouthful of dessert, always fruit salad, was eaten, George hurried out in to a nearby cul-de-sac where for an hour or so he and his friend, Freddie

Bell, played cricket with an old tennis ball and a bat roughly fashioned from a strip of wooden fencing.

Alone, Adam and Eva relaxed and were content. They had always been happiest in each other's company and their moments together were immensely comfortable and restorative. They still made love but not as frequently or as passionately; neither seemed any longer to need sexual excitement to reassure them. Eva wondered if all marriages accounted happy were simply an acknowledgement by two disparate human beings of friendship.

They conversed in Polish.

'Coming to South Africa was the best thing we ever did,' Adam said. He invariably began their conversations with this affirmation. The climate agreed with him. He still coughed but much less often. His only problem was that he tired easily but he put that from his mind. He was particularly sanguine on this evening because the settlement with Graham, added to his own savings, provided him with a decent amount of capital. He and Eva had often discussed how the money should best be used but so far no final decision had been made.

Adam said, 'I was thinking that the caricature of the Scots could not be more unfair or inaccurate. They are laughed at for being mean, yet no two people could have been more generous to us than Alistair and Donald Graham.'

'It's the same with the Jews,' Eva said. 'It's always a matter of individuals.'

'Yes, yes, it's all very unfair.'

They sipped from glasses of lemon tea.

'Eva,' Adam said at last, 'I have come to a decision about the future.'

'Yes?'

'I did not want to tell you before I was certain. But I have more or less made up my mind. I talked to Harry Kaminsky, you know, the young attorney.'

'Yes, I know,' she said. Harry Kaminsky was the cousin of Dr Kantor who had treated them in London.

Adam continued, 'Harry introduced me to a Mr James Carver, an Englishman, the best type, public school, Charterhouse, I believe. Mr Carver is a photographer and wants to expand his business into developing and processing. He needs capital. I think photography is a growing market, don't you?'

'How much capital?'

'Two hundred pounds for equipment such as enlargers and so on. We would get fifty per cent of the profits.'

'I'd like to meet this Mr Carver before you decide.'

185

'I knew you'd say that,' Adam said with a smile. 'He'll be here at nine.'

'Tonight?'

'Tonight.'

'Good. I think it best I give him the once over.'

It was not that Eva didn't trust Adam's opinion, but she was sure that when it came to Englishmen she was better qualified to judge. She could not rationalise this conviction but vaguely put it down to what she regarded as her comprehensive knowledge and love of all things English. In most other respects she deferred to Adam. Motherhood had softened her, but leisure, made possible by a servant, instead of liberating her to pursue her interests, seemed to sap her former energy. She still read and wrote occasionally for her own benefit but her passion for Zionism had almost entirely diminished. She attended occasional meetings of the local group, refused to stand for office and devoted most of her time to managing the family household with obsessive precision. She read to the children from Dickens, Shakespeare and Byron, and talked lovingly of London. The children adored her.

James Carver arrived on the dot of the appointed hour. He was in his late twenties, immensely tall and walked with a permanent stoop. He reminded Eva of photographs of Rupert Brooke, the soft blond hair, the flared nostrils, the dreamy eyes. His manners were courtly and Eva had the impression he belonged to the last century.

Adam proudly produced a bottle of Cape brandy and the three settled down in the living-room. Their conversation was punctuated by Selina washing up noisily in the kitchen and the raucous laughter of women out in the street. Later, an argument and agonised weeping erupted somewhere, but they ignored it.

'My husband tells me you were at Charterhouse, Mr Carver.'

'Good heavens, Charterhouse? Dear me no, good heavens, no.' He had a high-pitched giggle.

'I thought you said — '

'No, no, not Charterhouse. Hampshire House. Near Eastbourne. Hampshire House. I expect that's what confused you. Yes, Hampshire House. Not undistinguished. Laurence Brownlow was our most famous old boy. Double First at Oxford and all that sort of thing. He's a judge now. In Ceylon. Sir Laurence Brownlow.'

'Did *you* go to Oxford?' Eva asked.

'Oxford? Good heavens, no. Not nearly clever enough. Besides the war interrupted. I would have – perhaps – I don't know — '

'You served in the Army?' Adam asked sympathetically.

'Medical Corps. Not very pleasant. Rather not talk about it, d'you mind?'

186

George interrupted to say his goodnights. Adam introduced him to Carver. 'He is going to be a very fine cricket keeper.'

'Wicket-keeper, papa,' George said with a tinge of embarrassment.

Carver's face lit up. 'I used to play,' he said. 'Batted number three. Bowled a bit. Leg-breaks. Would you allow me to bowl at you one day?'

'Yes, thank you. That'd be fun,' George said.

He kissed his parents, and shook Carver's hand. Selina hovered in the doorway and ushered him to bed.

'He's a very bright boy,' Adam said. 'Good at arithmetic and figures. Don't know where he gets it from. I'm useless at that sort of thing and my wife is a linguist. She was a professor of English in Warsaw.'

'Not a professor, Adam, a lecturer. Very lowly, I assure you, Mr Carver.'

'Still, damned impressive, if I may say so.' He gave her a dazzling smile. 'No, I'm not the academic type. I've always been interested in poetry and art, that sort of thing. No talent, of course. Absolutely none. To be perfectly honest, I wasn't a very good cricketer either. But I was given a camera after the late conflict, when I was recuperating from – oh, well, it doesn't matter – and, d'you know, I found I had a knack. First time I discovered I was ever good at anything.'

'You are interested in poetry? Who are your favourites?'

'Well, I've only really got one favourite. Byron. I read a lot of Byron. Chap speaks to me as if he were sitting beside me.'

That, of course, convinced Eva. After the business affairs were discussed in more detail, and the future of photography explored in hopeful generalities, Eva said, 'Carver and Salt, photographers. Carver and Salt,' she repeated, playing with the names. 'You'd be better off opening a restaurant.'

'To *frizlitch*!'

Not far away, no more than a mile or so, at the top end of Upper Orange Street in the suburb of Oranjezicht, the Wildnowitz family were still seated around their walnut dining-table having finished their Sabbath meal. Solomon, now plump, almost cherubic, at one end, Leah, large and formidable, at the other nearest the door to the kitchen. The maid had cleared the table and finished the washing-up; the members of the family drank their own traditional toast. 'To *frizlitch*,' the Ionian word for freedom. After that they exchanged the week's news. They talked in Yiddish but, recently, the boys had introduced a sprinkling of English words.

Leah loved these moments after the Sabbath meal. She sat back and surveyed her brood with pride. At the far end, her husband, Solomon. Meek, hard-working, kindly Solomon. When she thought of the depths of despair to which he had descended in Hamburg, carrying a sandwich-board for Finkelstein's, she shuddered. Now, here he was, manager of Reuben Blumberg's furniture factory. Although unable to find work in the open air, his former trade of woodcutter had come in useful and he had started out sawing lengths of wood for Mr Blumberg's Sleep-eezy beds. Blumberg, who also hailed from Ploemyan – 'the 1898 vintage' he'd say – liked Solomon and soon promoted him to role of supervisor and then manager. Both the workmen and the customers warmed to Solomon. 'Your husband's a little darling,' Mr Blumberg had said. Yes, Leah thought, my Solchik hasn't done too badly.

And the boys? Her Baruch, she could squeeze him to death. Had he worked? My God, had he worked. God is good, it had to be admitted. Who'd have thought that working in Finkelstein's kitchen in Hamburg would be training for anything? But now look at him. Catering was his trade, and he'd risen from kitchen porter to hotelier before you could say Chaim Schmutz Poopick. He'd saved enough to put a deposit down on a small beach-front hotel in Sea Point called Seaview and was doing well. He owned a motor car and had his suits tailormade. Mind you, Leah did not approve of him changing his first name to Barnet. Now everyone called him Barney. She didn't like the name Barney. Baruch was such a noble name, meaning in Hebrew, praise. One day, please God, he'd meet a nice girl, have children, prosper.

And Julius? Now, he wants to be called Jack. Jack, what kind of a name was that? And she didn't like the idea of him wanting to go off to Johannesburg to represent a soft-furnishings company. She knew what would happen. He'd come back one day with some girl on his arm, too late for Leah to express disapproval, and in no time at all she'd be Mrs Julius Wildnowitz. Yes, Julius, Jack, he was a bit of a worry.

Not Isaiah. Isaiah, her little Ishkele whom, if she was honest, she loved more deeply than the others, he had grown into a handsome and attractive young man. Yes, she loved him most, and why not? He was her youngest, her baby, her little boy. And he wasn't noisy. He was the silent type, much less argumentative than his brothers, a little like his father, decent, yes, in short, also a darling. She hoped he would one day find a wife who would love him as much as she did. Not like that terrible Esther Sachs, with her make-up and scent and fancy hair-do. No, no, he'd find someone. One day. But, thank God, he was only a child, only twenty-one, and that day was a long way off.

Her only real regret was that he had become a commercial traveller, selling C to C cigarettes to shops and traders in the western Cape. She didn't like him having to be away from home during the week so she insisted he return each Friday night to attend the synagogue but, more importantly, to be with her. Still, you can't have everything, she decided. And she thanked God for all the blessings He had showered upon her. Yes, she regarded her family with pride.

Although smoking was forbidden on the Sabbath, Isaiah excused himself and went out on to the back porch to light a cigarette. Leah knew exactly what he was up to but turned a blind eye. Isaiah could do no wrong. Solomon, ever the innocent, thought the boy wanted air. His brothers paid him no attention.

Isaiah needed moments of solitude. He was timid and shy, qualities his mother mistook and admired for reticence. He felt some indefinable weight on his spirit which made him feel clumsy, especially in the presence of eligible young girls and this was a constant cause of concern. He wished he could display the bravado of Baruch or the easy manner of Julius. They could talk to girls, make them laugh, dance with them, but Isaiah became tongue-tied and helpless.

He had met a girl he particularly liked, Esther Sachs, whose father was an accountant. At first, he was more at ease with her than with any other young woman he had met. He was able to laugh and joke with her and she seemed genuinely to like him. He lay awake at night thinking about her and wondered if he was in love. Summoning all his courage, he asked his mother if he might invite Esther back for a meal. Leah was immediately anxious. 'Yes,' she said, 'you'd better.'

It was a disastrous mistake. Esther spoke no Yiddish, Isaiah was obliged to translate everything that was said. For most of the meal Leah was silent, eyes narrowed, appraising. Esther became more and more uneasy. Isaiah was in torment. After he returned from seeing Esther home and stealing a goodnight kiss, Leah was waiting for him. How could he bring such a person into the house, Leah demanded? It was an insult to his father. She'd only seen more make-up on a coloured servant girl, what was Isaiah thinking?

'I like her, mama,' Isaiah said.

'Stop liking her. Believe me, Ishkele, it's for the best.'

And he did as he was told. Esther, hurt and bewildered when he so suddenly avoided her, engineered a confrontation. 'You know your trouble, Isaiah? You're a mummy's boy, that's your trouble.' It was as if a dagger had pierced his heart.

He stood out on the porch, puffing his cigarette, thinking of Esther Sachs. And then, his Uncle Laban's face came into his mind. Hardly a day passed when he didn't think of Laban and on this night, his uncle's image was clear and vivid. He remembered Laban's words spoken to him the night he lay on the floor pretending to be dead. Hadn't Uncle Laban said something about honouring thy father and thy mother? Or was it that you shouldn't honour them? And then, as if the man were beside him, Laban whispered in his ear, 'Better an independent life than three score and ten of bondage.' Isaiah stubbed out his cigarette and heard Leah's voice, 'Ishkele,' she called, 'I'm going to bed now. Don't forget to come and give me a goodnight kiss.'

Laban smiled his idiotic smile and vanished.

4

'Lenin is dead.'

'No, he's had a stroke, but he's alive.'

'He may be alive but he's dying.'

'He's asked for a priest.'

'A priest? Lenin's asked for a priest?'

'He's paralysed down his left side.'

'You mean his right side, surely.'

'He can't speak.'

'He can't think.'

'I had it from the doctor attending him. Lenin is dead.'

'I know the nurse who gives him his suppositories. If she's sticking a suppository up his ass he can't be dead.'

'You never know.'

This hissing, first of the Moscow snakes, then others more numerous across the vast expanse of the new Union of Soviet Socialist Republics, was insistent, insidious and, for almost a week, unceasing. Both privately and publicly, in the spring of 1922, the topic of Comrade V. I. Lenin's health seemed to be the chief concern of two hundred and fifty million people bar at least one.

The one was Tatiana Sobeleva. Although she was on an urgent errand she walked at her usual stately and dignified pace along the narrow, winding streets of the Arbat. The city of Moscow was not yet fully awake. The sun had only just risen. Tatiana was determined to get her business over quickly, for she had a second more important appointment across the city and must be there on the stroke of eight o'clock. Carrying a discreet canvas bag, she made her way into an old crooked house and climbed the stairs to the apartment of Serge Cabrol, a Russian of French descent like his former employer, Peter Carl Fabergé, in whose workshop he had helped fashion, among other masterpieces of the jeweller's art, the Great Siberian Railway Easter Egg in 1900, before branching out on his own.

Even though he was woken from sleep and still in his dressing-gown, his silvery hair a mess, Serge Cabrol did not lose his unctuousness towards a former customer. He greeted Tatiana with a bow and led her along a short corridor like a hotel manager about to reveal a prize suite, his body slightly askew, one hand apparently on his heart, the other outstretched to show the way. They entered a small pentagonal room lined with empty shelves and devoid of all decoration; a rickety card-table and two chairs the only furniture. Cabrol raised the blind to let in the first faint rays of a cheerless sun. The day promised no heat.

'*Ma chère comtesse*,' he began, holding one of the chairs for her, and as she sat, said in Russian, 'What news of Comrade Lenin?'

'I have no interest in that affair,' Tatiana replied brusquely and in French.

Cabrol understood the reprimand and he, too, now used French. 'Ah, but I think his well-being is of the utmost importance to Russia— '

'To Russia, perhaps, but not to me,' she said.

'The people adore him,' Cabrol sang as though offering a warning or a criticism, but tempered it with 'not of course in the way His late Imperial Majesty was adored — '

Tatiana cut him short. 'I have come here to sell the Sobelev Small Tiara.' She saw his eyes narrow and sparkle. Looking all the while at Cabrol, she removed from the canvas bag the tiara which was wrapped in blue velvet and placed it on the green baize of the table. She did not dare glance at the heirloom, did not want to be reminded of the first time she had worn it, to the opera in Warsaw, or later at the ceremonies in honour of the Romanovs, now all murdered, or the countless other occasions on which she had set it on her head. She was consciously and wilfully learning to be unsentimental and practical. She needed money. The thing was a valuable object and now had to be sold.

Meticulously, Cabrol unwrapped the velvet. The jewels in the graceful uprights caught the early morning light. Tatiana closed her eyes. She did not want even the reflection to disturb her resolve.

'I remember it so well,' Cabrol said fondly.

'I have not much time. Will the English buyer be interested?'

Cabrol was a middle man for the English jeweller, Leslie Trasker who, since the *coup d'état*, had paid several visits to Moscow and Petrograd in order to purchase the jewels of the dispossessed aristrocracy and those who had once been wealthy. Trasker's special interest was in Fabergé but he was also in the market for objects of quality. He paid in foreign currency and Soviet officials either condoned or were bribed to condone the transactions.

Cabrol said, 'I'm sure he will be interested but, dear Countess, I may be able to arrange another buyer for you who will pay more.'

'And who is that?' She kept her eyes closed.

'A commissar. Very important. Very well-placed. I cannot mention names. He has a taste for fine things and his wife, I feel sure, would welcome an adornment such as this.' He tapped the tiara delicately.

Is this the new world, Tatiana asked herself? Is this the promised land, venal and already rotten? Has the same corrupt power simply changed hands? As in the famine, the party bosses fed while the people starved. Charity, abolished by the Bolsheviks, has been replaced by cynicism. She said, 'But this commissar, whoever he is, he would pay in roubles not in pounds sterling or in American dollars.'

'That's true. Roubles, yes.'

'I prefer to sell to the Englishman. May we come to an agreement, please?'

She thought that perhaps he was suddenly sad. Was he toying with the tiara, turning it slowly round with his little finger? At last he said, 'You realise I cannot possibly offer what it is really worth. There are so many risks. I am not sure when Mr Trasker will next pay us a visit. In the meantime I will have the responsibility of keeping — '

'I don't wish to discuss it,' Tatiana said severely. 'How much can you give me? I need the money at once.'

Cabrol was silent for a moment, making his calculations. 'I cannot do more than two thousand roubles. That's a thousand US dollars or two hundred and fifty pounds sterling. I can give it to you in the foreign currency, if you so wish.

She knew, and so, of course, did he, that it was probably worth much more, but Tatiana was not going to demean herself by haggling. She said, 'I'd like it half in roubles and half in pounds sterling, please.'

He rose and was about to leave the room when she said, 'Please take it with you.' He hesitated, returned to the table, quickly covered the tiara and left the room. The moment she was alone, Tatiana let out her breath as though she'd been winded and briefly lowered her head. The ordeal was over. She had done what had to be done.

When Cabrol returned with the money, he frowned sympathetically and asked, 'And what news of the dear Count?'

She ignored the question, took the money and stood.

'Please check it, Countess,' he said, but she hurried from the room, and although he trotted after her in an effort to open the door, she was gone before he reached it.

Tatiana hailed a taxi and placed herself in the corner of the back seat, hoping the driver couldn't see her in his rear-view mirror. Keeping the money she had just received inside the canvas bag as a further precaution, she counted it. The jeweller had added fifty dollars to the agreed price. She was neither touched nor pleasantly surprised. Guilt money, she thought.

The taxi came to a halt outside a nondescript, neglected building. A peeling, painted sign on rotting wood bore the word: HOSPITAL NUMBER 11. It was ten minutes to eight and she joined a long queue at a side door which was firmly shut.

She knew two women among those waiting. Silent courtesies were exchanged by a nod or a vague smile: the Countess Olga Beletskaya whom Tatiana had always dismissed as silly and inconsequential and the formidable Baroness Marina Dzhunkovsky, built like a battleship. The rest seemed to represent, in Tatiana's eyes, the new society, peasants, workers and those trying to look like neither. A young woman with sad, affectionate eyes, standing immediately beside her asked, 'Husband, son, father?'

'Husband.'

'I'm visiting my father. Nervous complaint. He cries a lot.' And then, as an afterthought, confidentially, 'They're better off where they are, your husband and my father, glory be to God.

Tatiana silently agreed. Lev had been ailing long before that night when he was driven away from Sobliki on the back of a horse-drawn cart. Oddly, his health not his whereabouts had been Tatiana's most constant anxiety. At first, she had no news of him until her brother, Grigory, turned up in Sobliki to say he was imprisoned in Moscow, in that grim edifice that once housed an insurance company, the Lubyanka. No charge, no trial, no sentence. How would he fare in prison? Would they let him see a doctor, would he be prescribed medicines or would they just let him die? And then, that eager, boyish, innocent American, Emmett Brumby, whose determination and obstinacy were strengths so well hidden that Tatiana had, to begin with, dismissed him as being of little account. Yet the young man had said he was committed to helping them and, to Tatiana's surprise, help them he did. Back and forth to Moscow he went, first to arrange accommodation for the family, then to secure confirmation that Lev was in prison and in so doing obtained permission from a high-ranking official for Tatiana to visit him and, lastly, to shepherd the entire family from Sobliki to Moscow, bearing the expense of the train journey and the two taxis to transport them and their belongings across the city. His energy and kindness seemed inexhaustible but Tatiana understood, of course, that his efforts were to a large extent fuelled by his feelings for Xenia. Tatiana did not, when thinking about her eldest daughter and the young American, allow the word love to enter her thoughts. She had no insights into Emmett Brumby's emotional life, he was too foreign a creature, too unlike anyone she had met. And Xenia was also difficult to understand. Although she was more outgoing than the others, she was still capable of concealment. Because of his father's sudden illness, Emmett had rushed back to Rome, promising Xenia he would return. Tatiana warned her daughter not to set too much store by the promise and furthermore, in Tatiana's opinion, there was no future in the friendship. Xenia replied with her maddening smile, 'We shall see what we shall see, mama.'

A nurse appeared, opened the door and the queue started to shuffle forward. The woman in front of Tatiana said, 'We mustn't get too excited. It could be hours yet before we see them.' Just before stepping into the building Tatiana noticed that the woman crossed herself and then looked round to make certain she had done so unobserved.

The hospital staff neither apologised for, nor explained the inhumane regulations which permitted only one visit a week for twenty minutes and even this visit was sometimes cancelled without warning. Although they were told that no one would be admitted after eight o'clock, the visitors were more often than not kept waiting at least an hour before the medical staff and nurses were ready. Even then, the visitors were not all allowed into the wards at once. They were called six at a time for no apparent reason and there was no logic either to the order in which they were summoned. This random, unsettling and cruel regimen encouraged anxiety in those already anxious. Perhaps, Tatiana thought, that is why they do it.

The visitors were herded into a small waiting-room. Those who knew the routine immediately found seats on the two narrow benches against the walls. Tatiana had come too late and stood.

She ached to see Lev. Whenever she entered the hospital, the fact that she was in the very building in which he lay excited her, but that excitement she would later describe to her children as pain. Standing near the door in the crowded, airless room, the desire to see him again suddenly overwhelmed her as it had never done before. She felt faint and inexplicably thought of Battistini. The giddiness passed and inwardly she smiled. Another age, another world, she reflected. Did I really behave like that over an opera singer? Did I really long to see him, to be in his presence, to hear his voice? How ridiculous it seems now. I did not know what longing meant then. Perhaps what they say about us is true. We were trivial people, insignificant, but we were people and what they have done now is to rob us of our right to be trivial.

'Tatiana, dearest — '

She turned to see Olga Beletskaya beside her. Olga's husband, too, had been taken ill in prison and transferred to the hospital. Olga had gone to a great deal of trouble with her appearance. She was carefully if rather too heavily made up, her dyed red hair swept stylishly to one side, and her fingernails were painted a deep crimson, but because she wore no jewellery she seemed somehow unfinished. Tatiana regretted that in the old days she thought of Olga as a frivolous creature. She seemed so painfully vulnerable now.

The two women kissed. Olga said, 'You're looking quite lovely, how do you manage it, you look so serene, so calm, yes, so beautiful.'

'Thank you. So do you.'

'I'm tense,' Olga confessed. 'I couldn't come last week. Ivan will be terribly upset, but I waited hours for a tram and when I got here, it was just gone eight fifteen and they wouldn't let me in. Do you think he'll be very upset?'

'No, no, I'm sure he'll understand.'

'I was up at five a.m. today. I wasn't taking any chances. Do I look very tired?'

'No.'

'I thought I'd try to look my best. It will reassure him, don't you agree? He'll think all's well on the outside, my little Olyishka looks a treat, he'll say.' She laughed nervously. 'He always likes me to look just so.'

The visitors were all talking now and the noise they made reverberated so that they were shouting to be heard above their own din. A young doctor appeared. 'Shut up, there are sick people in this place. You're not in a church now, you know.' Then he reeled off six names and six women followed him out.

Olga said, 'Where are you living?'

'With my parents,' Tatiana replied.

'How many of you?'

'Mother, father, and the five of us.'

'How many rooms?'

'Three.'

'Three? How did you manage that?'

'A young American friend of Xenia's was very helpful.'

'We are eight and only have two rooms.'

'I'm sorry.'

'Oh, don't be,' Olga said. 'I'm pleased for you. I've never been an envious person. How's your delicious brother, Grigory?'

'He's quite well, I think. He came to see us when we were still in Sobliki. He's in Petrograd now, I believe. He likes to keep moving.'

'Is he still so handsome?'

'He has a certain style,' Tatiana said, smiling.

'He proposed to me once, you know. But then I think he proposed to every girl he ever met. What a naughty boy he was.' She lowered her voice, and whispered, 'Do you think Lenin's dead?'

'I've no idea.'

'They say he was about to relax the rules and allow people to leave.'

'I don't think about leaving. If it happens, it happens.'

After half an hour or so, a nurse called more names, Olga's among them. She kissed Tatiana farewell and scurried away after the others. A moment later the door opened again and the woman who had been standing in front of Tatiana in the queue poked her head in. 'Lenin's alive,' she whispered to Tatiana. 'It'll be in *Pravda* tomorrow, official, he had a stroke but he's recovered. The man in the bed next to my father works in the Foreign Ministry. Pass it along,' and she disappeared.

With some reluctance Tatiana repeated what she'd been told to the man nearest to her and the news went round the room like an explosive fuse about to blow. Marina Dzhunkovsky, the battleship, ploughed a way through to Tatiana. In a booming voice she said, 'But surely, if it's to be in *Pravda* it means just the opposite. No, no, I believe the Antichrist is dead.'

A collective 'Sssh!' rose like the wind.

'I will say and do as I like,' Marina announced to the others. 'They can only take my life from me, nothing else.'

Tatiana said, 'I didn't know your husband was ill, Marina.'

'He's not ill. He was taken in for questioning and came out with a broken jaw. This is my first visit. How about you?'

'Lev was in the Lubyanka for almost a year. They transferred him here about eight weeks ago. I wasn't allowed to visit him in prison so this is my eighth visit.'

'How is he?'

'Not well.'

'Such a handsome man.'

Another half hour, an hour, two. There was no knowing when the nurse would next appear. Visitors were called, seats vacated, Tatiana sat now. At last, the nurse returned. She called the names, among them Dzhunkovsky and Sobelev.

They were obliged to wait again, this time in a narrow corridor that led to the ward on the third floor. The walls were painted the colour of urine. There was a smell of carbolic and ether. The cast-iron radiators were too hot to touch but hardly gave off any warmth. Tatiana was suddenly cold and her teeth chattered. Then, from out of a side door, his face heavily bandaged, came Baron Dzhunkovsky, Marina's husband. He wore a faded blue dressing-gown and, beneath it, green and white striped pyjamas. Marina sailed towards him, booming, 'Well, Baron, I can only say I'd rather be in Baden-Baden.' Everyone laughed. Tatiana watched them hug each other. The Baron laughed, too, even though it obviously hurt him, and then he burst into tears. Marina said, 'Don't fret, Baron, we'll go to Baden-Baden next year.' At that moment the others were allowed into the ward.

Tatiana had last seen Lev the previous week but when she now approached his bed she caught her breath. The deterioration in his condition was horribly apparent. His face had turned yellowish green, his eyes were open but vacant, his hair lifeless. She knew at once he was near to death. She forced a smile. He turned his head and saw her. He managed a smile, too, and when she reached him gave his cheek so that she could kiss him.

Her visits began always in the same way, not with words but with a look, a moment of absolute stillness in which both of them were lost, baffled, loving, tender, regretful, shared lives calling on an unspoken history of courtship, marriage, children, a house, tranquillity and terror.

He said, 'Is it a week since you were last here?'

'Yes,' she answered, sitting on the bed and taking his hand. Colder than mine, she thought, and I can feel his bones.

'I've lost track of time.'

'I had so much to tell you but it's gone from my mind,' Tatiana said.

'How are the girls and Valodya?'

'They're well.'

He stared at the ceiling. 'Are you going to Sobliki tonight?' he asked.

He had forgotten all she had told him about their long sojourn with Dunyasha's sister, of their journey to Moscow and of how Emmett Brumby had bullied or bribed a commissar to allow them to share three rooms with her parents in an old Souvritzin town house. She decided not to burden him again. She lied, and said, 'Yes, we may go back this evening. I haven't decided yet.' Lev nodded as though he agreed with her indecision. Then, he said in a matter-of-fact way, 'Tatiana, I love you more than life.'

She needed all her self-control. Again she tried to smile. She said, 'Oh my dearest Lev,' but could not hold back any longer. Tears filled her eyes and coursed down her cheeks. He freed his hand from hers and gently wiped her tears away. 'Please don't cry,' he said. 'All we can say is that this is our fate. This is what God always intended for us.'

A nurse marched down the ward. 'One minute,' she called. Marina complained, 'How dare you?' she cried. 'We've only had five minutes,' but there was no response.

'Tatiana,' Lev said, 'I'm dying — '

'No, dearest, no — '

'Yes, yes, we must face the darkness. The doctor, a decent chap, told me my kidneys are useless. I don't have long, he said. They won't let me see myself in a mirror. Or perhaps they haven't got a mirror. Do I look terrible?'

'You look as you've always looked, Lev. Handsome and strong.'

'Not like you to lie,' he said with a shadow of a smile.

'You'll get well, you'll see,' she said, leaned forward and kissed him on the brow. His brow furrowed. 'What's the matter? Are you in pain? What's troubling you?'

'Are you going back to Sobliki tonight?'

'We may.'

He closed his eyes and said, 'I think my father was right. Individuals matter.' Then he said what he'd said on each of her visits for the past month. 'I would love some fresh milk,' he said, 'but, of course, you need money for that. The doctors take bribes, you know.'

And Tatiana gave always the same response to reassure him. 'I have some money, you tell me which doctor to give it to, and we'll get you special medicines and food.'

'Where do you get money, Tatiana? I hope you've not become a thief.' Again he tried to smile.

She did not want to tell him about the sale of the Small Tiara. She said, 'Oh, the girls all chipped in. Father sold some jewellery — '

'Don't waste money on me. It's too late — '

'Time's up,' the nurse bawled, clapping her hands as if to scurry chickens.

She kissed him again and he held her hand tightly, but the effort tired him. He lay back and closed his eyes. Tatiana walked quickly away knowing she had seen her husband for the last time.

Lev died that night, alone, unattended. He'd called out for water but in a voice too weak for anyone to hear. A moment later his suffering was over. He was forty-one years old.

Baron Dzhunkovsky could not sleep because of the pain of his broken jaw. He found that pacing the ward was less agony than lying down. He happened to pass Lev's bed just after midnight and even in the dull glow of a night-light, saw that Lev was no longer breathing. A letter informing her of her husband's passing reached Tatiana two days later.

He was buried in the cemetery of the Novodevichy Convent. An old monk conducted the service. Tatiana, her children and her parents, Prince and Princess Souvritzin, stood at the graveside. After it was over, she remembered the words of a stranger and murmured, 'He's better off where he is, glory be to God,' and crossed herself. Tatiana left the cemetery, clutching Iliena's hand, telling herself she would mourn Lev for the rest of her life and this certainty gave her an inner stillness, a tranquillity, which, like her natural hauteur, some mistook for a lack of feeling.

*

Lev's death strengthened his grieving family as if, unspoken, a mysterious decision was made not to bow down to fate, human cruelty, caprice and, indeed, God's will. An understanding seemed to communicate itself, especially to the children, that in Lev's passing meaning must be found, and that the ruthless system which was responsible for his suffering must be defied. Their collective energy was released, directed towards one end, unwittingly constructing means of escape.

At the centre of the intricate design which determined the Sobelevs' future stood the eleven-year-old Valodya. The image of his mother, thin-faced, nose a touch too long, stone-grey eyes. Although he spoke Russian, French and English, in more settled times he would have been considered average at school, unlikely to have wanted a place at a university but, like Lev, would have made a good manager of the estate, a modest, just and likeable landowner. But in Russia, in 1922, other qualities were demanded of him. While living with the Kaltikovs in Sobliki, he attended the local school. Once the family reached Moscow, arrangements for him to continue his education were neglected. Tatiana had enough on her plate what with settling in, Lev's illness and the constant, tiring demands of a vicious, over-conscientious bureaucracy. Like many children of his age there was a need to earn, to increase the family's income, legally or illegally.

The building in which they lived, the former Souvritzin town house, was now occupied by a dozen families, fifty or so people, one of whom, Tratchikov, was a taxi driver. Valodya took to cleaning the man's cab each day for a few kopeks. On the evening the news first leaked out that Lenin had been taken ill, Valodya was at work on the car in the yard at the back of the building. Tratchikov came hurrying towards him followed by a good-looking young man in his late twenties, obviously a foreigner.

'Valodya, you speak English, don't you?'

'Yes.'

'This man's English, and he's trying to tell me something, needs me for a job, I think, but he speaks Russian like an Armenian, I don't know what the hell he's talking about.'

'You really speak English?' the man asked, squinting at the boy as though he doubted the claim.

He had an odd accent in English, too, Valodya thought. He said, 'Yes, I do. And French.'

'My name's Richard Webb. I'm a journalist. I work for Reuters. You known what Reuters is?'

'No.'

'It's a news agency. We gather the news, write it up, and send it out to the world.'

Valodya was impressed, Tratchikov impatient. 'What's he saying, what's he want?'

'He hasn't told me yet.'

'We need a taxi on call all day, every day. Ferry us round the city. Mr Tratchikov's been recommended. We had a bloke, Vyesevelod he was called, but he's – he's disappeared, currency offence, something like that. Ask Mr Tratchikov if he's interested. We pay well.'

Tratchikov accepted the offer without a moment's hesitation. He became the Reuters taxi driver and Valodya, because of his English, the agency's messenger boy. When the office telephonist, a Countess, elderly and frail, resigned and moved to Petrograd, Valodya recommended his sister, Darya, for the job. Invisible cogs turning invisible wheels.

5

Stepan Kessler stood on the platform of Chemnitz railway station waiting for the train that was carrying his parents and his younger brother out of Russia. Ever since his own escape, he had come to loathe railway stations and the sounds of trains; consequently his excitement at the prospect of being reunited with his family alternated between elation and despair. The Lohmeyers had bought him his first long-trousered suit, a dusty grey pin-stripe, and he stood, more or less to attention, gazing intently down the track, first apprehensive, then eager, then apprehensive again. The stiff collar of his shirt had been overstarched and cut into his neck so that every now and then he twitched his chin in the hope of lessening the irritation.

Liselotte Lohmeyer said, 'Stop that, Stepan. Your mother will think you've got a tic. Try to look cheerful. You're going to see your parents again.'

Karl Lohmeyer, who had been talking to a porter, joined them. He studied his pocket-watch. 'The train left Dresden on time. Should be here at any minute.' He paced up and down. His wife decided to sit on a bench.

Their son, Willi, had grown into a blond giant. The preciousness and effeminacy he displayed as a child had given way to gangling callowness. There was now something crude and ungainly about him. He sidled up to Stepan and said, 'See what I see?' and indicated a party of schoolgirls in uniform being shepherded down the platform by a pair of nuns. 'RCs, always good for a tit-tickle.'

Stepan grinned. Liselotte said, 'That's better, Stepan. You're looking cheerful now.'

Willi said, 'And keep looking cheerful because next Saturday, after the Sabbath's over, Rudi Rosensweig said he'd take us to the hostel where the RC nurses live. He says for fifty pfennigs they'll let us twiddle their nipples and for one mark they'll show us their jelly fish.'

Stepan laughed but as he did so heard the wail of the train's hooter, saw a puff of smoke and the engine snaking round a bend to nose slowly towards the station. The brakes screeched. Stepan winced. It made him think of a violin string snapping.

Shura was the first off the train, saw Stepan, ran towards him but stopped, overcome with embarrassment. Stepan barely recognised him, he had grown so much in the four years. But when his parents appeared, Stepan gave out a yelp of joy, ran past Shura, into his mother's arms and immediately burst into tears. Anya cried, too, and Stepan Senior squeezed his elder son's neck which aggravated the rash. His face buried in his mother's fur coat, Stepan heard Shura say, 'I had my tonsils out, Stiva, but they put me to sleep.'

Anya gently held Stepan's face in her hands. 'Oh my God, I can't believe it. You're a grown-up man. Oh, Stepan, my little Stiva. You're a hero, a real hero, and I'm so proud of you. You got here all on your own, my brave, brave boy.' He sniffed and shuddered. Then it was the turn of the Lohmeyers to greet the new arrivals, handshakes, kisses, a polite bow from Willi. Collecting the luggage took an age, and while they were waiting, Stepan, laughing now but still trying to catch his breath in the aftermath of tears, noticed that his father's semi-circle of hair and moustache had turned white. Anya's hair, too, had streaks of grey, and the lines on her face seemed deeper than he remembered. Beside Liselotte Lohmeyer she seemed so dowdily dressed, her fur coat showing bald patches, the woollen scarf round her neck threadbare, her shoes scuffed and worn. He'd carried a memory of her beauty and elegance and now he could not conceal his disappointment. Anya saw the look and knew at once what he was thinking. 'I've obviously aged,' she said with a twinkle. 'Don't worry, Stiva, there's nothing a hairdresser, make-up and a good little seamstress can't put right. You'll see.'

The restrictions governing immigration from the Soviet Union had always favoured celebrities or those with money to bribe their way out. In their wake, a backwash of the less-favoured managed to flood into Germany, France, England, Finland, Turkey, Canada, the United States, anywhere, indeed, that would have them. But the vast majority of Soviet citizens, those to whom the concept of homeland, *rodina* in Russian, was at the heart of their existence, or those who believed in the perfectability of humankind and therefore in the new society that was being violently hammered into shape to bring about that perfection, or those few whose lives were dependent on language, writers and actors, for example, remained. The Kesslers were among the aristocrats, bourgeoisie, musicians, dancers, the intellectuals and the intelligentsia who fled.

'Have you been happy, my darling boy?' Anya asked. Stepan was helping her unpack while Stepan Senior and Herr Lohmeyer talked in the study, and while Willi allowed Shura to try on his boxing gloves, a birthday present from his parents.

'Yes, mama, I think so.'

'You only think so? Haven't the Lohmeyers been kind? Has Willi been bullying you — ?'

'No, no, Willi's fine, he's my friend, he looks after me, he's not very clever but he's kind. And the Lohmeyers have treated me fairly, exactly the same as they treat Willi. I don't like all the praying we have to do, but yes, I've been happy, very happy, but – but — ' He stopped, unable to define his doubts.

'But what?'

'I don't know.'

'Did you miss us?' she asked playfully.

'Of course.'

'That must have been it, then.'

'I don't know.'

She tousled his hair and gazed at him. His hair, she thought, was already a little thin, the Kessler males' inheritance. He looked older than sixteen, so capable and mature. He wasn't exactly handsome, she decided, but immensely attractive, wonderful black eyes, straight nose and a strong chin; a little on the short side, but muscular, and he exuded energy; even now, in repose, thoughtful and reflective, she could sense his vitality. She sat beside him on the bed and again took his face in her hands and kissed his brow. 'Not a day passed when I didn't think about you, pray for you, ache to see you. When your first letter came to say that you were safe, the relief was so great, I had to go to bed. I couldn't think, I couldn't move, I just lay, staring at the ceiling, thanking God. Was the journey very terrible?'

'It was long,' he said.

Liselotte called, 'Dinner's ready.'

'I'm starving, I don't know when I last had a decent meal,' Anya said. 'Come, we can do the rest later.' As she opened the bedroom door, she asked, 'And do you and Willi still make music together? Have you found a good violin teacher? You still want to be a world famous musician, don't you?' His face darkened and his forlorn look alarmed her. 'What's the matter, Stiva?'

'I lost my violin on the train. It was stolen.'

'Oh, that's dreadful. But surely the Lohmeyers would have allowed you to use Willi's, or bought you a cheap one — '

'They wanted to but I wouldn't let them. I never want to play the violin again. Never.' And he hurried from the room.

Conversation at dinner was lively and spirited. Everyone seemed to speak at once. The Kesslers wanted to know everything that had happened to Stepan, his academic progress at the *Gymnasium* ('more than adequate' from Herr Lohmeyer), his social life ('the girls like

Stiva,' from Willi, spluttering, and being swatted on the head with a napkin by his father), his health ('excellent,' from Frau Lohmeyer, 'although he had trouble with his teeth and our dentist, Dr Rosensweig, was obliged to pull out two of them') – one question leading to another, Herr Lohmeyer vainly insisting on decorum, and Shura trying to butt in to tell his older brother of his own adventures ('I had my tonsils out — ' but no one took any notice). The Lohmeyers, in turn, asked about life in the Soviet Union ('is it really so hard?'), about Lenin ('is it true he is now a vegetable?'), his New Economic Policy ('how long will that last?'), his likely successor ('Trotsky, obviously, there isn't anyone else'), confusing, confused, animated.

'You can't buy make-up for love or money. I long to put a dab of good French scent behind each ear,' from Anya.

Herr Lohmeyer said, 'Do you agree with me about Trotsky? To succeed Lenin?'

'I don't think Russians will tolerate a Jew in charge. Mind you, they're all Jews, so what's it matter?'

'Papa, my best friend's a Jew,' Stepan said rather too aggressively, 'Rudi Rosensweig, his father's the dentist who pulled out my teeth — '

'I had my tonsils out, Stepya — '

'Really, really, well, if you can't find better friends than that — '

'The Rosensweigs are an excellent family,' Karl Lohmeyer explained, 'and he's an excellent dentist, a very brave man, Iron Cross first class on the Western Front — '

Willi said, 'We won't have anything to do with the RCs, Uncle Stepan, we give them a hard time — '

'Ah, boys are so intolerant,' his father said, pointedly.

'And what about clothes, Anya?' Liselotte asked.

'Clothes? What are they? We have rags and scraps and patches, not clothes — '

'Tomorrow, we will pay a visit to Frau Pfefferblum — '

'Sounds like another Jewess — ' from Kessler.

'Yes, but an artist with clothes. She's a widow. She makes all my things, we'll pick out some patterns and materials, she'll run you up an outfit to rival any Paris couturier — '

'Don't spend too much,' Kessler said mischievously. 'At any rate, not until I get back from Switzerland.'

A hush. Stepan asked, 'Papa, why are you going to Switzerland? Are we all going?'

'Little boys should be seen and not heard,' Anya said firmly and put an end to dinner.

A camp bed was put into the boys' room for Shura, who was quickly asleep. They lay in the dark, Willi and Stepan, talking with suppressed glee of the Catholic schoolgirls they had seen at the station, and how they would like to get their hands up their skirts, which led Willi to recount for the umpteenth time his adventure with a girl called Leni who had taken him to a woodland pool where they had bathed naked. And although Stepan never tired of hearing the tale, his mood suddenly plummeted.

He said, 'Shura, are you awake?'

Shura stirred.

'Shura, do you know why papa is going to Switzerland?'

'No. I had my tonsils out — '

'Yes, yes, you said, I'm asking about papa — '

'But they put me to sleep, Stiva. They put a mask over my face and made me count backwards.'

'You probably can't even count forwards so how could you count backwards?'

'Stiva,' from Willi, 'Saturday night, nurses' home, don't forget.'

'Why do you think my father's going to Switzerland?'

'I don't know. Perhaps he likes mountains.'

Presently, Shura and Willi were both asleep. Stepan lay awake a little longer. To his mother he may have given the impression of maturity, of a boy already a young man, but that was merely a deception, a stance, a manner he had developed to hide his uncertainty. He was mistrustful of continuity and had come to regard impermanence as his natural state. This expectation of imminent upheaval made him volatile, encouraged swings of temperament that forced him at one instant to be ebullient and expansive in an effort to embrace treacherous circumstances; the next to plunge him into gloom, a fearful acknowledgement of an indefinite future.

The news of his father's impending journey provoked all these insecurities. Would his mother go, too? Would they take him and Shura along? It didn't sound like it. It sounded as if his father intended to travel alone. Why? He'd only just arrived. Stepan didn't want to be parted from his parents again, ever. The memory of the men hanging from lampposts in a Moscow street entered his thoughts as it invariably did before sleep. That image marked for him the dividing line between the past, a golden age now lost for ever, and an unpredictable, disturbing present. Brave, brave boy, his mother had said. He wondered if he had any bravery left inside him? I'd like everything to be nice and settled, he decided. Like it once was. Before they hanged the men.

AK 1906. Varenka. Respectable, honest, worthy, reliable Stepan Kessler Senior, had kept only one secret from his wife in their twenty years of marriage. The secret, which he revealed on the train as it crossed from Russia into Poland, was that ever since young Stepan's birth he had been salting money away in a Zurich bank. Shortly after the boy was born, Kessler had occasion to visit Berlin to sort out some difficulty with the clothing manufacturer, Heinrich Naumann. When the matter had been resolved, Naumann, during dinner, playfully suggested that Kessler should open a Swiss numbered account. 'Many of the Russians I deal with are doing it. What with anarchists, Socialists and Communists, you never know. As a matter of strict confidence, Kessler, I have done the same thing.' Kessler thought what's good enough for a Jew must be good enough for me and returned to Moscow via Zurich.

He booked in, on Naumann's recommendation, at the hotel Baur au Lac, made his arrangements with Crédit Suisse and felt as though he was engaged in espionage. He chose to designate the account with Anya's initials and the year of Stepan's birth: AK 1906. Because the Swiss did not allow numbered accounts to attract interest, Kessler was advised to authorise an automatic transfer into a deposit account in his mother's maiden name which was Varenka. The money was then converted into sterling. He asked his few foreign customers to pay him in Zurich rather than Moscow. The export side of his business was not large but the scheme seemed nevertheless worthwhile. He had not dared keep a record of the deposits so he had no idea how much had been saved, but he guessed it would be a tidy sum, more than enough to start a new life.

He took a small suite at Baur au Lac, the hotel he had used on his first visit. He remembered its opulence and luxury, the fine food and wines, the correctness of the staff, the cleanliness of the rooms. If anything it was cleanliness he longed for. Kessler was not a sybarite, far from it, but after four years of living in two rooms, he had an uncontrollable urge to indulge himself, to take a dozen baths a day if he so desired, to sprinkle himself with *kölnischwasser*, to wear freshly laundered underwear and a clean shirt. And, he reasoned, it is not all that far to the Rathausplatz where his branch of the bank was located. He knew it was unfair to Anya to enjoy himself so ostentatiously and he decided that on his return he would tell her he stayed in a cheap *Gasthaus*.

On his first evening in Zurich he soaked in a hot bath for almost an hour. The tub with its elaborate gilt taps was enormous, enabling him to stretch full length, the water reaching up to his chin. He sipped a dry sherry while dressing in his pre-war dinner jacket which hung rather loosely on him. Odd, he thought, to have lost weight at my time of life. Feeling a little self-conscious about his appearance, he descended to the dining-room and admired the lavish but tasteful decoration before ordering his meal. He had entered a world he had once known well, the subdued chatter of his fellow diners, the hushed courtesy of the waiters, the pleasure of being served by those who took pleasure in service. This is not wicked, Kessler decided, but a mutually beneficial transaction that was both important and necessary.

He studied the menu with great care, ordered bouillon Henri IV, sole bonne femme, tournedos Rossini with pomme vapeur and ended with a small wedge of Camembert followed by grapes, his favourite fruit, but which he had not tasted for four years. The *sommelier* recommended the wines ('not too expensive, please'), a Chablis and a 1921 Château Talbot. He sipped a cognac with his coffee but declined a cigar. He tottered off to bed, a little drunk but gloriously content. He slept at once but woke at three and vomited his heart out. The meal had been too rich for a stomach accustomed to gruel. God has punished me, he thought, which confirmed his decision to lie to Anya.

In the morning, after bathing again, he walked to the bank. He had not gone very far when he stopped and tried to absorb the world around him. There was a smell in the air he could not at first identify. And then he supposed it must be the scent of freedom, an odd commodity, he decided, because he suddenly realised he could not only smell it in the air, but also see it in people's eyes, in their carriage and bearing, hear it in their voices. He wanted to reach out and touch it, grab it, capture it, but knew it was too ephemeral. He breathed contentedly, held his head high and continued on his way.

After his signatures had been verified by at least three of the bank's personnel, Kessler was ushered into the presence of the director, Dr Frick, a sad, lugubrious man in his fifties, who sucked peppermints and looked like an undertaker. Frick produced a leather-bound ledger and turned to the appropriate pages which, Kessler could see from the other side of the desk, were filled with columns of figures. So many figures, Kessler thought, this bodes well. Tell me how much, tell me, please, tell me, my life depends on it.

Dr Frick popped a peppermint into his mouth. He said, 'Just so, you are quite a rich man.' He pursed his lips.

Kessler's heart stopped. Quite rich, really? Quite rich? What does he mean? 'How much, please?' he asked.

'The last payment into AK 1906 was on the 18th July 1914. That is correct?'

'I expect so,' Kessler replied.

'So you have six years of activity and then zero.'

'Yes. There was a war and a revolution and my business was appropriated by the State — '

'Just so. We are dealing with many Russian people who have this problem. From AK 1906 authorised automatic transfers were made to the deposit account, Varenka, and coverted into pounds sterling.'

'Yes.'

'Just so. The sum standing in Varenka at this precise moment is, in pounds sterling, two thousand, four hundred and seventy six pounds, thirteen shillings and eight pence.'

Not rich, but well-off, comfortable enough, Kessler thought, yes, quite comfortable enough, a small fortune. 'I'd like it all, now, please.'

'All?'

'Yes.'

'You are closing the accounts?'

'Yes. I am making my home in Germany, so I'd like a cheque in German marks.'

Dr Frick winced visibly. 'Please, I beg you, not all in German marks, please. The German mark is very unstable and is likely to continue in this fashion. I do not rule out unbridled inflationary tendencies.'

'But I am going to make my home in Germany, I intend to set up in business again — '

'Just so. May I give you advice?'

'Of course.'

'Take some of your money now, a few Swiss francs, a few German marks. Leave the rest here. When you are needing some funds, you simply order me to make a transfer, always in pounds sterling, and thereby you will not be losing value. On the contrary, you will be gaining. Believe me, this is good advice.'

Kessler considered carefully. 'I don't think the Communists will ever gain a foothold in Germany. And I think one has to put one's faith in the country where one lives. So, I thank you for your advice, Dr Frick, but my answer is no. I'd like all my money now please. In German marks.'

Again, Dr Frick winced and broke the peppermint with his teeth. 'Please, please, not in German marks. At least let me give you a cheque in pounds sterling. I am Swiss. I don't like to see money worth less than the paper it's written on.'

Kessler nodded. 'All right. In pounds sterling. Thank you.'

6

An interlude in New York.

Nina Kaplanski was twenty-eight years old, petite, slim, with dyed blonde hair and huge, expressive brown eyes. She was a teacher of ballet, assistant to Vera Askenskaya whose studio near Columbus Circle attracted the daughters of the well-to-do. She was accounted an inspiring teacher although she had never had a day's formal tuition, a fact she and Madame Askenskaya kept secret.

Nina's father was a jobbing tailor and she had herself been a diligent seamstress. At the age of fifteen, she was employed by a theatrical costumier whose clients ranged from extravagant Broadway producers to amateurs existing on a shoestring. It was thought by all to be a glamorous job but was, of course, just another form of slave labour. Theatrical enterprise, at whatever level, seemed invariably to be dogged by crisis, and Nina worked longer hours than she would have done in the most gruesome sweatshop. In one such emergency, just before the Christmas of 1917, she had been obliged to travel up town to Columbus Circle in order to stitch tutus on to Vera Askenskaya's pupils so that what Askenskaya called, 'my little Pavlovas' would be ready to appear in her studio's annual display. Nina worked with speed and efficiency. Askenskaya, never one to miss a trick, suggested that the following year Nina should make the children's costumes herself, rather more cheaply than her employers, and put the money into her own pocket. For two years this arrangement continued and required Nina to attend early rehearsals in order to discuss designs and measurements and a hundred other details. Nina liked to put the various groups through their paces in order to see just what the demands on the costumes would be. Askenskaya was impressed by her ability to correct the attitude of the body, the line of an arm or the position of a foot. Never a stickler for technique – 'any mechanic can have technique, expression of feeling much more important' – Askenskaya invited Nina to become her assistant. This was another form of slave labour.

A week before the Christmas display of 1921, catastrophe struck. The premises which housed the makers of the children's dancing pumps burned to the ground and with it all their stock. 'They cannot dance in naked feet!' Askenskaya decreed and ordered Nina to scour the city in order to find someone who could make forty pairs of dancing pumps in six days at the right price. Using her parents' home as headquarters she began her quest on the Lower East Side.

Freezing wind whipped round corners. Snow flurries hampered vision. Treacherous black ice caused Nina to slip and flounder. But she persisted seeking out shoe manufacturers, wholesalers, retailers, any enterprise remotely connected with footwear, in the hope of finding someone, anyone who was willing and able to meet her demands: forty pairs of dancing pumps in six days. Five days. Four. Her request was greeted with laughter, shrugs, sympathy, astonishment but no pumps. With three days to go, her desperation increasing, Nina entered a small cobbler's near Rivington Street.

Behind the counter was a surly, scowling, swarthy man who barely looked at her but continued to cut leather for heels with savage intensity. Nina knew for certain she would have no luck here and in ordinary circumstances would have walked out at once. But these were not ordinary circumstances.

She said, 'I wonder if you can help me.'

'*Ikh red nit keyn english*,' the man growled.

Nor could Nina's parents speak English, so she resorted to Yiddish. The cobbler was impressed but chose not to show it. Nina explained her problem. 'I need forty pairs of soft dancing pumps in four days' time. Can you, or do you know anybody, who could help me?'

'Certainly,' the man said.

'You do? Who?'

'Me, that's who, who else?'

'You can make them or you know where to get them?'

'I can make them.'

'You can make them?'

'Lady, do me a favour, don't repeat what I say, it gives me a hole in the head.'

'You can make the shoes in three days?'

'That's what I said, that's what I'll do.'

'But it's a specialist's job, the material, the stitching, the soles — '

'Lady, don't give me a hard time. I said I can do it, I'll do it.'

'You're sure? You're absolutely certain?'

'Lady, when you were still a twinkle in your father's eye, I worked in a travelling circus and made and repaired pumps for acrobats. So don't ask any more questions. Just tell me the sizes and where to deliver.'

Nina, slightly shocked and disbelieving, gave the man the information he requested. As she was leaving, she said, 'By the way, my name's Nina Kaplanski, what's yours?'

'Benjamin Wildnowitz,' he said.

7

At nine o'clock on the morning of 27 January 1924, two members of the Communist Party's Central Committee and six ordinary workers entered the central hall of the former Nobles' Club, renamed The House of the Trades Union, and lifted the coffin of V. I. Lenin from a high couch with four columns that looked like a four-poster bed. The two committee members were Grigory Zinovyev and Josef Stalin. They carried their load out into the street. The temperature was thirty-five degrees below zero. The funeral procession took seven hours to reach Red Square accompanied by massed bands playing 'L'Internationale' in slow time. Darya Sobeleva, among an immense crowd, almost it seemed the entire population of Moscow, watched in silence. She was not there to pay her respects but because she was insatiably curious and because she felt she should witness a moment in history. She made mental notes of all she saw and thought that afterwards she would write a record of her impressions. So cold was it, she noticed, that all around her beards, hats, collars and eyebrows were white like the snow that clung to the trees. Few dared to take off their hats as the coffin passed. Most simply saluted with raised hands. Darya did not. The streets leading to the square were lined with tens of thousands holding high banners of mourning and from that vast multitude, Darya saw clearly, rising in the icy air a fog of congealed breath, like incense. After the cortège passed, Darya made for home, knowing that if ever she and the rest of her family were to emigrate, the time was now. In the wake of the leader's death there would be confusion, the realignment of Party forces, the crude struggle for power. Now was the time. She knew it for certain with every fibre of her being.

By the time she reached home, around four o'clock, the dead man's disciples were lowering the coffin into a crypt over which, the snakes insisted, it was planned to build a mausoleum to house the embalmed body.

Darya believed that the deceased's chief legacy to his fellow men was terror.

A week after the funeral, Emmett Brumby reappeared in Moscow. For months now he had been toing and froing from Switzerland. Because of his involvement in the American famine relief effort, he had attended in Geneva an international conference, called by the Red Cross, and had met for the first time an extraordinary man, a Norwegian, Fridtjof Nansen. On each of his many visits to Moscow, Emmett bubbled with enthusiasm for his new idol. Nansen was famed as an Arctic explorer, but was also an eminent scientist, an accomplished artist and a gifted statesman. He had headed the Norwegian delegation to the first assembly of the League of Nations and, Emmett said, 'Was head and shoulders above all the others. That's why they put him in charge of repatriating five hundred thousand prisoners of war back to Germany and Austria. He's a great man.'

But Emmett's real contact with Nansen came when the Norwegian was appointed High Commissioner charged with directing all aid to famine-stricken Russia. Later, Emmett was one of the team to negotiate with the Soviet government the opening of an office in Moscow of the International Russian Relief Executive and had the task of reporting back to Nansen the progress of the talks, hence his toing and froing. Emmett boasted, too, of having been privy to Nansen's initiative to introduce an identification card for refugees which was known as the 'Nansen passport'.

On that February night Emmett came loaded with gifts: make-up for Xenia and Darya, scent for Tatiana, a fountain-pen for Valodya, a fur muff for Iliena, gloves for Princess Souvritzin and cologne for the Prince who, for reasons known only to himself, put the bottle on the floor between his feet. Emmett also brought with him tinned and bottled delicacies – pickled peaches, strawberry jam, acacia honey, sardines and more, an assortment of what he called 'goodies'. A feast was planned for the following evening and Darya asked Tatiana if the Reuters man in Moscow, Richard Webb, could share the meal.

The table glittered. Not for many a month had it borne the weight of so much food. The only two who did not comment, indeed did not seem even to notice the abundance, were Tatiana's parents, Prince and Princes Souvritzin. The Prince sat sullen and hunched; his wife shook so alarmingly that little Iliena, now aged ten, was obliged to feed her.

During the dinner, while spoons and knives were scooping and spreading to an accompaniment of vodka, bubbling chatter and laughter, Emmett suddenly said with great formality, 'Countess, Prince and Princess, I have something to tell you all. Xenia and I are to be married.'

Xenia, glowing, looked at the others, but their silence caused her pleasurable anticipation to dissipate; she lowered her eyes, drew patterns with a fork on the tablecloth but did not stop smiling. Emmett said, 'I know this must come as something of a shock, Countess. We were going to tell you earlier but, well — ' He made a vague gesture.

Richard Webb, the Reuters man, said, 'Congratulations,' and shot a look at Darya who remained impassive.

Again the awkward silence descended. Apart from Princess Souvritzin's uncontrollable trembling all were still.

Presently Emmett said, 'We want your approval, Countess, and, if you give it, then you had better know we intend to leave for Italy as soon as possible. Xenia, being married to an American, you see — ' He did not need to finish the explanation.

As though she were mocking her mother Xenia said, 'Well, mama? And do you approve?'

All now looked expectantly at Tatiana. After what seemed an eternity, imperceptibly at first, and then with more conviction, she nodded.

They were married by a Soviet official and left Moscow for Rome the following day. All had grown used to partings. There were tears but somehow feelings had become hardened. Xenia, who could sense Darya's silent accusation of selfishness, made a good show of concern at leaving the others behind. Tatiana, as was her way, accepted her eldest daughter's departure without comment; as for the Prince and Princess Souvritzin, they were in no state to take in what was happening.

Their deterioration had been rapid; both seemed to weaken and decline at more or less the same pace, as though by mutual agreement they had decided to withdraw from the ugliness which enveloped them. Events had exacted a harsh price. They may have expected life to treat them more gently in old age, may have imagined a stately advance towards death, gracious perhaps, certainly dignified. Instead, they slept with Tatiana, Valodya and Iliena in what had once been the Prince's dressing-room; most appalling, especially for the Prince, was that they shared one bathroom with dozens of others less fastidious than he. For months he tried to preserve an immaculate appearance but finally, Tatiana noticed, he gave way and surrendered to wearing unwashed shirts and grubby suits; he no longer cared whether his fingernails were too long and he stopped cleaning the nicotine from his fingers with lemon juice and bicarbonate of soda. He shaved irregularly, his hair curled over his collar and dandruff peppered his shoulders. For a while Tatiana tried to mother him a little, brushing him down and cutting his hair, but she had other concerns, the daily queuing endless hours for food, fuel, clothes, the struggle, shared by millions of others, to survive. Prince Souvritzin lapsed into a black and morose silence, but on the last occasion Tatiana offered to cut his nails, he cried, 'Oh for God's sake, let me die with dirty claws.'

As for the Princess, the slight tremor that had developed before the Communist *coup d'état* degenerated into a grotesque and continuous shudder which meant she had to be fed and dressed and helped to the lavatory. Yet she smiled sweetly most of the time, even in her sleep, and asked after friends and relatives long dead.

Imagine a bunch of raving lunatics with names like Zinoviev, Kamenev, Evdokimov, Trotsky. The superintendent of the asylum discovers that they do not respond to treatment and cannot be subdued. So, he sets about destroying them. He deprives them of sleep, breaks their arms and legs, burns their flesh with red-hot pokers, and then obligingly shoots or hangs them. He then admits other lunatics with names like Voroshilov, Mikoyan, Ordzhonikidze, Kirov, Yezhov. In time, he will destroy most of them too because that's what the superintendent enjoys: killing his patients. His real pleasure, however, will come from breaking the arms and legs and of burning the flesh with red-hot pokers of sane human beings without giving a reason. The superintendent, Josef Stalin, learnt his trade from Lenin, but improved and refined the techniques, and then invented some of his own.

Richard Webb was thorough, persistent and conscientious. Reuters paid him two hundred pounds a year plus five shillings commission on the telegrams and letters he sent back to London. His Russian was primitive but serviceable. He was secretive yet never underhand and he had an inbred sense of decency. He, Darya and Valodya comprised the entire Reuters staff in Moscow. The head office, run by P. P. Schatokine, was still in Petrograd now renamed Leningrad and they worked a good deal through Tass, the Soviet news agency, with whom Richard had built a good businesslike relationship.

Two years after the Brumbys' departure and while the superintendent was having his fun behind the Kremlin walls, Richard asked Tatiana for Darya's hand in marriage. But unlike Emmett, he added, 'Don't worry, we're not leaving Russia without you. I have a plan. I know a bloke who knows a bloke who knows a bloke. The only thing is I won't be able to confide in you or even Darya. It's dangerous out there and it's best you don't know what I'm up to.'

A little later, Tatiana confronted Darya when they were out shopping. She said, 'I don't want to know what's going on, I know Richard's plans are secret and well under way, but if you are thinking that we are all going to emigrate, you had better realise now that I cannot possibly leave your grandparents.' Darya nodded but said, 'We shall see what we shall see.'

Secrecy played a great part in everyone's lives. Even within families caution was commonplace; no one knew who could be trusted. The unexpected was always fearful; the unannounced guest a harbinger of catastrophe. When Tatiana's brother, Grigory, turned up, Tatiana at first thought he had come seeking refuge. Only later was she told that Richard had made contact with him and urged him to come to Moscow. The approach had not been made by letter or by telegraph but by a Reuters colleague who was travelling to and from Leningrad. The phrase 'a good person' came into use to describe those few decent human beings who could be trusted.

Feliks Dzerzhinsky, Lenin's old friend, head of the Cheka, now named OGPU but still the secret police, had spies everywhere; nobody was safe. The Cheka – Extraordinary Commission for Combating Counter-Revolution and Sabotage – came into existence on 20 December 1917. Two months later, in February, its first execution without trial took place; in April, notorious three-man courts, the *troikas*, were set up to formalise its actions; in September came the infamous decree, 'On the Red Terror', which allowed for concentration camps and for the execution of anyone in contact with counter-revolutionaries. 'The Secret Police,' Lenin boasted, 'sprang from the very essence of the proletarian revolution of which terror was the inevitable consequence.' To those brave enough to criticise, those who, in Lenin's own words, 'sobbed and fussed' over mistakes made by the Cheka, he marvelled that when 'we are reproached with cruelty, we wonder how people can forget the most elementary Marxism.' Nikolai Bukharin and Leon Trotsky, too, expressed enthusiasm for the terror. And when word spread that the Cheka recruited sadists and criminals, Dzerzhinsky admitted, perhaps ruefully, 'Only saints and scoundrels can serve but now the saints are running away from me and I am left with the scoundrels.' Between 1918 and 1921 he consigned untold numbers to forced labour camps and, according to his own official figures, thirteen thousand to death. The younger Sobelevs were right to be obsessively secret.

Grigory was shocked by his parents' condition. He invited Tatiana to walk with him out of doors. 'But it's raining,' Tatiana said.

'Better wet in the streets than dry in the Lubyanka.'

Once outside, Grigory came to the point immediately. 'I have arranged for mama and papa to go to Novgorod.' Novgorod was about three hundred kilometres south of Leningrad, not far from the Souvritzins' former country seat.

Tatiana was wary, knowing full well that the plans to which she was not privy were now being put into motion. 'Are we leaving soon?' she asked. He made no reply. 'Perhaps mama and papa should come with us,' she said. 'I can perfecty well look after them.'

'No, you can't,' Grigory said. 'They are senile and will die soon.'

She was taken aback by his bluntness. She detected in him a trait she had neither known nor noticed before, a severity both of manner and purpose. He seemed to have lost something of his lightness, and she thought the way he talked of their parents callous and unfeeling. She stopped and turned to him. 'Are you coming with us, too?' she asked.

'Keep walking,' he said.

'Please tell me.'

'I don't think you knew papa's last steward, Kyril Denisovich. He and his wife will look after them. I sold some jewellery and gave them most of the money and two icons. There will be enough to last until mama and papa die. Kyril Denisovich and his wife are good people.'

'But why do we have to talk about these things in the street, in pouring rain? To see that our parents are taken care of can't be considered counter-revolutionary, can it?'

Grigory said, 'Let's go back now. Start packing their things at once. Kyril Denisovich will be here tomorrow.'

Yet another parting. God, Tatiana thought, how many more separations from those one loves? To her surprise, saying farewell to her parents was not as painful as she had imagined it would be. At the moment of taking their leave they seemed to her like a couple she had never known, a broken old man and woman so different now in appearance and behaviour from the people they once were, the people she preferred to remember: elegant, cultured, decisive, good. They seemed pleased to be going as though movement itself was in some way a mild confirmation of life. The Prince barked impatient orders as if he were still lord of a great estate and his former steward bowed and smiled and called him Excellency. Tratchikov, Reuters' taxi driver, took them to the station but Tatiana decided not to accompany them. She kissed them goodbye on the pavement. And they were gone from her life.

With two less the rooms were more easily manageable, there was more food to go round and Tatiana experienced relief which made her feel guilty. Darya and Valodya went out to work each day; Tatiana no longer had to worry about leaving Iliena in the care of her parents, or was it the other way round? But no sooner was she freed from one anxiety than another took its place: what if the local commissar discovered that her parents were no longer living with her? Would he order the family into smaller accommodation? She spent much time at the window watching the street for strangers.

Richard was a frequent visitor. Quiet and unassuming, he seemed an unlikely partner for Darya, who might have needed, Tatiana thought, someone more intellectually agile, at least someone as curious as she. Tatiana found it odd that a journalist, a reporter, should be so plodding and unimaginative, but she grew to admire his forthrightness and his inability to dissemble, qualities which gave him strength. All who came into contact with him understood at once they were dealing with a man who could be trusted, a man of integrity. With Emmett, Tatiana had always been ill at ease. She knew him to be kind and sincere but his enthusiasm, his naïvety, made her cautious. She wondered if beneath all the boyish charm and idealism there didn't exist a harder, more personally ambitious streak, but these misgivings she kept to herself.

Returning from work one evening, Darya said, 'Richard and I are going to be married one week from today, on March 18th. In church.'

Tatiana tightened her lips in what she hoped would pass for a smile. 'Thank you for telling me,' she said.

'Now, mama, you and I must go for a walk,' Darya said, which was the standard euphemism for those who had matters to discuss in private.

The two women, wrapped up against a cold March wind, set off in the direction of Pushkin Square. Tatiana waited for her daughter to speak, but Darya remained silent. There were other people on the street, mostly couples; they walked close together, talked earnestly and in whispers. Dusk had already given way to night. The cold was biting. Tatiana could not help feeling that life had become utterly ridiculous. She said, 'This is a funny world we live in. Here we are, two grown women, one of them a mother who has just been told her daughter is to be married in a week's time, and we are walking the streets and freezing to death. Do you think the Communists have got it quite right?'

They laughed. Darya linked her arm with Tatiana's, and kissed her on the cheek. When they reached the square both instinctively gazed up at Pushkin's statue as if intuitively paying their respects to a man who represented values now disparaged and debased.

Without looking at Tatiana, Darya said, 'I am sorry, mama, we have been so secretive but it was necessary. I know you understand. I don't even know what Richard has been up to but he seems to think it's now or never. On the 18th we are to be married. In the evening there will be a party. A farewell party. On the 19th, all of us are leaving for France.'

Tatiana barely reacted; she received the news as if she were being told of some minor shopping expedition. There had been so many surprises in recent years, one more, even one so momentous, seemed commonplace. 'But we haven't passports or permission,' she said dully.

Darya reassured her. Richard had, she believed, taken care of the travel arrangements. He had arranged for all the family to be issued with Nansen passports which were now deposited in Reuters' safe. Tatiana said, 'But I thought Nansen passports were only for refugees. We're not refugees.'

'We will be when we get to Paris,' Darya replied.

Whether by influence or bribery or both, Richard had obtained permission for Darya to marry a foreigner, a feat now more difficult than when Emmett and Xenia married. 'He won't tell me how he managed it,' Darya said, 'but we have all the necessary documents signed, sealed and, I hope, delivered.'

From the moment she woke on Tuesday 18 March 1926, Tatiana was filled with foreboding. She passed the day in a constant state of anxiety, looking over her shoulder from time to time, expecting to see the approach of grim-faced men who would brandish documents in her face and put a stop suddenly and viciously to all their plans. Darya, too, was patently nervous but Tatiana thought that only natural in the circumstances. She wore a borrowed bridal gown long out of fashion, loaned by older friends and relatives, who stiched and cobbled and patched to make it presentable. When Grigory came to the house and beheld her in her wedding finery, he burst into tears, and sobbed, 'Bastards, bastards!'

The couple was married first by civil authority; Valodya and the British Military Attaché acted as witnesses. Richard said the presence of a foreign diplomat would intimidate officials who were easily intimidated by officialdom. Afterwards, in the church of St Nikolai, they were married in accordance with the Orthodox rite. Grigory gave Darya away and Valodya was one of the crown holders.

That evening, into the Sobelevs' three rooms, the guests crowded to partake of some of the 'goodies' the family had hoarded: champagne, vodka and sweetmeats. Only the immediate family knew that this was the last time they would see these friends and relatives. There was much weeping but, fortunately, in Russia tears never need explanation. Tatiana tried to look as though she were taking pleasure in the event but it was difficult for her. The next day she would be leaving Russia for good, leaving behind her whole life, the earth she loved, the very essence of her being. She thought of Sobliki, white and shining on the hilltop. She thought of Lev's grave.

For Darya, too, the party was blighted. All gatherings were vetted by the OGPU. At the beginning of the month she had dutifully submitted a list of the guests. The OGPU officer said he would study the names and that she should come back the following week. On her return he kept her waiting for three hours. He handed over the list and said, 'Yes, you can have your party. There are at least three of our people on the list.'

She was appalled. The guests were either close relatives or dear friends. The thought that three of them were in the employ of the OGPU was chilling. Then it occurred to her that perhaps the man was lying in order to intimidate her. True or false, he succeeded in his aim. She dared not discuss the incident with anyone and she regarded all the guests with suspicion and caution.

Grigory lingered after the last guests departed. He was drunk and, of course, wept a good deal. He clung to Tatiana, saying, 'My God, we will never see each other again. A brother and a sister. This is what the world has come to. Oh, the bastards, skunks, degenerates — '

'Ssh!' from Darya.

'Never mind ssh! I'm going to sing a song.' He had a soulful bass voice and he crooned quietly a song for which his childhood friend, Yuri Veranadzhe, had composed the music, adapting the words of a poem by Stéphane Mallarmé, 'Brise Marine':

> The flesh is sad, alas! I have read the books,
> To escape! Far away!
> The birds are drunk to fly the unknown skies,
> Nothing, not old gardens reflected in the eyes
> Will keep this heart from drowning in the sea.

The newly-weds tidied up, helped by Valodya, who had been unusually silent all day. Iliena was fast asleep on the sofa, Tatiana beside her gently stroking her hair. Grigory sang and when he couldn't remember the words hummed, eyes closed, holding a twisted cigarette between thumb and forefinger, and using it like a conductor's baton.

Through the open door to the dressing-room, Tatiana saw the trunks and suitcases packed and ready. She smiled to herself, amused by the anguish she had suffered deciding what precious things to take and what to leave. The photograph albums? Essential. The painting of Sobliki by an unknown Italian artist? How could she part from it? Maria Obrunina's self-portrait? Not to take it would be betrayal. The few bits of remaining jewellery? How much space does a brooch or a ring occupy, and who knows when they will have to be sold? The miniatures of ancestors, Sobelev and Souvritzin? Of course. The two small samovars? She had known them for as long as she could remember. And the icons? Oh, yes, she would not leave without the icons. In the end, she had to acquire another case in the market, a good leather case, battered, but bearing the crest and initials of Count Piotr Orlov whom she had known in childhood. And Grigory sang:

> I shall depart! Steamer with swaying masts,
> Raise anchor for a journey to exotic lands.

There was yet to be another parting, unexpected and more anguished than anything Tatiana had known before. Over coffee and black bread which passed for breakfast, Valodya announced that he was not coming with them. 'I don't want to leave Russia, mama. This is my home. This is where I belong.'

All looked at him as though he had said something in a strange tongue. Darya asked him to repeat his words.

'I am not coming with you,' he said.

Grigory cracked him across the face. 'You little bastard,' he said. 'Why have you left it until now to tell your mother?'

'Because I didn't want any arguments. I didn't want crying and sobbing and begging. I'm staying here.'

Richard said, 'It's that girl, isn't it?'

'What girl?' Tatiana asked feverishly. 'What girl?'

Valodya lowered his eyes. He said, 'I, too, am going to be married.'

'But you're only fifteen,' Darya cried.

'I am marrying a Russian girl, not a foreigner,' he answered.

Iliena began to cry.

'Who is this girl?' Tatiana demanded.

'Her name is Ekatarina. She works for Tass.'

'How could you do this?' Darya asked, shaking her head continually, unable to believe what was happening.

His response was to kiss his mother on her forehead, then Darya, then Iliena. He shook hands with Richard. Grigory said, 'Don't come near me, you little Bolshevik bastard,' and before anyone could stop him, Valodya was gone.

> I shall depart! Steamer with swaying masts,
> Raise anchor for a journey to exotic lands.

At the railway station, Grigory said, 'I'll join you as soon as I can. Don't worry, Tatiana, I'll keep an eye on Valodya. I'll bring him out with me. Trust me!'

Oh Christ, what pain, what agony, Jesus Christ, teach me how to survive this suffering, Tatiana prayed, but she revealed no outward sign of her agony. At the carriage window she stood erect and watched Grigory waving until the train took a bend and he was lost from sight.

8

On 8 February 1926, James Carver, the photographer and Adam Salt's partner, was arrested by the Cape Town police for corruption of a minor. The offence took place at Three Anchor Bay, near Sea Point, a northern suburb on the Atlantic Ocean. Adam, always something of a prude, was shocked and mortified. He refused to discuss the event even with Eva. When later Carver skipped bail and disappeared, the newspapers carried reports of the police search, and Adam's embarrassment was made public and therefore more humiliating. As far as he was concerned the only saving grace was that he had not lost much money on the partnership, a little more than seventy pounds over the whole period, but that was paltry compensation for the scandal which had yet some way to run.

Six weeks after his disappearance Carver's badly decomposing body was found chained to a tree on the upper slopes of Devil's Peak. Even though a suicide note was discovered stitched to the lining of his alpaca jacket, murder was at first suspected. But the police investigation revealed that Carver had chained himself to the tree trunk, secured the chains with a padlock and thrown away the key, which was never found. The local CID concluded that James Carver died from self-inflicted starvation, dehydration and exposure.

Because Adam retreated into silence, Eva had the task of explaining the events to George and Isobel. The little they had seen of Carver they had liked. On the few occasions he visited the Salt home he never failed to bring them presents. He bowled leg-breaks to George in the cul-de-sac behind the house, and had taken formal studio portraits of them which they treasured. 'A very unhappy man,' was the line Eva decided to use and it seemed to satisfy. In private, she mourned deeply for James Carver and, although Adam absolutely forbade it, she attended his cremation with half a dozen others whom she did not know. For the truth was that she had been aware for some time of the shadow in which Carver lived, not because he had confessed to her but because of a piece of information George had supplied.

A couple of years before Carver's death, George reported seeing him at the General Post Office in Adderley Street, in a queue with several other Englishmen. They all seemed to know each other. They talked loudly, laughed a lot and, George said, behaved strangely.

'What d'you mean strangely?' Eva asked, intrigued.

'I can't explain but they – they – sort of – quivered and giggled a lot.'

'Quivered? What ever do you mean?'

'I can't explain,' George said. 'But a man behind me said, "Disgusting", and the chap with him said, "Remittance men", and then the other fellow said, "Nice boys, more like". What'd he mean, mama?'

Eva was alarmed. 'I've no idea.'

'What's a remittance man?'

'Oh, just somebody who gets an allowance from his parents in England, that's all.'

'But what did he mean by "nice boys"?'

'Exactly what he said, I suppose,' Eva answered irritably. 'That they were boys and that they were nice. Did Mr Carver see you?'

'I don't think so. Should I tell papa?'

'No,' Eva said firmly. 'I'll tell him.'

But she didn't tell Adam. The photography business was jogging along nicely, earning enough to cover expenses, to pay Carver and Adam modest salaries and to give Adam a small but satisfactory return on his investment. After the second year, they were able to employ a coloured girl, Eulalie, to man the studio and take bookings. More importantly, from Eva's point of view, Adam was free to construct his own timetable. He rose late, walked to the small studio near the City Hall, brought the books up to date, paid the bills, sent out invoices, banked the cash and the cheques, and returned home for lunch and an afternoon nap. His health was no longer a concern and he seldom coughed. But for Eva the most astonishing benefit Adam derived from his new way of life was to rediscover his artistic talent, which manifested itself in wood-carving for which he now revealed a passable gift. Fashioning walking-stick and umbrella handles into human and animal heads was his forte, and he spent the late afternoons of most days happily practising a skill he had once so much wanted to develop. Occasionally he sold his work to friends and customers and even received commissions.

Why, Eva, asked herself, disturb Adam's contentment with George's garbled account of Carver's behaviour in the General Post Office? She knew, of course, that 'nice boys' was the local slang for male homosexuals. She knew, too, that remittance men were often the black sheep of respectable English families, sent out to the colonies to avoid embarrassment at home. But she liked James Carver, he amused and interested her; she was beguiled by his good manners, enjoyed discussing poetry with him, admired his tuneful voice and exquisite English diction and on occasion had persuaded him to read aloud to her. He was reliable, hard-working and, something Eva set great store by, she had never detected the slightest hint of prejudice in him against Jews. On the contrary, he had once said to her, 'I feel a great affinity to the Jews. Outcasts, don't you know.' He smiled sadly but did not encourage her to pursue the remark. In short, Carver engaged her sympathy and that, Eva decided, was sufficient reason not to embarrass him by repeating what George had told her.

Carver's macabre death tortured Eva for weeks. His suicide note was to her especially harrowing. 'Jesus Christ was a Jew and of my persuasion. Why do you persecute us so? You have crucified me. I go to join my mother in Heaven. J. C.' The newspapers investigated and reported his past. His father was a professional soldier, a colonel, living in England, in Cheltenham, but he refused to comment except to say he was immensely proud of his son's war record. Carver, as he truthfully told the Salts, had served in the Medical Corps during the Great War. But he kept secret the Military Cross he had been awarded for bravery at Mons where he suffered severe wounds. After a long convalescence, during which he took up photography, he was discharged from the Army. A year later, he was arrested for soliciting in a public lavatory near Leicester Square but the charge, for reasons unspecified, was dropped. One charitable *Cape Times* journalist wrote that Carver's 'unnatural, disgusting and criminal behaviour could be attributed to the injuries he sustained during the late conflict.' But Eva knew better than that. Her intuition told her that James Carver's way of life, decreed criminal by society, was natural to him; he was powerless in the matter, a victim not a delinquent, and that his suicide was the result of shame and helplessness. She wished she had given him the opportunity to confide in her. Perhaps she could have been of some help. On the night after his cremation, for the first time since she had set sail from England she dreamed of Paul Ehrlich, who appeared to her like a savage demon mouthing words she could not understand but, as is the way of dreams, knew for certain he was castigating and warning her.

In the months following the discovery of Carver's body, Adam's behaviour turned erratic. On some days he rose early, long before anyone else in the house, and set off to the studio where he spent hours trying to teach himself how to develop photographic plates, make enlargements and prints. He dismissed Eulalie. A sign painter was ordered to replace 'Carver & Salt – Photographers' with 'Adam Salt, Photographer'. To Eva, most alarming of all, he visited the synagogue on two successive Friday nights. When she teased him by asking, 'Have you found religion, Adda?' he replied, 'My business.' She tried to remonstrate with him but he was too embattled to express himself reasonably and, anyway, showed no inclination to do so. He began to cough again and lost weight. He also returned to muttering more than ever before. Eva consulted their doctor, Norman Hurwitz. 'It's as if his whole personality's changed,' she said. 'He's a different person, someone I thought I knew, but I don't think I do. Everyone knows Adam's highly strung, but this is much more serious. He's changed and I don't know what to do about it.' Dr Hurwitz thought it was all a nervous reaction to James Carver's death. 'It'll pass. Don't worry, Eva, it'll pass.'

After three months of trying to acquire enough expertise to continue the photography business, Adam surrendered. 'I simply can't do it,' he confessed to Eva one evening. 'And anyway no one wants me to take their photographs. I'll have to find something else to do. There hasn't been a booking since – since — ' He fell silent for a moment, then exploded. 'Just when everything was going so well. I don't want any more upheavals, Eva. I'm sick of change! Oh, damn and blast that Nancy-boy!' Then, blinking furiously, he murmured, 'I don't want to be disturbed.'

A week later, on a cold, wet July evening, he returned home bubbling with excitement. He announced to Eva and the children at dinner that he had at last been presented with the opportunity to become rich. 'A business opening has come my way which will mean I shall have to work like a Kaffir for two years, but then I'll be able to retire and have nothing more to do with the hurly-burly,' and he then explained in greater detail.

Because he had begun the process of shutting down the photographic studio, much of his time was taken up with sifting through papers and with consulting Harry Kaminsky, his attorney, on the legal ins and outs. After a tiring morning, he retired to the studio and, by way of relieving tension, began to carve the head of a springbok on an umbrella handle. Just after two o'clock the bell rang in the front office. Adam emerged to find a man, probably in his late fifties, with a sing-song foreign accent and a kindly, avuncular manner, obviously prosperous, who introduced himself as Hyman Shapiro. Mr Shapiro was the owner of the Van Riebeck Tavern in van Riebeck Street, and he wanted a photograph to be taken of himself and his staff outside the tavern. 'I'm putting mine Van Riebeck on the market and I have a fancy for a memento.'

Adam informed Mr Shapiro that although the sign, 'Adam Salt, Photographer', had not yet been removed, he was no longer in business.

'Not in business? So, *nu*, what you going to do mit yourself?'

226

'I don't know. I'm looking for something.'

'Me, I'm going to sleep till I die,' Mr Shapiro crooned. 'I've made a few bob, I don't mind admitting, so me and Mrs S can live out our days in pieces of quiet. You don't want to own a tavern? I could sell to you a little cheaper because I won't have to pay commission to auctioneers.'

They talked. Mr Shapiro revealed the monthly profit he'd been making for the last five years. Adam was astonished at the large sums involved and Mr Shapiro was amused by the look of incredulity Adam did nothing to conceal. 'You don't believe me, you think I'm giving you a cockle-doodle story. *Nu*, okey-dokey, come back mit me, I'll show you mine premises and mine figures in black and white. The big night is Friday. Naturally, I'm in *schul* on Friday nights so I leave it to mine staff. I've got one hundred per cent honest people, they make for me a fortune.'

Eva listened to Adam with growing alarm. She could, of course, foresee the end of the story and she was more convinced then ever that her husband had suffered a severe mental aberration. At last he reached the predictable climax and said, 'So, the long and the short of it is, I shook hands with Mr Shapiro and I shall shortly be the proud owner of the Van Riebeck Tavern.' He looked at his wife and family with a triumphant smile and waited for their approval and enthusiasm. But all Eva managed was a hushed, 'Oh, my God!' The children remained silent.

Adam was genuinely dumbfounded by her reaction. 'What's the matter?' he said. 'It's the most wonderful opportunity that's ever come my way.'

Eva said, 'Adam, you haven't thought about this clearly,' and they began to argue. George and Isobel were immediately sent out of the room. Selina, the maid, wisely decided, and the children agreed, that they should not interrupt their parents and would go to bed without saying goodnight. But neither of them was able to settle. They were not used to their parents rowing, so the angry voices, arguing in Polish which they could not understand, were deeply disturbing and made sleep impossible.

Eva paced. 'Adda, please be sensible. You're simply not the sort of person to run a bar.'

'It's not a bar, it's a tavern.'

'Same thing.'

'Why? Why shouldn't I run a tavern? There's a fortune to be made — '

'Have you any conception of the hours you'll have to work, of the type of customer you'll have to deal with?'

'I said I'd work hard for two years — '

'It's wrong for you, Adam, I just know it, I feel it in every fibre of my being, your health won't stand it, you're not strong enough, it's outside your entire experience — '

'It's the chance of a lifetime, Eva — '

'It's a terrible gamble, Adda, you're not a gambler, you've never been a gambler, your father was the gambler not you. You know nothing about running a tavern — '

'I'll have Mr Shapiro's staff, all I have to do is supervise and count the cash — '

'And they'll cheat you out of every penny — '

'He vouched for their honesty and I'll be there on the big night, Friday night, I don't go to *schul* — '

'Never mind their honesty, never mind being there on Friday, you'll have to be there every day and every night, behind the counter, pouring drinks, are you going to wear an apron?'

'An apron? What's an apron got do with it?'

'Adam, I beg you, don't gamble away everything we've saved. You're not a gambler, your father was the gambler,' she said again, 'and think of how your mother suffered — '

'It's quite different, this is a respectable business proposition, not a roulette wheel — '

'Adda, I don't want you to do this — '

'I have made up my mind — '

'You'll end up just like your father, losing everything — '

On and on in repetitive, ever-decreasing circles, the storm raged. Even when they finally retired to their bedroom, their voices continued to rumble like distant thunder. Both lay awake for much of the night, tossing and turning, but no longer speaking. Eva finally dropped off shortly before dawn, slept for only a few hours and when she awoke Adam had already left the house.

After intricate negotiations with Mr Shapiro, a deal was concluded by which, in return for lowering the sale price, he would continue to share in the profits, with the expected provisos that the business would be well managed and the accounting honest. Harry Kaminsky helped Adam obtain a bond from the Standard Bank. All, Adam confidently predicted, was set fair and, towards the end of August, he became the legal owner of the Van Riebeck Tavern. Eva's disapproval, if by then unspoken, was all too evident and stubbornly unalterable. Between husband and wife there existed a smouldering, ominous tension, a resentful, uneasy truce.

Her certainty that Adam had made a disastrous decision prevented her from confessing to him her concern about his health, mental and physical. Had the friction not existed between them, she would have urged him to see Dr Hurwitz. Adam looked haggard and painfully thin, dark circles appeared under his eyes and his cough was more or less constant. Without telling him, she consulted Dr Hurwitz again. 'It's anxiety, that's all,' Dr Hurwitz said. 'When he's got the place open, the burden will lift and he'll be a new man.' The diagnosis did nothing to assuage her misgivings. She began to think more and more of her own emotional disturbance years before, in London, when she could not rid herself of the conviction that a terrible plague was about to destroy them all. She was convinced that Adam was suffering similar inner turmoil.

Adam's first week as a publican began modestly but he was not discouraged, for when he checked his takings against Mr Shapiro's figures, they seemed about average. Karl Uys, the manager whom he had inherited, was reassuring. 'Wait for Friday, Mr Salt, the only sound you'll be able to hear is the clink of cash.' And Adam was not disappointed. The moment he opened the doors on Friday evening the onslaught began.

Adam stood behind the bar watching his employees serve the noisy and boisterous pack of men, dockers, building workers, merchant seamen, who pushed and shoved and shouted to buy their drinks. They waved their notes and rattled their coins almost angry with impatience to quench their thirsts. He was at first alert to the constant sound of money changing hands but he soon began to lose awareness even of that sweet music, and was gradually consumed with dismay and repugnance. It was the sight of men tearing open their pay packets that triggered the crisis. His mother's form, in her rocking-chair, slowly began to insist itself, like the image on a photographic plate emerging. He saw her, waiting for his father, her cheeks tear-stained, her whole demeanour crushed by betrayal, saying, 'Don't worry, Adam, I have something put by. We won't wait, we'll eat. Thank God I've got a job. God is good,' and the squeaking of her chair sounded to him like terrified screams. Adam shook his head fiercely, trying to rid himself of the memory as if he were fighting nausea, but his mother's face remained, and her suffering and the vile, grating sound of the rocking-chair.

Adam pushed past Uys, took the nearest customer by the arm, a muscular Afrikaner with a luxuriant beard, and shouted at him, 'Go home, think of your wife, don't empty your pay packets, don't spend all your money here!' The astonished man brushed him aside, and so Adam climbed on to the bar counter and tried to yell above the din, 'Please! I beg you! Don't spend all your money here! Leave some for your families! Go to your homes!'

Uys looked up at him and cried, 'Hey, Mr Salt, you'll ruin the business — ' but Adam took no notice. He was too intent on making himself heard. One of the barmen tried to pull him down, but Adam eluded him, stepping like a dancer over the beer mugs and bottles, shouting, 'Go home to your wives and children! Leave something in your pay packets! Don't spend all your money here! Go home!'

As though given a direction by an orchestral conductor, the customers, to a man, fell silent. They looked up at Adam atop the bar, his eyes blazing, an evangelist in search of converts. He in turn looked down at them, pointed to the door, and said, 'Go home! Your wives are waiting.'

A glass hurtled through the air and missed him by inches, smashing into the elaborately scrolled mirror to his left. This was the signal for the opening of hostilities. A great roar erupted, and with the speed of an accident tables were overturned, chairs flew, bottles and mugs were smashed indiscriminately. Fights broke out among the customers and spilled into the street. Hands grabbed at Adam's legs but Uys managed to pull him down out of danger. The respite was temporary. Two burly dockers hauled themselves over the bar, saw Uys and Adam cowering under the counter, set about them mercilessly, kicking and punching, and then sat down beside them drinking anything they could lay their hands on. Somewhere outside a police whistle sounded.

'Christ, you're fucking crazy,' Uys yelled at Adam, wiping the blood from his nose, but Adam was in too much pain and too stunned to take any notice. By the time the police arrived, the Van Riebeck Tavern looked like a battlefield after the battle: men lay groaning amidst the upturned tables, the broken glass and what remained of the chairs. The police sergeant, who had seen action in France, said, 'God Almighty, this is worse than Dingle Wood.'

Adam spent the night in the Groote Schuur hospital, Eva at his bedside holding his hand. Their own doctor, Norman Hurwitz, appeared shortly after seven o'clock in the morning when Adam was still sleeping. He ordered Eva to go home to bed.

'No, I have to stay with him,' she said.

'Eva, there's no point,' Dr Hurwitz said, studying the chart that hung at the foot of Adam's bed. 'He's suffering from concussion and bruises. He's got to be X-rayed and I'll have David Rubin look at the plates. He's the best orthopaedic man in town. Don't worry, he'll be all right.'

Adam stirred. 'I want to see my attorney, Harry Kaminsky,' he murmured.

'It's Saturday morning, Adam,' Dr Hurwitz said, gently. 'It'll have .to wait until Monday.'

'I want to see him and I want to see him now,' Adam said, trying to rise.

'Don't be silly, Adda,' Eva said, 'rest, you'll see Harry on Monday.'

Adam threw back the bedclothes and tried to struggle out of bed. Nurses were summoned and Dr Hurwitz authorised a light sedative to be administered. When Adam finally calmed down, Eva, bewildered and distressed, left the hospital. The morning was foul. A ferocious wind had risen which made walking difficult. Rain beat down on her and when she reached home, she looked dishevelled and broken. She tried to reassure the children. She was fine, she said, just a bit tired and windswept, and their father was not seriously hurt but would have to be kept in for observation. She retired to her room, lay on the bed, too exhausted to sleep, too numb to think.

At eleven, Isobel rushed into the bedroom without knocking and said, 'Mama, Dr Hurwitz is here and wants to see you.'

Terrified, Eva stumbled out into the hall in her stockinged feet. 'What's happened?' she demanded. 'Is Adam all right?'

'He's disappeared,' Dr Hurwitz said. 'Can you think of anywhere he might have gone? I don't want to call in the police — '

'Oh my God,' she said, sinking down on to a chair. 'What have we done to deserve this? What have we done?'

Jews were meant to walk to the synagogue on Friday nights and Saturday mornings. Travel by motor car or public transport was forbidden by Talmudic law as was any other activity that might necessitate the use of money and thus cause the Jew to think of work. *Remember the Sabbath day, to keep it holy. Six days shalt thou labour and do all thy work: But the seventh day is the Sabbath of the Lord thy God: in it thou shalt not do any work*; the fourth commandment was taken literally. Harry Kaminsky, the attorney, in common with a great many others, parked his motor car, a 1926 Studebaker, the latest model, a block or two away from the synagogue and walked the remaining short distance, greeting his co-religionists who had, of course, broken the law in the same way.

Kaminsky, a bachelor, was in his early thirties but still lived with his parents. To many, especially to his clients, he gave the impression of being all-knowing and unnaturally calm, as though he had solved a spiritual mystery which contained the secret of life known only to him; others, chiefly his opponents and casual acquaintances, regarded him as arrogant, self-loving and smug. Discretion was his watchword.

On this particular Sabbath day in September, Kaminsky passed through the entrance lobby, greeted the *shammes*, Elijah Orenstein, and then entered the synagogue proper where the service was already in progress, the congregation rocking back and forth, chanting, praying. From a small, dark blue velvet bag, embroidered with the Star of David, Kaminsky removed his prayer shawl, his *tallis*, in which he enveloped his head, swayed to and fro, and murmured a short blessing. He then sat down, adjusted the black skullcap, the *yamalka*, on his head, the *tallis* on his shoulders and tried to find the place in his prayer-book. He glanced up at the women in their gallery above and then surveyed the males all round him, many more than the ten, the *minyan*, the minimum number required to form a quorum and without whom no communal prayers or rites could begin.

Kaminsky exchanged dignified nods first with those who were his clients or those with whom he had dealings: the millionaire, Reuben Blumberg, whose Sleep-eezy beds were sold from Cape to Cairo; Hyman Shapiro with whom only last week he had concluded the sale of the Van Riebeck Tavern to Adam Salt; Barney Wildnowitz, the hotelier, seated with his brothers, Jack and Isaiah, and their benign father, Solomon, all faithful and regular members of the congregation; Aaron Sachs, the accountant with whom Kaminsky did much business, and after whose attractive and still unmarried daughter, Esther, he lusted. He stole a look up at the gallery in the hope that she was present but was disappointed. And there, in the special box to the left of the ark, sat Rabbi Abramsky, whom many also regarded as smug and self-satisfied; and to the right of the ark, in their special box, in shiny top hats, sat the ill-tempered Zalman Mauerberger, now President of the Congregation, and his vice-president, Leonard Klingman, the swimsuit manufacturer, whom Kaminsky would have liked as a client. He tried to catch Klingman's eye but the vice-president was gazing heavenwards, praying perhaps for a good summer.

The fact that a synagogue was regarded not only as a place of worship but also as a communal centre was reflected in the way the congregation conducted itself during the course of the service. Most prayed, but others chatted or nodded to their friends and even moved nearer to them in order to exchange a few words. Young boys came and went, were often noisy and were hissed at by their elders. Silence was rare. The babble of the holy and the secular was a perpetual accompaniment, frequently but only briefly shattered by Cantor Katzen, the *chazzan*, tapping his tuning fork and singing out the opening words of a prayer in which the congregation then joined. Cantor Katzen was a virtuoso. Sometimes, he sang lengthy passages of the litany in a voice which could be either liquid and soft or anguished and fortissimo, but always expressing, it seemed, mourning and lamentation, unearthing from the complex Hebrew text its hidden yet implicit record of suffering, misery, acceptance, atonement, and, finally and inevitably, gratitude to God but for what no one was quite sure.

The one moment all respected was when the ark was opened and the Scrolls of the Law, the Five Books of Moses, the Torah, bedecked in silver and gold, was removed and paraded in procession. All stood. Kaminsky followed the custom, kissed a corner of his *tallis* and with it touched the Torah as it was carried past him, a small act of acknowledgement that the law was the heart and soul of Jewish life. Once the scroll was carried up to the *bimah*, a raised platform in the centre of the synagogue, the congregation sat and the hubbub continued as before.

Kaminsky resumed his seat and as he did so became aware of a disturbance in the entrance lobby: the sounds of a man ranting and then Elijah Orenstein's voice, 'Don't you dare, you stay where you are!' More ranting and then Orenstein again, 'All right, all right, you come with me.' A couple of boys ran in and made for their elder relatives, pointing to the entrance and whispering. A moment later Orenstein himself, clearly flustered, emerged through a private door beside the rabbi's box, and talked urgently to Rabbi Abramsky, who listened with an anxious expression, and then disappeared through the door with the *shammes*. A man behind Kaminsky leaned forward and said, '*Nu?*' Kaminsky shrugged. Cantor Katzen sang out a blessing while the Torah was being unfurled to the appropriate place and Kaminsky joined in, closing his eyes and swaying to and fro, *davening*, which means to pray.

He was disturbed by someone tapping him on the shoulder. He opened his eyes to see Elijah Orenstein. 'Mr Kaminsky,' the *shammes* said, 'the Rabbi would appreciate it if you come to his office.'

'What's the problem?' Kaminsky asked, but Orenstein was already half-way to the door. He had no choice but to follow and was aware that all eyes were on him, questioning, inquisitive eyes, hopeful of scandal.

At first, Kaminsky did not recognise Adam Salt slumped in a chair, moaning, coughing painfully and holding his side. He was unshaven, wore no tie, and both his eyes were badly bruised and swollen. The Rabbi made a helpless gesture and said, 'He demanded to see you — '

Adam said hoarsely, 'Harry, I have to sell the tavern — '

'But you've only just bought it — '

'Sell it, sell it, sell it — '

Even Kaminsky's well-known serenity was shaken. The Rabbi drew him aside and talked softly. 'He's your client, I take it?'

'Yes. He's Mr Salt — '

233

'I know him,' the Rabbi said. 'He's a *meshuggener*,' which means a lunatic. 'Please get him out of here and take him home.'

Adam died in his sleep in the early hours of Monday morning. His last words before lapsing into unconsciousness were, 'I don't want to be disturbed.' Eva bore her loss with dignity, comforting her children whose shock and grief was, Dr Hurwitz said, pitiful to behold. Her dominant concern was the funeral service. Should he be buried according to Jewish religious rite? Or, given that he was a convinced atheist and anti-religious, should some other form of service be adopted? Then she remembered that in recent weeks Adam had twice paid mysterious visits to the synagogue. She had asked him if he had found religion and he had said, 'My business.' What was she to make of it? She settled for asking Harry Kaminsky to consult Rabbi Abramsky.

'Found religion? Not exactly,' Rabbi Abramsky said with his self-assured smile.

'Well, Mrs Salt is anxious to decide how to proceed with the funeral,' Kaminsky said.

'Oh, I'll bury him with pleasure, but, in confidence, you know why he came here, to see me?' Kaminsky shook his head. 'I'll tell you. He twice burst into my office, without an appointment, and told me I was a charlatan and a criminal and that being a Jew was a curse. He babbled about oil and rocking-chairs, told me he was a Freethinker, who knows what? Found religion? I think not.'

'What do I tell Mrs Salt?'

'Nothing of what I've just told you, please. But assure her that I'll bury her husband. Oh, and I'll arrange for the *nakhtwachter* to sit with the body tonight and also, be so kind, Harry, to see if you can rustle up a *minyan* because I doubt if Mr Salt himself knew ten Jews.'

Fedya Katzenowitz, once Laban the Idiot's partner, kept company Adam Salt's corpse during its last night on earth. As was his habit, he swigged brandy, sat cross-legged on the floor beside the body wrapped in a shroud and said aloud in Hebrew:

'A pattern of stars on a quilted cradle,
Dictates the destiny of all mankind.'

The next morning there was a delay. Dr Hurwitz begged Eva to allow a post-mortem to be performed, but she refused. 'I do not want Adda mutilated,' she said. The exact cause of Adam's death was never known although Dr Hurwitz confided to Eva that he was convinced it was psychologically rooted. David Rubin, the orthopaedic surgeon, suggested that perhaps a splinter of bone pierced Adam's lung with fatal consequences. Eva said, 'The fact is you don't know and you will never know. My Adda is dead, and that's all there is to it.'

He was buried that afternoon. Apart from Rabbi Abramsky and himself, the other adult males Kaminsky managed to recruit to make a *minyan* and to intone the Kaddish, the prayer for the dead, included Hyman Shapiro, Dr Norman Hurwitz, Cantor Katzen, Elijah Orenstein, and the Wildnowitz men, Solomon, Barney and Jack. They were still one short. Barney Wildnowitz said he would persuade his younger brother to delay a business trip up country. Isaiah, therefore, was the tenth man. When it was over, he and the others shook hands with the dead man's family and, as is the custom in those parts, wished them long life. Isaiah was particularly struck by the beauty of the deceased's youngest child, Isobel.

9

LES ADIEUX DE
MATTIA BATTISTINI
CE SOIR

Tatiana saw the words *ce soir* being crudely stuck across the poster which was pasted up on a *pissoir* in the Boulevard St-Germain. Then, as she was about to cross the street, the name, BATTISTINI, caught her eye. She froze, one foot in the gutter, the other on the pavement, as if a hypnotist had snapped his fingers to induce a trance. An elderly man emerged from the *pissoir*, paused and stared at her expectantly while buttoning up his flies. Receiving no response, he tipped his hat politely before hurrying away. She did not notice. A motor car almost brushed against her. The driver hooted and shouted abuse. Only then did Tatiana come to herself and draw back.

She sat at Le Coq d'Or, a café on the Place St-André-des-Arts and ordered a coffee. The calm sunshine of the April afternoon was at odds with the excitement she now experienced at seeing the name that had once meant so much to her. She closed her eyes, turned her face to the sun and breathed deeply in the hope of recovering some sort of serenity, but to no avail.

In recent months Tatiana had discovered that when memories of the more distant past were triggered she was possessed of an inability to disentangle sequences of events; a product, she believed, of having to suffer so much tumult and upheaval. She had only to encounter an unexpected reminder, momentous or insignificant, and she became timid about chronology, almost cowardly; to put in logical order her experiences and ordeals required wilful, conscious effort from which, more often than not, she retreated. This confusion brought neither panic nor irritation, for she had decided that the past was not a country which she wished to visit too often or for too long. But the sight of Battistini's name was just such an incident to provoke recollections willy-nilly, and so she allowed memory to be deceitful, inaccurate, selective. Tonight. Lev dying. *Rigoletto*. Warsaw. Farewell party. Moscow. Darya and Richard. Lenin dead. A bald sailor in Sobliki. Grigory in the rain. The Small Tiara catching sunlight. Xenia and Emmett. Paris. Valodya – oh God, stupid, stupid Valodya. No, she didn't want to think of Valodya. No, no. She bit her bottom lip.

One method she had discovered of trying to restore clarity was to play a game, asking herself questions the answers to which she received like an incredulous child being told of unlikely adult adventures. Was it really more than twenty years ago that I first heard Battistini sing? Never! Twenty years? Really? 1927 now, and I am forty-one. Oh God, forty-one. Am I really? Yes, well, it must have been twenty years ago and more, certainly before I married. Was it 1911 when Lev and I were in Warsaw? And when did Lev die? 1922? And Lenin? In '24. January? Bitter cold and the city silent. And afterwards fear more terrible than ever. Better the devil you know. Only three years ago? Surely not. How long have we been in Paris? Two years? No, no, only one, more like one.

A waiter brought *café au lait* and slipped her bill under an ashtray. She glanced at the total, two sous, and that steadied her more abruptly and more surely than any game she chose to play. Of all the practical hardships she had been forced to endure Tatiana was least able to cope with her lack of funds and she realised, glancing again at the bill, the true underlying reason why Battistini's name had caused such an inward flurry. She knew the moment after she had taken in the poster that she would ask him for help, not a loan necessarily, but an introduction to professional musical circles, perhaps, or a recommendation, an influential word in an influential ear. Would he remember her after all these years? Would he be kind, she wondered? Would he make her life easier for old times' sake? Dare she approach him? Yes, provided she preserved her pride and dignity. She sprinkled sugar into her cup and stirred slowly as though the spoon were a key with which she was winding up her courage.

Tatiana tried to devise a plan. Leaving the table, she went inside the café, bought a *jeton* and telephoned her distant cousin, Countess Sophia Arkunina, with whom she and Iliena shared rooms in Saint-Cloud.

'Sophia? I'm going to be late this evening. I won't be back until eleven, perhaps even later.'

'Is everything all right?' Sophia asked breathlessly. She was a spinster, a nervous woman to whom any change of routine signalled calamity.

'Everything's all right,' Tatiana said. 'I may have another job. It's too complicated to explain. Madame Monge's accompanist has been taken ill and she may want me to play for her this evening. Be so kind as to see that Iliena's in bed by ten o'clock.'

She returned to her table on the pavement. From her music case she took pencil and paper, and wrote in French:

237

Dear Signor Battistini,

By chance, I saw your farewell concert advertised for tonight. I hope to be in the audience and would like so much to pay my respects to you afterwards, as I did all those years ago in Moscow. I wonder if you remember. You were kind enough to go riding with me, and later we were in contact once more, in 1911, I think, when my late husband was Military Attaché in Warsaw.

I look forward to meeting you again after all these years.

She hesitated, not knowing how best to sign herself. Deciding that modesty would do her no good at all, she wrote clearly, Countess Tatiana Sobeleva. Then, another agonising decision: should she buy envelopes? Would the stationer sell her just one? She even thought to ask the waiter if he could help. In the end, she folded the piece of paper several times so that it looked like a sachet and carefully printed Battistini's name in large capitals.

The hall where he was to sing was on the right bank of the Seine, in the rue Cambon. She was not going to waste money on a tram. She paid the waiter but did not tip him. He didn't seem to mind. She set off, walking in her slow and stately fashion, crossing the river by the Pont St-Michel, regretting all the while the circumstances that made this errand necessary.

Even with an objective, empirical approach it was impossible to attribute cause and effect in order to understand precisely the Sobelevs' odyssey. Some would account them fortunate but, to Tatiana at least, fortune played no part at all and, even if it did, was founded on incidents arising out of an inchoate past and present. Undoubtedly Valodya had played a key role: if not for him Darya would never have met Richard Webb; but then if not for her brother Grigory and the famine Emmett Brumby would not have entered their lives; if her elder daughters had not been attractive would the two foreigners have married them? And if Tatiana had not been able to play the piano how else would she and Iliena have eked out an existence? Tatiana soon came to the conclusion it was best not to question the caprice of existence for each answer only prompted a dozen more questions. To accept one's fate as the will of God, she decided, was both easier and more comforting.

Although she had daily to battle against poverty, Tatiana wholeheartedly loved this new life in Paris. She was at home in the city, was bound to it by spiritual and cultural ties. The émigré community was large and exuberant. The myth that all Russian aristocrats were now either taxi drivers, doormen, waiters or personal servants to the French nobility was only slightly exaggerated. In

Tatiana's own circle of relatives and acquaintances many had found work in department stores, were teaching Russian or, like Tatiana herself, giving music lessons and accompanying amateur singers. She knew of at least two Counts who had managed to smuggle out furniture and bric-à-brac, and so had successfully launched careers as antique dealers. Sophia Arkunina, her cousin, with whom she shared a flat, made a less than modest living as a translator. A Princess Troubetskoy had opened a lingerie shop and seemed to be flourishing. Paris was traditionally kind and welcoming to those whose lives had been dislocated, especially the titled whom Parisians treated with sympathy and respect, endowing their expulsion with romance. The exiled Russians found this particularly ironic in a city which had done to death so many of its own aristocrats. In Paris it was also possible to exist miserably poor yet not be victim to despair. Tatiana held herself erect, did not lose her well-known hauteur, and believed she would be able to make a life for herself and her youngest daughter. Yet, if not for Richard Webb's generosity her optimism would have been ill-founded.

After the flight from Russia, having seen Tatiana and Iliena settled in Paris, Darya and Richard returned to England. The offer of a job as a sub-editor on the *Manchester Guardian* drew the couple back to Richard's home town. Each month he sent a small sum, five pounds, sometimes more, sometimes less, which covered Tatiana's rent and bare necessities. Even after their first child, a boy, was born, the Webbs continued the allowance without complaint. When Tatiana wrote to Richard saying that perhaps he should now stop the payments, he replied:

Dear Mama,
We won't starve. You might.
Your loving son-in-law,
Richard.
P.S. Leo flourishes and has begun to walk like a drunk on pay day.

The Brumbys contributed nothing. Rarely, perhaps once a year, a gift would arrive, usually something useless, a photograph-frame or a tooled leather purse. They lived in Rome and Xenia's irregular letters told of Emmett's father's death, hinted at a large inheritance, explained Emmett's decision to become a dealer in Russian icons, described their apartment near the Piazza del Popolo and their visit to America. Tatiana was neither surprised by their lack of concern nor was she hurt. She had always been suspicious of Emmett's nature and suspected that Xenia, however much she might want to help, would find it difficult to ask him for money on behalf of her mother and sister.

Tatiana's own meagre earnings were spasmodic. She accompanied amateur singers and was occasionally employed as a rehearsal pianist for a ballet company. Princess Troubetskoy offered her a job in the lingerie shop but Tatiana did not find work behind a counter in any way agreeable. She sold odd bits of jewellery. The struggle to survive was hard but the struggle not to be debilitated by it, harder. Now, as she approached the rue Cambon, she hoped that some small favour from Mattia Battistini would, at least temporarily, make her lot easier. She had no idea what precise result she expected from the interview but had vague hopes of a letter of recommendation which would open doors and enable her to find more work.

When she reached the hall the sun had already set; the lights of the city began to sparkle and the prospect of a Paris evening, the expectations, the excitement, the bustle, the sense of pleasurable urgency were almost tangible. She had never any intention of spending money on a ticket for the recital and made directly for the artists' entrance, gave her letter and a small tip to the concierge, an old woman with scraped-back grey hair and a thin, cruel mouth.

'What time does the recital end?' she asked.

'Depends on how many encores he gives. About ten o'clock, thereabouts.'

'I shall be here again at about ten o'clock then,' Tatiana said. 'Please see he gets my letter. It's very important.'

Once outside in the street again she hesitated, not knowing quite how to while away the two or three hours before the recital's end. Then, she heard his voice. Somewhere in the building Mattia Battistini was warming up, singing scales first, and then repeating the opening phrase of Ponchielli's *La Gioconda*, '*Ebbrezza! Delirio!*' over and over again. She stood and listened to that rich, soulful voice, distant, muffled, as if filtered through gauze. She closed her eyes as though trying to remember a disturbing dream. When the voice was finally silent she set off, walking aimlessly, deciding she would save money and go without eating.

She lost all sense of time and only noticed how late it was when she happened to glance into a jeweller's window in the rue de Rivoli. Ten to ten. She hurried now and reached the hall just as the audience was pouring out, the ladies waiting demurely beneath the front entrance while the gentlemen went off in search of taxis. When she reached the artists' entrance there was a large group of admirers gathered, old and young, male and female, waiting for Battistini to emerge. Pushing her way through to the door, she heard the excited buzz of chatter and pleasure.

One old man said, 'He has the finest voice of anyone I've ever heard.'

'Yes, yes, he is a great artist.'

'The voice used to be fine but he's getting old.'

'Well, of course he's getting old, that's why it's his farewell performance.'

A dozen or so people were already badgering the concierge, calling their own names or handing over visiting cards, all demanding to see the singer. Tatiana waited. A man with an air of self-importance appeared. Battistini's manager, Tatiana supposed. After consulting with the concierge, he ushered a chosen few at a time through a heavy door that must lead, Tatiana decided, to the dressing-room. Ten minutes later the group reappeared glowing with pleasure and another few were allowed to pass into the inner sanctum. It reminded Tatiana of her visits to the Moscow hospital to see Lev. When the last visitors had been led away, Tatiana approached the concierge.

'Is there a message for me?' she asked. 'Countess Sobeleva.'

The concierge narrowed her eyes as though trying to bring Tatiana into focus. 'A message from whom?' she asked.

'From Signor Battistini.'

'Oh, yes! The note. I remember. Yes, wait for Signor Malgeri.'

The final group of visitors returned, escorted by the self-important-looking man who, now rather servile, bowed low to them as they left the building. When they had gone he glanced at Tatiana and then raised an eyebrow in the direction of the concierge.

'Countess Sobeleva,' the concierge said.

The man turned to Tatiana and gave a curt bow. 'I am Fausto Malgeri,' he said, 'the private secretary of *il maestro*. How is it possible I you can help?' He spoke in French.

'I left a letter for Signor Battistini.'

'But yes.' He searched in his pockets and produced Tatiana's note. He reread it to refresh his memory.

'You gave it to Signor Battistini, I trust,' Tatiana said, seeking confirmation not questioning.

Malgeri raised his eyes from the scrap of paper and looked at her. 'No,' he said, 'I am not always troubling *il maestro* with all letters.'

'But it was addressed to him.'

'I am, as I am telling you, the private secretary. All letters I am reading first.'

'Fausto!' A roar. Battistini's voice from the bowels of the earth.

He hurried to the door, opened it a crack and called, '*Si, si, maestro, momentino.*'

'I should very much like to see him,' Tatiana said. 'As you have read my letter you will know that Signor Battistini and I are acquainted.'

241

'Fausto!'

Malgeri took from his wallet a ten-franc note and stuffed it into Tatiana's hand. 'I must go now, excuse me.'

'What is this?' Tatiana asked, holding the note between thumb and forefinger as though it were contaminated. 'How dare you,' she hissed like a blast of cold air.

'Is ten francs, Countess,' Malgeri said with an apologetic smile. 'Is why you come, no?'

'How dare you,' she said again but more quietly, almost to herself. 'Fausto!'

Malgeri returned to the door and called again to his master to be patient, then he addressed Tatiana. 'Forgive me, please, but, understand, in recent years, there have been so many Russian countesses,' and with a shrug he vanished.

PART FOUR

Wheels within Wheels

(1932–1939)

1

Isaiah, not yet fully awake and still in his dressing-gown, opened the front door of his parents' home in Oranjezicht and padded down the path in his slippers to the letter-box which was attached to the wooden gate. There were three letters that Monday morning and all were addressed to him. The first was an invitation to attend a recruiting drive for the Junior Zionist Society. It was a circular letter, signed by Mrs Eva Salt, Secretary of the local Bnoth Zion Association, and whose name rang a distant bell. The second letter he had been expecting: confirmation of his appointment as sole agent for a new brand of cigarettes, Lord Somerset. The third puzzled him and quickened his interest. A German stamp. The postmark, Hamburg. He stood at the gate in hot December sun, trying to read the jumble of directions and redirections:

> Isaiah Wildnowitz,
> Kep Tovn,
> Südafrika

and then scrawled in ink and pencil: Not known, Try Cape Town, Return to Sender, Upper Orange Street??

Isaiah tore open the letter and held his breath.

'God Almighty!' he murmured, then cried out loud, 'Uncle Laban!' and ran back into the house. 'Mama, papa, there's a letter from Uncle Laban!'

Solomon, Leah and Isaiah huddled around the walnut dining-table trying to decipher Laban's Yiddish. He gave a *poste restante* address in Hamburg, and the letter was dated 2/7/32. It had taken five months to reach them.

Good day Isaiah!
Don't drop dead. It's your Uncle Laban writing. You remember me? Yes, I'm still in Hamburg but not for long.
Nu, it's nearly twenty years since we waved goodbye. You are now I'm guessing 32 maybe 33. I'm also guessing you are married with twelve children. All right, ten.

How are you? How is your mother and your father? Well and rich. I'm guessing again.

Why am I writing after all these years? I'll tell you.

Three reasons. Reason one. I am going to be married and I am telling everyone I know. Yes, getting married. Me. Now nearly sixty! Me! (I still feel sixteen never mind sixty!) My bride is Theodora von Tresckow. You met her. I call her Europa. She is not full Jewish but we discovered her grandmother was Sarah Levy. *Nu*.

Reason two. We are going to America next year. By then we will have enough money saved. This I always knew is what fate had in store for me. Your Uncle Benjamin is already there. Where exactly, who knows? But I'll find him.

Why after all this time to America at last? Zeus is the reason. For many years Europa never wants to leave. Now she cannot wait. Europa is no fool. Just take her word for it Zeus is in disguise again, this time he calls himself Hitler, a pimp, a rapist.

Reason three. I think of you a lot, Isaiah. I think of the days I taught you your bar mitzvah portion. You remember Circus Stoica? Ha-ha!

Please write to me if this reaches you which I hope to God it does.

Frizlitch!

Your ever loving uncle,

Laban.

P.S. I'm putting with this some thoughts on life.

And on a separate sheet of paper:

> Fate's a devil, a serpent with apples.
> Beware of bulls and eagles.
> Nothing you do changes your final destination.
> Be patient. Bow down. Your head will be raised.
> And remember your most important address.

After Isaiah read the last words, the three sat in silence, exchanging mystified glances, as though they had been visited by a supernatural being whose presence could not be explained. Leah was the first to speak. 'He's still an idiot,' she said and, for the first time in many a year, wept in fond remembrance of her brother-in-law.

'He's marrying a *shiksa*,' from Solomon, dully.

Isaiah simply smiled, a crooked smile, and subconsciously he was imitating Laban's grin, lopsided and idiotic.

Leah sniffed back tears and asked, 'You met this Europa?'

'Yes, but all I remember is that she gave me sweets.'

'Who's this fellow Zeus?' Solomon asked.

'A Greek god,' Isaiah answered.

'A Greek what?' Leah queried.

'A god, mama, I don't know, it's some sort of joke, I don't understand it either.'

'The only Greeks I know sell fruit and vegetables,' Leah said. 'What's this Zeus got to do with Hitler?' And she made a little spitting sound as if saying the Austrian's name gave her a bitter taste.

Then came a good deal of tongue-clicking and head-shaking. 'Laban! Tsth-tsth, after all these years! Laban! Tsth-tsth! God is good! And Benjamin in America! Tsth-tsth!'

Solomon picked up the sheet of paper with Laban's thoughts on life and, while Leah continued to marvel, he studied them. 'What's he mean your most important address?' he asked.

'Where a man lives inside himself,' Isaiah answered, continuing to smile Laban's smile.

'Apples, bulls, eagles,' Solomon muttered. 'Oimigott, my brother, Laban, is a real, hundred per cent *meshuggener*, the genuine article.'

Isaiah rose from the table. 'I'm going to write to him, this minute,' he said, and as he hurried to his bedroom, he heard Leah ask, 'Why does Laban write to Ishkele and not to us?'

Isaiah took up pen and lined paper, and tried but failed to bring Laban up to date; it was too daunting a task. Too much had happened, impossible to account for Barney and Jack, let alone himself. After a dozen attempts, he settled for a simple résumé: all were well and prospering, Barney was a rich hotelier, married to Rosie Minskoff, no children, Jack was a commercial traveller for a women's lingerie manufacturer, lived in Johannesburg, was married to Celia Platt, two children, a boy and girl, And of himself?

Crouched over the page, the pen poised in mid-air, Isaiah became motionless. What of himself? What was there to tell? Nothing had happened to him. He was thirty-two years old, living at home with his parents, making a decent living, but had he a life, any sort of life, or what Laban would call life? Should he tell Laban his secrets? Could he write them down? Could he confide his longings to find a girl of whom Leah would approve, with whom he could fall in love, marry, have children? A life, that was all he asked. Would he be able to express the constant feeling of a weight on his chest impossible to lift? Dare he confess his loneliness, nowhere to go, no one to see, only endless evenings alone or with his parents, smothering him with protection and love. He had some friends but all were married now, and he was the last, a bachelor, a *nebbish*, *drebshen*. Yet, Isaiah believed Laban would sympathise with his inner life, for after all that was the most important address, Laban's map which charted a path to the forest where magicians roam. Should he write of his longing to learn, to study? A short while ago, he could tell Laban, he had bought a second-hand set of encyclopaedias in English. True, they were only children's encyclopaedias, edited by Arthur Mee, but they opened Isaiah's eyes to a glorious universe – science, nature, music, literature, art, history. He loved history especially. Laban would smile at this. And Isaiah could curse history for thwarting his chances to acquire knowledge, and to be learned. Yes, perhaps he should tell Laban that there might be a chance of going to night-school, or —

He wrote. 'I am well. I am 32. I am a commercial traveller for cigarettes. I lead an interesting life. Please write again soon. Your loving nephew, Isaiah.'

Two weeks later, on a warm Sunday evening, Isaiah attended the recruiting drive for the Young Zionists, held in a room of the Zionist Hall in Hope Street. At the entrance, a young girl took his name. He remembered her instantly, and realised why the name Salt had stirred his memory.

'You're Miss Salt, am I right?' Isaiah said.

'Yes,' the girl said, and blushed.

'I attended your father's funeral,' he said, 'but you won't re-member.'

She shook her head, keeping her eyes down.

'And please, don't mind my asking, what's your name?' he asked.

'Isobel,' she said.

'Mine's Isaiah. People call me Is.'

He took a seat on the aisle of the last row which was unoccupied. He scanned the rest of the audience, all young people, most of them at least five or six years his junior. He knew hardly anyone present. On the platform, at a table, a handsome, grey-haired woman was busy sorting through a pile of papers. Isaiah kept glancing back at Isobel, still by the door, taking the names of the last arrivals. Presently, she closed the door, joined the woman on the platform, whispered to her and, with a flick of the eyes, indicated Isaiah in the back row. The woman looked up at him, nodded, and smiled. It made Isaiah feel awkward so he studied his shoes. Isobel then returned to the body of the hall, sat a few empty rows in front of Isaiah, but diagonally across from him and in his eye-line.

The woman on the platform opened the meeting by introducing herself as Mrs Eva Salt, Honorary Secretary of the Bnoth Zion Association in Cape Town. She explained the need for young people to become involved in the movement, especially now in view of the dangers threatening in Germany. Then, she said something that threw Isaiah into confusion. 'So it is very important that you, who are under thirty, should put some of your energy into our cause.'

Under thirty! But I'm thirty-two, Isaiah said to himself in panic. What do I do? Do I get up now and say I shouldn't be here? No, no, sit it out, wait. He didn't want to leave, not because he had any great desire to become a Zionist, but because he could not take his eyes off Isobel Salt. He thought she was the most beautiful girl he had ever seen. Slim, not too tall, long black hair framing a gentle face, pale complexion, slightly rounded cheeks, and sad brown eyes with heavy lids. She must have become aware of his penetrating stare because she glanced back at him. For the briefest moment their eyes met. They looked away. She sat more rigidly after that as if any movement she made would be indecorous. Isaiah took to staring at her again, transfixed, and paid little attention to the lecture being given by the girl's mother.

After Mrs Salt had answered a variety of questions from the floor, soft drinks and biscuits were served. The young people stood about in groups, chattering and laughing. Isobel and her mother went from one to the other handing out enrolment forms. Isaiah tried to position himself so that Isobel would be the one to hand him his form but, unluckily, her mother had the honour.

Eva said, 'Mr Wildnowitz?'

'Yes.'

'My daughter, Isobel, tells me you attended my husband's funeral.'

'Yes, I made up the *minyan*.'

'Thank you. Rather belatedly, but thank you.'

'Mrs Salt — ?'

'Yes?'

'I got a problem — '

'Oh dear. Can I help?'

Isaiah shrugged. 'I'm thirty-two. You said under thirties.'

'Oh dear.'

'You want I should leave now and not waste your time?'

'You can always join the senior group.'

Isaiah looked doubtful.

'Do you want to be a Zionist?'

'— '

'We need volunteers to help in the office. There's a lot of work to be done when you start a recruitment drive like this. Isobel and some of her friends work at weekends, it's very informal — '

He said quickly, 'Maybe I'll give that a try — '

'Good. Have a word with Belle. She'll tell you all about it.'

Belle. Is that what they called her? Belle? The name chimed sweetly in his ear. He looked for her. She had gone back to her table at the door and was counting the number of forms she had left over. She made notes.

249

'Miss Salt? I had a word with your mother. I'm thirty-two and a little old for this group but I'd like to give a hand in the office. She said it's with you I got to speak.'

Isobel did not look up at him at first, but continued to make notes. 'All right,' she said in a careless sort of way. 'We do one morning a week. Sundays. Will that be convenient?'

'Perfect. Because during the week, I'm up country, a commercial traveller.'

'We work from our house,' and she scribbled down the address on the back of one of the enrolment forms.

'I'll be there,' he said.

'I'll be there, too.'

The next morning he drove out of Cape Town, across the mountains, to visit Paarl and Robertson and Worcester, stopping at the general stores along the way and selling cigarettes. His heart was light. He could not remember when he'd been happier. What a fortnight! A letter from Uncle Laban, a new brand of cigarettes to launch, but most exciting of all, Miss Isobel Salt, Belle, beautiful Belle, who banished all other thoughts from his mind. Suddenly his future seemed bathed in a golden light. The weight on his chest lifted. Along the road he sang aloud, over and over again:

> 'Oi, Tsutsanna! Oi, don't you cry for me,
> I come from Ellybumma
> Mit mine banjer on mine knee.'

Isobel Salt did not sing songs but she took heart from poetry, from Browning and Byron, especially Byron, who had written what she believed then to be among the most beautiful lines of English poetry even written:

> Fictions and dreams inspire the bard
>   Who rolls the epic song;
> Friendship and truth be my reward –
>   To me no bays belong;
> If laurell'd Fame but dwells with lies,
>   Me the enchantress ever flies,
> Whose heart and not whose fancy sings;
>   Simple and young, I dare not feign;
> Mine be the rude yet heartfelt strain,
>   'Friendship is Love without his wings!'

She, too, was smitten. She had not remembered Isaiah Wildnowitz at her father's funeral, but the moment she glanced up at him on that hot Sunday night in December 1932, and their eyes engaged for a fleeting moment, she was instantly drawn to the handsome man with a foreign accent and a diffident manner. Like him, she could think of little else and looked forward to the following Sunday morning when she would meet him again.

Somewhere she had read that people were attracted by opposites: strong women to weaker men, introverts to extroverts, the garrulous to the silent. But she had detected in Isaiah a shyness similar to her own which she found beguiling in a man so many years her senior. The day after she met him she found herself practising a new signature – Isobel Wildnowitz. She confided to no one, not to her best friend, Jean Jaffe, and, more unusually, not to her mother; this inability to unburden what most mattered to her was a clue to her personality.

She was eighteen, in appearance an almost perfect mixture of her parents, especially the combination of her late-father's straight nose and her mother's heavily lidded eyes. She was more graceful than her mother and the question, 'Was she beautiful?' would not have been asked of her, for the answer was apparent: she was beautiful, and her beauty was much admired, especially by non-Jews who accounted her looks classically Jewish. Even to the least perceptive or sensitive of observers, such as her brother, George, for example, her eyes expressed a soulful quality, a vulnerability, what he called Isobel's 'hidden depths'.

Under her mother's influence, she took refuge in books, in occasional visits to the theatre or to the City Hall to hear the Municipal Orchestra. George had been fed the same cultural diet as Isobel but had not eaten as hungrily. Her mother naturally warmed to these leanings in her younger child, so they had much in common. Yet, Isobel's lack of confidence caused her to mistrust all affection and love. She knew, or thought she knew, that George was her mother's favourite; since he was the first-born and a boy, it was, she told herself, the way of things. She was not competitive. And although she knew her mother was unable to partake in George's world – principally engineering which he was now studying at the University of Cape Town, and cricket for which he had a passion and had won his blue – Isobel took for granted that she herself was in second place and did not complain.

Her achievements at school were average. She had been sent to Normal College which was run by nuns for whom she harboured affection and admiration. She had shown a talent for acting but it was not encouraged. She was well-read and well-informed, had shrewd political instincts and innate taste in matters artistic. She could be witty or what her mother called 'good at repartee'. But all these virtues, for they were virtues, she concealed, not deliberately but because she had no choice. It was the way she was made.

So, the coming together of Isobel Salt and Isaiah Wildnowitz was the mating of similar inner identities, both virgins not only sexually but also in their experience of the world. Neither of them had known the pleasure and the pain of a love affair however tenuous; both of them had only the love of their parents by which to test affection.

'Mama,' Isobel said one Friday evening, 'I want to invite Isaiah Wildnowitz to lunch on Sunday week.' She had screwed up her courage to make the request knowing full well that Eva would instantly understand its full import. And Eva did, for Isobel had forecast the look of concern that would cloud her mother's eyes.

The reasons for Eva's misgivings about Isaiah Wildnowitz were muddled. Ever since Adam's death, she had worried about her children's future in general and about Isobel in particular. Adam, despite the fiasco of his investment in the Van Riebeck Tavern, had left just enough money to buy an annuity, ensuring continuity of the life to which the family was accustomed: at least they could afford to keep both the house in Mill Street and the maid, Selina. Eva's personal needs were modest and so she accounted herself reasonably comfortable. But children were another matter. Education, while not expensive, was nevertheless demanding. Fees, school uniforms, sports clothes, textbooks had to be paid for. In her immediate encounter with grief at Adam's death, Eva had little energy to address what she instinctively knew would be a problem. She mourned for her husband and missed him intensely and painfully. Theirs had been a companionable marriage and now her companion was gone. But, after a shorter time than she anticipated or, indeed, thought decent, her strength began to return and she was able to harness her will and determination. She consciously reactivated her interest in Zionism and rediscovered the cause with a passion which proved to be a solace and an almost magical therapy.

Fifteen years previously, in 1917, Arthur Balfour, then the British Foreign Secretary, had issued a declaration giving British support to a Jewish national homeland in Palestine. This triumph of Zionist endeavour gave spectacular encouragement to Jews everywhere. In Cape Town, and in other cities both in South Africa and around the world, Zionism flourished. The need to raise funds to help those Jews already settled in Palestine, to finance a Hebrew university and countless other causes, became the driving force. When Eva returned to the movement there were women's groups, educational committees, all sorts of special interests hoping to influence national and international Zionist policy. There was, too, a political splintering within the ranks, left, right, centre, religious, secular, extremists, liberals, all vying to dominate in the hope of determining both how the reality of a Jewish State could be achieved, and the political complexion of the government that would necessarily and eventually be elected. Eva, committed to treading as liberal a path as possible, joined the Bnoth Zion, the women's society, which was then flexing its muscles, rebelling against subservience to the male groups, demanding and winning control over its own funds. After speaking from the floor at three or four meetings, her fluency and clarity impressed, and she was elected Secretary of the Cape Town branch.

Her sudden prominence in Bnoth Zion brought her to the notice of countless societies, small and large. It was discovered she had been a member of the English faculty of Warsaw University and so she was invited to speak on a great variety of topics, from literary criticism to practical advice on how to write a short story; for these she was modestly paid, but sometimes as much as five shillings, and the small fees were put into a separate account which Eva called grandiosely The Salt Education Fund.

Georgie's needs alone dented and then holed the fund within the first year of its existence. Eva didn't mind. She had a special affection for her son and although she would have been outraged to know that Isobel believed him to be her favourite, she would have been forced to admit that there was some truth in the assessment. She had confidence in Georgie, knew he would always be all right: he was socially assured, attractive to both sexes, was academically gifted and now training for a profession. But, and in a way more importantly, he was truly South African, at home in this beautiful land of his parents' adoption, and would never, Eva believed, experience her own or Adam's sense of perpetual exile from a country unspecified and unknown.

She was not so sure about Isobel. The girl had grieved for her father, talked of him often, wept and mourned his loss. Eva had once thought that the lack of a strong male influence would somehow damage Isobel; she read Sigmund Freud and Ernest Jones who confirmed this vague disquiet. It was an unpleasant moment when Isobel asked to bring the thirty-two-year-old Isaiah Wildnowitz to Sunday lunch but no real surprise.

This lunch did not go well. Isaiah's table manners were shocking. He ate crouched low over the table, slurped his soup, devoured the chicken just as noisily and ate at a speed that was breathtaking. He held the bones in his hands without permission, his mouth was covered in grease and, worst of all, poured his tea into the saucer to cool it. How outraged Adam would have been, Eva thought. But Isobel did not seem to notice. She looked adoringly on the object of her love as Titania did on Bottom with his ass's head.

Then, too, Isaiah had little conversation, at any rate to interest Eva. It appeared he had never read a book (except, he admitted shyly, that he had set himself the task of reading ten volumes of encyclopaedias, Aac–Zwi), took little interest in politics, was entirely bound up with his own family, especially his mother, and led a life that revolved round work and the synagogue.

Snobbery, too, played a part in Eva's disapproval of Isaiah. His accent, his inaccurate English, his general demeanour marked him out as distinctly foreign. Eva realised, of course, that she herself spoke with a Polish accent but it was somehow different. Isaiah was a Litvak, an almost derogatory term for those refugees from Lithuania, and she would have preferred someone for Isobel more socially acceptable.

Isobel anticipated her mother's objections before, during and after Isaiah's first visit. Eva asked her to take her time, to consider. But she was asking the impossible. It was beyond Isobel's power to bring reason to bear on what amounted to an obsession. She was in love, and wanted nothing else in this world but to marry the man who was the object of that love. She counted the days before she would see him next, and looked forward to meeting his mother and father.

Isaiah procrastinated. He did not want to disturb his own or Isobel's happiness. For there was no denying it, he was, he believed for the first time in his life, truly happy. He woke each morning full of anticipation and optimism; he relished the prospect of what the day held in store for him, good or bad, both were welcome. On Fridays he returned from the country, spirits soaring at the prospect of seeing his beloved. And Isobel took to going to the synagogue on the Sabbath eve. She sat in the women's gallery, looked down at him, and her heart tightened pleasurably each time their eyes met.

Saturday night was their time alone. They walked and talked of their future together, held hands, kissed, clung to each other, sat in cafés or visited cinemas – bioscopes, they were called – and afterwards lingered in shadowy places under the stars. Idyllic though it was, Isaiah's joy required him to keep at bay any thought of introducing Isobel to his mother. His memory of Leah's reaction to Esther Sachs was still fresh and Esther's accusation that he was a mother's boy still painful. But Isobel was persistent and when, one evening, she turned to him and said, 'I don't think you want to marry me. Otherwise you'd introduce me to your parents,' Isaiah knew the confrontation could not be put off for much longer.

She was invited to Sunday lunch, just the four of them, Solomon and Leah, Isaiah and Isobel. Isaiah prattled. Solomon smiled indulgently, for he was immediately taken by Isobel's beauty and dignity; subconsciously he warmed to her reticence which was so like his own and sensed in her a kindred spirit. Isobel, shy in company at the best of times, was cautious, demure, a touch aloof; she contributed little to the conversation but was aware of Leah's narrowed eyes on her, knew she was being scrutinised as though she were an object under inspection for flaws.

By this time in their lives Leah and Solomon had improved their English vocabulary if not their syntax. Leah was, as ever, polite, almost unctuous, Solomon mostly silent. They questioned her about her family, seemed impressed by Eva's Zionism and sympathetic regarding Adam's untimely death. The evening, Isaiah thought, must be considered a success all round. It was only after he returned from seeing Isobel home that, as with Esther Sachs, Leah unleashed her full maternal fury. Dismayed, Isaiah sat at the table burying his face in his hands, allowing Leah's monstrous weight to crush his spirits. She had just got going, first accusing the Salts of not really being part of the Jewish community, of not knowing what it was to maintain the traditions which had kept Jews strong and united, and then launched forth into rhetorical questions about Isobel's ability to cook, to bring up children when, to Isaiah's astonishment, Solomon intervened vehemently on the young couple's behalf. He confronted his wife in an almost unprecedented display of firmness. If Isaiah was astonished, Leah was shocked. She backed off instantly, retreated into silent resentment like a bully who bolts at the first show of retaliation. She knew that, in trying to find fault with Isobel, she was clutching at straws and the straws slipped from her grasp.

In December 1933, Isaiah Wildnowitz and Isobel Salt were married. Isobel's brother, George, led her down the aisle. Without daring to tell his parents, Isaiah paid for the reception at the Salts' home. The couple had no honeymoon and moved to Muizenberg, a suburb on the eastern seaboard of the peninsular, into a flat which overlooked a railway line. For a time they were happy and, although she called him Isaiah and he called her Belle, they were known to their friends as Is and Is.

2

Stepan Kessler fled Chemnitz for Berlin in September 1931. He travelled at night and in secret. A few days later he wrote to a few friends and acquaintances explaining that he had left so hurriedly because he could not bear goodbyes; he told them he wanted to see and experience life in the big city and that he needed to escape the suffocating confines of his parents' home. Ater all, he said, he was now twenty-six years old and the time had come to spread his wings. The truth behind his departure was uglier and entirely devoid of platitudes.

In the spring of 1931 Stepan was taken aback to see his cousin, Willi Lohmeyer, changing into the uniform of the SA – *Sturmabteilung*, the strong arm of the Nazi party, the storm-troopers. After the party's spectacular success in the 1930 election – they had increased their vote from eight hundred and ten thousand to six and a half million – membership soared but, even so, Stepan was surprised that Willi had enlisted in its most militant wing. Willi had in fact joined the local SA not as a storm-trooper but as bandsman, a trumpeter, and was issued with a brown uniform, a cap, jackboots, a leather belt and a Nazi armband. The Chemnitz SA marched to old martial airs and the rattle of side drums; the storm-troopers themselves trailed behind and bawled out new Party songs and other older marching tunes which were just as strident. Their favourite was the new 'Horst Wessel Song'. Horst Wessel was a Berlin *gauleiter*, son of a Protestant chaplain, who had abandoned his family and his studies to live in a slum with a prostitute and to dedicate his life to National Socialism. He was murdered by Communists in February 1930 and would have been forgotten had he not left behind the words and music of a song which became the Nazis' anthem. Horst Wessel was hailed by members of his Party as an idealist and a martyr. Non-members said he was degenerate and earned his living as a pimp.

By 1931, the Kesslers had moved into their own house not far from the Lohmeyers so Stepan was a little out of touch with Willi's activities. Kessler Senior had bought into Herry Lohmeyer's textile factory and the partners prospered. Even with the unrelenting inflation afflicting Germany, the two men somehow managed to keep their heads above water and enjoyed comfortable lives, helped from time to time by Kessler's Sterling reserves. Both men, first privately and later publicly, condoned the policies of Adolf Hitler, for principally they saw the Nazis as a buffer against Communism. To Kessler a defence against the greatest evil he believed the world had known was an historical necessity. Had he not seen with his own eyes the havoc Communists wrought? Had they not instituted a reign of terror as savage as any in recorded history? Had he not lost everything at their hands? He was also not opposed to the Nazis' anti-Semitism. After all, the Communist revolution, as he was fond of saying, was little more than a revolution inspired by Jews. Herr Lohmeyer agreed with him, ceased to be a patient of Dr Rosensweig and instead visited a non-Jewish dentist.

Stepan took little interest in politics. He, his younger brother, Shura, and Willi were all employed in the offices of the textile mill and it was one evening, after work, while the three of them were washing before setting off for home that Stepan saw for the first time Willi changing into his new uniform.

'What's that?' he asked.

'What's it look like?'

'It looks like an SA uniform,' Stepan said.

'That's what it is,' Willi replied.

Stepan and Shura watched him in silence and Stepan noticed, pasted on the inside of Willi's locker door, a photograph cut from a newspaper or magazine of Adolf Hitler, Ernst Roehm, Hermann Goering and another man in army uniform, Eric Ludendorff. Stepan recognised them easily, for they were all national figures now, infamous or renowned depending on your point of view. Ludendorff especially caused him to shudder, for he remembered the first time he had seen the general's likeness, in the kitchen of the policeman, Alfred Schmidt. Stepan was suddenly overwhelmed with a memory of Frau Schmidt's sickly sentimentality and it made him uneasy.

'You should join us,' Willi said, pulling on his boots.

'No, it's for Germans not Russians.'

'You'll be sorry,' Willi said in a sing-song voice.

Stepan made no reply but doused himself generously with *kölnischwasser* as though there was a bad smell in the room.

For a short time, a couple of months at most, Stepan continued to be friends with Willi. But the gulf between them quickly widened. At work they exchanged words only when necessary. In the evenings Stepan went his own way, remained friends with Rudi Rosensweig, the Jewish dentist's son, and continued to enjoy himself drinking, flirting, going to dances and spending as much time as he could in the countryside. Nature was one of his great passions.

Willi, by contrast, attended SA band practice on weekday evenings or helped his comrades collect funds for the Party. At weekends he also visited the countryside, there to set up camp in the woods, to play the 'Horst Wessel Song' and learn the goose step.

But Willi's membership of the SA was not the only reason for the rift between them, although it played a part. Stepan could not wholeheartedly accept Nazi ideology and not because he was prescient or particularly high-minded. He was neither virulently anti-Communist like his father, nor did he feel a pressing need to defend Jews, democracy or the Weimar Republic. His antipathy to Nazism surfaced simply because he was uncomfortable with any rigid doctrine of faith. He did not like being told what to do or what to think. He rejected Lutheranism and ceased going to church for precisely that reason. His instinct, which he dared not voice, told him that Nazism was just another religion, like Communism or Christianity, and that made him draw back. He decided his belief, for want of a better word, was vested in a vague sort of decency, in his own individuality and not in brutality imprisoned in a collective straitjacket. A voice, no more than a whisper, told him that Nazism was crude and stifling.

There was, too, something else about Willi which made all he did suspect in Stepan's eyes, for he had come to learn, in the last year or two, that Willi was homosexual. Willi had ceased to be a member of the gang, the friends – Rudi Rosensweig was one of them – who since *Gymnasium* days were the boys about town, the lads who hung around the extrance to the nurses' hostel and afterwards exchanged details of their sexual adventures. Willi, the blond giant, with his lavatorial humour, who had always boasted so noisily of his prowess with the opposite sex, gradually seemed to remove himself from the group. He seemed also to lose his boisterousness and was for some reason unhappy. Stepan knew that Willi spent many of his evenings wandering from bar to bar, drinking too much. On one occasion, when Stepan himself was returning late at night by taxi, he saw Willi, apparently drunk, sitting on the pavement's edge in the yellow glow of a streetlight, weeping, and being comforted by a young man. As the taxi passed, Stepan looked back and was certain that the young man was wearing make-up, his lips and cheeks a bright, unruly crimson. He appeared to Stepan like an animated but melancholy gargoyle.

Willi's detachment from his former friends and his obvious depression more or less coincided with the Kesslers' move into their own house so Stepan had not the ready-made opportunity to question him. Soon, however, rumours began to circulate although Stepan was never a direct recipient of the gossip. One evening, walking alone with Rudi Rosensweig, he asked why the others had been whispering and giggling about Willi and yet excluding him. Rudi was embarrassed. Even though he was in his mid-twenties, handsome, self-assured – the girls called him Rudi Valentino – he was still capable of blushing.

'You don't want to know,' he said.

'What kind of an answer is that?' Stepan demanded.

'It's the best answer I can give.'

'Tell me.'

But Rudi stopped to light a cigarette and didn't respond.

Stepan said, 'It's about Willi, isn't it?'

'Yes,' Rudi said, blowing out a thin stream of smoke.

'So, what are they saying?'

'They say he hangs about with Hans Ritter and his mob.'

'All right, so Hans Ritter's a Nazi and Willi's a Nazi, so what?'

Rudi summoned his courage. 'Ritter's a bum-pirate, Step. So are his friends.'

'I thought they were all just Nazi big shots.'

'No, I'm telling you, they're bum-pirates.'

'Yes, but what I'm saying is, not all Nazis are bum-pirates and not all bum-pirates are Nazis.'

'No, but Ritter's both.' He studied the glowing end of his cigarette, adding, 'And so is Willi.'

Then, on a glorious summer's day in July 1931, a Sunday, Stepan, one of his girlfriends, Brigitte von Bock, and Rudi Rosensweig bicycled out into the country. Somewhere along the way Rudi left them because he was to lunch with cousins but the three had arranged to meet again in the late afternoon and so return to Chemnitz together.

Stepan and Brigitte headed for the von Bocks' weekend retreat, a comfortable chalet in the woods. Her father, a military man, was away in Berlin that weekend and Brigitte thought it a good opportunity to introduce Stepan to her mother. They arrived in time for lunch which was stiff and formal. In the afternoon the couple said farewell to Frau von Bock, wheeled their bicycles through the woods, making for an old barn where they had arranged to meet Rudi. They heard from somewhere in the woods, not all that far away, the emphatic strains of a brass band. When they reached the barn they immediately mounted to the hay-loft where they kissed, cuddled and grew overexcited. At a moment of high passion they heard voices and sprang apart. The voices grew louder. Stepan and Brigitte peered through the hay bales which formed a wall at the end of the loft. They saw a half-dozen uniformed SA men, Willi and Hans Ritter among them, dragging into the barn a young man, his hands tied behind his back, his mouth gagged. Stepan and Brigitte froze. The prisoner was Rudi Rosensweig.

The storm-troopers pulled off Rudi's trousers and underpants. Ritter said, 'Now, let's all fuck the Jew bastard.' There was unanimous agreement. Ritter began to remove his own trousers, saying, 'Turn him on to his stomach so we can see the little Jewish asshole.' There was much laughter. Ritter was standing directly beneath Stepan and Brigitte, who were clutching each other, terrified. Rudi grunted and struggled but Willi and his comrades held him down while Ritter continued to undress, having difficulty slipping his trousers over his jackboots. At that moment, Stepan let go of Brigitte and with all his strength heaved over the edge of the loft a bale of hay which struck Ritter in the small of the back, flooring him.

Instantly Willi and the others let go of Rudi while Stepan and Brigitte clambered down the rickety wooden ladder, Stepan shouting, 'Run, Rudi, run! And you, too, Brigitte, run!' Rudi, naked from the waist down and gagged, his hands still tied behind him, scrambled out of the barn, Brigitte after him. But a moment or two later, she returned, grabbed Rudi's trousers, saying, 'Excuse me', and fled. Meanwhile, Willi had gone to help Ritter, who was gasping for breath, but after Brigitte's intervention the other SA men grabbed Stepan and mindlessly began to punch and kick him.

Willi cried, 'Stop that, he's my cousin!' but they took no notice. They beat Stepan savagely, loosening two front teeth and cutting him above the eyes. Blood choked and blinded him. While he lay on the ground moaning and struggling they kicked him with their jackboots until Ritter, himself in pain and still trying to recover his breath, called, 'Let's get out of here, they'll be going to the police.' When he reached the door of the barn, he turned back and waved a threatening finger at Stepan, who lay semiconscious on the ground. Ritter said, 'You're a marked man, Kessler. We'll get you, don't worry, we'll get you.'

Near by, hidden in undergrowth, Brigitte and Rudi watched the Nazis depart. Then they hurried to the barn and took care of Stepan. The three decided it was best to return to Chemnitz by train. Pale and shocked, they sat in the luggage-van with their bicycles.

Stepan, still bleeding and holding a handkerchief to his mouth, asked Rudi what had happened.

'I was cycling along, coming to meet you as arranged,' Rudi said. 'The path was overgrown so I got off and started to push the bike. I thought I heard voices, footsteps, snapping twigs, you know, but well, it didn't worry me because I just thought there were other trippers about on a nice summer's day. Then, they jumped me. That's all.'

Brigitte said, 'You didn't provoke them?'

'I've told you what happened. I was minding my own business.'

'Yes, but you're a Jew, Rudi, you mustn't provoke them,' she said.

'I didn't provoke them! I was minding my own business — '

'You must have done something — '

'I didn't! All I was doing was walking in the woods.'

She was about to respond but held back. They sat, gloomy, all three in shock, rocking gently with the movement of the train.

Rudi asked, 'Are you going to tell your parents?'

Brigitte and Stepan shook their heads.

'I'm going to tell mine,' Rudi said.

'Not me,' Stepan said. 'I don't want trouble with the Lohmeyers. I'll say I fell off my bike.' Then suddenly he laughed.

'What's so funny?' Rudi asked.

Stepan said, 'I liked it when Brigitte came back, took your trousers and said, "Excuse me."' They all laughed then, saying 'Excuse me' over and over again, almost hysterically, until their laughter ran dry.

Later, back in Chemnitz, after Rudi had left them and they were pushing their bicycles through the dimly lit streets, Brigitte said, 'Jews cause trouble. They will have to stop walking in our woods.'

The next morning Stepan visited Dr Rosensweig in the hope that somehow the dentist could save his loose front teeth. Dr Rosensweig said, 'Rudi told me what you did for him yesterday. Thank you.'

Since his mouth was stuffed full of instruments, Stepan could only reply with unintelligible grunts.

Dr Rosensweig said, 'I mean this, Stepan, if ever I can do anything to help you, in any way whatsoever, you must not hesitate to come to me. You understand?'

'_'

'You are a brave man and there are not many about. There. That should hold the teeth steady until they settle. And you should have that eye looked at. Come again at the end of the week.'

Events moved swiftly. In the afternoon Stepan returned to work. Willi avoided any contact, never once even looked at him, but afterwards, in the locker room, while both were standing side by side washing, Willi said quietly, 'Stepan, you must get out of Chemnitz. Don't ask any questions. Just go.'

'And if I don't want to?' Stepan asked defiantly, looking directly at Willi in the small cracked mirror above the basins.

'Then you're a dead man.' He reached for a towel and mumbled, 'I'm sorry.'

Stepan now felt he had no choice but to confide in his parents. Embarrassed, omitting the crudest details of the incident and any

261

mention of Willi's homosexuality, over dinner he told his parents what had happened in the barn. He told them of his intervention and the warning both Ritter and Willi had given him. Throughout the meal and for more than an hour afterwards the discussion raged. For most of the time Kessler Senior repeatedly accused Stepan of recklessness and stupidity. Anya sat like a statue, one hand covering her mouth as though she were trying to stifle a scream.

'Anyway,' Stepan said, 'I want to leave. I'd like to go to Berlin — '
'Berlin?'
'I'm not a child any more, papa — '
'What would you do in Berlin?'
'I'll find work — '
'There's a depression, inflation, every other day the banks have to close their doors and you say you'll find work, just like that.'
'I've no choice, papa, they'll kill me — '
'Nonsense!'
'Papa, you didn't see what I saw — '
'Nonsense, the Nazis are not barbarians — '
'Well, they behave like barbarians — '
'Nonsense, they're just high-spirited, over-conscientious — '
'Papa, Willi risked a lot to tell me that they were going to get me — '
'Stop talking like an American gangster — '
'He wouldn't have taken such a chance if there wasn't something in it — '
'I told you, you should not be seeing that Jew-boy, Rosensweig — '
'He's my friend, papa — '
'Friend, friend, he's a Jew. You should join the SA, then they won't kill you.'

That was too much for Stepan. Angry and sullen he stormed off to his room and locked the door. He sat on his bed trying to formulate a plan. But struggling to find a solution to his troubles only made him more and more uneasy. He caught sight of himself in a mirror and said aloud, 'This isn't happening.'

After hearing his parents retire, he stole down the stairs in the dark. Just as he was opening the front door as quietly as he could, the landing light came on and he saw Anya, in her dressing-gown, looking down at him.

'Sweetheart, where are you going?' she asked anxiously.
'Out.'
'Where?'
'Just out.'
'Be careful.'
'Yes.'
'Please don't be late.'

'No.'

'I shan't be able to get to sleep until you're back. Please be careful.'

Stepan walked quickly, keeping to the shadows. He was angry with himself for feeling frightened but he couldn't help it. Any unexpected sound or movement alarmed him. He passed the Lohmeyers' house and was relieved to hear Willi practising the trumpet. He told himself that if Willi was at home then his SA comrades can't be out in the streets waiting to pounce. He reached the Rosensweig residence and rang the bell. A maid answered the door. Stepan was shown into the large living-room where Rudi and his father were stretched out on the floor, playing with a clockwork train set like two children. They looked up at him, startled. The older Rosensweig knew at once that Stepan was in trouble. 'You're pale, Stepan. What's happened?' he asked.

'Stepan, are you all right?' from Rudi.

Stepan recounted Willi's warning and said, 'I think I have to leave town. I know it sounds melodramatic, but why take a chance?'

Dr Rosensweig poured each of them a brandy and soda. He said, 'I thought something of the kind might happen.'

'God help us,' Rudi said. 'This is Germany, for God's sake, this is the twentieth century, and one of my friends is going into hiding for helping me — '

'Ssh, Rudi, please. We must keep our voices down. My wife's resting upstairs. She's been very upset by these events.' He held up his glass and said, 'To better times.'

'To better times,' the boys repeated.

Stepan said, 'The problem is, where can I go? That's why I'm here. I don't know who else to turn to. You did say, Dr Rosensweig, that if I needed help — ' His voice trailed off.

Dr Rosensweig, tall and energetic, nodded and began to pace, hands behind back, chin on chest. The boys watched him. Stepan could not help noticing how similarly furnished this room was to his parents' sitting-room: the Persian rugs on polished floors, the Bechstein upright piano, the photographs of relatives, the knick-knacks and bric-à-brac, even the engraving of Frederick the Great and the glass-fronted bookcase – but were the books the same, he wondered? On their spines he saw the names of Heinrich Heine and Stefan Zweig and did not think those authors graced his parents' shelves.

Abruptly Dr Rosensweig stopped and turned to him. 'Are you willing to go to Berlin?' he asked.

'Berlin? Of course, that's where I'd like to go most in the whole world. I just said to my father I'd like to go to Berlin, he thought I was crazy.'

Dr Rosensweig nodded to himself. 'All right,' he said. 'What do you know about tea?'

'I beg your pardon?'

'Tea, you know, tea, the stuff you drink — ' His eyes twinkled.

'I drink it, that's all I know about it — '

'How would you like to go into the tea business?'

'In Berlin?'

'In Berlin.'

'I'd love it,' Stepan said with his engaging smile.

'Give me a day or two. My brother-in-law, my wife's eldest brother, Heinrich Liebermann, is an importer of tea. In Berlin. I'll book a telephone call to him in the morning. I'm sure he'll help if he can. He's a widower. He has one son in Ceylon. You may even be able to live in his house. He's a kindly man.'

The weekend following Stepan was on the night train bound for Berlin.

Above his desk Heinrich Liebermann had, in a plain black frame behind glass, the following words beautifully inscribed by a calligraphist:

> I have often felt a bitter sorrow at the thought of the German people, which is so estimable in the individual and so wretched in the generality. A comparison of the German people with other peoples arouses a painful feeling, which I try to overcome in every possible way.
>
> – Johann Wolfgang von Goethe

Liebermann lived alone, attended by two servants – a married couple, Franz and Lotte – in a large mansion in the Grünewald where many of Berlin's richest families had their homes. Stepan decided not to take up Liebermann's offer to lodge in his house even though he would not have been charged rent. But he had no intention of exchanging one father for another and found rooms in a boarding house at the poorer end of the Kurfürsten-Allee, an area with classically named streets, Nestor, Achilles, Sybil and Cicero, and not far from Hallensee. But once a week, on Thursday evenings, Liebermann sent Franz to fetch Stepan in the car and the two dined together in candle-lit luxury.

Heinrich Liebermann was in his early seventies, always immaculately dressed and always looking as if he had just stepped out of a bath which he probably had. He spoke French and English fluently, and spent most of his days reading philosophy and history or writing essays in which he tried to analyse contemporary events. He had no formal education but was possessed of a remarkable memory and a real thirst for knowledge, so his commentaries were pitted with quotations and references to the giants of the past and his conclusions were often half-baked. He would have liked to have attended a university but his father's early death forced him into the business of importing tea at which he became highly successful, transforming a small firm into a large and flourishing enterprise. He loved the theatre and the opera and had set up a small trust fund to help aspiring playwrights and composers. When Stepan was asked by Anya what this Herr Liebermann was like, he replied, 'He's like a monument to culture.'

He was a lonely man who did not make friends easily. He missed his son, Bruno, who managed the Ceylon end of things. The advent of Stepan suited Liebermann for several reasons. He liked Stepan's warmth and enthusiasm, so at odds with his own austere nature, admired him for saving Rudi from the SA, and thought of him as a defender of Jews. Modestly, Stepan tried to explain that he was defending Rudi in particular not Jews in general, but Liebermann brushed the objection aside. It pleased him to regard Stepan as a hero. It also pleased him to treat Stepan like a disciple, for the old man liked to try out his thoughts and theories in lecture form. After their Thursday evening dinner, over the port and Havana cigars, he would launch forth.

'Do not be too alarmed by the Nazis,' was invariably the main thrust of his discourse in the early months of 1932. 'This is the country of Goethe and Schiller, of Leibniz, Kant, Herder, Humboldt, Schopenhauer, Lessing – the list is endless. This is the country of Beethoven and Bach. The Nazis are full of sound and fury but just consider this: Dr Karl Lueger, whom I met on two occasions, the burgomaster of Vienna, was a dreadful anti-Semite, but, and it's a very big but, only officially. It's true that he brought anti-Semitism into politics but he was always helpful and friendly to the Jews. Even Stefan Zweig, who was a child in the city when Lueger was mayor, testifies to the fact that the city administration was perfectly just and over-conscientiously democratic. Zweig went on to say that even the Jews who trembled at the triumph of Lueger's anti-Semitic party continued to live with the same rights and esteem as they had always done.

'So it is, I believe, with the Nazis. They need a popular platform and anti-Semitism is always popular. But, mark my words, if ever they become the elected government, which I pray to God they won't, they will make a lot of noise but we will go on living, as Zweig says, with the same rights and esteem as we do now. They are nationalists first and second, and anti-Semites a poor third. And I have to say, with one of their policies I agree absolutely. The Versailles treaty, what Hitler calls the *vriedensdiktat*, is an infamous document in European history.

Always remember, Stepan, we Germans in 1918 did not lose the war, we were betrayed by our leaders and therefore forced to surrender.

'You see, Stepan, cultured people, and the Germans are undeniably cultured, cannot throw off centuries of civilisation on the orders of a demagogue. It is simply impossible and unthinkable. There will always be enough individual Germans who will stand up and say, "No!"'

He liked to trace the philosophical roots of Nazism beginning with Johann Gottlieb Fichte and then Hegel, the ultimate idealist, the dialectician, the inspiration of Karl Marx and Lenin. Liebermann was fond of repeating one particular Hegelian observation: 'Periods of happiness are the empty pages of history because they are the periods of agreement, without conflict,' and he would chuckle. 'Well, that's what I want most for the world. Empty pages of history.'

From Hegel he lept to Heinrich von Treitschke, the man from Saxony who became a professional Prussian, he who said it does not matter what you think so long as you obey. And then he touched on Nietzsche. 'The interesting thing about Nietzsche is that he was never an anti-Semite. He believed both Christians and Jews were responsible for what he called the "slave morality". He's become the Nazi god. Why? Because they haven't read him, that's why.'

His optimism was infectious and Stepan was warmed and reassured by the old man's discourse. 'And let me say this,' Liebermann concluded. 'Although I don't deny Hitler is an arch anti-Semite, anti-Semitism is not a specifically German phenomenon. As a matter of fact, the Germans are not good anti-Semites, which is more than one can say for the Austrians or the Poles. The truth is anti-Semitism is weaker here than in most other countries. And Hitler knows this. Have you noticed how in recent months he's softened his anti-Semitism? You know why? Because he knows it finds only a faint-hearted response in the German people. No, no, I believe with all my heart and soul that civilisation will triumph, the cultured élite of this land will, if necessary, overcome the barbarians. Now, next week, I want to explore German mysticism, so I will tell you about a man of genius who was both a god and a devil: Richard Wagner.'

3

The first weeks of January 1933 were filled with excitement for Tatiana and Iliena. They had three events to celebrate: first Iliena's name-day, then Russian Christmas two days later and, perhaps the most keenly anticipated of all, a family reunion, for the Brumbys were travelling to Paris from Rome and the Webbs from Manchester. Emmett and Xenia had reserved a suite at the Crillon – a hotel beloved of Americans – but Richard and Darya were unable to afford such luxury and so had no choice but to stay with Tatiana and Iliena in Sophia Arkunina's small flat in Saint-Cloud.

The Webbs arrived first. To make room for them Tatiana moved in with Sophia, and Iliena slept on the narrow sofa in the sitting-room. The chatter was incessant, the passing of photographs constant, for the Webbs now had two children, Leo aged six, and David, aged four, whose progress in every imaginable and unimaginable mood and pose had been preserved in black and white from birth. Richard's parents were looking after them which enabled the couple to escape for the week.

Tatiana was amused to see that Richard had filled out a little. Marriage obviously suited him: it was plain that he doted on Darya and the boys, and he confessed that he was more than content in his job as a sub-editor on the *Manchester Guardian*. But Tatiana was a little circumspect when it came to assessing Darya's moods and attitudes. There was an uneasiness about Darya which, Tatiana believed, hid her disappointment at not being able to take a university degree, to work in a chosen profession, in short, to express her intelligence which was the hallmark of her individuality. She was tolerant and more than affectionate towards her husband, yet Tatiana detected a certain restraint in her daughter, the causes of which were impossible for her to diagnose accurately.

Xenia and Emmett arrived like royalty. They hired a car, an ancient Rolls-Royce, driven by an aged chauffeur in pale fawn livery, the former Prince Dmitri Dolcharov whose parents had kept both the car and the chauffeur's uniform in Paris for their annual pre-revolutionary visits. When Prince Dmitri escaped, he remembered the car, headed for Paris and set himself up in the automobile rental business.

He was short and emaciated with failing eyesight, so he sat on two cushions and peered under the rim of the steering-wheel to see the road as best he could. But, being a prince, he knew how a chauffeur ought to behave and with remarkable agility hopped out into the street and opened the passenger door while Emmett and Xenia were still removing the rather threadbare plaid rug from their laps.

On recognising him, Tatiana said, 'Dmitri Dmitrovich, come indoors, keep warm, drink Iliena's health. It's her name-day.'

'No, thank you, Tatiana Sergeievna,' he said cheerfully, 'I know my place,' and clambered into the back seat where he stretched out, covered himself in the rug and went to sleep.

Outwardly, Emmett had hardly changed. He had neither lost any more hair nor put on an ounce of weight, but wealth robbed him of his youthful, innocent air and he had adopted a pompous, deliberate tone which made even his most commonplace pronouncements, a greeting for example, or a comment on the weather, seem like weighty aphorisms. No longer did he talk of noble causes, of serving humanity or of self-fulfilment. He smoked Havana cigars, wore dark suits in all seasons, rattled the change in his trouser pocket and breathed noisily.

His ponderous manner had in no way dampened Xenia's vitality. She was as lively as ever and money allowed her to dress in a style both individual and timeless. Darya once said of her, 'Xenia can do more with a scarf than the average couturier can do with a bolt of silk.' Fashion was Xenia's domain and she had infallible and indefinable chic. But Tatiana noted that neither Xenia nor Emmett once offered to contribute to the cost of feeding them all during their visit, nor did they suggest inviting the family out to a meal. Although she would never voice any criticism of her children publicly, she was inwardly censorious and Xenia's preoccupations with clothes and jewels both irritated and tired her.

For dinner on Iliena's name-day, the second night of the visit, Tatiana hired for a few sous an old servant of Princess Troubetskoy's, a bald Cossack called Yevgeny. The Princess had somehow managed to bring him out of Russia. She called him her Holy Man because, she said, he had extraordinary powers of predicting the future. He made a little extra pocket-money by helping out at dinner parties and soirées. The old man, a former groom who spoke no French, was miserable and lonely in Paris and spent most of his afternoons in cinemas, watching films whose plots and stories were entirely lost on him. He welcomed therefore any and every opportunity to speak his native language. Because of his reputation as a seer he had become something of an attraction in *émigré* circles. He told fortunes by reading palms and so, after dinner, before he cleared the table and started on the washing-up, he needed only the encouragement of a large glass of vodka to study Iliena's palm and to predict what fate had in store for her.

Yevgeny bent low over her hand so that Iliena was transfixed by his shining, yellowish pate. After grunting and muttering, he looked up sharply and said, 'You will know contentment,' which was greeted by a collective sigh of relief and approval. 'You will also know a new life.' Again he peered at her hand, again he grunted and muttered. 'You will marry a bald man, not as bald as me, but almost.' Laughter. 'A good man. A kind man. A difficult man. A brave man.'

'Is she going to marry one man or four?' Emmett asked and chuckled alone.

Yevgeny turned to him. 'These are the qualities of one man, Excellency. A rare spirit. Now, let me see, yes, here, ah, yes, a journey across water. Yes. I see a journey across water. And, o-ho, a-ha, a secret. Iliena Lvovna, you have a secret wish.' At this Iliena flushed a little and Xenia said, 'Tell us more.'

Yevgeny glanced at her sideways. 'Xenia Lvovna, I never tell secrets, but this one, this one of Iliena Lvovna, concerns children.'

'First you've got to find the bald man, Iliena,' Richard said.

'Oh yeah,' Emmett said, 'the good, kind, difficult guy.'

Yevgeny ignored the interruptions. 'You will live a long, healthy life,' he continued. 'You will hold Russian earth in your hands but you will never see Russia again,' and his eyes filled with tears as if he was also predicting his own bleak destiny.

His sadness touched the others. All eyes, even Emmett's, flickered with regret and loss until Tatiana said, 'Enough, you may clear the table now, Yevgeny.'

He rose, gave her the peasant's bow, and began to clear away. Presently, after pleading a headache, Tatiana retired, to be followed by Sophia Arkunina. While Xenia and Darya prattled, Emmett turned his attention to Iliena, who was sitting on the opposite side of the narrow table.

'Putting aside the bald guy, Iliena, have you thought about what you're going to do with your life?' he asked, nodding sagely.

Iliena shrugged awkwardly. 'I think – I don't know, I – I think I'd like to be a nurse.'

Richard said, 'Oh, that's a fine ambition. Good for you, Iliena.'

'Wait a moment,' Emmett said. 'It's maybe a fine ambition but shouldn't you be considering something more – more practical?'

'I'd have thought,' Richard said, 'that there's hardly anything more practical than being a nurse.'

'Practical? Really?' Emmett said, not to question but to contradict.

'Nursing the sick?' Richard said. 'Of course it's practical.'

'Sick children,' Iliena said. 'I'd like to study to be a children's nurse. That's why, when Yevgeny said I had a secret about children, I was amazed. It's not to have children, you see, it's to nurse them,' but she stopped there, overcome with embarrassment.

Her sisters broke off their conversation and expressed admiration for Yevgeny's mysterious gifts, and then Richard said, 'There you are, Emmett, what could be more practical than being a children's nurse?'

'I am somewhat reluctant to bring this up,' Emmett declared, 'but nursing requires training and training requires money. Shouldn't you be thinking of making a living?'

Although they had resumed their chattering Xenia and Darya caught the gist of this last remark and fell silent. Xenia played nervously with her rings; Darya flicked glances from Richard to Emmett to Iliena. Iliena remained composed, eyes downcast so that it was difficult for the others to judge her reactions.

Emmett continued expansively. 'The way I see it, Iliena, is like this. Your mother and you simply do not do enough to support yourselves.'

'Emmett — ' a hiss from Xenia.

'No, no, I think it has to be said. I know your mother plays the piano now and again, gives lessons, sells family heirlooms and so on and so forth, but I don't believe it's good enough. I believe in the ethic of work and saving. Now, I realise your mother, given her background, is unaccustomed to working for a living but she has to take into account present circumstances. As for you, Iliena, I honestly believe you cannot possibly entertain thoughts of training for a career in nursing.'

Again from Xenia, 'Emmett, please — '

'Somebody has to say it,' Emmett answered, now shaking his head as if he regretted the burden being his.

'Well, if somebody has to say it,' Darya said tartly, 'then perhaps it ought to be Richard since he's the only one who contributes anything at all to their living — '

'Darya,' Richard said angrily, 'that's nobody's business but ours, and mama's. I don't want that mentioned again.'

Emmett swivelled in his chair to face Darya, who was next to him. 'I deliberately do not offer support to your mother and Iliena, not because I'm miserly – I don't think anyone can accuse me of being miserly – but because I believe that both of them would gain self-respect, not to mention a better way of life, by going out to work like other people and having the satisfaction of a wage packet at the end of each week.'

'Please, I can't bear this,' Xenia said, 'let's change the subject — '

270

'Take note of my words, Iliena — ' Emmett persisted but again Xenia interrupted. 'No, Emmett, I said I don't want to hear any more of this and I meant it.'

Emmett grunted and puffed at his cigar. Xenia continued to twiddle the rings on her fingers each in turn. Darya lit a cigarette. Iliena remained motionless. The silence was broken by Richard, who reached across to Iliena and placed his hand on hers. 'I think nursing's a damn fine thing to do and I hope no one will stop you from going full steam ahead.'

Iliena glanced up at him and smiled gratefully. Immediately Emmett rose, said perfunctory goodnights, and announced his intention of returning to the hotel Crillon.

Iliena lay on the uncomfortable sofa unable to sleep, rehearsing over and over again Emmett's criticisms and strictures and trying to hold on to Richard's encouraging words. She was nineteen but still a child, fragile and unconfident. The upheavals she had known, the expulsion from Sobliki, the sojourn in the village, the moves to Moscow and then to Paris had, of course, served to undermine her perception of security but she was by nature insecure; the repeated disruptions only reinforced her vulnerability.

She had never attended school but was a good linguist. When a child she had been taught the rudiments of English by Miss Muck, and Tatiana almost always talked to her in French. She read avidly, novels and memoirs mostly, but hated newspapers; the very mention of politics or politicians caused her to withdraw. She had inherited Tatiana's trait of being able to retreat into herself, to bolt into a blank, empty world where nothing moved. In these moments, misinterpreted by others as repose or, more frequently, as Sobelev hauteur, she was at her most beautiful, having inherited more of Lev's looks than Tatiana's: straight nose, generous mouth and none of her mother's severity.

More than anything, Iliena wanted to enter the world in a real and proper way, as if she were struggling to be born. She was aware that her life in Paris was artificial. Much of her time was spent with her mother, knitting, sewing, chatting, walking. When alone, she read. On a few occasions she had helped out in Princess Troubetskoy's lingerie shop but found the work dull. She had once suggested that she learn to become a secretary but Tatiana dismissed the idea. This was a selfish reaction on Tatiana's part which had nothing to do with false pride; she dampened Iliena's initiative not because she thought a lady should not work, but because she had an uncontrollable possessive impulse to cling desperately to her youngest child.

Was the longing to become a nurse a reality, Iliena asked herself, twisting and turning on the sofa? How could her ambition be achieved? Should she start making enquiries? Perhaps she would need qualifications? What would the authorities say when they learned she'd had no schooling? How could the years of training be afforded? Wasn't Emmett right to admonish her for such foolishness? What would Tatiana say to it all? Was the idea so silly, unattainable, impossible, that she should now this moment dismiss it from her thoughts?

She began to pray for guidance and help, but fell asleep before the prayer was finished. She dreamed she was in a canoe being ferried across a tempestuous strip of water, Yevgeny at the oars, head down, his bald head shining like a beacon.

In the morning, Richard contrived to be alone with Iliena. He said, 'How did you sleep?'

'Not well,' Iliena replied. 'And you?'

'Not well either. I was thinking about what you said. Are you serious about becoming a nurse?'

'Yes,' she replied, 'but I know now it's impossible.'

'Don't talk daft, as we say in Lancashire. If you're serious, we'll find a way. I'm not saying any more now, but I think I've had an idea that may just do the trick.'

His certainty bred optimism in Iliena. For weeks after the Webbs' departure she watched from her window for the postman and hoped for a letter postmarked Manchester.

4

Barely three weeks after the marriage of Isaiah and Isobel, tragedy struck. Eva, hurrying out to a Zionist meeting, slipped on the front steps of her house and broke her hip. She was rushed to hospital where two days later she developed pneumonia, lapsed into unconsciousness and died. Isobel was at her bedside; George, summoned from the Transvaal, arrived in time for the funeral. She was buried beside Adam. Neither had reached the age of fifty.

Isaiah insisted that he and his new wife sit *shivah*, a Hebrew word meaning 'seven' that has come to denote the seven solemn days of mourning which begin immediately after the funeral in the home of the deceased. Isaiah would have liked to have followed the traditions rigidly – the removal of shoes, the donning of cloth slippers, the sitting on low stools, the covering of all mirrors. Isobel objected. 'It's hypocrisy,' she said, 'my mother would have hated it.' But she gave in to covering the mirrors and to her husband's insistence that each evening ten adult males must visit, forming a *minyan*, so that the Kaddish, the prayer for the dead, could be said with its final wish, 'May the Father of peace send peace to all who mourn, and comfort all the bereaved among us.'

Reluctantly, Isobel was bound to admit that the rituals were comforting: from the ancient and bleak funeral, which she accounted barbaric in its crude simplicity, to the nightly intoning of prayers in her mother's home, while not assuaging her grief, seemed somehow to ease the shock which quickly gave way to a suspended state as though she were observing another's sorrow and pain. Friends came each day and she particularly welcomed the visit of her closest friend, Jean Jaffe, who had an instinct for other people's moods. Jean seemed to know if Isobel wanted to talk or remain silent, and her presence was a further comfort.

Eva left a few hundred pounds which was equally divided between her son and daughter. Isobel had the task of sorting through mountains of paper – agendas, minutes, standing orders, lecture notes; she found, too, letters from Uncle Max in Warsaw, occasional confessions – about Eva's breakdown in London and the visitations of Paul Ehrlich's image. The last such intimacy was written in English a fortnight before her accident:

I am not given much to prayer but I pray for Isobel's happiness. I think Isaiah is a good man. There is a sweetness about him that is attractive. But I fear he is not cultured enough for Isobel, who has such wonderful and sensitive qualities. To him Browning is something his mother uses in gravy.

I feel a milestone has been reached. Isobel married. And what of me? Well, I enjoy my life now although I still miss Adam dreadfully. I feel young and energetic but have no interest in remarrying or even having a male companion. My Zionism is now, I suppose, my escort. How odd it is to have ended up here at the bottom of the world. So unpredictable. When I think how driven I was by ambition in Warsaw and how I longed to live in London – for which I still have occasional longings – and then consider my present circumstances, I cannot help feeling that destiny and personal will somehow contrive to walk hand in hand, conjoined, indistinguishable, inseparable. The conclusion must be I suppose that I have the spirit of a wanderer, a restlessness which collaborated with outside events, large and small, to send Adam, me and our children hurtling into the southern hemisphere. I have never felt truly at home here. I have never felt truly at home anywhere. But there is no choice for people like me, only the task to accept the struggle in the hope of victory. I am an eternal expatriate.

5

Stepan Kessler was suspicious of the vitality and tumult of Berlin. The great metropolis was invigorating and confusing yet he never felt completely in tune with himself. The rhythm of Berlin jarred, like the syncopated jazz to which Berliners sang and danced. True, he enjoyed his weekly dinners and discussions with old Herr Liebermann; true, he loved the tea trade, the sniffing, the sifting, the tasting, the swilling, the spitting; true, he loved his new-found freedom; but he did not like the fashion then to anglicise first names so that Stepan became Steve. Ironically, and herein lay the baffling nature of the city, Berlin's neurotic tempo forced him into renewing his feeling for Russia and Russians.

He lived on the third floor of Frau Winzer's boarding-house at Sybelstrasse 43. Frau Winzer, whose husband had been killed on the Somme, ran a strict establishment: maximum of two hot baths per person per week, no music after eleven, no parties except on Saturdays, no unaccompanied women at any time. In return, she allowed her lodgers to come and go as they pleased, kept the house spotless, changed the linen and towels once a week, saw to it that breakfast was always on time. Steve's fellow lodgers were mostly, like him, young business types, a bank clerk, a commercial traveller, a shoe salesman; the Leuschners, a middle-aged couple, occupied two rooms across the passage from him: their house had recently burned down and they were temporary residents awaiting the settlement of their insurance claim. Herr Leuschner was a Nazi who most evenings went out in uniform. He claimed that Communists had set fire to his house. In the beamed attic room directly above Stepan, on the top floor, lived Fräulein Naomi Kahn, a frail Jewish spinster in her late fifties, who was secretary to a lawyer. Stepan hardly ever saw her: she never came down to breakfast and left the house before most of the young men were awake. He sometimes heard her in the evenings pacing to and fro on a diagonal line above his head. Once, when he was on his way out and she was returning from work, he met her on the stairs and exchanged a few words with her.

'I hope my music doesn't disturb you,' he said.

She smiled crookedly or, perhaps, Stepan thought, lopsidedness was the natural disposition of her mouth. 'On the contrary,' she replied. 'I find it rather calming in these worrisome days.'

Each evening, after work, Stepan would return to Sybelstrasse 43, climb the stairs to his room, wind up his gramophone, play the music of Rachmaninoff or Tchaikowsky or Chopin, pour himself a large Scotch and water, flop on his bed and smoke a cigarette. This was the hour when he tried to shed Steve Kessler, trainee tea-taster, Berliner; for the other side of Stepan's Berlin sojourn was his Russian life, after dark, when he was once again Stepan Stepanovich. Almost from the moment he arrived he found himself gravitating towards the large Russian community in the city. He had developed, not unnaturally, an inbred suspicion of the Germans which, after his recent experiences in Chemnitz, had deepened. He admired their clichéd cleanliness, efficiency, diligence and refined good manners; most of the people with whom he came into contact seemed well-educated and cultured. Yet, they alarmed him. For one thing they were too easily reduced to sentimentality, unlike Russians who, when they cried, cried tears of blood wrung from them in pain and suffering and cruelty. Russians cried for their love of life and for their fellow human beings. Not the Germans: they cried for themselves; their tears, Stepan thought, were ersatz like the emotions which produced them, soft-centred and sickly. He was also not enamoured of their humour, especially the famed *Berlinhumor*: it was too forced, too black, too lavatorial for his taste. He preferred a different kind of vulgarity, the Russian variety, crude, yes, but of the earth not of the urinal. And the Germans, Stepan found, were unable to shed their inhibitions except when drunk and that, to him was despicable. He himself could dance like a Cossack at any time of day or night, drunk or sober; he knew Russians who, stone-cold sober – admittedly a rare state for a Russian – would unburden their darkest secrets at first meeting or invite you back to their homes and share the little they had as if you were a long-lost brother. You never knew what a German was thinking and they seemed to agree with whatever view was being expressed. They had the mentality of the herd whereas Russians, Stepan believed, despite their present slavery, preserved their individuality and nourished their souls.

The centre of his night world was a large basement room just off the Potsdamerplatz, in Bellevuestrasse, a cabaret called Tzigane, where Stepan was to be found most evenings and where the *habitués* called him Stepan Stepanovich. Here, a balalaika band played until midnight. At the stroke of twelve they were replaced by a gypsy orchestra, mother, father, their two sons and sixteen-year-old daughter, Alyona, who was accounted to be, not just by Stepan but by all the customers, male and female, the most beautiful creature in the entire world. When she sang, old men wept for their lost vigour, and the eyes of the younger ones glowed at the thought of possessing the unattainable.

In Tzigane, Stepan's nights were passed in a swirling haze of vodka, cigarettes, laughter, sadness, nostalgia, assignations, music – a sort of intensity of emotion and gusto that was not to be found as far as he knew anywhere else in the city. Here, they talked of what they had lost, family, friends, houses, estates, possessions and most heartfelt of all, the very essence of Russia, the eternal homeland, the spiritual dimension which, like the music, accompanied and informed every word, every rapidly changing mood, and sweetened their tears. Here, too, it had somehow been tacitly agreed that politics were taboo, so that the daily preoccupations of Germans – the incessant talk of Socialists and Nationalists and National Socialists and Communists, of street battles, demonstrations, elections – were forgotten. Here, the names of von Schleicher, von Hindenburg, von Papen, von Neurath, Hitler, von Hammerstein and Hugenberg were seldom if ever uttered. Tzigane, a cipher for all that was pleasurable, was a refuge from reality.

Reality smashed all that was pleasurable on the last weekend of January 1933. On the Saturday, 28 January, the Chancellor of the Weimar Republic, Franz von Papen, was summarily dismissed by the geriatric President, Field Marshal Paul von Beneckendorf und Hindenburg. The leader of the National Socialists, Adolf Hitler, whose party had won a majority of seats in the Reichstag, was himself demanding to be Chancellor of a republic he had vowed to annihilate. The snakes hissed as they had rarely hissed before and that was a measure of the city's mood. Hitler as Chancellor was an impossibility, for the snakes insinuated that von Hindenburg himself had said that he had no intention whatsoever of making that Austrian corporal Chancellor of the Reich. Then, the word spread that two generals, both Kurts, von Schleicher, a former Chancellor, and the Commander in Chief of the Army, von Hammerstein, were planning to seize power and install a military dictatorship. But still another rumour had it that a *putsch* was being planned by Hitler himself if he was not given the power for which he craved. Talk also of a general strike and, on the Sunday, a hundred thousand workers did indeed mass in the Lustgarten to protest against the possibility of the Nazi leader as Chancellor.

On Monday, 30 January, 1933, just before noon, the snakes were silent. A knot of people at the entrance to the Kaiserhof hotel on the Reichskanzlerplatz witnessed the Austrian corporal enter his limousine and drive the short distance to the Chancellery. Von

Hindenburg had relented under the influence of his son, Oskar, and was now to name the next and last Chancellor of the Weimar Republic, the self-same Austrian corporal, Adolf Hitler.

That evening Stepan lay on his bed, smoking and listening to a recording of the *adagio sostenuto* from Rachmaninoff's Second Piano Concerto in C minor. In the room above him Fräulein Kahn paced with greater agitation than usual. Around eight o'clock he set off by tram for Tzigane. But on nearing the city centre he became aware of the sound of drums beating. Presently, the passengers were told that the tram could go no further. A huge parade was in progress and had brought all traffic to a standstill.

Stepan decided to cross the Tiergarten towards Kemperplatz and with each step he took the drums grew louder like the thunder of an approaching storm. He heard the music now, the same tunes that Willi had played in Chemnitz, the 'Horst Wessel Song' and all the others, but blaring out from massed bands, more strident than ever but, he was bound to admit, stirring. From every corner of the Tiergarten, it seemed, people were hurrying and Stepan was caught up in it all, first trotting, then running, then stampeding, he, too, one of the herd.

As the noise swelled, he was aware of another sound beneath the music and the drums, the sound of marching, jackboots pounding the streets in disciplined precision. Then he saw the glow of flickering torches lighting up the night sky and, on reaching the Wilhelmstrasse, came upon an amazing, breathtaking spectacle. Thousands upon thousands of Nazi storm-troopers, holding high flaming torches and banners, marched like robots to the thundering drums and the martial music, singing as one the 'Horst Wessel Song', arrogant, vainglorious, a terrifying river of flame. In celebration of their leader's ascendancy, they had begun their parade at dusk. Out of the Tiergarten they emerged, rank upon rank, to the frenzied cheers of onlookers. They marched, tens of thousands of them, until well past midnight.

There was no visit to Tzigane that night. The Nazi demonstration of power triumphant had more or less closed down the city. Just after the parade ended, Stepan returned to Sybelstrasse, poured himself a Scotch and sank into the armchair. The house was silent except for Fräulein Kahn, who was still pacing above him, more quickly now than usual, with sudden stops, only to resume again. These sounds of agitation were in keeping with Stepan's own mood. The true meaning of what he had seen was not yet intelligible to him, and he was not alone in that. He was unable to think clearly; his head was too full of drums and torchlight. It occurred to him that now men like Hans

Ritter and Willi Lohmeyer would have the running of things and that perhaps he was in danger once more. No, he decided, it was still possible to be lost in a big city like Berlin. They would never find him. No, his own personal safety was not what disturbed him. Something else. But what?

He downed the Scotch, stood and was unbuttoning his shirt when he heard the noise from Fräulein Kahn's room above him. The sound of something falling, a chair perhaps, and then, quite clearly, a brief, strangulated scream followed by short, ugly grunts. Perturbed, he went quietly out on to the landing. A gas mantle, turned low, gave off an uncertain light. He looked up the stairs and called softly, 'Fräulein Kahn, are you all right?'

No reply.

He crept up the stairs. He could still hear her making these harsh, irregular grunts. He reached her door and knocked gently. 'Fräulein Kahn?'

Then the sounds ceased and were replaced by creaking, but Stepan was at a loss to indentify the cause: not floorboards, no, no, but as though something needed oiling. He knew the sound but could not remember where he had heard it before. He knocked again, 'Fräulein Kahn, it's Steve Kessler, please open your door.'

Nothing. Even the creaking softer now.

He tried the handle. The door was unlocked. He opened it a crack and saw her. The emaciated, spidery woman was hanging by a rope attached to a beam. Gently she swung to and fro, the creaking rope tight about her thin neck, and an overturned chair lay on the floor. Her tongue lolled out of her crooked mouth and her eyes bulged. And Stepan saw again the distended corpses of the men the Pharaohs had hanged, the three corpses with elongated necks and swollen tongues spinning slowly on an October afternoon in Moscow. That was where he had heard the sound before, the creaking of rope stretched taut. Involuntarily, he said aloud, 'They're one and the same.' He turned and pounded down the stairs to find Frau Winzer. When he reached his own floor, Herr Leuschner opened his door. He was in his SA uniform which was stained with sweat. 'What's up, Kessler?' he asked. Stepan didn't answer, reached the ground floor and woke Frau Winzer.

By the time the police arrived all the residents of Sybelstrasse 43 were awake. Frau Winzer wept. Stepan thought that her tears were for the dead woman who had been her lodger for almost seventeen years. But Frau Winzer said, 'Oh God in Heaven, will they punish me now for having a Jewess in the house?'

Herr Leuschner comforted her. 'Don't cry, dear woman, we only would have made you evict her, nothing more. It's our turn now.'

They're one and the same, one and the same.

A note written in a beautiful copperplate hand was found pinned to the hem of Fräulein Kahn's skirt:

I have no relatives. I thank God. This is no time to be alive. I apologise for any trouble I may cause. I am of sound mind.
Naomi Kahn

Two ambulance men carried her body down the stairs. It was covered in a brown blanket but her stockinged feet were visible. All the lodgers gathered on their landings to witness the pathetic cortège pass. Herr Leuschner said, 'Well, one Jewess less in the world is a cause for rejoicing.'

Stepan did not sleep that night. The cold, dark hours were spent gazing at the ceiling of his room. He was unable to rid himself of the memory of Naomi Kahn, suspended from a rope, dead. In his mind she was transformed into a pendulum, but not a marker of time passing; rather was she a dreadful herald of a sinister future. The image of the woman dangling was accompanied by the beating of drums, the pounding of marching feet and trumpets whinnying, and the refrain, they're one and the same, one and the same, one and the same.

6

When the trains did not pass, Isobel could hear the sound of the Indian Ocean lapping the soft white sands of Muizenberg. She was pregnant and spent her days knitting and reading – Jane Austen mostly – which she enjoyed doing simultaneously. Isaiah was away up country from Monday to Friday, selling his cigarettes, C to C, which stood for Cape to Cairo, and the new brand, Lord Somerset, that was selling briskly. She was glad the only contact she had with him was at weekends, for she had decided, after not quite one year of marriage, that the less she saw of her husband the better.

There were two main roots to her discontent: the one, she believed, was obvious, there for all to see; the other submerged, gnarled and best not thought about. The overt cause was her mother-in-law, Leah. From the moment Isaiah defied her and went ahead with the marriage, Leah expressed her disapproval of Isobel in ways both subtle and shameless. Leah was expert in silent disapproval and had an extensive armoury which included the sour smile, the glance to heaven, the helpless shrug, the apparently inadvertent tut-tut and countless other secret weapons. The stings and arrows of implied criticism were loosed on almost any pretext – from Isobel's fear of spiders to her morning sickness, from the way she arranged her furniture to her taste in clothes. Leah's life was dedicated to endless skirmishes, aimed at driving wedges between her son and his wife. Open warfare, however, was waged on the battlefield of food.

Isobel loathed cooking, despaired of thinking up meals for Isaiah and did not enjoy shopping. Their maid, Margaret, was an adequate cook but her day off was Sunday, when Isaiah expected a three-course lunch, always beginning with soup which he slurped noisily; weekend menus were torture. Leah saw to it that when the couple came to visit, which they did once a week, usually on Friday evenings, the abundance and variety of food was dazzling. Then, too, Isobel had no knowledge or interest in Jewish dishes and this Leah found particularly contemptible. The opening shots were fired during the couple's engagement.

'You can't make potato *latkes*?' Leah asked incredulously, referring to one of Isaiah's favourites, fried potato cakes.

'I don't even know what they are.'

'You don't know from a *latkes*?'

'No.'

'Don't tell me, you don't know from *gefilte* fish?'

'No, I don't know from *gefilte* fish.'

'*Tsimmes* you don't know also?'

'No.'

'*Tsimmes*,' she repeated as if it were the best known dish in the world. 'You make mit the grater a carrot, you add the sugar, what's there to know?'

'You tell me,' Isobel answered tartly.

'Ishkele, bubbela,' Leah said to Isaiah, 'you married practically a *shiksa*,' which is an insulting term for a non-Jewish girl.

Leah insisted that she teach Isobel how to prepare these delicacies and other specialities for the Sabbath, Passover and New Year. She would use the lessons to inform Isobel of how she cooked in the hostel in Hamburg ('mit out a pfennig for a grain rice'), how she struggled and fought to maintain standards of decency. Isobel must learn, she insisted, what it means to be a Jewish wife.

Isobel's only confidante was her friend, Jean Jaffe. They were the same age and had similar backgrounds, Jean's mother hailing from Belfast which, as far as Isobel and she were concerned, was the next best thing to London. Her father was an accountant and Jean acted as his receptionist which meant that she could take days off more or less when she liked. Although she lived on the other side of the Peninsular, in Sea Point, she visited Isobel at least one evening a week, spending the night in the Muizenberg flat. And when she was not visiting, hardly a day passed when the two did not talk on the telephone. Slight and timid, Jean was a loyal and adoring friend and so naturally supported Isobel unquestioningly and encouraged her to stand up to her mother-in-law. From all she had heard she was convinced that Leah was overbearing, possessive and destructive. Jean had taken Isobel to see the play *Dear Octopus* performed by a visiting company from London. Afterwards they agreed that the central character might have been based on Leah whom they referred to thereafter as 'Mine Yiddishe Octopus', for, the friends concluded, she enwrapped not only Isaiah in her tentacles but also Barney and Jack. 'What's more,' Jean said, 'she is really ugly which doesn't help.' At this, Isobel laughed and found further respite. From then on Leah was known as 'Mine Ugly Yiddishe Octopus'.

Leah, not surprisingly, was also the subject of the first row between Is and Is. One Friday, Isaiah telephoned Isobel from the country to say he would be late home and asked her to advise his mother. Isobel dutifully telephoned Leah and gave her the news.

'So,' Leah said, 'the moment he's home, you'll come over, I'll keep things warm.'

'No, don't,' Isobel said. 'If it's all the same with you, we'll have dinner here, just the two of us.' There was a silence broken only by the sound of Leah's heavy breathing. Isobel said, 'He'll phone tomorrow. Good *shabbes*. Goodbye.'

When Isaiah returned some time after nine o'clock, his first concern was to tell his mother he was home safely.

'She's probably waiting dinner for us.'

'I don't think so,' Isobel said. 'I told her we'd be eating here.'

Isaiah shot her a worried look, then dialled his parents' number. Isobel decided this was the moment to lay the table, which she did while listening to the conversation. There was not much to hear from Isaiah's end apart from 'Yes, mama, no, mama, yes, mama,' and when he finished he turned to Isobel. 'Oi Gott, she's furious.'

'Good.'

'We could have gone over.'

'I didn't feel like it.'

'She kept the dinner warm.'

'I told her not to.'

'You told her not to?'

'That's what I told her.'

'Isobel, she's my mother.'

'Yes, I know she's your mother.'

'She's an old lady.'

'Yes, I know she's an old lady.'

'She's my mother.'

'You're repeating yourself.'

'We owe her respect.'

'I owe her nothing.'

'Isobel, how can you say such a thing?'

'Like this, this is how I say such a thing, I owe her nothing, you see? That's how I say it.'

'Isobel, I wouldn't be here if it wasn't for my mother.'

'And your father, don't forget your father.'

'My mother struggled and slaved — '

'Yes, she told me — '

'Got us half-way across the world — '

'Only half-way? A woman like her, you'd have thought she'd have gone the full distance — '

'Isobel, I owe my life to this woman — '

'You don't owe her a thing, you've paid in full.'

'I'm going to see her now.'

'You dare.'

'I'm going.'

'Go, only I'm staying here.'

'You're coming with me — '

'I'm staying here — '

'Isobel, if you don't come with me, I'll – I'll — '

'You'll what? You'll what?'

He stood, shaking, clenching and unclenching his fists. She held his gaze, steadily and coldly. Then he stormed out of the flat, slamming the door. She ate alone and while she ate she read *Persuasion*.

But Leah was only the superficial cause of the dispute, the objective focus of Isobel's deeper, more secret unhappiness which lay embedded in the gnarled roots which she did not care to think about let alone discuss. She abhorred the sexual act. Until their marriage Isaiah and she were both virgins; his ardour was clumsy, rough, inept. To Isobel the act of love was a brutal invasion of her being, indistinguishable from rape. Her reluctance to submit, founded on revulsion and fear, stoked the fires of Isaiah's frustration and helplessness. When they argued about Leah it was because she had become the symbol of the irreconcilable tension between them.

After Isobel fell pregnant her relief was great, for the condition allowed relief from the weekly ordeal, the thought of which paralysed her. Despite her nausea and tiredness she revelled in the prospect of giving birth. Between husband and wife, it was little more than a temporary truce.

The couple decided that when the baby was born they would need an extra bedroom. Isobel was keen to move to Sea Point, to be near Jean, and a flat was found in Victoria Road, not far from the sea, backing on to Cape Town's smartest hotel, The Queen's, where the Prince of Wales had stayed. On the day preceding the move, a second letter arrived from Laban Wildnowitz in Hamburg, dated 2/7/34.

Isaiah my nephew!

Oivey! Have we got trouble! Here Zeus is back in charge. Watch out!

You know my Europa/Theodora went to such trouble to find out she's got a Jewish grandmother. For my sake, she did this so we could be married and go to America. Now, they are saying she's as good as Jewish like me. Her business is closed down. We live on the smell of an oil rag. We struggle for an American visa. Times are not easy. But! I know, I just know Uncle Benjamin is waiting on the quayside for us in New York City and we will see him soon. I KNOW IT!!!! *FRIZLITCH!!!*

Help, please. There are good Jewish people helping. Like the ones who settled us in Hamburg. Believe me now, they too are frightened. See what you can do. Give them our names. God help me, I may reach America via Keptovn. No wonder they called me Laban the Idiot.

My friend, a journalist, Kleiber, a member now of the Zeus gang, he once wrote about me, is trying to help also. He's a good man really. Europa cries a lot. Here is my latest poem:

> Statue with a torch!
> Burn me.
> This will mean, dear lady,
> That I am near your flame.

I like this poem a lot. Your loving uncle,
Laban. (Idiot, yes, Idiot.)

Isaiah was thrown into a state of alarm. He wished his mother-in-law, Eva, was still alive for she would have known the right people to approach. Neglecting Isobel, he spent that day and the day following, visiting influential Cape Town Jews, telling them of Laban's plight and asking for their assistance. All were sympathetic, all promised to help. When he returned at sunset to the unpacked tea-chests and the unmade beds, Isobel was blazing with indignation. 'How could you leave me on a day like this?' she demanded. 'I'm exhausted, why weren't you here to help?'

'I had to see people, Belle, my uncle is in danger.'

'I'm in danger! I'm going to have your child and you leave me to fetch and carry like a labourer. If not for Jean and Margaret — ' She burst into tears and fled to the small second bedroom, locking the door. There, alone, weeping, she spent the first night in her new home. They never slept in the same room again.

Her baby, a boy, was born on 9 November 1934 and was the cause of what was to prove the final showdown with Leah, who declared hostilities over Isobel's insistence that he be named Harrison. Leah was outraged. 'What kind name is Harrison?'

'It's a family name,' Isobel said.

'Harrison's a family name? It's a *goyische* name, that's what it is. Better you should call him Adam after your father, or Moses, like my father, or Isaac after Solchik's father. Harrison! I never heard a name like Harrison.'

'You have now,' Isobel said.

Telephone calls between Leah and Isaiah were a daily occurrence; the moment he replaced the receiver, as if talking to his mother had given him instant courage, Isaiah would turn on his wife and beg her to change her mind. She refused. There were meetings too. Solomon, for whom Isobel had true affection, sat by her bedside and pleaded gently with her. 'For my sake, darling,' he said. Still she would not move. Barney and Jack arrived for the *bris melah*, the circumcision, and they too pleaded. To no avail. 'He is to be called Harrison,' Isobel said.

And so it was. Harrison Wildnowitz was duly circumcised. He was adored by his parents. His arrival, however, did nothing to soothe the troubled waters of a doomed marriage.

On the eve of Harrison's first birthday, his grandmother, Leah, suffered a stroke and a week later died. None of the immediate Wildnowitz clan dared voice their thoughts, but all believed that the aggravation surrounding the naming of Harrison contributed to her end. Hardly a day had passed since the baby's birth when she did not rail against Isobel for her obstinacy and defiance. This was the main theme of her lament, stated and restated; the variations were similarly repetitive and, to Isobel at least, ridiculous:

'Me, who wept over mine son, Isaiah, to make people believe he was dead so we should escape from the Tsar, me, who followed his coffin, who slaved in a circus wagon to keep a family together, me, who had to work like a *schvartzer* to scrub and clean and cook, me, who kept mine poor Solchik from going mad, me she tells a name like Harrison. Where goes her respect? You know her trouble? Too hoity-toity, that's her trouble. And her father a *meshuggener* barman. Oi mine Gott, what kind name is Harrison Wildnowitz?'

Her husband and sons filed past the open coffin and looked for the last time on her face, unexpectedly sterner in death than in life. They stood at the graveside and intoned the Kaddish. For a week they sat *shivah*. Barney, Jack and their respective wives came and went. Solomon appeared somehow cheerful, many thought indecently so. But not Isaiah: he could not control his weeping. He cried perpetually, it seemed, his whole body was weighted down by grief. In the living-room of the small flat in Sea Point, he sat crumpled in an armchair, staring into space, tears racing down his cheeks. He refused food and barely slept. Dr Hurwitz was called and advised rest. Isaiah was put to bed. Privately, to Isobel, the doctor said, 'I think your husband is suffering a nervous breakdown.'

And then one morning, when Isobel, with Harrison in her arms, went in to take Isaiah his morning cup of tea, she found him sitting on the edge of the bed, bewildered and frightened.

'What's the matter?' she asked.

'Belle,' he whispered. 'Something's happened. I can't move my left hand. It's paralysed.'

'Nonsense.'

'Look for yourself.' He used his right hand to lift the other. 'I can't move the fingers, Belle. If I pinch I don't feel anything. It's dead, Belle, dead. My hand is dead.'

Two letters and one cable.

From Richard Webb in Manchester to Countess Iliena Sobeleva, Saint-Cloud, Paris, dated 8 December 1933.

Dear Iliena,

At last I am able to give you some news that will, I trust, be welcomed by both you and mama.

Ever since our visit earlier this year and our conversation about your future, I have been making enquiries concerning the possibility of you training to be a nurse in this country. Through the good offices of a friend, a surgeon, Mr John Elliott, (all surgeons are Mr in England) a place has been secured for you at the Manchester Infirmary, one of the best hospitals in the country. It will mean, of course, that you and mama will have to be here not later than January 31st next.

Although mama may find yet another upheaval unwelcome, I feel sure, and so does Darya, that this opportunity is too good to miss. Furthermore, I have no doubt that life will be easier for her (and you) here in Manchester.

Darya has written a long letter to mama about these matters which I shall post at the same time as I send this to you. Please let me know as soon as possible what you and mama decide.

Your devoted brother-in-law,

Richard

From Stepan Kessler in Berlin to Bruno Liebermann, in Colombo, Ceylon, dated 12 February 1935.

Dear Mr Liebermann,

I write further to my cable of yesterday's date informing you of the death of your father, Heinrich Liebermann.

Sadly, Herr Liebermann died alone, his two servants, Franz and Lotte, having left his employ without warning, but apparently under pressure, some months ago. Dr Zuckermann assured me, however, that his passing was peaceful and without pain. He was buried this morning. The service, which I, most of his employees and many friends attended, was conducted by Rabbi Pfeiffer.

Your father was a fine man, a generous employer and, to me especially, a good friend. I cannot help feeling that in present circumstances his passing was a blessed release.

The writing of this letter has fallen to me because the General Manager, Ludwig Gottlieb, has emigrated to the United States. He left Germany suddenly late last week and without telling anyone. Although we knew he and his family had disappeared, the first real news we had of him was contained in a letter written by him and posted in Le Havre. Your father's lawyer, Herr Klaus Zalmann, will, he tells me, be writing to you.

In the meantime, for reasons I will explain at a later date, I have also decided to emigrate. I shall be leaving shortly for London having received the promise of employment from Mr Lionel Kingsley of Messrs. H. L. Kingsley and Co., Tea Merchants of Mincing Lane, London, EC3. The matter was discussed and finalised during his recent visit to Berlin.

I wish you and your family my deepest sympathy.
Stepan Kessler.

And the cable, dated 16 April 1935, from Stepan Kessler to his parents in Chemnitz.

Arrived safe and well stop Address here is 12A Queen's Club Gardens Barons Court London W14 stop Stepan

When Berliners called Stepan Steve it jarred, but the same sobriquet from English mouths he found delightful and welcoming, and that was because he felt immediately at home in London in a way he never did in Berlin. He journeyed each day by Underground from Barons Court to the offices of H. L. Kingsley, tea merchants, in the City and was entranced by the other worker bees who thronged the honey-comb of streets and alleyways, the passages and lanes through which he had to find his way. Each time he said the words Mincing Lane he had the impression his English was improving.

He had stayed his first few nights in a temperance boarding-house near Bedford Square but soon made contact with the Russian Club where, in the entrance hall, a mosaic of postcards pinned to a board advertised local accommodation. The offer of his own bedroom in a small flat near by seemed promising, and by the end of his first week he was ensconced at 12A Queen's Club Gardens in Barons Court.

Stepan shared the flat with a bicycle salesman, Nikolai Kazanyov, whose family had once been the St Petersburg agents for the Birmingham bicycle manufacturers, Raleigh. He was a year or two older than Stepan, tall and elegant. He wore clothes well, adored the company of women, was an inventive linguist and liked people to think he was English. His insouciant charm and studied detachment concealed a fierce ambition to succeed.

They lived on the top floor of a modest Victorian house. The rooms were small and oddly shaped; the doors did not quite close, the floors and ceilings were, to say the least, uneven. The bath stood in what passed for a kitchen but when not in use was boarded over with a hinged plank of wood. There were gas and electricity meters which were fed with sixpences and shillings. A public telephone which took pennies was situated on the first-floor landing; a system of buzzers summoned the residents when required to take their calls. All the other units were also occupied by émigrés except for the ground-floor garden flat where Mr Arnold Dingley, a typewriter repairman, lived with his wife, Prunella, the manageress of a local stationer's. Since the couple were childless and enjoyed company they made no complaint of the almost nightly celebrations for which the Russians apparently needed little or no excuse, and to which the Dingleys were inevitably invited. Indeed, they seemed positively to feed on the buoyant melancholy that invariably pervaded the house after dark. 12A Queen's Club Gardens, Barons Court, W14, was, to Stepan's mind, apart from the variety of coins needed for daily existence, an ideal residence. But its greatest asset was its proximity to the Russian Club which was five minutes' walk away.

The Club, like Tzigane in Berlin, was the centre of Russian *émigré* life. The Russians made Barons Court their *quartier*, and although some lived in other Russian enclaves, such as Grove Park where they had a Sports Club, and Chiswick, pronounced by them Chyee-zik, many were to be found in the evenings and at weekends playing bridge, chess, talking, drinking of course, and in numerous ways assuming consciously but mostly unawares the manners and mores of the English middle class. Stepan wore a navy-blue pin-stripe suit and a bowler hat by day, a Prince of Wales check in the evenings, a tweed sports jacket and suede shoes at weekends, grew a discreet moustache, and brushed the little hair he had left straight back. He had begun to lose his hair in his teens as his father had done before him but it never in any way undermined his con-fidence. Women found him electrifying much to Nikolai Kazanyov's annoyance.

Stepan remembered his father once telling him of a visit to Zurich shortly after escaping from the Soviet Union; of how, on taking the morning air, he had become aware of a scent he was at first unable to identify until he realised it was the scent of freedom. In London Stepan was similarly affected. Each morning on stepping out of the front door he breathed deeply, hoping to be made light-headed by that sweet and deceptive smell.

There were other activities undertaken by certain members of the Russian Club regarded by some as ridiculous and comic but thought of by others as sinister and dangerous. On Stepan's second or third visit to the Club in the summer of 1935 he heard others address a middle-aged portly man with a neat beard as 'Prime Minister'. This was puzzling for the man had been pointed out to him as Ivan Kiyushin, son of an impoverished merchant. He claimed he was 'something in the City' until it was discovered that he was the doorman of a private bank, obliged to wear a green livery and a black top hat. Kiyushin had great bulging eyes that seemed to suggest they had witnessed some horror from which they had never recov-ered. After dinner, when members were gathering in the bar, Kiyushin entered and said, 'To work! To work!' in a hoarse monotone as though he were asking members to volunteer for a firing squad. A dozen or so of the men excused themselves and mounted the stairs to an upper room.

Stepan asked what was going on. An elderly woman beside him said, 'The Duma in Exile,' and raised her eyes to the ceiling.

It was explained that some *émigrés* had formed a parliament complete with two parties, Royalists and Democrats, whose purpose was to assume the reins of government after the inevitable overthrow of the Communists. The Barons Court Duma had began as a debating society, an election being held once a year at the same time as the election of the Club officers. But, with mounting evidence of Stalin's brutality, their deliberations turned serious as though the ferocity of the tyrant they opposed made their resolve more necessary and urgent. In no time at all they began to believe that Stalin could really be overthrown, either by force of arms or by being undermined in other subtler ways which no one was ever able to specify succinctly.

In 1935 the Democrats were the majority party; the main plank of their policy was that, after the destruction of the present Soviet regime, a democratic system following closely the constitution of the United States would be instituted in their former homeland. Kiyushin, liveried doorman and Prime Minister, appointed his cronies to ministerial portfolios – finance, foreign affairs, defence, home affairs, heavy industry, agriculture, and they were treated with a deference that Stepan found rather disturbing. They took themselves and their mission with great solemnity and seriousness.

'What about the Royalists?' Stepan asked.

'Ah! Next year they'll form the government,' someone said.

'Don't be so sure,' said another. 'Kiyushin won't give up power that easily.'

'What power?' Stepan asked.

'What do you mean what power? He's Prime Minister.'

'Yes, but what power does he have?'

'But he's Prime Minister.'

Nikolai Kazanyov took Stepan aside. 'Allow me to explain, my dear fellow,' he said. 'It's best not to be naïve in these matters. Just think about it. The doorman of a bank by day is called Prime Minister by night. He and his so-called Cabinet control the club. They vet prospective members, keep people in line. They even have informers, a sort of secret police, just like the Tsar's Okhranka or Uncle Joe's OGPU. You'll find out. Yes, one could say the Prime Minister has power.'

Stepan was mystified but realised the Duma in Exile was not to be publicly mocked. He nodded and simultaneously shrugged in the hope his response would be regarded as non-committal. Kazanyov laughed and then lowered his voice. 'I'm on your side,' he said. 'And if you think the Prime Minister's mad, wait until you meet the Leader of the Opposition.'

'Who's the Leader of the Opposition?'

'Andrei Bulkarov, leader of the Royalist Party. He's a kitchen porter at St Charles Hospital, Ladbroke Grove. Says he was a doctor before the Revolution. He's on holiday in France at the moment, says he's seeing some Grand Duke or other. He'll ask you to join his party. Be careful because he's *really* mad.'

To begin with Stepan was an object of curiosity in Russian circles as a result of his recent departure from Nazi Germany. 'But why did you leave?' he was frequently asked, mostly with amazement. 'The Nazis are determined to destroy Communism.'

'Nazis may be worse than Communists,' Stepan said.

'Worse than Communists?'

'Well, if not worse, no better.'

This response was overheard and recorded by one of Prime Minister Kiyushin's spies. Stepan was duly summoned to the upstairs room where the Duma met. Small upright chairs were arranged in a rough horsehoe shape to mirror European parliaments; a trestle-table served as the Speaker's desk and the Prime Minister sat deep in the only comfortable leather armchair from which the stuffing protruded like an uncontrollable weed.

'Certain matters have been reported to me concerning your political beliefs,' Kiyushin began, staring wildly at Stepan. 'I am told you are sympathetic to the Bolsheviks.'

'That's not true,' Stepan said quietly.

Kiyushin glanced at his notes. 'Not true, not true? You are quoted as saying that if the Nazis are not worse than the Communists they are certainly no better.'

'I believe that to be true.'

'That is a provocative remark,' Kiyushin said, returning his maniacal gaze on Stepan. 'Kindly explain.'

'Prime Minister,' Stepan said feeling slightly ridiculous addressing him in that way, 'I have lived under both systems. Believe me, there is nothing to choose between them. In my opinion they are both criminal. They both believe in killing people who do not agree with them or destroying those they hate. I endured two years of the Nazis and could take no more of it. I felt as though I were being choked to death. I do not think one has to be a Nazi in order to oppose Communism.'

Kiyushin made a strange humming noise that Stepan thought might signal agreement. 'You believe in democracy, then?'

'Yes.'

'In the monarchy?'

'Which monarchy?' Stepan asked. 'I certainly believe in the English monarchy. I think it's an institution which gives stability and continuity.'

Kiyushin's eyes bulged more fiercely. 'No, no, no, the Russian monarchy.'

Stepan hesitated. 'It no longer exists,' he said.

'Would you like to see the Tsar restored?'

'The Tsar is dead.'

'His heirs then, his heirs, the Pretender, the claimant, whoever leads that rotten pack, would you like to see a Romanov back on the throne?' Kiyushin barked irritably, shifting in his chair.

'I would like to see the Communists overthrown. I would like our people to have a better life.'

'Then you must join my party, the Democratic Party.'

'Forgive me, Prime Minister, but I don't want to join any party. I'm not a political animal. I want a quiet life, that's all.'

'You mean you want us to fight your battles for you so that you can enjoy your quiet life, that's it, isn't it?'

'I don't think everybody has to be consumed by politics,' Stepan answered simply. 'That's what's happened in Russia and Germany. Everyone is forced to sleep, eat and breathe politics. There is no other life for them and that is awful.'

Kiyushin continued to stare unblinking as though trying to read Stepan's thoughts. At last he said, 'All right, Kessler. As long as you don't join the Royalists.'

To Nikolai Kazanyov, one evening, Stepan said, 'A lot of people in the Club don't believe me about the Nazis, you know. Even decent, cultured people. They'll support anybody who promises to destroy Bolshevism.' They were drinking vodka and eating pickled onions.

'And the other way round,' Nikolai said.

'How do you mean?'

'Here in England, for example, a lot of decent, civilised people sympathise with Communism because they believe the Communists are the only bastion against the Nazis.'

'They're also wrong,' Stepan said. 'One should oppose both of them.' He knocked back his drink, bit on the onion and stood. He raised his empty glass. 'One should oppose any system that destroys individual freedom. You don't have to be a Communist to hate the Nazis, and you don't have to be a Nazi to hate the Communists.'

'I'll remember,' Nikolai said with a smile.

'Don't make fun of me,' Stepan said, resuming his seat. 'Just believe me.' He recounted his memories of the three men hanging in

Moscow, and of Fräulein Kahn's suicide. He told Nikolai of his encounter with Willi Lohmeyer and the SA gang who tried to rape Rudi Rosensweig. He described the Nazi celebration on the night Hitler became Chancellor. He said, 'Whether it's Nazis or Communists, you wake up each morning frightened. You pass your days believing that something terrible might happen to you or to those you love. Your sleep is filled with nightmares. In short, you are the definition of fear personified. It's unbearable. And it's no way to live. Yet, my father, a decent man, supports them. And so too, I think, does my brother.

'They came to Berlin to say goodbye to me and all they talked about was catching a glimpse of Hitler. And when I made any criticism of the regime, they stiffened, looked over their shoulders, begged me to keep my voice down. No, believe me, Nikolai, in England one is not frightened. A man can always think what he likes but in England you can actually say what you like. And that's a big difference. As far as I'm concerned, the best system of government is the one you don't notice. Now, come, let's go to the Club and get really drunk.'

In no time at all Stepan was described by his fellow members as simple-minded.

'Have a good holiday, doctor?'

'Holiday? Holiday? I was in meetings morning, noon and night with the Grand Duke. It was hard labour from start to finish. We are formulating our plans. It won't be long now. Holiday, indeed.'

Dr Andrei Bulkarov had aged gracefully and his energy and ebullience were little diminished. He never confessed his true age but he must, by 1935, have been at least seventy if not more. He looked much the same and was physically vigorous, but anyone who had known him in his Warsaw days might not have been aware of a subtle change in the man's demeanour. What once had passed for professional discretion was now transformed into obsessive secrecy. His diary, which he had resumed on his arrival in England in the autumn of 1929, he now kept in code but even to those private pages he confided nothing, for example, of his escape from Russia or the circuitous journey he must have undertaken to reach a safe haven. If and when questioned about these events he would hold up a hand, close his eyes and shake his head slowly as though to repeat that history would be too painful. He was less reticent about his role in the Civil War and positively effusive when describing his life as medical adviser to Georgy Skalon, the Tsar's representative in Warsaw. But regarding his more recent past he remained guarded and evasive.

He had hoped to resume his medical practice but he had arrived in England without any documents to prove his qualifications and the British Medical Association were not inclined to accept his word for them. It was suggested he might sit examinations but he declined. He found work as a hospital kitchen porter and threw himself with a passion into the politics of exile. On his return from France, although it was only early September, he began canvassing votes for the election at year's end. On hearing that there was a new member who had declined to join the Democrats he made a beeline for Stepan Kessler.

In contrast to Prime Minister Kiyushin, Bulkarov was pragmatic. When Stepan gave him the same answer he had given Kiyushin – 'I am not a political animal' – Bulkarov swept aside this defence, saying, 'I am not asking you to join my party. I am demanding your vote. Promise me, Stepan Stepanovich, that you will vote Royalist in December.'

'I'd like to think about it,' Stepan replied.

Bulkarov unexpectedly hugged Stepan tightly. 'Ah, Stepan Stepanovich, it's men like you who are the guardians of Russia's soul.' Stepan smiled and disengaged. The doctor smelt of disinfectant. 'Look,' Bulkarov continued unabashed. 'I don't care if you're a member of the Politburo or an Obergruppenführer in the SA. I am not concerned with your beliefs. I am only interested in your vote.' He suddenly tensed and looked back over his shoulder. Stepan followed his gaze but could see no one. Bulkarov gripped his elbow and propelled him out into the small back garden.

'I cannot say too much,' Bulkarov confided urgently, 'but if my party is elected and I assume the burden of the highest office, let me assure you that you will number your return to Russia in days not months or years. Days! It is imperative I have your vote. Remember these words, Stepan Stepanovich. I should like to be summoned by the democratic process but I must warn you, that if I am not, one way or another I shall be the next Prime Minister. Vote Royalist for a Free Russia.'

Stepan later said to Nikolai, 'You're right. He's absolutely mad. And worse, totally immoral.'

In October Bulkarov launched his election campaign by giving a party. The Royalists took over the Club for the evening. The guests each brought a bottle and the drink flowed. Wives of party members prepared *zakuski*, a stuffed cabbage dish called *golubtsy* and an abundance of rice. Gianado and his Gypsy Band provided the music. No one knew exactly how the event was financed. Bulkarov hinted that the Pretender had made a generous donation, implying that he viewed Bulkarov's party as the only hope for his restoration.

Stepan and Nikolai, both regarded as undecided voters, were invited to join in the festivities. In any event, to them a party was a party. They arrived in high spirits but it so happened that as they entered Gianado, the gypsy band leader, was playing a solo on his violin, a miserable rendition of a tune by Lehár. Stepan's mood instantly plummeted. It was not the music itself which depressed him but the sound of the instrument so appallingly played. He shut his eyes and lowered his head.

'What's the matter with you?' Nikolai asked.

'Nothing.'

'Nothing? You were in such a good mood and now you look as though you've come to a funeral.'

'I'm Russian,' Stepan answered belligerently and went off to skulk in a corner. As though he were on the train again he remembered the terrible panic when he first realised his violin had been stolen. He thought of Valentin Manishowitz, his old teacher, and wondered what had become of him. He wondered what had become of his violin.

Nikolai thrust a vodka into his hand and Stepan downed it in one. Presently the drink and more agreeable music, both potent seducers, began to work on him; in no time at all his good temper revived and he entered into the spirit of the evening with abandon.

'My God, you *are* Russian!' Nikolai called to him as they cavorted on the dance floor. Stepan was soon improvising Russian folk dances, bending his knees, kicking out his feet and clapping his hands. But when Gianado broke into *Ochi Chornya* – 'Black Eyes' – played sadly and badly, Stepan was again brought low. The violinist wandered from guest to guest with a sickly self-satisfied smile, playing into their faces. And again Stepan was on the train in a darkened tunnel consumed with panic; he wept. Nikolai ignored him, sniffed around for attractive females but most of those present had at one time or another already seen through his charm.

Disconsolate and tipsy, he said to Stepan, 'Let's get out of here, this is no bloody good.'

'Right,' Stepan said, wiping away his tears.

'I thought there'd be some new talent here tonight but they're all the old crowd.'

'Nothing plays better than an old fiddle,' Stepan said, stretching out his arms, eyes closed, snapping his fingers and swaying in time to the music. And he remembered his travelling companion, Count Belaev, with his long thin face and beard. 'In hell do as the damned.' Where was the Count now?

'Let's go up to the West End, I know a place where we might just be lucky.'

'Yes,' Stepan said, 'yes, let's get out of here. I can't stop thinking the most upsetting thoughts. God knows why. Yes, let's get out of here.'

They were about to leave when Bulkarov spotted them getting their coats. 'Where are you going?' he asked. His eyes were unusually bright with drink and, presumably, the promise of power. He put his arms round both men's shoulders and hugged them close.

Stepan said in English, 'No crumpet,' and giggled.

'Crumpet?' Bulkarov repeated. 'You want crumpet? But *blini* is better, no? We serve *blini* in a moment.'

'No, no, no, not *blini*, crumpet, girls, bits of fluff.'

'I will never speak English,' Bulkarov said and then, understanding, bellowed, 'A-ha! I have a solution. Across the road lives Maria Denman, a widow. I often visit her although she does not use the Club much. She has I've been told a beautiful young woman and her beautiful old mother visiting from the north of England which is why she is not here tonight. Let's go over and invite them. She lives just across the road.'

'Good idea,' Nikolai said.

The moment they emerged from the Club the fresh air made them reel. Laughing and staggering they crossed the dimly lit street. 'As a matter of fact,' Bulkarov said, 'the widow Denman, despite her name, is not English but Russian. A very talented person. And very grand. She was formerly Countess Maria Obrunina, an artist of outstanding gifts,' and he rang her doorbell.

Maria Denman, née Obrunina, stylish and serene, opened the door. She burst out laughing. 'Ah Dr Bulkarov,' she said, 'don't tell me you've run out of drink again.'

'No, no, dear Countess, we have simply ventured across the street to entice you to my party.'

'Thank you, you are very kind, but I think I told you I have guests — '

'But we invite them, too,' Bulkarov said expansively, and then introduced Stepan and Nikolai. They bowed. Maria inclined her head graciously.

Stepan said, 'We are told one of your guests is a beautiful young woman and — ' but Nikolai nudged him sharply and Stepan fell silent, drunkenly aware of his clumsiness.

Maria laughed again. 'Yes, yes, she's very beautiful, so come in, come in, I'm sure she would prefer two handsome beaux to the company of two old gossiping women.'

Maria led them into her small drawing-room, the walls covered in her paintings and drawings, the tables and shelves bearing photographs and miniatures of people and places belonging to times past.

Bulkarov breezed in but the instant he saw the older of Maria's guests he stopped dead and sucked in his breath. 'My God!' he cried. 'Countess Sobeleva!'

'Dr Bulkarov!' Tatiana said, smiling at first but her face darkened as if remembering something unpleasant.

The doctor bowed low and kissed her hand.

'You two obviously know each other,' Maria said.

'Know each other?' Bulkarov repeated incredulously. 'I diagnosed the Countess's happy condition in Warsaw in 1911.'

'You, Iliena, I suppose,' Maria said with a smile.

'No,' Tatiana said. 'Valodya. Iliena was born three years later in Sobliki.'

Stepan looked on Iliena Sobeleva and was stricken. Her beauty sobered him. When the doctor came to introduce him he was barely able to move. His energy seemed to evaporate and he became almost timid. He kissed Iliena's hand and then retreated, content just to look on her while Nikolai chatted to her easily, smothering her with his smiles and courtly manners. Iliena kept her eyes downcast as though she were studying the patterns of the rugs, but she glanced up once to catch Stepan's lost look and her interest in him was quickened.

Bulkarov said, 'Please, please, dear Countesses three, join us and add lustre to the celebrations.' Maria and Tatiana were at first reluctant but Bulkarov was not to be discouraged. 'Come, Countess,' he said to Tatiana, 'and we will once again dance a mazurka together.'

'Did we dance one before?' Tatiana asked.

'I can't remember,' Bulkarov said, chuckling. 'But we will dance one tonight.'

'You have an orchestra?' Maria asked.

'A band. Gianado and his Gypsies. Actually, his name is Archie Levine. He works at my hospital as a morgue assistant. He's from Hackney and is an extremely fine fellow.'

'Please, mama, may we?' Iliena asked unable to hide her excitement. 'I'd like to go.' Nikolai imediately gave her his arm but she did not take it. 'I'll have to change,' she said.

'No,' Stepan said, more emphatically than he'd intended. 'Come as you are. You will be the best dressed woman in the place. You look absolutely perfect.' He realised he had been immodest and he, too, took to studying the patterns of the rugs. Maria smiled. Tatiana did not. But there was little discussion after that, the three women each in turn adjusted their appearance in the looking-glass that adorned the mantelpiece. Nikolai escorted Iliena, Bulkarov Tatiana, and Stepan brought up the rear with Maria, née Obrunina, on his arm.

While crossing the street to the Club, Maria said to Stepan, 'This is the most extraordinary evening. I have not seen Tatiana Sergeievna for almost twenty years and then out of the blue about a month ago I heard from her. Our reunion deserves a party, believe me. What a to-do!'

'Yes,' said Stepan. 'It is an extraordinary evening in every way.'

The new guests were quickly the centre of attention. On learning Tatiana's identity old men wept. 'A Sobelev formerly a Souvritzin,' they exclaimed, shook their heads in disbelief and blew their noses. A sort of elegant charade ensued, the Royalists paying obeisance to the three newcomers as though the women somehow represented the entire lost Russian aristocracy of whom they, the Royalists, were the natural champions. Stepan found the women chairs in a corner of the Card Room. He sat himself beside Iliena. And, as is the way with *émigrés*, the conversation turned to tales of escapes and journeys, to the remembrance of lost friends and relatives, the litany of exile. Stepan begged them to tell the story of how Maria and Tatiana had come together after all these years. Between the continual interruptions, in fits and starts, the story emerged of the reunion.

'You tell them, Tatiana,' Maria said.

'There's not very much to tell. We live in Manchester now — '

'Why Manchester?' Stepan asked.

'I'm training to be a nurse at the Infirmary,' Iliena explained. 'A children's nurse.'

'My God, how wonderful,' Stepan said.

'Not so wonderful. I enjoy it but it's awfully hard work. I cry a lot. They call me Nurse Sob. Believe me, it's not only because it's short for Sobeleva.'

'The English are very bad at foreign names,' Bulkarov said, missing the point.

'Go on, Tatiana,' Maria said.

'My son-in-law, Richard Webb, is a journalist on the *Manchester Guardian*. One evening, about a month ago, he showed me an article that he'd seen in the *London Evening News*. They seem to get all the newspapers from everywhere in his office. But he'd read this article on a Russian *émigré* artist and thought it would interest me. I first saw the name, Maria Denman, and thought nothing of it but then I saw her photograph — '

'And who can forget a face like mine?' Maria interjected.

'Exactly,' Tatiana said.

Iliena took up the threads. 'I've never seen mama so excited and she asked Richard if it was possible to find out where Maria lived. I don't know but journalists seem to be very clever at that sort of thing and a day later we had her address here in London.'

'What a glorious story,' Stepan said.

'There is no understanding fate,' Bulkarov decreed. 'What some people call coincidence and others luck is of course nothing of the kind. It is all part of having a belief in the Great Design.'

And from Maria: 'And from having a son-in-law who is a journalist.'

Nikolai seized the moment of everyone's laughter to invite Iliena to dance. Stepan watched enviously from the shadows, waiting his turn. Archie Levine, alias Gianado, played '*A mir bis du shehn*' but the guests did not want a Yiddish love song and so he played 'Tangerine' instead. Stepan decided that this was his moment. He tapped Nikolai on the shoulder, said, 'Excuse me', and for the first time held Iliena in his arms.

'So, Iliena Lvovna, tell me, why haven't we met before?'

'You tell me.'

'Geography.'

'I expect that's the reason.'

'I've never been to Manchester.'

'There you are.'

'But I assure you, if you'd lived in London, I'd have found you much sooner. I think this is the most wonderful night of my life.'

She blushed.

'My God, you're beautiful.'

'Stop talking so much,' she said. 'Just let's dance.'

Stepan was not much of a ballroom dancer so they stood more or less on the same spot, barely shuffling their feet, but staring into each other's eyes until Gianado and his band struck up 'Jealousy', an opportunity for Gianado to wander around the room again, playing passionately and staring into the eyes of the onlookers, males and females, with indiscriminate fervour. Nikolai, who prided himself on dancing the tango like Rudolf Valentino, advanced like a predator.

Seeing him approach, Iliena said quickly, 'Perhaps we should sit this one out,' and led Stepan away. Nikolai found another partner, the youngest Princess Dobrekova, whom everyone said was 'fast'.

Tatiana appeared at the door and beckoned to Iliena. 'Oh dear,' Iliena said, 'I think it's time to go.'

They stood momentarily forlorn, buffeted by the dancers. Stepan could not bear the thought of being parted from her and was overwhelmed by that same feeling of panic he had known on the train and which he had remembered so vividly earlier in the evening. If I lose her now, he said to himself, I shall never see her again. Just then, Gianado approached, his violin tucked under his chin, sawing away with sublime self-satisfaction. As though it was the most natural thing in the world, without a moment's thought, Stepan seized the violin and the bow from a startled Gianado – ''Ere,' he said, 'what's your game?' – and Stepan played, like an insane descant, a slow, loving rendition of 'Kalinka', never for one second taking his eyes from Iliena's face. Gianado waved to his gypsies to abandon 'Jealousy'. The dancers cried an 'Ah!' of disappointment but when they heard what Stepan was playing, they murmured an 'Ah!' of sentimental approval and began to clap softly and slowly at first, then more loudly and faster, eventually forcing him to increase his tempo so that the music Stepan played became wild and frenzied.

Stepan, lost in love and music, was unaware that it was the first time he had touched a violin since he made a vow that day on the train in the darkened tunnel in the middle of nowhere. He faltered occasionally but he was playing again, playing for Iliena Lvovna Sobeleva and for no one else. Her beauty had bewitched him. His whole being informed every note he coaxed from the instrument. His tears ran freely and unashamedly. And Iliena, embarrassed at first, found the courage to look up and return his gaze. Then she noticed, as if for the first time, that he was bald. She recalled the prediction of the old Cossack, the Holy Man, Yevgeny, on her name-day in Paris, and that made her smile.

'What a to-do!' Maria said, but Tatiana did not repeat the catchphrase of their youth. Instead she asked, 'Do you believe in love at first sight?'

Maria considered before answering. 'Since it exists as a phrase, I expect it exists in reality.'

'There is another phrase,' Tatiana said. 'Whirlwind romance. That I believe in but not in love at first sight.'

The two old friends sat in Maria's drawing-room. Their reunion had enlivened them; they picked up the threads of their broken lives and were once again affectionate and intimate as though they had never lost touch. Maria had asked Tatiana to sit for her and so now Tatiana sat, head erect, straight-backed as always, hands folded on her lap, her eyes troubled. She had confided her concern about the speed at which, it seemed, her daughter's future was being decided.

'She is so inexperienced,' Tatiana said.

'Keep still.'

'I like Mr Kessler but I know so little about him.'

'I like him, too.'

'He has very good manners.'

'And I have the impression he has a very good heart.'

'I did not like his friend, Mr Kazanyov.'

'No. He seemed very full of himself.'

'Very.'

'Where are they this evening, Mr Kessler and Iliena?' Maria asked.

'He is giving a party to introduce her to his friends.'

'Has he spoken to you yet?'

'About what?'

'About what, you ask. About marrying Iliena, of course.'

'Certainly not.'

'Don't be so vehement, Tatiana. You may expect him to ask for Iliena's hand, believe me.'

'But they've only known each other a week.'

'You were the one who talked about love at first sight and a whirlwind romance. Turn a little to me.'

Maria tried to catch the look of anxiety in Tatiana's eyes, and both women were silent. Then Tatiana said, 'Perhaps I am making too much of all this.'

'Perhaps.'

'We go back to Manchester on Monday. It'll blow over.'

'Perhaps. Relax your mouth. Don't look so grim.'

Tatiana tried to do as she was told but her thoughts commanded her expression. What, she asked herself, would Iliena's destiny have been had the earth not collapsed beneath our feet, had the tempest of history not swept away our world, had we not been blown here, there and everywhere. She thought of Lev dying alone in a Moscow hospital and wondering how he would have reacted had he still been alive. 'A tea-taster? Really, my dear.' But that now was a meaningless censure. Tea-taster, prince, sub-editor, count, doctor, what did it matter? Was Stepan Kessler a good man, a faithful, honest, decent man? Would he be kind? Would he give Iliena his life?

'Chin up,' Maria said.

Raising her chin so that she looked defiant, Tatiana said, 'This will all blow over. I know it.'

'Perhaps,' Maria said.

Perhaps not. There was no escape from the whirlwind. Stepan asked for Iliena's hand on the Sunday before her planned return north. They had known each other less than a week. Tatiana gave her conditional consent. 'Yes, provided you wait a year,' she said but knew the condition would be ignored. Stepan saw Iliena off at Euston; the following weekend he visited Manchester; when apart, they wrote to each other every day.

In reply to the news of the impending marriage, Stepan Kessler Senior issued a warning from Berlin. 'You will be marrying out of your class,' he wrote. The advice was ignored. The wedding was planned for early the following year in London.

In the election of the Barons Court Duma, the Democrats were re-elected. Reluctantly conceding defeat Bulkarov made a graceless speech which contained a veiled threat. 'This may not be the end of the matter,' he said. His words turned out to be not quite as prophetic as he had hoped.

On an icy evening in January Bulkarov turned up at 12A Queen's Club Gardens unannounced. Stepan was alone and invited the doctor in for a drink. The doctor's mood was wild and unpredictable and his state of alarm greater than ever. He went often to the window to peer down cautiously at the street; he paced; he stared into the gas fire as though it would provide the meaning to the universe.

'What's troubling you, doctor?' Stepan asked.

'It's too dangerous for me to say. I don't want to compromise you. But, because you are a neutral party, I want you to keep these for me.' From his briefcase he took three hard-covered Lett's diaries. 'Keep these for me. Hide them. They contain highly secret information. Don't worry, they're in code.'

Stepan took the books. 'Is there anything I can do to help?'

'Yes, tell no one I was here.'

And with that he left.

Two days later his body was found on the tracks of Barons Court Underground. Eyewitnesses gave differing accounts. Some said they had seen him throw himself in front of an oncoming train; others, that they were certain they had seen a man push him. The police investigated and, because he had left no suicide note, the coroner's jury returned an open verdict.

Some members of the Russian Club decided that the cause of death was the election defeat. Bulkarov did not want to go on living under Prime Minister Kiyushin and his Democratic Party. The doctor's own adherents hinted that it was political assassination, for it was widely believed that Bulkarov had been planning his own *coup d'état*. His death marked the beginning of the end of the Russian Club and the Barons Court Duma.

Stepan and Iliena were married in the Orthodox Church in Buckingham Palace Road, London, in March 1936. Princes and counts held the ritual crowns over their heads. Bishop Antoni consecrated and blessed their union. The couple moved into furnished rooms in Turnham Green and a few months later, when Iliena fell pregnant, into a furnished flat in Chiswick. Their first daughter was named Vera; their second, born fourteen months later, they named Natalya.

Isaiah's days were spent watching motor cars pass by. He stood, leaning on a low brick wall that protected the small block of flats in which they lived, on the main road to Clifton and Camp's Bay. Left hand lame, he could no longer drive a car and could not afford to be driven. He had ceased to be a commercial traveller.

Things had not gone well for him ever since Leah's death. First, the nervous breakdown; then the paralysis; and finally the need to find another way of making a living. Borrowing money from his brother, Barney, the hotelier, Isaiah purchased a fishmonger's in Sea Point, a thriving concern, the seller said, a money-maker, a gold mine. Isobel served behind the counter. She hated the smell of fish. In less than eighteen months they were bankrupt. The recriminations were savage and repetitive. Isobel, unforgiving, never forgave him. She found work as a clerk in Electricity House. The one thing husband and wife now shared was their love for their only child, Harrison.

A lonely, failed life. He watched the cars; occasionally, he exchanged the time of day with a passer-by. The maid, Margaret, prepared his lunch and he napped in the afternoons. In the evenings, he read his encyclopaedias and accumulated a vast store of useless information. Isobel read and knitted in her own bedroom. If they were not arguing and shouting at each other, there was between them an implacable, hostile silence.

Ever since his sojourn in Hamburg Isaiah had acquired the habit of writing down his dreams. One afternoon he recorded in his graceful handwriting, and in English:

1st October, 1938. Afternoon dream, having just woken.
I was in a field, green and luscious. But I could hear the sound of wood being sawn and that frightened me. Although I was as I am now, forty years old, with a paralysed left hand, I was in feeling a child again. I could hear also my Uncle Laban singing one of his American songs. Suddenly, I was face to face with Ion Stoica, the circus man, only he was dressed as a Christian priest. He said these words which I did not understand: 'Stickali punateri Kristiano.' I

said, '*Frizlitch?*' and he laughed and shook his head. Then Uncle Laban called. I had to cross the field. The grass was very high and the going hard. There was a hut. Somehow I knew Uncle Laban was inside, so I went in. There was a skeleton lying on the bed whom I knew to be Uncle Laban. Uncle Benjamin was also there, hammering nails into the bones of Laban's feet which Laban seemed to enjoy. Laban said, 'This is what fate has in store for me.' Then I noticed that Europa Altona was lying beside him. She was naked and said, '*Shligalick,*' and then I woke, sweating, and with tears on my cheeks.

10

In the early hours of Tuesday morning, 22 August 1939, a German radio programme of light music was suddenly interrupted by an over-excited announcer. 'The Reich government and the Soviet government,' he bleated, 'have agreed to conclude a non-aggression pact with each other. The Reich Minister for Foreign Affairs will arrive in Moscow on Wednesday, 23 August, for the conclusion of the negotiations.' It was a triumph for Joachim von Ribbentrop; and, in a way, for Stepan Kessler.

For Ribbentrop, champagne salesman, snob, lickspittle, immoralist and hoodlum, it represented the greatest moment in his tawdry life. The lapdog of power wagged his tail when Josef Stalin said, 'I know how much the German people love their Führer. I should therefore like to drink his health.' Ribbentrop may even have realised as he put the glass to his lips that Adolf Hitler was the only man Josef Stalin trusted. On his return to Berlin Ribbentrop reported ecstatically to his lord and master. 'I was made to feel completely at home,' he said, 'just as though I were among old party comrades.' His lord called him 'a second Bismarck'.

Stepan also crowed but not in public and with little pleasure. Had he not always said that the Nazis and the Communists were one and the same? Now was he not proved right? For a year or two people no longer called him simple-minded.

'What now?' Maria Denman asked him.

He was holding his babies, Vera and Natalya, one in each arm. He said, 'I'm not a prophet. All I know is they both want power so that they can satisfy their lust for order. Between them God knows what they'll do to us,' and he kissed each daughter on their foreheads as though bestowing on them protection from evil.

PART FIVE

Full Circle
(1945 and after)

1

The war was the landscape against which Harrison Wildnowitz grew to adolescence. The war invaded his consciousness and served as fuel to his imagination. The war indelibly marked him. In its shadow he lived his childhood. The inevitable topics of adult conversation, death and oppression, were a constant accompaniment to which perforce he listened, not always understanding, but somehow always aware. Certain words, names and phrases – Dunkirk, Churchill, Eden, HMS *Hood*, route marches, HMS *Ark Royal*, Montgomery, Alexander, Tobruk, repatriation, missing believed killed, D-day, Hitler, Goering, Goebbels, Himmler, Streicher, Tojo – were his familiars. And later: Belsen, Auschwitz, Dachau, genocide.

And Isaiah's scream.

Year's end, 1946. Harrison has just turned twelve. In blazing heat the Jewish community of Cape Town show newsreels of the Nazi death camps, fragments pieced together as a macabre duty by elderly Dr Hurwitz.

Isobel refuses to attend the showing and objects when Isaiah insists on taking Harrison.

'A twelve-year-old boy shouldn't see such things.'

'He must,' Isaiah says and for once there is no argument.

They sit beside each other, father and son, in the darkened hall adjacent to the Sea Point Synagogue. To the whirring of the sixteen-millimetre projector they watch the ghastly evidence of unimaginable barbarism. Men and women weep; there is the constant flickering of handkerchiefs. Dr Hurwitz reads a commentary he has written himself: 'This is Heinrich Himmler visiting a concentration camp in 1943.' The agent of death, the former chicken farmer, passes along, gazing serenely at the doomed prisoners behind barbed wire, chickens for slaughter.

Isaiah screams.

A terrible scream, long, attenuated, degenerating into a strangulated guttural moan. He faints, comes to, moans again. Harrison, shocked and momentarily immobile, fears his father is dying. Dr Hurwitz refuses to interrupt the showing or his commentary so a colleague, a Dr Wolman, helps Isaiah out, Harrison following like a bewildered mourner.

Once in the warm fresh air Isaiah begins to breathe more regularly but he is still ashen. 'What is it, Mr Wildnowitz?' Dr Wolman asks. 'What is it, Dad?' from Harrison.

'My Uncle Laban. I saw my Uncle Laban. He was behind the wire, smiling.'

'No, no, you must be mistaken — '

'It was my Uncle Laban!' Isaiah cries with such vehemence that there is no doubting him.

Laban the Idiot, behind the wire, never identified for Harrison because Isaiah refuses to experience the ordeal again. But later Barney sees the film, and so does Jack, and they confirm the sighting. Laban the Idiot, the tall one, but no longer strong, the haggard one with missing teeth, behind the wire, inspected by Heinrich Himmler.

Sixth, remember that we can change our lives. Fate can be fought, as the poet says, and if you ask which poet, I answer, the poet Laban Wildnowitz. Life is not a curse it is a blessing. So, if life becomes cursed transform it. This can be done. Believe me.

A pattern of stars on a quilted cradle dictates the destiny of all mankind. Isaiah talks much of Laban to his son, Harrison. Why didn't he practise what he preached? Why didn't he go to America with Benjamin? Why? Why? Why did he allow fate to murder him? Why did he submit to an insane conviction of sanity?

> I'm down dere mit mine hat bust in,
>   Doodah! Doodah!
> I'm go beck hoim mit a pucket full tin,
>   Oi! doodah day!
> Gunna run all night!
> Gunna run all day,
> I bet mine geld on de boptail neg,
> Tsomebody bet on de bay.

2

Among the six million and more who were slaughtered by the Germans in extermination camps or by other means, these must be included:

Reb Yankel of Ploemyan, Max Ehrlich, Lela Krantnik, Anita Posniak (Mrs Max Ehrlich), Konrad Blokh, the Dickensian scholar Dr Chaim Shapiro, of Warsaw; Ion Stoica, Raina Stoica, Chivu Stoica, Arpad Stoica, Constanta Stoica; Adam Salt's brother, Dr Karl Salz of Vienna; Abraham and the other unnamed Pasym Jews; Reb Grossman of Danzig; the banker, Alfred Bronstein (Iron Cross, second class), Katarina Bronstein, Reb Leitermann, Sigmund Frankfurter of the Frankfurter Bank, the shipping agents Ludwig Kahn and Adolf Wassermann, shoe-shop owner Jakob Dobermann, bookseller Adolf Adler, Yitzchak the *shammes*, Rabbi Levi, kosher restaurateur Samuel Finkelstein, the newspaper editor Josef Herbstein, Pastor Naupert of the Society for the Conversion of the Jews, all from Hamburg; the dentist Dr Rosensweig (Iron Cross, first class), Frau Rosensweig, Rudi Rosensweig, the dressmaker Frau Pfefferblum, of Chemnitz; from Berlin, Heinrich Naumann, clothing manufacturer, Alyona and the gypsy orchestra from Tzigane, Dr Zuckermann, Rabbi Pfeiffer, the lawyer Herr Klaus Zalmann; Europa Altona, formerly Theodora von Tresckow, and Laban Wildnowitz also known as Laban the Idiot.

3

At about seven o'clock on Thursday morning, 3 May 1945, Stepan gathered up the written reports of interrogations of German prisoners of war he and his colleagues had conducted. He then commandeered a jeep and a driver and made the forty-five minute journey to Field Marshal Montgomery's headquarters at Lüneburg. The day promised heat.

He was Captain Stepan Kessler now, an Intelligence Officer in the Canadian Black Watch which he joined five years before because he learned the Canadians paid their soldiers more than the British. He was very drunk at the time.

He knew the German surrender was imminent but he was not prepared for what happened on his arrival at Tac HQ. It was obvious something big was about to break. A Union Jack was being run up outside Montgomery's caravan and Stepan was ordered to keep out of sight. He jumped from the jeep and made his way into a hut where other officers were crowded around the windows, peering out. He pushed his way through. Nothing much was said because no one knew exactly why there was such tension in the air, but all seemed to be aware that something momentous was about to take place.

At 8.20 four German officers arrived escorted by Military Policemen who were immediately dismissed. The Germans were lined up under the Union Jack. They stood to attention. Two were Navy and two Army. They looked like the caricatures of Allied propaganda. The Navy officers wore long black leather greatcoats; the Army men, one of whom was a General with dazzling red lapels, wore grey greatcoats.

In the hut Stepan and the others were trying to identify the delegation but not having much success when the door of Montgomery's caravan opened and out stepped the Field Marshal, short, slight, steely, wearing battledress and a black beret but with a General's cap badge. The Germans saluted smartly. Monty did not acknowledge them at once so they had to remain at the salute. He walked slowly towards them, a distance of about eight yards. He then seemed to flick his beret with his right hand rather casually; the Germans dropped their arms. He approached the first naval officer.

'Who are you?' he asked in his most austere nasal military tones.

'General Admiral von Friedeburg, Commander-in-Chief the German Navy, sir,' came the reply.

'I have never heard of you,' Monty said loudly. Stepan and the others watching suppressed laughter.

Monty passed on to the next officer and followed the same procedure. 'Who are you?' he asked, establishing the identity first of Rear Admiral Wagner, Flag Officer to the Admiral of the Fleet, then General Kinzel, Chief of Staff of the German Army, North, a magnificent-looking man, enormously tall, in his late forties, complete with monocle. He came to the last of them, another tall man, young, late twenties, with a cruel, brutal face.

'Who are you?' Monty asked again.

The officer replied, 'Major Friedl, sir.'

'Major!' Monty barked. 'How dare you bring a major into my Headquarters!'

In the hut, someone beside Stepan said, 'The Chief's putting on a good act this morning.'

And someone else said, 'Balls. The son of a bitch has been rehearsing this all his life.'

'What do you want?' Monty asked the Germans.

Von Friedeburg explained that they had come to surrender the German armies facing the Russians in Mecklenburg.

'Certainly not. Those armies are fighting the Russians. If they surrender to anyone then it must be to the Russians. Nothing to do with me.'

The sun was higher now and the Germans in their coats were sweating.

Monty then gave them his demands. 'Surrender to me all German forces on my western and northern flanks.' He listed the German armies. When he said all he meant all. The German delegation were unable to agree but they expressed concern about the civilian population in those areas and wanted to come to some agreement about looking after them.

Monty's face became sterner than usual. 'Do you remember a little town in England called Coventry, which six years ago was blown off the face of the earth by your bombers? The people who took the brunt of it were the women, children and old men. Your women and children get no sympathy from me – you should have thought of all this six years ago.' He then launched into a bitter tongue-lashing about the concentration camps, recounting in detail the horrors he himself had witnessed. 'Have you seen them?' he asked. 'The crematoria, the gas ovens, the helpless victims? Have you seen the suffering you have caused?' He paused, twitched his lips, then continued, 'Unless you surrender unconditionally I will order the bombing and fighting to continue with the inevitable loss of German civilian and soldiers' lives.'

Stepan whispered, 'They'll agree, I bet you.'

Monty turned and walked towards two of his own officers and talked to them out of earshot of the Germans, who saluted Monty's departure. 'We'll give them lunch to reflect on what I've said,' Monty murmured. 'Lay on the best possible food in the Visitors' Mess. Give them all the drink they want.'

Only the British, Stepan thought, would take such delight in organising the charade that followed. Whether or not Monty had ordered and orchestrated it was not clear. The Visitors' Mess became the centre of activity. A bedsheet was used as a tablecloth to cover the table at which the Germans were to sit. An officer who could speak German was instructed to act as Mess Sergeant and a white tunic was quickly found for him. The Germans were given a splendid meal accompanied by red wine, and with their coffee cognac. The officer who was pretending to be the Mess Sergeant, while pouring the cognac, said, 'Sorry about the poor meal, gentlemen, but the day's rations haven't arrived yet.'

The Germans looked at him astonished. One of them said, 'We haven't eaten food like this for months.'

'Really? Well, our private soldiers won't touch this muck.'

The following day the Germans agreed to Monty's demands. Three days the later, on Monday 7 May, peace came to Europe when General Jodl signed the unconditional surrender of all German forces to General Eisenhower in Reims.

For Stepan it was not quite over. From the moment he had landed on European soil, on 12 June 1944, there was a terror of a world divided, the war he was helping to fight on the battlefields and the one within himself. Stalking him was a constant fear that he would come face to face with his brother, Shura, or Willi Lohmeyer and be obliged to kill them. Perhaps there would be other German soldiers who were once friends or acquaintances. How would he react? What was right? How should he behave? He was dogged, too, by concern for his parents. Chemnitz had been taken the Russians. If the Kesslers were still alive would they be sent back to the Soviet Union to freeze to death in labour camps? These anxieties which he kept well-hidden were nevertheless a constant presence and he decided that before going home he would try to discover what had happened to his relatives.

He had several advantages: he spoke German and Russian fluently which was why he was in Intelligence in the first place; he also had access to a variety of Allied Intelligence reports and it was while sifting through these that he gained his first piece of information. The Lohmeyer textile factory in Chemnitz, which had been turned over to making German military uniforms, had been bombed. The knot in his stomach tightened. A week later he learned that a large number of civilian refugees from the Dresden area had made their way into the British Zone. The hunt for important Nazis was under way and no one was above suspicion so the refugees from the east were being questioned in a camp near Braunschweig. Stepan thought a visit might be worthwhile. He spent the unfolding days in a state of dread at what he might discover.

With Corporal McKay as his driver he set off in a jeep and headed south. They drove past long lines of defeated German soldiers, thankful probably to have surrendered to the British; past refugees, thankful to be alive, through smouldering villages and towns whose inhabitants were at work among the ruins, sifting the debris for anything that might be of value. Stepan had the impression they were already rebuilding their homes.

He could not help feeling a certain satisfaction at having been a small part of the victory. He had entered the concentration camp of Belsen three days after its liberation; the living were barely distinguishable from the dead. Stepan fainted and came to, vomiting. He had no pity for the Germans. 'Your women and children get no sympathy from me,' Montgomery had said. Nor from Stepan.

Apart from the routine of interrogating prisoners and decoding German signals, he had performed one act for which he had been awarded an MBE Military Division. In late November 1944, he was stationed just east of Eupen in Belgium, close to the German border and the front line. All through the day and well into the night he questioned prisoners. It was known that the Germans were re-grouping or preparing for a counter-offensive. To discover the size and composition of the German forces was the task in hand. If a prisoner proved recalcitrant, the standard routine was to threaten him with the Russian Front. That usually did the trick. Only one man, in all Stepan's experience, a cliché of a young blond Nazi officer from an SS panzer division, was indifferent to the threat; the rest, the canaries, confessed all they knew. On that particular night, however, the prisoners yielded little, but one man talked casually of a large deserted château about two miles down the road to Schleiden where, he said, his officers had looted a splendid wine cellar.

'Did they take all the wine?'

'No. You would need trucks to take all the wine. No, they took all they could but there's enough there to refloat the *Graf Spee*.'

'Is the château behind your lines?'

'It was but I don't think it is now. I think you pushed us back. I'm only guessing.'

Just after midnight he returned to the office where his batman, Tony Johnson and his driver, Corporal McKay were brewing tea. He told them what he had learned and called for a map. 'Of course, it must be on our side by now,' Stepan said. 'Schleiden was captured two weeks ago. Come, let's go and get ourselves a decent bottle of wine.'

Clouds obscured the moon and the rain was incessant. The three men, wrapped up warmly and with a large sack concealed under Johnson's waterproof, marched down the road. Far away they could hear artillery pounding, and the drone of distant aeroplanes, but in their immediate vicinity it was deathly quiet apart from the sound of the rain. Presently, they saw the château silhouetted against the dark sky and made their way up a long, winding drive towards the main entrance. The house was shuttered with broken windows boarded up.

Corporal McKay was all for breaking down the door. 'No, no,' Stepan whispered. 'We must find a way into the cellar.'

Tony Johnson discovered the stone steps at the back of the house. They descended. A wooden door was unlocked. They crept in. Corporal McKay lit a match. The flickering light was briefly reflected on a vast army of bottles.

'Housey-housey!' Tony Johnson said.

'Safe to use the flashlight, sir?'

Château Margaux, Château Latour, Château Haut-Brion, Château Ausone, Château Pavie, Clos des Amandiers, Château d'Yquem, Schloss Johannisberg, Niersteiner, Zeltingen. A 1929 Château Lafite.

'My God!' from Stepan.

'Any good?' from Corporal McKay.

Stepan had a pocket-knife with an attachment that passed for a corkscrew. He drew the cork of the Lafite, sniffed it and then let it stand for a minute or two, meanwhile opening a Johannisberg and the Château d'Yquem.

'I'll show you how to taste wine,' Stepan said.

'I thought you were better at tea, sir.'

They went through five bottles and were very quickly very drunk. With meticulous clumsiness, they filled the sack. Tony Johnson heaved it on to his back to an accompaniment of 'Sssssh! You'll break 'em, ssssh, carefully now.'

Staggering and reeling, the bottles clinking, they slithered back down the drive and thought they had found their way to the road when machine-gun fire opened behind them spraying the ground at their feet. Stepan and McKay dived for the side of the road and rolled into a ditch. Tony Johnson dropped the sack and followed them.

German voices. Running footsteps. More firing. The sound of a motor-bike starting. A volley of rifle shots. An American voice, 'Got the motherfucker.' Silence.

Tony Johnson asked, 'Should I go back for the wine?'

'Fuck the wine,' McKay said.

They crept along the ditch up to their knees in water, Stepan leading them. He stumbled. 'Shit.'

'What, sir?'

He had tripped over a dead body. McKay produced the torch. A German despatch rider, his skull shattered, bleeding from bullet holes in his chest, soaked in blood and rain.

'What's a despatch rider doing behind our lines?' Johnson asked.

'He's not behind our lines, you fool, we're behind theirs.'

They searched his leather pouch and found a package wrapped in a dull green oilcloth. Stepan tore it open. Several pages. Top Secret. In cipher. He had difficulty focusing but, even as drunk as he was, he recognised the codes for 6th SS Panzer Army, 5th SS Panzer Army, and the name, von Runstedt.

Somehow they managed to return to their base. Stepan ordered Johnson to make hot black coffee but the batman passed out and lay on the floor, snoring heavily. McKay made the coffee. Stepan began the task of decoding and translating his find, labouring until dawn. What he had stumbled on was the disposition of von Runstedt's forces in the Ardennes and to him they looked threatening. At first light McKay drove Stepan to Montgomery's Headquarters. The documents were delivered, the intelligence circulated and assessed. The Americans believed the Germans were in defensive positions. Montgomery thought otherwise. When the Germans began their offensive, what became known as the Battle of the Bulge, on 16 December 1944, the Americans failed to respond to the gravity of the breakthrough. But Monty, because he had information from the find of a drunk Intelligence Officer in the Canadian Black Watch, believed his troops were in danger of encirclement and took appropriate action. It was to prove a decisive tactic.

Stepan was told he could expect to receive his MBE from the King on his return to London.

Stepan and McKay travelled along the line that separated the British and Russian zones. Just south of Braunschweig they came upon a vast camp. The Germans had used it as a transit camp for Allied prisoners of war but now it was filled with their own civilians, the wooden towers on stilts manned by British soldiers. Someone had scrawled a sign which was attached to the barbed wire at the main gate: Displaced Persons.

Stepan asked to see the camp commander, a Colonel Anderson, early fifties, short and muscular; he affected an upper-class accent, clipped, military. Before the war, he claimed, he'd been a first assistant to the film director, Alfred Hitchcock.

'I'd like to see the list of inmates,' Stepan said.

'Haven't got one,' Anderson said.

'How are these people being processed?'

'They're not. Waiting for the Red Cross.'

'Shouldn't you be making a start, sir?' Stepan asked. 'After all, there may be high-ranking Nazis among them.'

'They're all high-ranking Nazis far as I'm concerned. Not letting anyone go so it doesn't matter who the hell they are. They'll stay here until I'm told to release them.'

'May I take a look around, sir?'

'What, hoping to spot Martin Bormann and get yourself a gong, is that the game?' Anderson asked, his upper lip curling.

'I'd like to look, if you don't mind, sir.'

'Please yourself.'

Stepan walked into the main compound where only men were kept, and knew at once his task was futile. Hundreds of them. He scanned the faces of the defeated and the displaced but they became a blur of broken, hopeless creatures, brought low, humiliated, lost. Stepan turned to McKay. 'Let's get the hell of here,' he said. 'This is pointless.'

As they made their way back to the jeep, Colonel Anderson approached. 'If you're looking for anybody in particular it's easier to see from one of the guard towers. High angle always best for crowds. Looking down on them easier than looking at them.'

Stepan and McKay mounted one of the towers near the main gate and surveyed from on high the teeming mass of what seemed to him like the damned. The guard offered him binoculars. Stepan put the glasses to his eyes and adjusted the focus. He recognised his father's bald head, watched him as though he were a stranger, shuffling, hands behind his back, head bowed. Stepan felt nothing but McKay saw him stiffen.

'Seen anything, sir?'

'Yes,' Stepan grunted. Keeping the glasses trained on his father, he said, 'Get down there, I'll point him out to you.'

'Have you found him, sir?'

'Yes.'

He could not control the trembling of his hands.

4

When Harrison Wildnowitz was twelve years old he was already certain what he wanted to do with his life. Because Isobel, like Eva before her, paid blind allegiance to the country of her birth, she determined that Harrison should be taught to speak like an Englishman. When he turned six, she arranged for him to have elocution lessons so that he should rid himself of the dreadful South African accent. He soon revealed, as she had once done, a talent for recitation. From 'There's a mouse in the house' he went on to '"Is there anybody there?" said the Traveller,/Knocking on the moonlit door', and later:

> Now the sunset breezes shiver,
> And she's fading down the river,
> But in England's song forever
> She's the Fighting Téméraire.

He was entered for speech competitions, known in Cape Town as Eisteddfods, and he won many medals, mostly gold, and cups, mostly silver. A visiting examiner from Trinity College declared that he was outstandingly gifted. From recitation he graduated to plays in which he showed even greater facility. His future career was now certain: he would go to England and become an actor.

'If you want to know how good you are,' Isobel said, 'you had better find out in a place where it matters. London. That's the centre of the world. There is no point in staying here and being a big fish in a little pond.'

Mother and son discussed the future often and obsessively. In the evenings, when she returned from work, they sat at the dining-room table in the octagonal entrance hall of the small flat in Sea Point, and she would talk not only of her hopes for him but also of what it meant to be an artist. 'You have to be cultured,' she'd say. 'Generally cultured. You have to read novels and poetry, listen to music, visit the theatre, appreciate painting. You have to acquire knowledge, real knowledge, not like your father's bits and pieces, no, I mean real knowledge and use it properly.'

'What do you mean properly?'

'I mean to use it for your good and for the good of others. You don't acquire knowledge just to show it off. To be cultured, knowledge, taste and talent must be deeply embedded in you. It's the only way to be a *mensch*.'

One evening, when Harrison and Isobel were reading scenes from *King Lear* and trying to unravel their meaning, there was a commotion in the street, the sound of screeching brakes and a thud. Then a neighbour's voice called with alarm, 'Mrs Wildnowitz!'

They ran out to find Isaiah sitting on the kerb, dazed. He had walked down to the local general store to buy cigarettes and on his return, attempting to cross the busy main road, a bus had knocked him down. Dr Hurwitz was sent for. Apart from a bruised arm and a gash on his forehead Isaiah was not apparently badly hurt. But the day after the accident he awoke to discover that his left leg, like his hand, was lame. X-rays followed and tests, but no organic or physical cause could be found.

'You see, Mrs Wildnowitz, I have this theory about your husband,' Dr Hurwitz said. 'I believe his condition is psychological or what I prefer to call "mind over matter". First, we have his grief over his mother's death and his hand goes lame. And then this accident, and he loses the use of his left leg. Yes, I'm afraid it's mind over matter.'

Now, Isaiah, his left leg useless, shuffled from the front door of the flat to lean on the wall and watch the cars pass by. Harrison used to wonder what went on in his father's head, day after day, standing there, hardly ever seeing a friend or a relative. His brother, Barney, and he were not on speaking terms ever since the fish shop fiasco. Isaiah had lost everything and was therefore unable to repay the money Barney had lent him, and Barney never forgave. Isaiah, ever the dutiful son, occasionally found the energy to make the journey into town to visit his father, Solomon, in the old aged home. And after the old man died, gentle, sweet, senile Solchik, Isaiah, for most of the time, was solitary and silent. What did he think about?

Once, when Harrison was feigning illness to miss school, Isaiah sat on the bed, and asked, 'Have you got pen and paper? Good. Because I want you to write something down.' He closed his eyes and, haltingly, related to his son the circumstances surrounding the family's flight from Ploemyan. 'Now, what I'm going to tell you is the most important of all. Take it down carefully,' and he repeated Laban's seven commandments that had been told to him when he lay on the floor pretending to be dead: don't get too involved with God; behave decently to your fellow-men; be independent of your parents; honour the mysteries and the unknowable secrets and remember all humankind lives in a secret place where spirits roam free and magicians haunt the forest; beware politicians who say they are there only to serve; remember we can change our lives, fate can be fought; and, last, if you are unlucky enough to fall in love with a woman do not blame her, blame only yourself. When he finished he kept his eyes shut and bit his bottom lip as though trying to bear unbearable pain.

Harrison gazed at his father in amazement. Never had he heard Isaiah touch on these things or on any matters remotely like them. Was this what he thought about during his long, lonely days? His Uncle Laban? His conterfeit death and his coffin?

Isaiah's eyes snapped open as though a sudden revelation had been visited on him. He said, 'I know what I have to do now. And I do it in honour of mine Uncle Laban. Yes, we can change our lives. He must have forgotten that fate can be fought.' He heaved himself up. 'Keep what you've written down safe,' he said, and hobbled from the room. Harrison wondered in a moment of panic whether or not to tell his mother, for he thought that Isaiah meant to divorce her and that frightened him.

Harrison soon realised that what his father had in mind had little or nothing to do with Isobel but to do with Isaiah's own pride and dignity. The Sunday following, over the usual lunch of soup, roast chicken, roast potatoes, green peas followed by fruit salad, and lemon tea, Isaiah made known his intentions.

'I am going to leave the Orthodox *schul* and join the Reform.'

Isobel, pouring the tea, said, 'You're mad.'

'Why am I mad?' he asked, instantly belligerent. 'Let me tell you something, I'm doing this not only for me but for Harrison — '

'I didn't think you were doing this for me,' Isobel said.

'Shut up and listen, you're always so clever.' Now, when he talked, he addressed his remarks directly to Harrison. 'All my life I've gone to the Orthodox *schul*. The only thing they ever asked me to do was to form the *minyan* at your late father's funeral. Why,' he demanded, 'have they never asked me to draw the curtains of the Ark, the Holy of Holies? Why have they never asked me to carry the Torah or to say a blessing from the *bimah*? Why? I'll tell you why. Because I'm broke, because I'm a failure, because I'm a discard. If they thought for a moment that I'd give them a donation, they'd make me Governor-General.'

'What do you know about the Reform?' from Isobel.

'They're starting up here, that's what I know. And I know it's new, it's different, it's modern, it's – it's – it's — ' He struggled to find the words. At last he said, 'It's change, Belle, that's what it is, it's change.'

'And what about Harrison's bar mitzvah?'

'He'll have it in the Reform.'

'You know nothing about the Reform — '

'I know they don't talk business while they pray, I know they believe in decorum. I know they don't talk cards, I know they don't talk stocks and shares. Last Friday you know what I heard Lionel Epstein say while he was supposed to be praying? I heard him say, "I was beaten on three aces last night!" I'm sick of it. Enough. I want to be regarded as a *mensch* not as a failure — '

'Yes, you want to be regarded as a *mensch* — ' Isobel began in tones of disparagement but Isaiah slammed down his teaspoon so that it bounced off the table. 'Don't talk to me in that tone of voice, Belle, I won't have it. I'm telling you now, that's what I'm going to do. We're joining the Reform. To you it doesn't matter, to me it matters. And it matters to Harrison. In the Reform they say most of the prayers in English, in a language he can understand. The women and the men sit together. And I'll tell you another thing. I'm sick of the world pushing me around here, there and everywhere. This is me, Isaiah Wildnowitz in charge, doing what I want to do! *Gottmeiner*, this is *frizlitch*, Belle! *Fritzlitch!*' and he limped out of the front door to the wall to watch the Sunday afternoon traffic on its way to the beaches of Clifton and Camp's Bay.

Isobel said quietly, 'This is like a Catholic becoming a Protestant.'

Isaiah carried out his threat. Briefly, the family was ostracised and condemned. But Isaiah stood firm and erect. 'What I did is right. For me, for Harrison, and in memory of my Uncle Laban.'

Harrison celebrated his bar mitzvah in the new Reform Synagogue at Green Point. He gave his parents *nakhes*. And, if he learned from his mother to love and admire the arts and all they expressed, then from his father he learned, as if by a mysterious osmotic process, that the currency of change is courage.

Isobel's determination to make Harrison's future possible also required courage; and sacrifice. She scrimped and saved but without complaint. He would go to England, study at the Royal Academy of Dramatic Art and become a famous actor, of that she had no doubt. Such was her certainty that Harrison felt able to take his future for granted. He wanted nothing more than to succeed, to be the big fish in the big pond, but, had he the insights, he may also have realised that he was being driven by a need to escape his unhappy, loveless parents. And there was in him, as in his immediate forebears, a strong sense of not belonging, of not being rooted, as if the final destination chosen by his grandparents at the bottom of the world was accidental, haphazard, a half-way house not a terminus, a place he would never be able to accept as home. England represented to Harrison what America did to Laban: escape, renewal, rebirth. His future seemed

324

assured. Then, returning home from school on a wet day in April 1950, he found their old maid, Margaret, weeping.

'What's the matter?' he asked.

'It's the master,' she said, meaning Isaiah. 'He's had a heart attack. Oh, Master Harrison, I didn't know what to do, I couldn't phone madam at work, I didn't know what to do — '

'Where is he?' Harrison demanded.

'In the nursing home, I phoned Dr Hurwitz — '

But it wasn't a heart attack. A specialist diagnosed a tumour on the brain. Isaiah's skull was trepanned; the tumour was non-malignant. Meningioma. Dr Hurwitz was in part right in his diagnosis. The emotional shocks, it seems, accelerated the tumour's growth. Mind over matter, matter over mind. Two days after the operation Isaiah died and was placed for the second time in a coffin. Isobel did not weep and was not able to dissemble. As for Harrison, only when the funeral rites obliged him to spade the first sod of earth on his father's coffin did he break down. The dull thud seemed to open within him a gaping hollow, like his father's grave, in which his sobs found neither echo nor resonance. Isobel helped him away and he was aware of others wishing him long life but he was not comforted.

The future was temporarily halted, but only temporarily. A month was all Isobel needed to gather her strength. Harrison said, 'It doesn't matter. If it's not meant to happen — '

But Isobel cut him short. 'Don't speak like that. I have enough saved. I'll work to the end of the chapter. I don't mind. It's something I have to do for you.'

A schoolmaster, Mr Flynn, said, 'I think you ought to change your name. Harrison Wildnowitz won't look too good on the bills. You need something short and snappy. I've been thinking. How about Harrison Wilde? Wilde's a good name for a theatre man, yes, indeed, it's a fine name, Harrison Wilde.'

5

Dressed in her Brownie uniform Natalya witnessed her father receive the MBE from King George VI at Buckingham Palace. For Stepan the ceremony marked both the end of one way of life and the beginning of another. He wanted to find a new occupation.

Pulling strings, he had managed to bring his father back from the camp in Braunschweig. From the old man Stepan learned that his mother had died of cancer in 1943; the Lohmeyers had been killed during an air raid; of Shura and Willi Lohmeyer there was no trace. Shattered, lost lives and Stepan found it impossible to mourn in any profound or proper sense.

He had moved his family to Cobham, a village south-west of London, in the early days of the war and to Cobham he returned to start his new life. Here, old Stepan Kessler and Tatiana Sobeleva lived with their children and their children's children. Old Kessler, manufacturer of German army uniforms, twice in his lifetime had lost all he possessed to the Communists he so hated, but of these things he never talked.

Tatiana kept her distance from him. She did not care for his austerity and his brooding silences. The antipathy was mutual. They conducted their dealings with polite, uneasy suspicion. The burden fell on Iliena, the arbiter, keeper of the peace; and on Stepan, who had now to find a way of making a living that would support six people.

Insulated by a gratuity and a demob suit, he visited the offices of H. L. Kingsley, the tea merchants, his former employers, to give notice that he would not be resuming his old job. He was shocked by the devastation London had suffered; whole streets blown away leaving ugly, gaping holes. Unlike the Germans the British had not yet begun rebuilding. He was disorientated and had to ask a policeman the way to Mincing Lane.

'Captain Kessler!' one of the older men greeted him. 'There's a letter for you, been here about a year.' The writing paper was headed: Cazanove and Dingley, Office Machinery, 18 Church Street, Kensington, London W8, dated 18 January 1946.

My dear dear Steve,
The moment you receive this please get in touch with me. In case
you're wondering who is writing this letter, it's your old flatmate,
Nikolai Kazanyov, only I've just changed my name by deed poll to
Cazanove – more English, don't you think? And in case you're
wondering who Dingley is: remember Arnold Dingley who lived
on the ground floor of 12A QCG? The typewriter salesman?
Please make contact on your return.
I won the DFC in Burma. How about you?
Your loving friend,
Nicky.

The reunion took place in a restaurant called the Hungaria near
Piccadilly Circus.
    'What took you so long?' Nicky asked.
    They talked of the old days and of war. Then Nicky filled in the
blank spaces.
    'I was sent to Canada for training, then to the Far East. And who
should be one of the maintenance mechanics but Arnold Dingley.
Small world, eh? We were together all the way through. It was all his
idea. Typewriters, adding machines, duplicators. He's the mechanic,
I'm the visionary.'
    'You were never modest,' Stepan said.
    'Join us, Steve. We already employ twelve people. We're on the
brink of being really big. I want you to be Sales Director, organise
distribution, soft-talk the customers. Will you? No one could do it
better. Apart from me, you're the most charming man I know. Please
say yes.'

Cazanove and Dingley prospered and so did Stepan Kessler. His
father died and was buried in an English churchyard. His mother-in-
law grew old gracefully, remained straight-backed and steely-eyed.
His daughters matured apace: the elder, Vera, his beautiful Vera, the
scholar, and Natalya, his beautiful Natalya, well, she would be a ballet
dancer. It seemed to Stepan appropriately Russian. She was sent to a
ballet school where she boarded and grew more beautiful.

But she also grew too tall; and the physical strain was not to her taste.
Besides, she hated performing, being on show. She was self-
contained and retiring, like her mother and grandmother, exuding
dignity and the ability to unsettle others with her hauteur. Her ballet
training had given her discipline and a need for perfection in all she
undertook. Her gift for drawing and for languages she dismissed
because neither were of the highest order. She loved music and was,

even when young, knowledgeable; she read voraciously. She was, by Isobel Wildnowitz's high standards, truly cultured.

But what to do with her life? Secretly, Stepan nursed the hope that she would meet some English aristocrat or, if not an aristocrat, someone from a respectable upper-middle-class background, marry, have children. Through her, or Vera, he could lay claim to a sense of belonging. Natalya, however, had other ideas.

'I'd like to do something in the theatre, but backstage, not in front of an audience,' she said.

The Bristol Old Vic offered a course in stage management.

'Perfect,' she said.

6

Harrison Wilde arrived in England on a cold, wet, misty day in December 1951. There were still bombsites in London, and food was rationed, but he entered the land of promise, confident, ambitious, high-spirited, vigorous, ebullient, quick-witted and resourceful – qualities the English would find both attractive and distasteful.

Deus ex machina, a German policeman, the adulterous wife of a banker, a Reuters man in Moscow. An actor.

Rupert Gough-Martin, when not working which was most of the time, produced the occasional play with students of the Royal Academy of Dramatic Art in Gower Street. Small, pixie-like, impish, he accounted one of his pupils not especially talented but nevertheless unusual.

'What's your name again?' Rupert asked, one hand thrust into the waistband of his trousers. He talked very quietly, almost mumbled, and smoked his cigarettes jerkily as though he were unsticking the end from his lips.

'Harrison Wilde,' the pupil answered.

Always shabbily dressed, frequently in polo-necked sweaters, Rupert had a fey manner which was described then as 'camp', a word much in use and applied mostly to describe the extravagant gestures and behaviour of male homosexuals. Rupert muttered, 'There is something about you,' he said, 'I'm not quite sure you'll end up an actor but there's something about you.' And then as an afterthought, 'It's your Adam's apple, you see. It's a little large.'

When Harrison repeated the remark to his girlfriend, Bonnie, an American, she said, 'Watch out, buster. The guy's a fruit,' and Harrison secretly agreed. But a few days later, to his astonishment, Rupert said, 'Harrison dear, I want you to meet my wife, Monica. She's a theosophist and can see *into* people, and I want her to see into you.'

Harrison was invited to dinner at their house in Paultons Square in Chelsea. Having expected the Gough-Martins to live in something approaching poverty, Harrison was surprised by the size of the house, the high quality of the furnishings, the fine food and the wine.

He would have to learn that there is a sort of Englishness which prides itself in the shabby exterior concealing the riches within.

Monica Gough-Martin was tall and gaunt, with a long face, a generous mouth and large bucked teeth.

'Green,' she said. 'Your aura is green.'

'Told you so,' sang Rupert.

'Oh yes, yes, yes, *yes*,' she said, 'green!'

'What does that signify?' Harrison asked timidly.

'It means you are here and not here. You have found a world and not discovered it. Perhaps you never will. Green is the rarest aura of all. Rupe's is indigo. Mine is orange. Both *frightfully* common. But you, Mr Wilde, are only the second person I have met whose aura is green, and you will travel far.'

'Who was the other with a green aura?' Rupert asked beadily.

'That would be telling,' she replied.

Harrison wanted to question her further but sensed that she believed she had made herself crystal clear.

Rupert smiled without showing his teeth. He said, 'Green! I knew it. We must never lose touch. Promise me.'

When he left RADA Harrison worked as an actor spasmodically. Isobel sent him money when she could, but that, she confessed, was proving a struggle. He took work in Lyon's Corner House in the Strand and survived. In 1958 a telephone call from Rupert gave him cause for hope. He was once more summoned to the house in Paultons Square. Monica opened the door and shied away. 'My God,' she said, 'the green is *blinding*!'

Rupert interviewed Harrison in the first-floor drawing-room. 'I've been invited to be Artistic Director,' he said, 'of the Chesterfield Civic Theatre. A weekly rep.'

'Where's Chesterfield?'

'Derbyshire. A small town. It has a church with a crooked spire. I want you to come up and play as cast. I won't need you till the third play which is *The Diary of Anne Frank*. You're to play the father. Nine pounds a week, all right?'

'All right.'

'Oh, I am pleased. We'll be doing a lot of Agatha, of course, but I've one or two surprises for the citizens of Chesterfield.'

As Harrison was leaving, Rupert let out a mournful sigh.

'What's the matter?' Harrison asked.

'I simply can't make up my mind between two girls for the job of stage manager. One's extremely experienced, the other's extremely beautiful. What should I do? You tell me.'

'Oh, take the beautiful one,' Harrison said.

*

He first saw her on the stage of the theatre. He'd arrived in the late afternoon to begin rehearsals the following day. She was making a bed for the current play which was to open that night, *Intimate Relations* by Jean-Paul Sartre, one of Rupert's surprises, no doubt, for the citizens of Chesterfield. Harrison decided then and there that she was the most beautiful creature he had ever clapped eyes on: tall, dark, perfect.

'I'm looking for Mr Gough-Martin,' he said.

'He'll be in the office in the foyer.'

He stood, transfixed, watching her cross the stage to fetch the second bedsheet. Wanting to make an impression, he said, 'You look like a ballet dancer.'

She paused to glance at him with icy hauteur.

'Were you a ballet dancer?' he persisted.

'Yes, but I grew too tall,' she said, flicking the folded sheet as though she were dismissing him with a grand gesture.

He said, 'My name's Harrison Wilde. What's yours?'

'Natalya Kessler.'

First Epilogue

First Epilogue

The image of the wheel: the cogs, the turning, the wheels within wheels; the tracks made from Ploemyan and Sobliki, from Moscow and Warsaw, across the world, converged in the middle of England, in the small market town of Chesterfield, Derbyshire, whose church, St Mary and All Saints, has a crooked spire. When Harrison arrived in the town he invented a myth. He said that when a virgin married in the church the spire would straighten. On leaving the town, the myth was told to him by a taxi driver who said it was an ancient legend.

Lives run their course. These are the last loose ends.

When Harrison first met the Kesslers they had moved to a large house near Godalming, with a garden Stepan and Iliena had created out of a wilderness. In the drawing-room hung the painting of Sobliki, romantic and mysterious, the self-portrait of Maria Obrunina, and the portrait Maria had done of Tatiana in London before the war.

Harrison first saw Tatiana in 1959 when she was in her early seventies. She was vigorously cutting long grass with a sickle. She wore a grey smock and a bright blue scarf tied round her head. He might easily have mistaken her for a peasant until she straightened up, stood erect and held out her hand for him to shake. He had the impression he was not so much being introduced as presented.

Over the years, until senility overtook her, they developed if not an intimate relationship then an understanding founded on his interest in her past. He had always been fascinated by the turmoil that had caterpulted his own parents and grandparents across the earth; now, on meeting the Kesslers, he was equally fascinated by their experiences. Tatiana was reluctant to speak about herself but Harrison begged her to record her memories and eventually she wrote down in pencil an account of the night the Bolsheviks occupied Sobliki and other, small details. She taught him the Russian alphabet and made him read the opening of *War and Peace* to her but after a sentence or two she begged him to stop.

Stepan and Iliena, who could not at first have been overjoyed at their daughter's choice of husband – a Jew, an out-of-work actor, penniless – took him into the family and made him welcome. Later, when he began to write for his living they seemed proud of him and were, as his career prospered, doubtless relieved. With both he enjoyed a warm, relaxed intimacy. Stepan, generous and expansive, a giver of life, was particularly important to Harrison, for he seemed to fill that hole within which had opened up at Isaiah's graveside. They welcomed Isobel, too, who returned to England for the wedding and stayed a while. Never wanting to be a burden she found work; she was, Natalya always said, an ideal mother-in-law; Isobel admitted that her memory of her own guided her. In time, Harrison could afford to make her an allowance which enabled her to stop work, to return to Cape Town and there to live into a contented old age, proud of her son and justly proud of her own part in his progress. She died in 1986.

Stepan dominated the family. Sunday was his day. The vodka flowed and he became wonderfully, expansively drunk. He would burp often and loudly, and say with a twinkle, 'My soul spoke to God.' Always, towards three o'clock in the afternoon, he would lift the telephone, dial the operator and growl, 'Put me through, please, to Nikita Sergeyevich Khrushchev in the Kremlin. Make it person to person! I want to tell that man what a skunk he is!' Presumably the Godalming operators became used to these demands, for they never rang back and Stepan never seemed to remember he had made the call in the first place.

In the evening he played his records, and once, in summer, when the sounds of the Schubert Piano Quintet floated through the open windows of his study into the garden where the family was sitting, Harrison observed Tatiana stiffen. As the slow movement began she rose and slowly walked into the house. In her bedroom she sat at her dressing-table and, for the last time, recorded a memory:

> I heard the slow movement of Schubert's Piano Quintet tonight. Stepya was playing it on his record-player but it sounded as though ghosts were teasing me with it. It was unbearable for, Proust-like, I was in Sobliki again, in the park, listening to the Jewish musicians. Not a memory. I was there, physically, emotionally, in every way. Oh, Sobliki, Sobliki. Home.

Still simple-minded, Stepan clung to his theory that Communism and Fascism were born of the same impulse: a lust for order which is an impossible demand on the human spirit. Order is what humanity most craves and most resists. When drunk, he put it graphically: 'Lenin, Stalin and Hitler were moulded from the same piece of shit, a turd passed by the devil when he had constipation.' And Harrison, also perhaps simple-minded, came to similar conclusions but refined them, for he believed, too, that the misery of the century into which he was born was created out of the insanity Voltaire identified: the madness of those who are certain. The madmen may have been motivated by hunger for power and what Stepan called their lust for order, but what drove them was their certainty. Protect us from those who are certain.

There is a definition of Russian farce which goes like this: a man possesses a beautiful vase knowing that it is one of a pair. All his life he searches for the match until he finds it. He brings the second vase back to put beside the first. As he lifts it up it slips from his fingers and breaks.

In about 1960 the Brumbys received a Red Cross postcard in Rome telling them that Xenia's brother, Vladimir Sobelev, Valodya, was alive and trying to make contact. When she heard the news Tatiana smiled grimly. The memory of that dreadful morning when her son refused to accompany her to Paris sprang to life as though it had happened yesterday. Meanwhile, Stepan made enquiries and wrote letters to the British Home Office, appealing on compassionate grounds. 'Mr Sobelev's mother is aged and so we hope that she and her son may be allowed to meet again in the very near future.' At last, after six or seven years of applications, refusals, promises, Valodya was given a visa. A month before he arrived, Tatiana died. She had gradually descended into a vague nether world in which time and faces were meaningless; she no longer asked after the son she had not seen for almost fifty years; the pills the doctor prescribed she dropped into a narrow silver vase intended for a single rose; her once steely gaze softened and her eyes seemed shielded by a perpetual mist. Her death was painless and unremarkable: she slipped away in sleep in a Guildford nursing home. Those who nursed her remarked on her dignity.

Valodya was gaunt and painfully thin. Shortly after the family's departure for France he was arrested and imprisoned. He had worked for Reuters and any contact with foreigners was accounted a crime. He spent twelve years in the Gulag, was released and then conscripted into the Red Army when Adolf Hitler betrayed his twin, Josef Stalin. ('Poor Hitler,' Stalin had said in 1943 when the Germans were being driven out of the Soviet Union.) He fought bravely, was awarded medals for gallantry, reached the very environs of Berlin. The moment he returned to his country he was rearrested and spent another eight years in the Gulag. Only when Khrushchev denounced Stalin at the 20th Congress of the Party was he finally free.

337

He talked obsessively to Stepan and Iliena of the camps in which he had served his sentences. He had been brutalised into submission. No matter what the Kesslers showed him of England, be it a stately home or a view of glorious English countryside, his response was invariably, 'We have better in Russia.'

Stepan died in 1982, aged seventy-six. Smoking and drinking, the doctors said, did for him. He declined first into irrational outbursts and then into premature senility. He recognised neither Iliena nor his daughters. He suffered a heart attack and departed more or less peacefully.

Harrison, in seeking to record the history of the four families, was attempting to chart the totally unpredictable movement of his and Natalya's forebears, wrestling with a massive insult to demography. His starting-point was the families themselves, the witnesses, the oral historians, the repositories of family gossip, fragments of careless chatter upon which folk memories are built.

During the course of his work, he and Natalya returned to the Soviet Union several times. They looked for Lev's grave in the Novodevichy Convent but without success. They found the graves of Khrushchev and Mikoyan, of Stalin's first wife whom it was said he murdered, and other Soviet notables. They saw the graves, too, of Anton Chekhov and Konstantin Stanislavsky. But not Lev's. The graves of the aristocrats who died in the twenties had long been covered over; but he lies there somewhere.

Wherever he went Harrison asked after Sobelevs and Souvritzins. Late one afternoon, the dramaturg of the Russian theatre at which his play was being performed, telephoned. She was obviously excited. 'There's a Souvritzin here in Moscow. He says he'll see you.'

'What name?' Harrison asked.

'Grigory. He's very ancient.'

Tatiana's dashing brother, Grigory.

He was more than a hundred years old and he still smoked incessantly. His drooping moustache was white and stained with nicotine. Completely bald, almost toothless, his shrivelled eyes were alert and watchful. He was looked after by an elderly woman whom he introduced as his daughter. She said little. They lived in a one-roomed apartment where he never rose from his bed. Throughout the interview he held Natalya's hand. 'My God,' he said, 'if you were not my great-niece, I would sweep you off your feet. Girls, my God, that's my speciality.' He wheezed alarmingly.

Natalya asked about her great-grandparents.

'Dead,' Grigory said. 'Senile. Pee-pee like babies. Better dead.'

He, too, had served in the Gulag, but his life, his survival, remained a mystery. He asked after Tatiana and her daughter but would not speak of Valodya. 'Skunk,' was his only comment. 'How is that American Brumby?'

'Rich,' Harrison said.

'You know the best of the bananas? Richard Webb. Englishman. True hero. God knows how he got them out. Great, good man.'

After an hour he grew weary. But as they were taking their leave, with one bony finger he beckoned them back and urged them to come close. Harrison and Natalya leaned over him. Tonelessly, he said, 'Freedom, you know, is not abstract ideal. No. It's disease. It's infection. There's no cure. If you catch it, beware. It gets into your stream of blood and you are doomed. Here, here, closer. Ssh. Secret. Freedom gets the nervous system, makes numb all other parts of body, oh yes, believe me, I know what I am talking. You know what is drug addict? Okay. Freedom is drug. You crave, crave, crave. I know many, many people who died from craving freedom.'

The work taught Harrison, who was not ordinarily an envious man, that he envied permanence. He envied those who could say that they had lived in the same house for a hundred years, two hundred, three. He envied those who could trace their ancestry back into the distant past. He envied those who had never been victims of cataclysms. He envied those who could say home and mean it. Given man's precarious foothold on his planet, permanence may, he realised, be nothing more than illusion but it was an illusion he longed to share.

Another cataclysm: 9 November 1989, Harrison's fifty-fifth birthday. Television cameras recorded an event so momentous that it was as if they were bearing witness to Martin Luther nailing his thirty-nine theses to a church door. Human hands, also armed with hammers, began to chip away at a monstrous edifice, the wall that encircled West Berlin, and by nightfall the breach had been made. Not just bricks and cement and concrete and rubble crumbled; the rotting body of a corrupt regime exploded and disintegrated, following its twin which had been buried in a nearby bunker.

A new spirit abroad, fears dissolving, candour abruptly the fashion of the age, a longing to unburden, the outpouring of unsolicited memories. All these Harrison attempted to gather, calling upon a mighty network of people across the world, like a spy ring, dedicated to unearthing the truth. Academics, translators, amateur historians, like Harrison himself, sniff out and devour articles and pamphlets, documents once secret, tracts and diaries that touch on the century's horrors. Official and unofficial papers surface. Chance plays a part.

An interview in a Chicago newspaper in which Harrison happens to mention the name Ehrlich, produces a letter from a Mrs Betty Goodman who gives him Lela Krantnik's letters written from Warsaw to Mrs Goodman's mother in Peoria, Illinois.

Over the period Harrison developed an instinct for what might or might not be useful, and occasionally he benefited from a sort of insane inspiration. Watching television he saw an old black and white film, a musical. When the credits rolled, he noticed that the shoes were made by Benjamin of Hollywood. This instinct stirred. When next in Los Angeles he asked his friend, the film historian, Ben Levene, if there was anything known about the shoemaker. Two days later, a telephone call. 'His widow lives in Santa Monica.'

'What was his surname?'

'I don't know. Benjamin, I guess. She calls herself Nina Benjamin. Says she was a dancer.'

The apartment overlooked the ocean. Nina Benjamin, née Kaplanski, was in her eighties but spry, fit, pink hair, plucked eyebrows, what Americans call feisty. 'Have some champagne,' she said. 'I always keep a bottle on ice. You never know when a cute guy like you is going to turn up.'

Sipping Dom Perignon, Harrison explained the reason for his visit. 'My father, you see, escaped from Lithuania in 1911 with his family. They were called Wildnowitz.'

'Jesus Christ,' she said, 'that was my Benjamin's name. He hated it, so you know what the son of a bitch called himself? Benjamin Benjamin. The guy was crazy. I said to him, "Who has a name like Benjamin Benjamin? The President's not called Roosevelt Roosevelt." Jesus, or imagine someone called Reagan Reagan. Obstinate? I swear this guy was the most obstinate man who ever lived. But could he make shoes? I'll show you.'

She produced from her bedroom a pair of tap shoes, put them on, pulled Harrison into the hall which was tiled and proceeded to do a soft shoe shuffle. 'Not bad for an old hoofer, huh? He must have made these pumps fifty years ago.'

On Benjamin Wildnowitz's history before they met, she knew little. 'Yeah, yeah, I seem to remember some brother he left behind. Who knows? He hated talking about the past. As a matter of fact he hated talking, which suited me fine, because I did enough for both of us. He left me a bundle. Benjamin Benjamin was a good guy in every way. See this rock? He gave it me. Yeah, yeah, I just loved that son of a bitch.'

Then, there was Kolya Bulkarov, the doctor's son, a cinema projectionist in St Petersburg, the guardian of his father's early diaries. He had been recommended to Harrison by Piotr Kaltikov in

340

Sobliki. Kolya's excitement that his father's words might be published touched Harrison and when he returned to England he told Iliena of the interview.

'Bulkarov,' she said, 'but I knew him. He was killed in mysterious circumstances.' She put a hand to her mouth. 'Wait a moment, I think Stepan knew him, too.' In a drawer she found the diaries Bulkarov had kept in code and when next Harrison visited Kolya he gave him photocopies. Kolya grinned, 'I know this code. My father taught it to me.'

There was one passage of interest:

December 1935
If we lose, I shall seize power. I know I am followed everywhere. If they get scent of this they'll kill me. But I am preparing carefully and in secret. God give Russia strength.

He was, of course, talking of the election of the Duma in Exile in Barons Court, London.

Of these and other witnesses was the history recorded.

Second Epilogue

Second Epilogue

For Harrison the question that plagued him was the one, of course, that was unanswerable: what was the dominant force in the tide that buffeted the people who had made him and Natalya? The waves of history or the individual will, Tolstoy's theories or old Count Boris Sobelev's instincts? Do individuals affect history, change it, stamp it indelibly? Or is that, like permanence, an illusion? But if not a counterfeit death, then what? If not dignity preserved, or the courage of parents to send their twelve-year-old son alone on a dangerous journey, or if not a restless spirit, then what? And who can explain the priapism of a self-styled poet, the kindly act of a policeman, the indecision of an out-of-work actor, an adulterous wife, the doggedness of an English journalist, the help given by the wife of a British diplomat? Countless small favours, individual acts to confound the historical imperative.

God, Harrison thought, let the world be still, let there be Hegel's blank pages. Enough movement, enough upheaval, enough uprooting of people, individuals all, and tossing them across continents and oceans, from one end of the earth to the other. Let there be stillness.

The image of perpetual motion.

When he and Natalya emerged from the splendid white house called Sobliki on that chill day in May 1983, Yuri, the Jewish photographer, managed to draw Harrison aside on the pretext of taking yet another photograph. He lined up Harrison and clicked his camera. Harrison was about to rejoin Natalya when Yuri stopped him. 'I know you help refusenik writers, Mr Wilde. I have a brother in Israel, I have been four years waiting for visa, always I am refused. Help, please, a refusenik photographer.' He pushed into Harrison's hand a slip of paper with his name and address.

'I'll do what I can,' Harrison said.

'Hide, please, the paper,' Yuri urged. 'You know,' he said, 'one day we'll be free, I know it in my bones. But then it'll be somebody else's turn to suffer.' He smiled and his gold teeth sparkled in the pale sunlight.

The image of earth.

Natalya asked if she could take a scoop of earth from Sobliki back to her mother, Iliena Lvovna. The Chairman of the local soviet was moved and ordered the Jewish refusenik photographer, Yuri, to record the scene. From her handbag Natalya took an empty cassette that had held a roll of film, and gracefully, with enormous dignity, she bent down and scooped up the earth of Sobliki. Piotr Kaltikov, who had played with Iliena as a child, sobbed painfully. In due course, Natalya presented the symbol of permanence, the capsule of earth, to her mother, the last of the Sobelevs born in that place. It may have been at most, Harrison reflected, an act of reconciliation, at least a gesture towards tranquillity.